Texas Lawyer

MANGAN BOOKS
6245 Snowheights Court
El Paso, Texas

Texas Lawyer

The Life of William H. Burges

by
J. F. HULSE

First Edition

Library of Congress Catalog Card No. 81-84678
ISBN 0-930208-12-9

To my wife
Macie
whose help
as to content
and form
of this book
has been invaluable

Preface

THE IDEAL LAWYER of the ages has been one who defended the poor, advised the rich, was successful in court and wise in his office, and who took an active part in the political and civic affairs of his community. Such a man was William Henry Burges—a lawyer of eminent scholarship and practical ability, who was excelled by none and equaled by few.

His history is largely the history of El Paso, Texas, from 1889 to 1946, from the date he arrived in El Paso until his death. He represented rich and poor alike, and was a political and civic leader over a long period of years. He was city attorney from 1893 to 1895. During the 1890s and early 1900s, he was a leader of the reform group who fought open gambling and the ills that accompany it. During the 1890s he knew many of the famous two-gun men of the West, many of whom came to El Paso at one time or another during that era. In 1897, he and W.W. Turney entered into the partnership of Turney & Burges, which rapidly became one of the great institutions of the town and of the Southwest, not only in legal circles, but in civic work, and in the business and political community as well.

William Henry Burges was an avid reader, with a photographic memory. He was instrumental in collecting the law library of Turney & Burges, which was unequaled in the Southwest. He also collected a private library of approximately seventeen thousand volumes. The rare-book librarian of the University of Texas wrote the Burges' library had only a few rare books, but was full of scarce books, and was remarkable in that it contained not a single piece of trash. He had 1,100 volumes of various editions and works of Shakespeare, although he made no effort to acquire a special collection of Shakespeare. He frequently quoted at length not only from Shakespeare, but from numerous other authors including Byron, Tennyson, Kipling,

Longfellow, Poe, Bret Harte and Mark Twain. And he knew not only the contents of their books, but their monetary value as well.

He was a devotee of the drama and music, and had seen and heard the great actors and actresses and singers of his day, including Caruso, Galli-curci, Tetrazzini, Edwin Booth, Patti, and Geraldine Farrar.

He was the unofficial advisor of various librarians of the El Paso Public Library, who frequently passed on to him inquiries they received about various books, the source, identity, and location of various quotations, and like questions.

He was one of the leading spirits of the celebrated Toltec Club, which yielded nothing in its manner of being to metropolitan clubs.

He was onetime regent of the University of Texas, and was the person consulted on legal questions by the president of the Texas College of Mines (later Texas Western College, now the University of Texas at El Paso).

He was president of the Texas Bar Association, served on the Executive Committee of the American Bar Association from 1912 to 1915, was one of the group of lawyers who sponsored the formation of the *Texas Law Review,* and was on the advisory committee of the original edition of *Texas Jurisprudence.*

He was a charter member of the El Paso Symphony Orchestra sponsors. He watched it grow, with pride, and served as its attorney—as always in community and civic matters—without monetary remuneration. He also represented the Woman's Club, and prepared its charter when it was incorporated in 1910.

The cultural life of El Paso is deeply indebted to him for helping lay many of the foundations on which it is built.

His home was the center of all those things which are mentioned above. It was graced by his wife, Anna Pollard Burges, who, although handicapped by poor health, was the charming center of their household. From 1907 on, it was located at 1302 Montana Street, a two-story brick house with a full basement, the south side of which had several high windows above ground level. It was not an imposing house on the outside, but once one stepped inside, there was a feeling of warmth, vitality, and intellectuality. The dining room was larger than most for a house of its kind, and the highlight of social entertainment was a dinner at his home, with a round table at which sixteen people could be seated. After a cocktail or soup was served, he carved the meat or fowl, and the conversation flowed brilliantly, continuously, and entertainingly, the largest part of it coming from him. When dinner was finished, everyone retired to the library, which occupied most of the lower area. As one descended to the library level, he saw near the foot of the stairs a bust of Beethoven and another of Napoleon. Along the wall among them hung several autographed pictures, including one of General John J. Pershing. The doorway into the library from the small entrance way at the foot of the stairs hung with red silk, brocaded curtains, a gift from his long-time friend and client, Mar Ben Chew. The library itself ran the length of the house, and except for the window area on the west side, the entire walls were lined with shelves filled with books. There were other interesting paintings, pictures, and objets d'art, one of which was a print showing men and women in evening clothes coming out of a theater, with the title printed at the bottom of the picture, "Society." A closer look at the picture, however, showed the figures of the men and women in it, and clothes they wore, actually made a picture of Mephistopheles.

He was the advocate in a myriad of lawsuits. In them he represented such clients as The First National Bank, The Atchison, Topeka & Santa Fe Railway, the Mountain States Telephone & Telegraph Company.

There were the numerous Chinese Exclusion Act cases, many criminal cases which he tried during the early days of his practice, land title suits, extradition cases, cases involving international law, particularly those growing out of the Mexican Revolution, the celebrated Bisbee I.W.W. (Industrial Workers of the World) Deportation case, the Banco cases, and antitrust suits. At the same time he represented those who were poor, widows, orphans, and the destitute. There is hardly an end to the list which could be made of these cases. At the same time, he was a generous monetary contributor to those in need, usually giving anonymously.

He was active in politics for many years, and during the early part of this century, was a dominant figure in a small group who controlled the politics of El Paso.

His representation of clients took him to such widely separated places as New York and San Francisco. It brought him an offer to become general attorney for American Telephone & Telegraph Company in New York, which he declined, an offer of a partnership in a top Chicago law firm, which he accepted, and it took him to San Francisco, representing the Standard Oil Company of California in some of its important litigation.

It is of such a man this biography relates.

–J.F. HULSE

Contents

I	*Early Life*	15
II	*El Paso, 1889*	20
III	*Early Lawsuits and Practice*	29
IV	*Gambling and the Reform Movement: The Election of 1895*	39
V	*Reform Still Elusive*	50
VI	*John Wesley Hardin*	58
VII	*The Fitzsimmons-Maher Prizefight*	62
VIII	*Anna Pollard Burges*	67
IX	*Turney & Burges*	71
X	*Chinese Exclusion Act Cases*	82
XI	*Extradition*	91
XII	*The Twentieth Century: Early Years*	98
XIII	*The Henry Ward Beecher Episode*	110
XIV	*Gambling and the Election of 1903*	115
XV	*The Case of the Lost Record*	127
XVI	*1905: Reform Triumphs*	136
XVII	*The Case of the Ticket Scalpers*	139
XVIII	*Appomattox: Laying a Trap for the District Attorney*	142

XIX	*A Hat Full of Diamonds*	*147*
XX	*The International Water Co. Case*	*151*
XXI	*Intertwined with Mexico*	*155*
XXII	*Chicago Interlude*	*175*
XXIII	*The I.W.W. Calls a Strike*	*184*
XXIV	*Gathering the Evidence from Bisbee to Chicago*	*194*
XXV	*The Law of Necessity*	*203*
XXVI	*The Scarlet Standard*	*221*
XXVII	*The Ku Klux Klan and the School Board Election of 1922*	*244*
XVIII	*A Reasonable Fee: $300,000*	*250*
XXIX	*The Rio Grande Boundary Litigation and Other Cases*	*261*
XXX	*Litigating over Millions: The Yates Oil Field Cases*	*277*
XXXI	*The Ateca Case: Suitcases Filled with $750,000*	*303*
XXXII	*Thomas B. Love: "Tellest Thou Me of Ifs"*	*320*
XXXIII	*The Banco Cases*	*326*
XXXIV	*The Jimmie Allred Antitrust Case and The Blue Buzzard*	*336*
XXXV	*Wanted: A Day in Court*	*358*
XXXVI	*Politics, Demagogues, and Public Utility Rates*	*369*
XXXVII	*Last Years*	*388*

Texas Lawyer

WILLIAM H. BURGES

I

Early Life

Ah, happy hills, ah, pleasing shade, . . .
Where once my careless childhood strayed.
—Gray

IT WAS TEXAS in 1867. The terrible ordeal of the Civil War was over, and the more brutal and tyrannical ordeal of Reconstruction was in full swing. President Andrew Johnson had prescribed the acts to be taken by each of the Southern States as a condition precedent to being recognized anew as one of the sovereign states of the Union, but a Congress dominated by the evil genius of Thaddeus Stevens in the House and Charles Sumner in the Senate, undertaking to follow the proscriptions of Sulla, had inaugurated a regime of oppression and violence. General Philip A. Sheridan had been appointed Military Commander of the Fifth District, with headquarters at New Orleans. The military government of the Fifth District included Texas, and he had removed the first Reconstruction Governor of Texas, A.J. Hamilton, and installed another one, E.M. Pease. Under Sheridan and General J.J. Reynolds the right to the writ of habeas corpus was suspended, citizens were tried before military courts, the recently freed Negro slaves were enfranchised, and most of the white citizens were disenfranchised. Liberty, freedom and democracy, as well as law and Constitutional Rights were ruthlessly overridden.

Into such a state of affairs William Henry Burges, Jr. was born at Seguin, Texas to William Henry Burges and wife, Bettie Rust Burges on November 12, 1867. His father fought throughout the Civil War in the Army of Northern Virginia, and returning home to Seguin, Texas, after Appomattox, entered the practice of law. He was a distinguished citizen and a leading lawyer in his area of Texas, where he held at different times, the offices of district attorney and state senator.

Seguin, a small rural county seat, situated on the banks of the beautiful Guadalupe River, was surrounded by historic Texas. Thirty-seven miles to the west lay San Antonio, where stood the Alamo. Eighty-eight miles southeasterly stood Goliad, scene of the tragic massacre of Fannin's command in 1836. Fifty-one miles to the north lay Austin, the state capital. The early grants from Mexico to Stephen F. Austin lay to the east, the early German colony of Prince Solm-Solm at New Braunfels was only fourteen miles to the north. Other early-day colonies, settled by empresarios, were to the east and south. The frontier was not over a hundred miles or so to the north and west, and whoever ventured beyond was subject to raids by the Comanches. Young Burges grew up in Seguin, amid the stories he heard from his father and other Confederate veterans, not the least of which involved incidents occurring during his infancy, when the people of Texas were engaged in the struggle to overthrow a corrupt and arbitrary militarily supported government, and to restore a government that fit the boast of being "of the people, by the people and for the people."

His brother, Richard Fenner Burges was six years younger than he, being born on January 7, 1873. Their mother died six days after Richard's birth, and before she died, she said to her sister, "Nannie, take care of my boys." Nannie was faithful to the trust, and when later, she married Dr. W.M. Yandell, she kept the boys with her at the Yandell residence much of the time. It was about two miles out of Seguin, and the Yandell household was a second home to them.

His youth was relatively uneventful, being described by one writer of doggerel, as:

> Billy Burgee
> Sitting on the banks of the Guadalupe
> Beneath the shade of a pecan tree.

William Henry Burges, Jr. suffered with asthma from the time he was two years old, and it bothered him the rest of his life. When he was sixteen, his family sent him to Tom Green County, in the neighborhood of San Angelo, to see if he could get any relief by a change in climate, but with the real expectation that he would die, so severe was his asthma. He said he was raised on the hurricane deck of a mustang pony, and this, no doubt, stood him in good stead that summer, for while in Tom Green County, he went on some hunting trips and recalled that on one of them they sighted some Indians, apparently unfriendly. At least they were chased by them, but he succeeded in escaping.

He went to the University of Texas, at Austin, after finishing school at Seguin. The university was then a comparatively new school, but had on its faculty some men of great personality and excellent scholarship. His asthma was so bad while he was attending the university that he sat up in a chair more nights than he slept in bed. Nevertheless, he made top grades. And although there were no chapters of either Phi Beta Kappa or the Order of the Coif established at the university prior to his graduation from the School of Law, when chapters were established later, he was made a member of both orders. He received his LL.B degree June 19, 1889. He always recalled with pleasure Dr. R.L. Dabney, a professor who had been the chaplain and one time chief of staff for Stonewall Jackson's Army, and who left a lasting impression on his students at the University of Texas. Former Governor Oran M. Roberts was on the Law School faculty, and he, too, left his indelible imprint on his students. His father was at one time a law partner of Governor Ireland, and through his father he knew, while attending the university, most of the state officials.

He particularly recalled with pleasure two of the great men in the judicial history of Texas, Chief Justice Reuben R. Gaines, of the Supreme Court of Texas, and Judge James M. Hurt of the great Court of Criminal Appeals.

He recalled that in warm weather, of an evening after dinner, a number of leading citizens, including Judge Gaines and Judge Hurt sat in front of the entrance to the Driskill Hotel visiting and swapping stories. He told of the time Judge Gaines' married daughter, and her family, came from Chicago to Austin for a visit at Christmas time. Judge Gaines had a sizable group for dinner on Christmas, with the table set on the mezzanine floor of the Driskill Hotel. In due time, one of the waiters brought in a large turkey, set it on the table in front of Judge Gaines, and to have working room, he stood up to carve it. Unbeknownst to him, the waiter who stood behind him pulled his chair back about two feet to give him more room. The conversation was lively as Judge Gaines carved the turkey, and guests were served. When he had finished carving, and not knowing his chair had been pulled back, he started to sit down. But when he should have felt the chair beneath him, he felt no support, and continued on the downward path. Involuntarily, he clutched the tablecloth with both hands, but it was not secure enough to hold him. As he went on down to the floor, he pulled the tablecloth, together with the turkey, dressing, gravy and whatever else was on the table, on top of him. He arose, carving knife in hand, and looked around. The waiter, seeing the look on Judge Gaines' face, tarried not, but went down the stairs to the lobby three steps at a time, with the Chief Justice, knife in hand, right behind him. The waiter fled at a speed greater than the speed Judge Gaines could muster, and so was way ahead as he went out into Sixth Street and safety.

He also repeated a story about Judge Hurt, who was the presiding judge of the Court of Criminal Appeals at the time when it was known as one of the greatest courts of criminal appeals in the English-speaking world. On an evening when Judge Hurt had tarried late with the group sitting in front of the Driskill Hotel, he arrived home after 11:00 P.M. The front door of his house was locked, and he knocked for admittance. Mrs. Hurt, a fine, estimable lady of seventy—about the same age as Judge Hurt—called out, "Who's there?" and with ready tongue he replied, "who in the hell were you expecting?"

He also told of the young lawyer who was arguing his first case on appeal before the Court of Criminal Appeals, and was obviously nervous, which was intensified by members of the court interrupting to ask him various questions about the case he was arguing. Judge Hurt, seeing that counsel was about to lose his composure, leaned forward in his kind and fatherly manner, and said, "Counsel, you can talk to us just like you would to the justice of the peace in your home precinct."

The rejoinder was instantaneous: "In that case, I'd say, 'Keep your mouth shut until I get through'."

He remembered with great pleasure Governor Roberts, as a teacher in the Law School, and quoted him on occasion. He told of Governor Roberts saying to a class, "Young men, if someone comes into your office and wants to buy a legal form, don't sell it to him, give it to him. I had a man come in one day and ask how much I would charge to write a deed to some land. I told him, 'Ten dollars', and he asked if I didn't have a form for a deed I could sell him. I said, 'Yes, I have a printed form. I won't sell it, I'll give it to you.' Six months later he was back and paid me $250 to defend his title to his farm."

As the class of 1889 of the School of Law, University of Texas, filed out of the old courtroom of the Supreme Court of Texas in the Capitol Building where they had just been admitted to the bar, one of the Supreme Court Judges said: "The Justices of the Peace in Texas are going to catch hell this summer."

Burges returned to Seguin and entered into the general practice of law. The Supreme Court Justice was correct—the justice of the peace in Seguin was busy that summer. Among other things, a constable was busy on Saturday night arresting some of the local citizens for crap shooting and other forms of extralegal local Saturday night entertainment. Burges represented a great many of these brethren, obtaining small cash fees from them, and from those who could not pay the cash fee, he took notes in small amounts, secured by chattel mortgages upon such property as a calf, or a pig, or perhaps a few chickens.

But he was not to practice law in Seguin long. Asthma continued to bother him so badly there was some doubt he could continue to live with the climate of that area. He and his father were told that the climate of El Paso, Texas, nearly six hundred miles to the west, because of its altitude—3,780 feet—and its dryness—in a semi-arid region—would give him relief from asthma. So it was that in September, 1889, he and his father took the train to El Paso, Texas, which, as it turned out, was to be his home, except for a twenty-month interlude in Chicago, for the rest of his life.

II

El Paso, 1889

The earth was made so various, that the mind of . . . man . . . might be indulged.
—*Cowper*

THE *EL PASO TIMES* of September 17, 1889, reported that "Will H. Burges, Jr., son of Will H. Burges of Seguin, Texas, a distinguished lawyer, has come to our city to practice law, and is stopping with his uncle, Dr. Yandell." Dr. W.M. Yandell, from whom, no doubt, the Burges family had received a recommendation that Will H. Burges, Jr. would find relief for his asthma in El Paso, was a distinguished citizen of that frontier city. So Burges was not alone as a complete stranger in the city that stands on the banks of the Rio Grande at the Pass of the North.

The El Paso to which he came was a unique and interesting city. It was situated on the north bank of the Rio Grande, the Rio Bravo del Norte of the Spanish explorers and the Mexican historians, across from the Mexican city of Juarez, at the foot of the Franklin Mountains just below the famous Pass of the North. The Rio Grande, having risen in the snow-capped Rockies of Colorado, and flowing almost due south through the center of New Mexico, makes its turn just above El Paso, and flows through the Pass southeasterly to the Gulf of Mexico. It is a tremendous river in length, some 2,200 miles, but was often capricious, and sometimes devastating. On occasion it carried disastrous floods which often changed the location of the channel of the river in the broad valleys that lay both above and below the Pass of the North, and occasionally overwhelmed the lowlands, including a large portion of the city in its early years.

The route of the conquistadors lay through the Pass of the North, and through here came Onate, Espejo, and DeVargas, enroute from the interior of Mexico to Santa Fe. To this area came a little group of Spanish colonists, seeking refuge following the great Indian uprising in Santa Fe and northern New Mexico in 1680. They, and a group of Isleta Indians who accompanied them, founded the little town of Ysleta, some twelve miles down the Rio Grande Valley from present-day downtown El Paso, making it one of oldest towns in Texas. Its church, known as the Ysleta Mission, is one of the oldest churches in continuous use today in this country.

Juarez, Mexico, so long-known in earlier years as Paso del Norte, later changing its name to honor the great Mexican patriot, Benito Juarez, lay just across the river. In fact, the two towns constituted a single urban area, divided only by the Rio Grande. On the one side was Juarez, with a Spanish and Mexican background and culture, while on the other side lay El Paso, with the same background, but on which was superimposed, as the dominant culture, that of the Americans of the United States. The two were connected by a ferry at the foot of Santa Fe Street, and carried pedestrian and vehicular traffic to and from El Paso and Juarez. Josiah Gregg in 1838 described El Paso del Norte—now Juarez, there being no El Paso on the north side of the river at that date—as follows:

> The valley of El Paso is supposed to contain a population of about four thousand inhabitants, scattered over the western bottom of the Rio del Norte to the length of ten or twelve miles. These settlements are so thickly interspersed with vineyards, orchards, and cornfields as to present more the appearance of a series of plantations than of a town; in fact, only a small portion at the head of the valley, where the *plaza publica* and the parochial church are located, would seem to merit this title. Two or three miles above the *plaza,* there is a dam of stone and brush across the river, the purpose of which is to turn the current into a dike or canal, which conveys nearly half the water of the stream, during a low stage, through this well cultivated valley, for the irrigation of the soil. Here we were regaled with the finest fruits of the season; the grapes especially were of the most exquisite flavor. From these the inhabitants manufacture a very pleasant wine, somewhat

resembling Malaga. A species of Aguardiente (brandy) is also distilled from the same fruit, which, although weak, is of very agreeable flavor. These liquors are known among Americans as 'Paso Wine' and 'Pass Whiskey' and constitute a profitable article of trade, supplying the markets of Chihuahua and New Mexico.

W.H.H. Davis, the United States District Attorney for the territory of New Mexico, described El Paso as it looked to him in the Spring of 1854. Of the El Paso wine he wrote,

"It is a good article, and is said by those who are judges to be superior to many of the wines that are imported from Europe. That made in the Valley of El Paso has become quite celebrated, and is thought to be a better article than is manufactured elsewhere."

He wrote of being received at the hospitable mansion of Judge Hart, of giving his tired horses into the care of Hart's majordomo, of supper, following which they retired to the library for some most agreeable conversation. He wrote that El Molino, the home of Judge Hart, was situated on the east bank of the Rio Grande, three miles above the Mexican town of El Paso del Norte, and a short distance below the Pass. Near the place where his house was located, there was good water power, and he erected a large flour mill at that point. Hart was a Kentuckian by birth, his wife a Chihuahuan of fine Spanish blood, and a lady of intelligence and refinement. Davis went three miles further, to Magoffinsville, where Fort Bliss was then located, and where Mr. Magoffin lived in a large Spanish built house, somewhat in feudal style. He extolled the virtues of the El Paso valley, its productiveness and its salubrious climate.

He also described the Mexican town of El Paso del Norte, referring to the plaza, the old cathedral, custom house and other public buildings. He was favorably impressed by its charming appearance.

In 1881, the railroads arrived in El Paso, and a Scotsman who visited El Paso in late December of that year reported the town was booming. This was evident in many ways: in the demolition of the low, Mexican houses with their pillared verandas, which were giving way in the principal street to brand new American stores with sloping roofs and plate glass windows; in the busy crowd of nondescript and rather rough-looking characters who thronged the hotel entrance, and whose talk was principally of mines, ranches, and stores of groceries and dry goods; in the numerous hack-wagons with canvas tops, drawn by seedy mules, which plied between the American town and El Paso del Norte, across the Rio Grande. He went to El Paso del Norte crossing on a rough bridge, partly constructed of wooden piles and partly of pontoons, crossing a "turgid yellow stream," at a charge of "a shilling" a head, which included being driven over in a hack-wagon, and the bridge toll. He wrote for *Blackwood's Edinburgh Magazine:*

> I have never visited a place more typical of American progress during wanderings which have taken me through every state in the Union . . . A fellow-traveler who was on his way from an Arizona mining city to Boston . . . informed me a few hours after our arrival that he had given up his eastern journey, and was on his way to a lawyer to sign a deed of partnership with a friend whom he had accidentally met, and who had already persuaded him to go into the grocery business with him. It is this extraordinary versatility and readiness to abandon plans, form new combinations, and make new decisions, which enables the pioneer of civilization in the West to rise and fall with such rapidity. The present population of El Paso is estimated at over 3,000, of whom probably about two-thirds are American, and the remaining third are Mexican, who lounge listlessly at the street corners watching the stir and enterprise which have overtaken their once sleepy village, without apparently being stimulated thereby to take part in the competition for sudden wealth which has been excited.

El Paso, having become the county seat in 1883, following the coming of the railroads, had indeed become of age, and was booming. By the time of Burges' arrival in September, 1889, it had become to some extent, a modern city of that age, boasting a population of ten thousand. Juarez, at the same time, had a population of about six thousand, strung out along the southerly bank of the Rio Grande for approximately six miles.

The main line of the Southern Pacific passed through El Paso, enroute from Los Angeles to New Orleans via San Antonio and Houston. The western terminus of the Texas and Pacific Railway Company was in El Paso, from whence it ran eastward to Dallas and on to St. Louis. The Santa Fe Railway had a branch line that ran northward out of El Paso to Albuquerque, New Mexico, connecting with the main line at Belen; and southward, the Mexican Central Railway ran from Juarez to Mexico City.

El Paso was already advertising itself as a health resort, extolling the virtues of its high, dry climate, and mild winters. It was to be, during the 1890's a booming, bustling frontier city, with a Southwestern flavor of gunmen and gamblers, of businessmen and travelers, of politicians and of performers of the arts, the era of the McGinty Band, bicycle clubs and the Bloomer Girls.

While the streets were all unpaved as yet, making the sandstorms raised by the spring winds particularly bad, and becoming avenues of mud in event of rain, they were as yet untraversed by automobiles, which had not come into general use. Transportation was by buggy or carriage, or by the mule-drawn streetcars. One line of the little mule-drawn cars went out San Antonio to Cotton Street and back on Magoffin, while the other made a circuit west on Mills, down El Paso and Santa Fe streets to Juarez, and back on Stanton.

Although a large portion of the population, numbering some ten thousand souls, of which sixty percent was of Mexican origin, lived in comfortable, if unattractive-appearing adobe houses, and some business buildings were adobe, there was an attractive part of the city. The main business street in town was South El Paso, stretching from San Francisco Street and Pioneer Plaza southward to the river. The center of the business area was where East San Antonio intersected South El Paso Street. On the southeast corner of this intersection stood the Wells Fargo Building, where, until April 1, 1897, Burges had his office. Beyond it, just past the alley on San Antonio Street, was the old Wigwam Saloon, and next to it stood the leading restaurant in town, the English Kitchen, run by Dock Sing. On the corner of this block, adjoining Oregon Street, was The State National Bank. Across San Antonio Street stood a two-story building known as the Bronson Block, and which, in 1897, was to have in it the first office of the celebrated law firm of Turney & Burges.

The most imposing structure in town was the four-story Sheldon office building, later converted into the Sheldon Hotel. It abutted on Pioneer Plaza, which was then a little larger than it now is, and was a center point of downtown El Paso. Across the street, where the Mills

Building is today, stood the Grand Central Hotel, an imposing structure for a town of this size, some four stories in height.

San Jacinto Plaza was already in existence and facing it at the northeast intersection of Mills and Mesa streets, then known as Utah Street, stood the Vendome Hotel, a well-known hostelry in that era. Two blocks to the east on Main Street, between Stanton and Kansas streets, was the old Southern Pacific Railway passenger depot. Beyond it, on Mills, between Kansas and Campbell streets, stood another famous early-day hostelry, the Pierson Hotel. There were two banks, one the First National Bank, capital $100,000, surplus $25,000, run by Joshua Raynolds, which was soon to become one of Burges' best clients, and The State National Bank, "resources $434,770.97," run by C.R. Morehead, with whom he notably tangled in the city election of 1903.

The City Hall stood at the southwest corner of Santa Fe and Overland streets. One of the most magnificent buildings in town was the County Courthouse, which stood, as does the present one, between San Antonio and Overland street, and Campbell and Kansas streets. Its courtroom was used as the ballroom for social events, and many a gala affair was held in it. Those who attended, both the men and their ladies, walked to the courthouse for these occasions, except on those rare times when it had rained. Then the streets were muddy, and cabs were in great demand—but not in great supply—as a means of getting to and from the ball.

The new United States Customs House, which housed not only the customs offices, but also the Post Office and the United States District Court was being built at the corner of Mills and Oregon streets. Congressman S.W.T. Lanham, of Weatherford, whose district included El Paso, had sought an appropriation of $300,000 for it, but had to be content with $150,000 allocated to its construction.

Mention must also be made of the elegant Myar Opera House, built in 1887 and destroyed by fire in 1905, on South El Paso Street. Here, while it stood, came most of the great musicians and actors of the world who toured and performed in United States. It opened December 15, 1887, the first performance being James Neil in Dumas' *Count of Monte Cristo*. It was a sell-out. Not long afterward

Edwin Booth appeared in *Julius Caeser.* Adelina Patti performed here a little later, as did many other leading musicians and actors. A group of Italian artists, under Luis Donizetti, performed *Norma* one evening, and *Il Trovatore* on the next evening. The California Opera Company played *Said Pasha,* and followed it the next day with *Fra Diavolo.* There are later notices of performances of *Faust, Lohengrin, Il Trovatore, Rigoletto, Tannhauser,* and *Carmen.* In between there were travelling troupes who performed comedies. Of one of them was the J.M. Hills Union Square Company. In *Possible Case,* the *San Antonio Express* was reported to have said it was the best show seen in Texas in five years. Nor were these the only musical performances in El Paso. Concerts were given in Chopin Hall, and, in warm weather, the Fort Bliss Orchestra played of an evening in San Jacinto Plaza from time to time. Chopin Music Hall was situated on Myrtle Street,

The elegant Myar Opera House was one of El Paso's most famous theaters. It was built in 1897 and destroyed by fire in 1905.
[*Aultman Collection*]

where the Federal Courthouse now stands. It was a center of musical performances, and was a cultural hub of early El Paso.

We need hardly mention the saloons and gambling halls. The town was full of them, and several have had their names preserved in history by the actions of gunmen in the early days—the Gem, the Wigwam, and Coney Island, among others.

The main residential areas, where the houses were mostly built of red brick, were on East San Antonio, East Magoffin, and East Myrtle streets, betweeen the main part of town and Cotton Avenue. Most of the population lived south of the railroad tracks which ran just north of Main Street, there being only scattered residential dwellings north of the railroad tracks, as far north as Arizona Street.

Some 150 to 200 yards north of the river flowed the *acequia,* a canal which, from a point on the river above the city, carried water from the Rio Grande to give life to the fields and gardens growing in the valley area. Here was an oasis, where trees gave welcome shade in the summer, and where fruits and vegetables, and most especially the famous El Paso grape, grew.

Burges was soon to meet a number of public officials.

One was Joseph W. Magoffin, around whom much of the early history of El Paso revolved, and who was elected mayor in April, 1889. That his election was not unanimous was reflected in the fact the *El Paso Herald* commented it was the triumph of boodle, booze, and treachery; and the *Herald* dwelled on the statement that voters by the wagon load were purchased body and soul. It was common, in the 1880s and 1890s to hear one side, or both, in the local elections had brought over a large number of Mexicans from Juarez, supplied them with poll tax receipts, and paid them to vote.

Other local officials included A.G. Foster, city attorney, W.M. Yandell, city physician and health officer, and T.C. Lynn, city marshal, with nine regular policemen. The district judge (34th District Court) was T.A. Falvey, a real pioneer, and a giant among lawyers. O.A. Larrazola was district clerk, later succeeded by Ike Alderete.

T.S. Maxey, of Austin, was United States district judge, and held court in El Paso in October and April of each year. Colonel George W. Baylor was clerk of this court.

James E. Townshend was county judge, James H. White was sheriff, and B.G. Thomas was county clerk, with J.A. Escajada and Miss Jeanne Clark as deputies.

All of these were people with whom Burges would soon be dealing, as public officials, clients, or opponents in politics or lawsuits.

He would also become acquainted, not only with the gunmen, gamblers, prospectors, pioneers, and other such rugged souls, but also with the people who made up the business community. Newspapers of that time show they included:

Lightbody & James, a men's clothing store, which advertised a sale on shoes for $3.50; J. Calisher's California Store, 208-10 South El Paso Street; Ullman's Furniture Store, 507 Lower El Paso Street; E.B. Fatman, Grocer; John B. Watson, Grocer, corner of Stanton and Myrtle Streets; Momsen & Thorne, wholesale and retail pumps, stoves, refrigerators, tinware, etc., Nos. 76 and 78 South Oregon Street; A. Goodman, Wholesale Grocer, 315 S. El Paso Street. There were also Pomeroy's El Paso Transfer Co., "Hacks, Bus and Baggage," 113 San Francisco Street; Longwell's Transfer; A. Solomon's Store; Krakauer, Zork & Moye, wholesale and retail dealers in hardware, agriculture implements and mining supplies, and agents for Studebaker Wagons; the Palace Dining Hall, "The Most Elegantly Appointed Restaurant in this City," 123 South El Paso Street; Delmonico's Restaurant, 320 South El Paso Street "Opposite the Opera House," one time advertising dinner for 75 cents, then dropping the price to 50 cents. A most unusual ad was Andrew & Hills, offering a three-barreled gun, a double-barreled shotgun and a rifle. W.G. Walz Co., Juarez, quoted "Cigars cut, $2.25 per hundred," and M.J. Kohlberg, Mgr., advertised the Mexican and Indian Curio company.

When he arrived in El Paso, Burges looked around, particularly at the adobe houses to which he was unaccustomed and said to himself, "Is this the place where I have come to spend the rest of my life?" If he could have foreseen the future, he would have answered affirmatively. At least it was home, but his busy and far-flung practice took him away from El Paso often and to far distant points spread from New York to Chicago and San Francisco.

III

Early Lawsuits and Practice

And do as adversaries do in law—
strive mightily, but eat and drink as friends.
—Shakespeare

BURGES OPENED an office on the second floor of the Wells Fargo Building, located at the southeast intersection of East San Antonio and South El Paso streets. Clients were not long in coming.

He was employed shortly after his arrival in El Paso on some business by the First National Bank of El Paso, and soon became its regular counsel and represented that bank until it failed in the Great Depression of the early 1930s. His diligence and ingenuity was illustrated in a case referred to him by the First National Bank. It recommended him to handle a claim by an out-of-city bank for debt against a local resident, with the request that an attachment be made of some personal property in the southern part of the city. The debtor had several creditors, and Burges hastened to file his petition, his affidavit for a writ of attachment, and attachment bond, and to have the writ of attachment issued. At the Courthouse he discovered another attorney had filed a suit just ahead of him against the same debtor and also had issued a writ of attachment. Judge Kemp placed his writ in the hands of a deputy sheriff and they took the old horse-drawn streetcar for the location of the property to be attached. Burges hurriedly placed his writ in the hands of another deputy, hired a cab, and raced past the streetcar for the location of the property, and succeeded in having the deputy with him actually take into his possession the property to be attached before Judge Kemp could arrive with his writ.

There is no record of his very first clients, but *The El Paso Times* of March 7, 1890, reported he was in Marfa trying a lawsuit. The same paper reported, on Februrary 26, 1891, that during the trial of the Williamson case, Attorney Will Burges lost his usual serene temper, and that he entered the fray with fire in his eyes, and a large and healthy cane in his hands, when Judge T.A. Falvey commanded order. Burges, who never seemed to give the appearance of a small man, actually was of less than average height—about five feet seven inches tall—and never weighed over 140 pounds, so he was apt to be overmatched in any physical encounter. All was not serene in the trial of cases in those days. *The El Paso Times* of January 1, 1893, reported the trial of a case before Justice of the Peace Farrell. Arthur Destor, a young boy, was tried for riding a horse belonging to L.C. Chriss. The evidence showed it was due to a mistake, and at the close of the trial, Destor, who was represented by Burges, was found not guilty. Mr. Chriss thereupon made an offensive remark to Burges, who responded by hurling a heavy inkstand at Chriss. Fortunately he missed, and the constable quickly restored order.

The *El Paso Herald* reported, November 19, 1891, that William H. Burges, Jr. was in San Antonio arguing Chinese cases. This was probably the first of many interesting and profitable Chinese Exclusion Act cases which he tried.

There was other news of interest in daily papers. On January 1, 1890, Adelina Patti, the famous singer, was enroute to El Paso for a concert in the Myar Opera House. On February 3, 1893, a contract was reported let to build Hotel Dieu at a cost of $34,800. On March 15, 1893, the paper carried an advertisement: "Dr. Burrow will guarantee to cure cancers. No cure, no pay." A February 10, 1893, article showed the national gold depletion of the present times is not news, for the headline stated, "U.S. Treasury Empty of Gold." Prices of merchandise were indicated by an advertisement of January 28, 1893, "Isaac Blumenthal—The Great European Store. Retiring from Business. Selling at and below cost for cash: $6.00 men's suits for $4.00, $10.00 suits for $6.00. Our $10.00 and $12.50 men's suits are worth $20.00 and $25.00, $5.00 overcoats for $3.00."

Early in 1892 Burges married Ada Dean, whose brother was

district attorney at El Paso. She was beautiful and charming, and it was a great tragedy when she died in November 1892 of pneumonia.

Sometime after his arrival in El Paso, Burges formed a partnership with A.G. Foster, an older, established lawyer. This partnership lasted until January 1, 1896, when he and his brother Richard F. Burges, who had recently been admitted to practice, went into a partnership with each other. During these years his office remained on the second floor of the Wells Fargo Building. This partnership was dissolved March 31, 1897. W.H. Burges said it was dissolved because he being the older of the two brothers, and having been in practice longer, the clients who came to their office usually wanted to see him, and that the arrangement, therefore, was not fair to R.F. Burges. Effective April 1, 1897, he formed a partnership with W.W. Turney, and the famed firm of Turney & Burges, long an outstanding institution of the Great Southwest, came into being, and lasted for forty-one years.

Burges said when he began the practice of law, he thought if he were not a member of Congress within ten years he would be a failure, but after he had practiced law for ten years he would not have taken the office of congressman, if offered him. But he did "hit the ground running" in politics when he came to El Paso, for he not only started with the ambition to become a congressman, but he held the additional thought, somewhat in the alternative, that the person who was the town's social leader could be the community's political leader, and the combination would put him in position to draw unto himself a very substantial part of the town's law practice. In other words, it was a path to a great law practice.

He was not long in getting into politics, not as a candidate, but as an active participant, and he soon became a dominant figure in it. In July 1892, the Democrats were engaged in a row—not unusual—and he was elected by one faction as a delegate from the Third Ward to the County Convention. The tenor of El Paso politics in those days is seen in reporting of the meeting of the Democrats of the Second Ward on the night of July 20, 1892, stating:

> The Democrats of the Second Ward met last night and made good their claim as a fighting ward. There was no contest over who would be Chair-

man or Secretary, and all present agreed to the proposal that they should elect eleven delegates to the Democratic Judicial Convention.

W.H. Austin and T.R. Hasam were appointed as challengers to see that none but Democratic votes got in the hat. Several votes had been received, including those of four Mexicans. The fifth vote that was offered received a challenge from a Mr. Hasam. Charley Patterson claimed that the Mexican was as good a Democrat as Mr. Hasam, which statement was not relished by Mr. Hasam, and he in vigorous and picturesque English declared to the contrary.

In the argument that followed, Newman intimated that Patterson was in the packing business, to which Patterson replied that Newman was as well up in the line as anyone.

"You are a liar," came from Newman.

"And you are a damned liar," said Patterson.

The debate did not proceed further under the rules due to the fact that Newman grabbed his walking stick and hit Patterson over the head with it. Only the interference of bystanders prevented the effusion of blood other than what was coming from Patterson's head. With the request to Constable Lyons to "do his duty," editor Page ventured to render the part of the Good Samaritan towards Patterson, and during his absence Barney Harmsen, one of the Democratic warhorses of the Third Ward, was requested to throw into elegant Castilian the invitation of "Come up and vote if you are a Democrat, live in the Second Ward, and will support the ticket." The quiet of the meeting was disturbed by the return of Patterson with a knife up his sleeve, which friends prevented his using. It was reported some Democrats in the city, even in the Second Ward, regretted the circumstance, and entertained the hope that at some future day, the Second Ward Democrats would be able to do business in harmony. Some, however, thought a killing would be the price of harmony.

In October 1892 Judge Foster appointed Burges judge of the election in the Third Ward. On November 11, 1892, it was announced there would be a "Democratic Jollification Tomorrow Night", and there would be a procession to march on the Plaza, where the crowd would be addressed by T.J. Beall and W.H. Burges. It was later reported, however, that Burges was out of town, and was unable to be present at the "Jollification". By early 1893 he was acting city attorney, on occasions, when City Attorney Barnhart was out of town. In the meantime a politico-legal matter arose. The *Dallas Morning News* reported, February 16, 1893, the Senate Judiciary Committee was redistricting the state, with respect to the Supreme Judicial Districts, i.e., the districts for the respective Courts of Civil Appeals. There was no Court of Civil Appeals in El Paso then, and the report was that El Paso would be placed in the same district with Abilene, Brownwood and San Angelo, and should the court meet at either of these places, it would, as one lawyer expressed it, necessitate one having business with the Court of Civil Appeals taking his blanket and camping on the bald prairie. A meeting of the El Paso Bar was called, and after electing Major B.H. Davis chairman and W.H. Burges secretary they unanimously passed a resolution requesting El Paso be placed in the 4th Supreme Judicial District, in which the court sat at San Antonio. The protest must have been heeded, as El Paso remained in the 4th District until the 8th Supreme Judicial District was created in 1911, putting a Court of Civil Appeals in El Paso.

H.B. Barnhart was city attorney, but when he could not be on hand, Burges substituted for him and performed the duties of city attorney on such occasions. It was during this time the city issued $205,000 in bonds for the Water Department. Opponents of the bonds brought suit to declare them invalid. On January 26, 1893, the firms of Davis, Beall & Kemp, Edwards & Neill, and W.H. Burges jointly offered the city to assist the city attorney in upholding the validity of the bonds for a fee of $1,500 and travel expenses, if any. The offer was to fight all cases brought against the validity of the bonds, half of the fee to be paid at that time, and the other half when the first case was disposed of. The offer was accepted by the city, by a motion which carried four to two.

The city was soon in the throes of the election of 1893. A Democratic meeting was called for the night of March 22, 1893, at which A.M. Loomis was nominated for mayor. J.J. Stewart had been talked of as a candidate, but it soon was reported he was out of it, and W.H. Austin was nominated.

There was an active campaign, in which Burges supported Austin.

He was away from El Paso part of March, and the *Herald* reported he was in Austin. He was waiting on the Legislature, where a bill was pending to amend the El Paso City Charter, principally with respect to city council procedure in issuing bonds, and levying taxes to pay for them. The emergency clause referred to the necessity for the city of El Paso to enlarge its waterworks, showing the bill was especially for that purpose. He was quite active in the city campaign however, and not long after the election, which Austin won 1,073 to 253 for Loomis, Burges was prominently mentioned for city attorney. The *Times* reported, shortly after the election, "They want Pie," and named several, including Burges, who wanted the city attorney post, but stated Burges had been for Austin first and last, and inferred he had the inside track. As fate would have it, Austin took a leave of absence for sixty days on account of illness, and J.B. Badger became acting mayor. The council got around to selecting a city attorney on May 26, 1893. Alderman W.F. Payne nominated W.H. Burges, paying a high compliment "to that young attorney for his ability, energy and honesty." The nomination was seconded by M.W. Stanton. Alderman Magoffin nominated Judge T.A. Falvey, a great lawyer, a highly respected citizen, and a former district judge. He eulogized Mr. Burges, and said Judge Falvey would give equally good service. This nomination was seconded by Mr. Kohlberg. The vote was five to three for Burges, and on motion by Magoffin was made unanimous.

The office of city attorney was not a full-time position, but it had the great attraction of a monthly salary, $125 per month. The panic of 1893 was on, money was scarce, many people were out of work, and families were destitute. Mr. Burges was a single man at the time, with no one dependent on him for support, and he gave a substantial part of his city attorney's pay to the needy. When Christmas came in 1893, he gave his entire month's pay to the poverty-stricken, mostly in baskets of groceries, with a few special items such as candies and toys for the children. The gifts were anonymous and deliveries were made by the grocerymen, as Burges did not want the recipients to know the source of the gifts. It was enough thanks for him to know that these gifts were received by deserving people, who were greatly in need of assistance.

The City Hall was in a rented building at the southwest corner of Overland and Santa Fe streets. Here the city council met during the two-year period 1893-1895 that Burges was city attorney. While J.B. Badger was the first acting mayor, due to W.H. Austin's illness, he was succeeded in that capacity first by A. Solomon, and later by R.F. Johnson. The council worked on the committee system, and had the following committees:

Finance	Streets and Grades
Building	Ordinance
Fires. Water	Parks
Acequia	Police

One of the principal assets of the city was the acequia—the main canal, leading off from the river some distance up river, above Santa Fe Street, and flowing through South El Paso, and beyond into the Lower Valley. In earlier days its waters had served for drinking and domestic use, but now its sole purpose was to supply irrigation water for yards, gardens, orchards, and farms, and it was responsible for creating an oasis in the midst of a desert. Its importance is verified by the fact the city council had an "acequia" committee. The committee received complaints, on occasion, of shortage of water in the acequia, or about dilapidated buildings on its banks which threatened to fall in it, and similar complaints.

When Burges took office as city attorney, the suit against the city on its authorized issue of $205,000 of water bonds was pending. This suit constituted one of the first problems facing the new city council in 1893, and it called upon its lawyers for a report. They reported (1) the city can win the suit; they might have to go to the Court of Civil Appeals to win it, and this would take twelve to eighteen months' and (2) the city could pass a new ordinance to issue bonds, and, considering the new amendment to the City Charter, this is the best course to follow. Burges also pointed out to the council a new amendment to the General Laws of the State of Texas, effective in August, 1893, which required the certification of the validity of the bonds by the attorney general of the State of Texas, and that his certification would make the bonds more saleable. The Council acted on his recommendation, and on August 11, 1893, passed an ordinance annulling the water bonds previously authorized, and then passed an ordinance providing for the issuance of water bonds in the sum of $175,000.

The money was to be used in the construction and completion or purchase and extension of a system or plant of water works for the city and its inhabitants. On February 13, 1894, O.T. Bassett, et al., filed a Bill in Equity against the city of El Paso seeking to enjoin the issuance of the bonds on the ground the city ordinance exceeded the powers conferred by its Act of Incorporation, and alleged the ordinance, in several respects, violated the Constitution and the laws of the State of Texas, and that the bonds, if issued, would be void. On the same day the bill was filed, it was presented to C.N. Buckler, judge of the district court, who set it for hearing on February 20, 1894. When February 20 came around, Judge Buckler held he was disqualified, being a citizen residing in and a taxpayer of El Paso. On February 22 the Bill was presented to the Honorable Walter Gillis, Judge of the 41st District Court. Judge Gillis heard it, and refused to issue the injunction. Thereafter, the Honorable A.M. Walthall, later a district judge in El Paso, was commissioned as a special judge to try the case. He was something of a frontier character himself, having moved to El Paso from Pecos, Texas. His saltiness can be inferred from a story about him to the effect that while sitting on the district court bench in El Paso one day, he heard that a friend was in trouble two blocks or so down San Antonio Street from the Courthouse, apparently in an argument that threatened to erupt into gun play. He hurriedly adjourned court, descended from the bench, and went back in his office, strapped on his .45 and hurried down the street to help protect his friend.

On May 1, 1894, the plaintiffs filed their second supplemental petition, and the case went to trial, at the conclusion of which, on May 3, the injunction was refused. It was appealed to the Court of Civil Appeals for the Fourth Supreme Judicial District at San Antonio. Appellants' brief stated the taxable value for the city in the year 1893 was $5,359,190 and the city taxes, at the rate of $1.85 per $100 valuation, amounted to $99,145. Plaintiffs in the case were represented by J. M. Dean and F. B. Sexton, while the City was represented by William H. Burges, Jr., Peyton F. Edwards, and Davis, Beall & Kemp. In due time the trial court's judgment denying the petition for injunction was affirmed by the Court of Civil Appeals at San Antonio on November 7, 1894, the opinion appearing in *Bassett v. City of El Paso,* 28 S.W. 554. The case went to the Supreme Court of Texas, and Burges reported that following the arguments in the case, the judges discussed the case informally with counsel, and he found it most interesting. The Supreme Court affirmed the lower courts on April 15, 1895, and the case had been won for the city.

There was other litigation by the city, the minutes of the council reflecting it authorized the city attorney to appeal the case of *City of El Paso, Appellant v. James Ashford, Appellee,* and that City Attorney Burges reported he had filed suits against ex-collector Merrill for the years 1890-92, but most of the city's affairs were routine. The city attorney's duties included such things as preparing a contract between the city and Thomas Howard relative to a driveway on East Overland Street; contracts for grading Tays Street, and for grading and graveling Second Street. There were no paved streets in El Paso at this time, and gravel was the best hard surface material available. His duties also related to other matters before the council: passing on the title to property to be purchased from James Burns for a pesthouse, reporting on the advisability of codifying the city ordinances, preparing a new lease for the City Hall, preparing an ordinance to prohibit the riding of bicycles on sidewalks, and forbidding hack drivers, cab drivers, transfer agents, and their solicitors from soliciting and harassing persons at the railway depots. Another ordinance was to regulate public laundries, and there were others relating to mad dogs and their owners, and so on.

In the midst of his career as city attorney, the newspapers of June 22, 1894, reported Burges had been elected president of the University of Texas Alumni by acclamation, with the comment "this shows he is highly thought of in educational circles, and is a compliment to this part of the State." There was added: "The State University is steadily rising in public estimation, and its graduates are achieving more or less renown."

El Paso County Courthouse in 1891.
[A.J.T. Joslin]

IV

Gambling and The Reform Movement: The Election of 1895

Some play for gain; to pass time others play
For nothing; both to play the fool, I say.
—Heath

FROM 1889 TO 1903 the division of El Paso, politically and otherwise, was largely along the lines of for-or-against open gambling. There were a large number of saloons and open gambling halls in the city, most of them being on South El Paso or San Antonio streets. There were more mercantile businesses in Juarez than El Paso, and El Paso's business area, with its saloons, gambling halls, and the brothels on South Utah, now Mesa Street, suffered by comparison with Juarez. It was the day of the frontier. The town had its quota of Indian fighters, ex-peace officers, gunslingers, prospectors, range riders and similar characters who were a hard lot. But the swelling tones of the cry for reform would not be stilled.

A state law, passed in 1881, prohibited betting and wagering at a gaming table, and provided for a fine of $10 to $25. It also provided the person permitting the use of a house as a place for public gaming should be fined $25 to $100. This law was not enforced in El Paso, so on December 30, 1889, the city council passed an ordinance to restrain gambling by means of licenses, the license fee to be paid quarterly in advance; and before the license was issued by the tax assessor and collector, the applicant was required to get a permit signed by the mayor and a majority of the councilmen. They would designate the person to whom the license would be issued and the house in which gambling could be conducted. For violation of the ordinance a fine of $25 to $250, and imprisonment in the county jail from ten to sixty days was provided.

Two weeks later the first license was issued to the Wigwam. In reporting the action of the city council, one of the local newspapers started its article:

"A full Council (no invidious distinction in the word 'full') met last night . . ."

But licensed or unlicensed, open gambling continued, and the fight against open gambling went on. It was attacked again in the January 26, 1893, issue of the *El Paso Herald,* which, in its lead editorial took the gamblers to task. It said there were three classes of gambling houses paying license to the city, of which there were three licenses to each class. The first class included the three houses run in connection with three of the largest and best patronized saloons—The Wigwam, Gem and Mint. The three houses paid the city $200 per month, and the editor calculated they paid out in salaries to their dealers, and conductors of games $3,500 per month, and rent, etc., so the total cost of operating the three houses was $4,000 per month. It then figured if the profits were twenty-five percent this meant taking in $5,000 per month "from the hard earnings of our mechanics, clerks, and businessmen," and added, generally there were several professional gamblers hanging around each house who lived off of winnings, which had to be added to the "take."

The next class included the Chief, on lower El Paso Street, the Monte Carlo, on South Oregon Street, and Charlie Townshend's place, on East Overland Street which, the newspaper said, was frequented only by the laboring classes, Mexicans and Negroes—and the same arguments applied about taking hard-earned money from these people in this class of gambling house.

The third class included the three Chinese joints which were run for the benefit of the four hundred Chinese in city. The editorial attacked licenses that brought the city $800 each per annum, at the cost of such a drain on the wages and earnings of those who patronized the gambling house.

Nevertheless, it was to be awhile before any action was taken against the gamblers. Mayor Johnson was urged to close open gambling, and on August 4, 1894, he issued a proclamation barring it. Jeff Milton, chief of police, was called in, and was told to close up gambling. "What authority is there behind me?" he asked. "The authority of the city of El Paso, Bob Johnson, and myself," replied City Attorney Burges.

"That's sufficient. Every gambling house in this town will be closed by night," said Milton.

Hardly anyone believed it could be done, but within twelve hours not a roulette wheel was spinning, nor was a card turned, or a pair of dice rolled in the city.

For about two months the town was closed to open gambling, but this seemed to hurt the town's business, and after a time the gamblers gradually were allowed to reopen their halls.

This was the situation when the city election of 1895 approached, with two issues uppermost in the minds of the people, open gambling, and a municipal water system. The faction in control of the local Democratic party machinery favored open gambling, and it also backed Watts, owner of the El Paso Water Works. The other faction split off, calling itself the Non-Partisan Independents, striking out for reform on both issues. One of the leaders of the Independents was W.H. Burges. They nominated E.A. Shelton, a highly respected merchant, for mayor, with an aldermanic ticket. They had not only the Democrats to consider, but also the Republicans, who, seeing in the Democratic split a chance for victory, nominated for mayor a gambler named Robert Campbell, with an aldermanic ticket.

The election started off with a bang. The *Herald* stated, "The Democratic Primaries was a Romantic Racket," reciting that in the First and Bloody Second wards the "straightouts" carried the day, but in the Third and Fourth the Non-Partisans carried off the plums. That paper observed, "And the band played Annie Laurie," and,

"The next day it snowed," these refrains being suggested by the Democratic primaries in the Second, Third and Fourth wards. Chairman Blacker of the Second Ward casually observed, during a lull in the proceedings while Bill Fewel and Charlie Patterson paused for a new supply of wind, that the racket reminded him of the good old times when it was a regular thing to have just such Democratic primaries as this right along.

Everything was quiet in the First Ward, but, as Sol Schutz said, "The blamed fools ought to have charged admission to the Second Ward primary, as it would have been paid cheerfully." It was pandemonium from start to finish, and "monkey and the parrot" were not in it at all. Judge Blacker was chosen chairman, and Justice of the Peace W.D. Howe, later district judge, was named secretary. The acrimonious debate which followed was said to have been just like the racket at Ephesus, where "some cried one thing, and some another, and the whole city was thrown into confusion." The Third Ward had a similar, but less noisy meeting, as those opposed to strict party regularity were in a majority of five to one, and the minority held a rump convention. The Fourth Ward's meeting was about like the Third's.

The City Democratic Convention was held that night in the District Courtroom. It was due open at 7:30 P.M., but at that hour the courtroom was quiet as a grave. Soon the crowd began to stream in, and by 8:00 P.M. the room was full. Several little groups of two or three hunted corners where they could talk privately. Bill Fewel and Sheriff Simmons held a political tete-a-tete and Charley Patterson found a corner where they whispered words of learned counsel, and blew tobacco smoke around each other's heads. Another whisper group was formed by J.D. Ponder, Judge Townsend and W.D. Howe. Dick Staples sailed up to Judge Loomis, and asked Loomis if he would run for alderman, but before he got his answer, Bill Fewel called out, "Where's Ed Fink?"

"Herding Mexicans," was the prompt rejoinder from someone, implying he was corralling them to vote. It was common practice for both sides in early day elections to round up Mexicans from Juarez, as well as from El Paso, keep them overnight, with plenty of beer and sandwiches, and herd them to the polls on election day. If they came out wearing a certain colored ribbon, they received two dollars. Those who could not read were given strings in which knots were tied. When the string was laid down on the top of the ballot, the knots showed them how to mark the ballot. These practices continued until the enactment of the Terrell Election Law in 1903.

Chief of Police Jeff Milton, W.W. Mills, A.P. Coles, and Judge Coldwell were also among those present.

City Recorder Clark was elected temporary chairman, J.H. Harper, secretary, Chief Milton and Alderman Howley, sergeants-at-arms. The chairman, expressing appreciation for his election, said:

> We have met here as Democrats and in our party have we always placed our trust and faith, a party that has always advocated the greatest good of the greatest number. But we are in the throes of a political upheaval, in which Democratic brother appears arrayed against Democratic brother, and this sad condition of affairs can only be explained by the fact that Democrats are falling away from their allegiance.

The meeting adjourned at 10:30 P.M., to meet again at 7:30 P.M. the next day without having nominated a candidate for mayor.

On April 3, 1895, at 8:00 P.M., the City Democratic Convention resumed its meeting in the District Courtroom. It fizzled, and the oppositon paper led off its news article on it with:

> It was the animals' fair, the birds and the
> Beasts were there,
> And the old baboon, by the light of the moon
> Was combing his auburn hair.

The chair did put the question, and with spectators as well as delegates voting, it seemed to be about equally divided.

"The ayes have it, and this convention stands adjourned," declared the chair.

The attendance was small, compared to the previous evening, but on roll call, it was discovered a quorum was present. Among those present were Joseph Sweeney, later county judge, Dick Caples, and "Redlight" Jim Burns. The convention was soon embroiled in an acrimonious debate, but it did not last long.

Mexican voters being paid off in front of Chopin Hall.
[Aultman Collection]

"I move this convention adjourn," yelled Charley Patterson, springing to his feet. A half dozen delegates shouted a second to the motion. The chair hestiated, and fifteen or twenty men cried out, "A motion to adjourn is not debatable! Put the question; put the question!"

And so it ended. But the election campaign was in full swing, for if the Democratic party had failed to nominate candidates, the Non-Partisan group's ticket, headed by E.A. Shelton was in the field, as was the Republican ticket headed by Bob Campbell, a gambler, and for the first time they were hopeful of success at the El Paso polls.

The Non-Partisans drew first blood. They held a political speaking on the night of April 4, 1895, where about five hundred people gathered to listen. Dr. Yandell presided, and introduced first Judge Peyton Edwards. He said:

> . . . for the first time, I appear before you in support of an independent ticket. I have in the past been . . . what some call a yellow-dog Democrat [laughter], so it made no difference who was put up, I supported him. But of late it seems to me the most open and shameless trades were made in the Democratic Convention (to crowd down one man and crowd up another), until I have come to the conclusion that there shall be no more party strings on me [applause] . . . The Republican party pretends to be Republican, but it is so only in name. The Independent movement is solely to maintain good moral government in El Paso and good waterworks . . . It seems to be in the air that gambling is to reopen as soon as Campbell is elected . . . The people you talk with on the street all appear to agree that as soon as Bob Campbell is elected mayor of El Paso, gambling will be started again . . . It seems the highest recommendation given him is that he is a gambler and stays sober while the poor fool who plays against him gets drunk, and Bob gets all the money [laughter and applause].

He then spoke of the Republican candidates for the city council:

> There is W.W. Mills up Campbell's sleeve [laughter]. There is J.J. Stewart, the silent monk. No one knows what J.J. Stewart thinks at any time (if he ever thinks he never tells anyone about it). Adolph Schutz is the very young man who won a prize in dancing. He is the Queen of Diamonds . . . There is John O'Keefe, the Knave of Diamonds [laughter].

He then returned to a discussion of the waterworks issue, and linked

Campbell to Watts, as being in favor of having the city pay an exorbitant sum to Watts for the waterworks system.

Alderman Stanton was introduced as the next speaker. He said Campbell was opposed to investigating courthouse frauds, as he was a county commissioner at the time the frauds were committed. An admirer of Campbell declared to Stanton that Colonel Campbell had a national reputation, and in Washington was considered a very big man. "I read an interview with him in one of the Washington papers written by one of the brightest reporters there, who gave his readers to understand what he thought of Colonel Campbell by referring to him as Poker Bob, every few lines, and he quoted one of the colonel's wise sayings, 'If you open a jackpot on less than queens, you will come out loser.' " He also quoted James H. Marr as having said, "All that can be said against Colonel Campbell is that he plays poker. Yes, my friends, he does play poker, but he plays to win: and always keeps sober and when the soft pated, brainless suckers besotted with whiskey play with him, he usually gets away with the pot, and that's what he'll do in the election." [laughter and applause]. The speaker asked if Marr did not say that Colonel Campbell was a good hand to roll a drunken man? [laughter and applause].

Thus the tenor of the election campaign is seen.

The big night, however, was on Monday, April 8, 1895. San Jacinto Plaza was crowded with people there to hear the speakers on behalf of the Independent ticket. Dr. Yandell again was chairman of the meeting, and introduced the first speaker, City Attorney W.H. Burges. In introducing him he said the young man's only sin was that he was the chairman's nephew.

Burges made a forceful speech, which was devoted to the water company and the necessity of municipal waterworks, stressing that if Shelton and the candidates for the Independent ticket were elected, the demand for a good waterworks system would be met. He then turned his attention to a card, which Colonel Campbell's people had been circulating, alleging statements by prominent Independents which the latter had never made, and Burges declared that the man who got up that card was a literal descendant of Ananias and Sapphira, in fact, he was their most promising son [laughter]. There was a signed agreement (which he exhibited) between committees representing the Independents and the Republicans for a joint discussion, and the Republicans should be at the meeting this very night, but instead were holding a Star Chamber session in the opera house with thirty-two Mexicans in the gallery, and Chipman, Fink, and Archer holding down the front seats in the parquet. [laughter and applause]. The opposition was engaged in its favorite little game of poker, but had been called down, and was showing a bobtail flush, seven high [laughter]. He then turned his attention to the water question, stating that one of the chief opponents to a good water system in El Paso was R.F. Campbell. He riddled the Republican platform, especially its claim to "safe business methods and conservatism," yes, the safe business methods and conservatism of Jim Burns, Chipman and Archer [laughter]. On further paying his compliments to Jim Burns and his redlight dance house, Schoonmaker called out from the crowd, "You're an old one, you are." The only reply Burges made was, "If the scavenger will remove that thing, I will thank him." [prolonged laughter]. He roasted the candidates on the Republican ticket before closing by urging the voters of El Paso to support the Independent ticket and give the people of El Paso cheaper water.

Following Burges, A.G. Foster spoke, making a polished address, and he was followed by J.A. Harper and Judge Edwards.

But the reform movement had not come to fruition, and Poker Bob Campbell was elected mayor.

However, the election of 1895 did not mean Burges was through with Poker Bob. Campbell, represented by J.A. Buckler, on September 1, 1891, filed a libel suit against George Knapp & Company, publishers of *The St. Louis Republic,* and the defendant was represented by J.M. Dean and W.H. Burges. Campbell's suit was based upon an article in the *Republic,* printed in its issue of July 16, 1891. The article all related to activity in Washington to oust F.P. Clark from the position of collector of customs at El Paso, and it was said that Campbell was behind this effort, with a view to securing the appointment to that position for himself. Tenor of the article was generally unfavorable to those seeking to oust Clark, and among other things, referred to them as smugglers and Pharisees, but the paragraph which was the basis for the libel suit read:

> It is hinted here that "Poker Bob" Campbell, a character of more or less notorious reputation in the Southwest, who was a candidate for the collectorship himself at the time Clark was appointed, and who has been indicted several times in El Paso County for maintaining a gambling house, is the active spirit behind the charges against Mr. Clark.

Campbell alleged that the statements in this paragraph were false, scandalous and constituted a malicious libel upon him.

For some reason, not now known—unless presumably the plaintiff's attorney did not ask for the case to be set for trial—the case was not called up for trial until December 13, 1895. The trial was held before Judge C.N. Buckler, who was a brother of the plaintiff's attorney, J.A. Buckler.

There was much testimony about Campbell being a professional gambler. The testimony tendered in the case which was offered by defendant, and excluded by the judge, was to the effect that Campbell had lived in El Paso since 1882, but had spent much of his time in Chicago and New York; he had been in the drugstore business in El Paso from 1883 to 1889, and he had speculated in real estate in El Paso. There was considerable testimony to the effect that he was generally known as Poker Bob. In view of the fact that the article complained of said that he was a character of more or less notorious reputation in the Southwest, defendant offered the testimony of W.W. Turney, who then lived in El Paso, but who had lived in Alpine, Texas, in 1891, to the effect that he had heard of him in that part of the state, and he was generally known as Poker Bob. It appeared Campbell owned a house in which gambling was carried on, and he had been convicted and fined for playing cards in a public place in El Paso. There was also testimony offered, some of which was excluded, to the effect that Campbell owned a building which housed the Fashion Saloon—later the Wigwam Saloon—and this places it as being in the corner of the alley and San Antonio streets, just west of Oregon Street, where the State Theater now stands. It also appeared gambling was regularly carried on in this building, and that Campbell, himself, gambled there almost daily when in El Paso.

It was too much to expect to win a case in the District Court in El Paso, in which the mayor of the city was the plaintiff, his attorney was a brother of the judge, and the action was against a St. Louis newspaper. The jury brought in a verdict of $3,000 actual damages, and $2,000 exemplary damages, and judgment was entered against defendant for $5,000.

The defendant appealed to the Court of Civil Appeals, El Paso, at that time being in the district of the Court of Civil Appeals in San Antonio. The appeals court held Judge Buckler was not disqualified to try the case, and that the newspaper article was libelous per se.

The court did hold, however, the trial court had erred in excluding testimony as to Campbell's reputation as a gambler, saying any testimony that tended to show the appellee was a gambler and permitted a gambling house owned or controlled by him to operate was admissible in mitigation of damages. The gist of the action was in the injury done to the reputation of Campbell, and if he had no reputation to be injured, in the line of the accusation, he would not be entitled to substantial damages. Especially would the testimony be admissible on the cross-examination of the appellee. Actual bad character, such as would be shown by proof of commission of other crimes of the same nature, may be shown in mitigation of damages. This, of course, was material on the questions of damages to be assessed by the jury, and for this error, the judgment in favor of the plaintiff was reversed and the cause remanded to the District Court of El Paso County. There is no further record of the case, and it is a fair assumption that after this ruling by the court, the case either languished on the docket until it was dismissed for want of prosecution, or else, was settled by the defendant for some comparatively small sum.

During the period of time covered by the trial and the appeal of this case, W.H. Burges and Richard F. Burges were partners, under the firm name of Burges & Burges. Their accounts show that on January 10, 1896, they were paid $250 as a fee in this case, no doubt for their services in the trial court, and on January 26, 1897, they received $250. Presumably, the case had been either dismissed or settled by this time, and this fee, no doubt covered their services in the Court of Civil Appeals and for concluding the case.

V

Reform Still Elusive

Formless themselves, reforming do pretend,
as if confusion could disorder mend.
—Daniel

STILL THE REFORM MOVEMENT would not die. Although the election of Poker Bob as mayor was a victory for the gamblers, and quickly resulted in Burges' dismissal from the post of city attorney, and Jeff Milton from the position of chief of police, there was, nevertheless, more than one string to the reform bow. The *El Paso Herald* of July 18, 1895, spread the news in an article entitled, "Bombshell In The Gambler's Camp," and stated:

District Attorney McGown and ex-City Attorney W.H. Burges took a little trip to Del Rio (400 miles via Southern Pacific Railroad—two-thirds of the distance to San Antonio) a day or two ago, very quiet; and put in an appearance at Judge Gillis' Court. Mr. McGown had a petition which he presented to the Court, stating how the state laws had been honored more in the breach than the observance; and after detailing the premises and where gambling is carried on in this city and the parties who are engaged in it, prayed for a temporary writ of injunction restraining J.J. Taylor from renting his premises on El Paso Street to Patterson or Burris, or anybody else for gambling; also, asking for an injunction restraining Gus Lee, J.P. Dieter, George Sauer and Park W. Pitman from permitting any gaming prohibited by the States from being played, dealt, kept or exhibited at the said Gus Lee's place of business; also an injunction restraining Ben Patterson, Sam Burris, and their agents, servants or employees from keeping, playing, dealing or exhibiting any game, device of any description at the Gem Saloon, and in the Gem building on El Paso Street in this City . . .

The article then copied the injunction order issued by Judge Gillis, whose 41st District Court included El Paso. The news article rejoiced that there was no opportunity for the miscarriage of justice through the chances of a jury trial, since the judge granting the injunction is judge both of the law and of the facts which constitute a violation of it.

Among those specifically enjoined were "Curly Bill Brewster" and "Gushy Jim Baker," along with fifteen or sixteen others.

The reporter interviewed Burges on his return from Del Rio, and quoted him as stating there was little to be said, as the newspaper had a copy of Judge Gillis' order. He added, this order is all the good people of El Paso could desire, and they may rest assured Judge Gillis will see it is enforced. The judge has the power to punish anyone violating the order by fining them any sum not to exceed $300, and by imprisoning them for any time, not to exceed three days, or by both fine and imprisonment.

The Gillis injunction had been issued in a case styled *The State of Texas v. Ben M. Patterson, et al, Appellees.* The State was represented by W.C. McGown, district attorney, and by Burges & Burges. The defendants, in addition to Patterson, numbered some twenty-five other residents of El Paso. The bill sought to restrain the defendants from violation of a penal law of the State of Texas, to-wit: the exhibiting of gaming tables, gaming banks and other devices for the purpose of gaming in the Gem Building in the city of El Paso; second, to prevent and restrain a violation of the revenue law of the State of Texas, namely, the maintaining of a gaming house and the exhibiting of games, gaming tables, gaming banks, and gaming devices for the purpose of gaming on premises occupied by defendant Gus Lee as a retail liquor house, and to prevent acts which he, the said Gus Lee as Principal, and J.P. Deiter, George Sauer, and Park Pitman as sureties, executed their bond to the State of Texas in the sum of $5,000 conditioned said acts therein complained of should not be permitted on or about the said premises; and third, to refrain and abate the maintenance of public nuisance, to-wit, a public gambling house in the said Gem Building in the city of El Paso, Texas.

Judge Gillis granted the injunction when the bill was presented to him on July 17, 1895. On the following day, the petition was filed in the District Court of El Paso County. On September 23, 1895, the defendants filed an answer. On September 24, 1895, the defendants moved to dissolve the injunction upon various grounds such as: (1) the allegations in the petition did not show a cause cognizable in equity; (2) there was no authority for bringing this suit by the district attorney; (3) the bill was not sworn to by the relator or by any agent for the plaintiff; (4) the bill is sworn to before the attorney who represented the plaintiff; (5) and the injunction was issued without any authority on the part of the court to order the same, in that the injunction only restrains the violation of penal statutes. The defendants were represented by W.B. Brack and W.M. Coldwell.

On further hearing before the court, the judge ruled that there were no equities in the bill entitling the state to the relief prayed for, and the State of Texas appealed. The appeal went to the Court of Civil Appeals at San Antonio, which on October 7, 1896, handed down an opinion affirming the judgment of the trial court. This judgment was rendered on the basis that criminal statutes were expected to be enforced by the criminal process, and not by an injunction; and that while violation of criminal laws could be enjoined, it was only where they interfered with someone's personal or property rights as distinguished from a general violation of the law amounting to a public nuisance.

The opinion of the Court of Civil Appeals was written by Judge Neill, a very able lawyer and judge, who was practicing law in El Paso at the time he was appointed to serve on the Court of Civil Appeals in San Antonio. On the merits of the case, Judge Neill wrote, before holding that there was not equity in the bill:

> It is well established that a common gaming house is, at common law, a public nuisance, and the keeper thereof punishable criminally for the reason that persons attracted to it, especially youths, are there lured to vice . . . It draws together evil disposed persons, encourages idleness, cheating, and

other corrupt practices, and tends to public disorder . . . And that Courts of equity have jurisdiction to abate public nuisances is equally as well established.

But in the end, the court left the state to pursue the matter by criminal process and not by injunction under the facts of this case.

He did add one thing of general interest, stating:

> Before entering upon this consideration, we will remark that when a State appears before a judicial tribunal, though it may be a creature of her sovereign authority, she appears as a suitor, and not in her sovereign capacity, and, as any other litigant, can only invoke such powers and jurisdiction as she has by her Constitution and laws conferred upon the Court before whom she has brought her action. For Courts to recognize her in any other attitude, or draw a distinction in her favor against the humblest individual who appears before them, would be to stultify themselves, and subject their judges to the condemnation of the laws of the State in whose interest they sought to violate them.

Even before the district court held a permanent injunction would not issue, the reform group found enforcement of the temporary injunction next to impossible. It was reported July 30, 1895, that gambling was going on at the Gem, regardless of the injuction. The news comment was made that it remains to be seen what Judge Gillis will do. "The gambling fraternity seems determined to run the town, but time will tell which is the stronger, the law of Texas or the lawbreakers. Continuance of gambling at the Gem shows the gamblers have no regard for the laws of the state, and they are determined to set at defiance the order of the court." The paper called on Mayor Campbell to act to enforce the law.

It was generally known that gambling continued to run at the Gem, but the doors to the gambling hall were guarded so closely it was impossible to get in unless you were known to the doorkeeper to be someone who wouldn't peach. As a result, it was impossible to get evidence to prove gambling was being carried on.

Burges and his group decided to appeal to the governor for help. He went to Austin, and called on Governor Culberson, and asked him to send Texas Rangers to El Paso to enforce the law against gambling. The governor asked for a letter from the district attorney and the sheriff with respect to their need of the Rangers. A few days later Governor Culberson received the following letter:

El Paso, Texas
July 31, 1895

Hon. C.A. Culberson, Governor
Austin, Texas

Dear Sir:

In connection with the request heretofore made by me to you, for the assistance of the State Rangers in enforcing the laws against gambling in this City, and in addition to the statements made to you by Wm. H. Burges of this place, in conversation with you on Monday last, I have to report.

1st. Public gambling is carried on in the City of El Paso at this time in open disregard of the laws of the State of Texas and in violation of an injunction heretofore issued by Judge Gillis at the suit of the State, and now pending in the District Court of El Paso County, Texas;

2nd. In all cases in which it has been practicable, process has been issued to bring the violators of the law to justice, which process has been promptly served by the Sheriff of El Paso County, Texas, but owing to the fact that the gamblers keep a guard out who report the approach of officers and offer objections to their entrance to the gambling hall, it has been impossible to get full and adequate proof of the violations of the law and injunction.

3rd. That the number of men employed in violating the gaming laws of the State in El Paso, and banded in conspiring together to that end, is between forty-five and fifty.

4th. Although these laws are openly violated along the principal streets of the City, the police of the City have made no effort to prevent the violations of the laws of Texas, which are at the same time violations of the ordinances of the City of El Paso, but have remonstrated with citizens for prosecuting the offenders.

5th. The Constable of the Precinct has rendered no assistance whatever except to serve a few subpoenas and warrants placed in his hands. No assistance can be looked for from either the Constable's office or the police force.

6th. The Sheriff and two deputies are the only available officers to assist in enforcing their laws.

7th. Acting upon the testimony of the gamblers themselves, good and creditable citizens of El Paso have filed complaints against the gamblers, charging vagrancy and various offenses against the gaming laws. In one instance already one of our citizens, a quiet, law abiding man, has been attacked on the street for filing such complaints. Many others have been threatened. The gambler who attacked the citizen was not even arrested though the offense was committed in the presence of a policeman, who caught and held the attacked citizen when he endeavored to resent the insult and assault.

8th. I have every reason to believe, and do believe, that citizens whose only offense is an effort to enforce the laws of this State are liable to attack at any moment and their lives are in constant danger from this lawless set of men, who have no interest in this community except to violate its law and plunder its people.

9th. On account of the large number of men of this class and the very small number in the Sheriff's office, (the only protectors we have) it is impossible to cope with these lawbreakers and to enforce the law unless assistance is received from you. I am strengthened in this belief by the fact stated to you on Monday last by Mr. Burges, among which I may mention the effort to prevent the officers from obtaining evidence of the commission of offenses, the often repeated threats of suing officers on their bonds, should any mistake be made in arresting supposed offenders, and the open and repeated threats to institute prosecution against citizens and officers for malicious prosecution. All the prosecutions heretofore instituted have been based on the testimony of the gamblers themselves. With a hardihood which I believe is without parallel, they announced that they are engaged in violation of the laws of this State and they propose to continue so to do, and boldly make their threats of personal violence towards officers and citizens who endeavor to have them brought to justice. The Sheriff has used the means at his command, but has not been able to bring these violations of the law to an end. I do not believe he can do so without the assistance of the Rangers, be he ever so active and efficient, in fact, the situation has become more aggravated, they now not only violate the gaming laws but endeavor to do personal violence to those who oppose them. I therefore most urgently request the immediate assistance of Capt. Hughes and his men. This request is made as a last resort, to the end that the law may be enforced, the lives of good and peaceable citizens saved and violence prevented.

Very respectfully,
W.C. McGown
Dist. Atty. 34th Jud. Dist.
of Texas

Governor Culberson, I hereby endorse the foregoing statements and most urgently and sincerely request that you grant the assistance therein asked for. I know of no reason why it should not be granted and every reason why it should. The enforcement of the law and the lives of our best citizens depends on it.

W.W. Turney

I hereby endorse the foregoing statement so far as it pertains to what my office has done and can and will do, and am perfectly willing to have the Rangers sent here to act in the matter.

F.B. Simmons
Sheriff El Paso County
July 31, 1895

Hon. C.A. Culberson, Governor
Austin, Texas

Dear Sir:

I enclose herewith the letter from the District Attorney and Sheriff you mentioned, this needs prompt attention. Violence is hourly threatened. As the Sheriff states in that letter, his office cannot cope with it. This is stated in the District Attorney's letter, and the Sheriff endorses it.

Please let me hear from you at once.

Very respectfully,
Wm. H. Burges

Fighting the gamblers was not always a peaceful or safe activity. Burges' office was on the second floor of the Wells Fargo Building, at the southeast corner of South El Paso and East San Antonio streets. He had a room, for his living quarters, next to his office. On one occasion one of the tough supporters of the gamblers came into his office, where he was alone, and threatened to do him great bodily harm. Burges was less than average size, and no match physically for a bully such as this one was, and he was not in a strategic position to get his Colt .45, which was in his desk. He determined, if the man made a hostile move, to snatch up a metal letter opener lying on top of his desk, and defend himself with it. It turned out, however, that his belligerent caller was all talk and no action.

Every night about 10:00 P.M., he went from his office to the English Kitchen, the leading restaurant in town, run by Dock Sing. It was just east of the alley, on the south side of San Antonio Street, in the same block with the Wells Fargo Building. He was tipped off that two of the gamblers planned to hide in the alley, and do him in as he crossed it on the way to the English Kitchen that night. At 10:00 P.M. he put on his .45 and went towards the English Kitchen, keeping well out to the outside of the sidewalk, for more room to see into the alley, and to maneuver. Whatever the gambler's plans were, they did not develop, and he had no untoward experience.

On still another occasion a state official of the Y.M.C.A. called on him, and urged him to let up on the gamblers, his argument being they did so much good by their contributions to the Y.M.C.A. Burges rejected the suggestion with a deep feeling of contempt for a man ostensibly using his life in the service of a moral-uplift organization, but who would stoop to serve the gamblers. Years later, in 1908, when the new Y.M.C.A. building erected at the corner of North Oregon and Missouri streets was completed, a member of its Board of Trustees, who obviously had not heard this story, came to see Burges, and asked him to be the speaker at the dedication ceremony of the new building. He answered he'd be glad to speak on that occasion. A few days later his caller returned, and said the dedication had been postponed to a later date, not yet set, and that he would let him know when it would be held. He never came back. No doubt, someone had put him wise.

But the edge was off the antigambling fight, and it would be nearly ten years before the reform forces would finally win out.

VI

John Wesley Hardin

His guns were his mouthpiece.
—Anonymous

THE 1880s-1890s was the era of the two-gun men in El Paso. Most of the best known ones of that time came to El Paso to stay a few days or months. Among those who were in El Paso for shorter or longer periods in the 1890s were Bat Masterson, John Selman, George Scarborough and John Wesley Hardin. Burges knew all of them, and none better than John Wesley Hardin.

Hardin had quite a career as a gunman before coming to El Paso early in 1895. He had served a term in the Texas Penitentiary for murder. There were stories extant that after being freed from the penitentiary, he hoped to leave behind him his old gunslinging habits, live down his reputation as a gunfighter, and become a respectable citizen. Whatever his hopes were, he arrived in El Paso wearing his guns, and his reputation, which had preceded him, diminished not one whit. He was known as a dangerous man, and was reputed to be the fastest man with a gun in that part of the country.

Among other characters who came to El Paso at that time was Martin M'Rose, who was wanted in New Mexico for cattle stealing. He went on across the Rio Grande to Juarez, and lived there to avoid extradition from El Paso to New Mexico. At the same time a buxom woman known as Mrs. M'Rose came to El Paso, and passed as being the wife of Martin M'Rose. But there seemed to be some uncertainty whether he and she were married to each other. In any event, she busied herself with trying to help take care of M'Rose's troubles in

Juarez, and to arrange for his return to El Paso, and his safety and welfare once he was back on the north side of the Rio Grande. During this time John Wesley Hardin got to know her, and became enamored of her. They apparently lived together, or spent considerable time together, although she was busily engaged in arranging for M'Rose's return to El Paso.

Eventually arrangements were made, and although M'Rose seemed to have some doubts about his safety, he decided to return. In accordance with the plan, he, with Scarborough, on the night of June 29, 1895 walked over the Mexican Central Railroad bridge across the Rio Grande after dark. They had hardly set foot on the soil of the north bank of the Rio Grande, when from out of the shadows of darkness they were accosted by two officers, who called on M'Rose to surrender. He whirled, drew his gun, and fired. The officers returned his fire, and M'Rose fell mortally wounded. The two officers were Captain Jeff Milton, formerly chief of police in El Paso, a Texas Ranger before that, and again commissioned as a Ranger at the time of this event. The other was Ranger Frank M. McMahon. Milton, who was a "good man with a gun" himself, and a good officer, with a fine reputation for being a gentleman and a fearless man, had, while chief of police, become a close friend of Burges. It was against this background that the following story unfolds.

Burges was a bachelor at this time, and lived in a room adjoining his office, which was on the second floor of the old Wells Fargo Building. There was a stairway leading from the sidewalk to the second floor. On the day in question, Captain Milton came striding into Burges' office, and said:

"Burges, I hear John Wesley Hardin is telling around town that he hired me to kill Martin M'Rose. That's a lie, of course, and I am going to find him, and make him take it back. I wish you would go with me to see no one shoots me in the back. Will you come along?"

"I certainly will," Burges answered. He arose, picked up a Colt .45 he kept in his office, stuck it in his belt, and away he and Milton went, looking for Hardin, the fastest man with a gun in town.

It did not take long to find Hardin. They walked down San Antonio Street to El Paso Street, and there, about one-half block down

El Paso Street stood Hardin, talking to two of his friends. Captain Milton and Burges marched in step down El Paso Street until they were within six or eight feet of Hardin, where Burges halted, to be in position to protect Captain Milton from the rear. Milton walked on up to the group, facing Hardin, and said:

"Hardin, I hear you've been telling around town that you hired me to kill Martin M'Rose."

"Well, what of it?" asked Hardin, in a tone that implied he could not be called to account for whatever he did.

"Well," said Milton, "I want you to tell these gentlemen here that when you said that you were a goddamn liar."

This was when the shooting was expected to begin. But Hardin, instead of pulling his gun, said, "Go on Milton, I don't want to have any trouble with you."

"I mean what I said, Hardin. You tell these gentlemen that when you told that you hired me to kill M'Rose, you were a goddamn liar."

"Go on, Milton, I don't want any trouble with you. And besides, I am unarmed."

"That's a damn lie. You never go out without your gun. But if you say you don't have it, go over to your room, it's only two blocks from here, and get it, and come back shooting."

"No, Milton, I told you I don't want any trouble with you. Now go on away."

"Hardin, I mean what I say. You tell these gentlemen that you were a damn liar when you said you hired me to kill Martin M'Rose, or I am going to count three and when I get to three, you'd better start shooting, because I'm going for my gun."

Captain Milton started counting.

"One"

"Two"

"All right," said Hardin, "When I said I hired you to kill Martin M'Rose, I was a goddamn liar," Hardin said.

Their mission was accomplished, but at this point the question in Burges' mind was how were they to get away, without running the risk of being shot in the back. Captain Milton, however, never hesitated. He took three steps back, and when he was even with

Burges he turned on his heel, about face, and Burges did likewise. They marched back, side by side, to San Antonio Street, turned the corner, and down San Antonio Street to the stairway leading to his office. They were out of sight of Hardin. Captain Milton leaned limply against the door facing at the entrance to the stairway, and said,

"What do you know about that? He's so much faster with a gun than I am, that if he had gone for his gun, I wouldn't have had a chance."

VII

The Fitzsimmons-Maher Prizefight

Hath his belly full of fighting.
—Shakespeare

IN JANUARY, 1896, the great news in El Paso was the announcement that the next heavyweight championship prizefight was to be held in the city. The champion was Bob Fitzsimmons, and his challenger was Peter Maher. The town was agog with the news that the fight would be held there, as it would not only enable the local sports and interested people to see it, but would bring a crowd of people to town for the event.

There was one hitch about it, however. The legislature of the State of Texas, at its session in 1895, passed a law forbidding prizefights in Texas. Burges had supported the bill, and he was also a supporter of Governor Charles A. Culberson, who had favored the antiprizefight law. No sooner was the announcement made that the fight was scheduled to be held in El Paso than he announced there would be no prizefight in El Paso. He cited the law against it, and declared he would see the law enforced. He knew he would have no support from the city administration, for Mayor "Poker Bob" Campbell and his council welcomed it, and the rowdiness, and rowdies, who went with it.

Almost immediately rumors began to circulate the fight promoters were bringing in some gunmen to see there was no interference with their plans.

This was a challenge, not a deterrent. Burges sent a telegram to Governor Culberson, apprising him of the situation, and requesting the governor to send some Texas Rangers to El Paso to enforce the law against prizefighting. The governor issued a statement he would not permit the fight to be held on Texas soil. Dan Stuart, the promoter, retaliated with a manifesto that the fight would be held "in or near El Paso." There was Juarez, just across the river in Mexico, and there were the then territories of New Mexico and Arizona within easy reach.

Ten days before the fight the rough element, who .were camp followers of the ring in those days, began to drift into El Paso. New gambling halls and variety shows were opened. Gamblers and gunmen were rampant. You could not afford to win in the gambling halls—for above the noises of the nightlife could be heard gunfire and the dull thud of lead pipes as some camp follower with the robber instinct relieved a winner of both his roll and his life.

Fitzsimmons established his training quarters in Juarez, where he gave exhibitions, wrestling with his pet lion, Nero, while Maher began training at Las Cruces, New Mexico.

On February 10, Adjutant General Mabry came into El Paso with ten grim and well-armed Rangers. During the next few days others arrived under Captain Bill McDonald, and reported to Burges, as instructed by Governor Culberson. Burges again announced there would be no prizefight, adding that Governor Culberson had sent the Rangers to see to it.

The city hummed with excitement when the press reported Bat Masterson was bringing one hundred Pinkerton detectives to El Paso to aid Dan Stuart in pulling off the fight in defiance of the law.

At about the same time the Arizona National Guard mobilized to prevent the fight being held in Arizona. Federal officials gathered in Las Cruces, and Delegate Tom Catron of New Mexico rushed a bill through Congress barring fights in the Territories. Mexican troops were dispatched to Juarez to prevent the fight from being moved over the border. General Mabry conferred with the governor of New Mexico, and then announced, "The Rangers will act on all soil in dispute between Texas and New Mexico and the United States and Mexico." This covered the situation created by a rumor the fight would be held on disputed territory as a means evading the authorities.

About this time Bat Masterson arrived from Denver with his Pinkertons, and a United States marshal with twelve deputies came from Santa Fe. Governor Ahumada of Chihuahua, Mexico, reached Juarez on February 12, with a detachment of Mexican cavalry. These were stationed along the south bank of the Rio Grande. Colonel Parker, in command of the United States troops at Fort Bliss, issued orders no officers should leave the post after 6:00 P.M.

The town seethed with newspapermen from all over the country and with all manner of sports celebrities, including John L. Sullivan, who had been dethroned from his championship four years previously. The El Paso fight was to decide which one of the men involved would meet Jim Corbett, Sullivan's conqueror, and Sullivan was there to see it.

Being a reporter was not a safe occupation, especially if the newsman asked too many questions. One reporter was approached by a fellow with hawklike features who fixed him with a cold gray eye that sent a chill down into his shoes and said, "You'd better forget this kid, if you want to keep healthy." The speaker was one of the notorious gunmen who had been brought in to overpower the anti-prizefight movement.

Texas Rangers followed Fitzsimmons in El Paso and Maher was shadowed by deputy marshals in Las Cruces. Bat Masterson and his men hung around, ready for any emergency. The town was boiling. In one faction resentment grew over the presence of the Rangers without a request from the sheriff. The El Paso City Council passed a resolution condemning the governor for having sent the Rangers.

It was amidst these scenes of riotous and near-riotous conduct that the fight against holding the prizefight in El Paso—or Texas—was carried on. The prizefight crowd felt like they had the upper hand in any show of force, and they could pull it off successfully. But Burges held the trump cards; for his final and compelling announcement was: "There will be no Fitzsimmons-Maher fight in El Paso or in Texas, for Governor Culberson has placed the Texas Rangers at my disposal, and if the fight cannot be prevented in any other manner, my instructions to the Rangers are to shoot the principals as soon as they climb into the ring. I know there will be no prizefight here."

It began to dawn on the fight promoters that he meant exactly what he said, and the fight could not be held there. So they made arrangements to hold it in Mexico, just across the Rio Grande from the little station of Langtry, on the Southern Pacific Railroad (then the G.H. & S.A. Railway Co.). Langtry is best known as the home of Judge Roy Bean, "The Law West of the Pecos." It is some 359 miles east of El Paso, and the fight crowd arranged with the railroad for a special train to take the crowd from El Paso to Langtry for the event.

When the day came for the train to make the run from El Paso to Langtry, and while the crowd of fight enthusiasts were getting aboard, Burges and the Rangers at his command appeared with tickets for Langtry. He proposed to go along, and take the Rangers, to see it was not held in Texas. The fight promoters told him he could not go, that this was a special train, secured by them, at their request, and that he and the Rangers could not go. His reply was, "This railroad is a common carrier, and under the law it must carry any passenger who pays the fare." So he and General Mabry, Captain McDonald and the Rangers went.

The fight was held on February 20, 1896. The crowd that went down on the train to Langtry streamed across the river to a sandbar on the Mexican side which was the site of the "World's Championship Heavyweight Prizefight," and took their places around the ring. But not for long, for in the middle of the first round, Fitzsimmons knocked out Maher, and the fight was over. Among those who went from El Paso to see the fight were Judge T.A. Falvey, the district judge, and John M. Dean, the district attorney. The fight was over so quickly that Dean did not see it. When Maher was counted out, Judge Falvey said:

"Come on, let's go."

"Go where?"

"Back to the train."

"No sir," said Dean, "I made this trip down here to see a prizefight, and I'm going to stay until they fight."

But Judge Falvey persuaded him to leave.

The crowd streamed back across the river, and into Judge Roy Bean's Jersey Lilly Saloon, the only place to get something to eat. Bat Masterson, two guns swinging below his hips, strolled in and strode up to the counter at the head of the line. He was exercising what he apparently deemed was his God-given prerogative of pushing ahead of all the ordinary folks standing in line. But he reckoned without Ranger "Wild Bill" McDonald. Hardly had Bat Masterson reached the head of the line, hungry and looking for preferential service, than he felt the end of the barrel of a Colt .45 in his back, and heard McDonald's command, "Back to the end of the line. Everybody takes their turn here." Masterson did not argue the point. He knew only too well that if he gave McDonald any provocation, or excuse, the Ranger would shoot him where he stood. He meekly turned, became the last man in the rear rank of the line.

The crowd, feeling cheated of seeing a real fight, and half-hungry, boarded the special train, and returned to El Paso.

Burges had seen to it that the fight was not held in El Paso, or in Texas.

VIII

Anna Pollard Burges

She was a phantom of delight.
—Wordsworth

IN THE MID-1890s, the leading drugstore in El Paso was Kelly & Pollard. It was owned and run by Henry Kelly, later mayor for several terms, and Joseph H. Pollard. Pollard had come to El Paso from Fulton, Missouri, where his father had a drugstore. In the late fall of 1895, Burges discovered there was a particularly pretty and charming young lady visiting in town. He saw her and quickly learned that she was Joe Pollard's sister. He told Henry Kelly that he would like to meet Miss Pollard, and Kelly promised to introduce him to her. Several days went by without this promise being fulfilled, and although the promise was renewed on several occasions, the introduction did not materialize. Finally, he told Kelly once again that he wanted an introduction to Miss Pollard, and that he was anxious to meet her. This was on a Saturday. Kelly said, "Several of us are going to the bullfight in Juarez tomorrow afternoon. If you will be just outside the entrance to the bullring when the bullfight is over, I will introduce you to her."

So, the next day in the late afternoon as the bullfight was drawing to an end, Burges stood outside the entrance to the bullring waiting for the introduction. As the crowd came out when the bullfight was over, here came a group which included Henry Kelly and Anna Pollard. Burges lost no time in making his way to them, and Kelly introduced him to Anna Pollard. He began calling on her immediately afterwards, and found her as lovely and attractive as he had thought when he first saw her. It developed that she had come to El Paso for her health, as

ANNA POLLARD BURGES

did many other people who had lung trouble. She had an arrested case of tuberculosis, with only one good lung left. It was not long before he proposed to her, and they looked forward to their marriage at an early date.

Later, Miss Pollard returned to Fulton to be at home until the marriage should take place. Burges went up to call on her, and meet her parents and the other members of the family in advance of the wedding date. He arrived in Fulton while a William Jennings Bryan campaign for president was in progress. Burges was orthodox in his views about politics, public affairs and economics, and he did not subscribe to the populist proposals of William Jennings Bryan. When he stepped off the train at Fulton, he found himself in a hotbed of Bryan supporters. He afterwards said that when you got off the train in those days in Fulton, and asked some stranger standing by the depot how to get to Pollard's drugstore, the stranger would take his hat off, throw it up in the air and holler, "Three cheers for William Jennings Bryan! Pollard's drugstore is two blocks that-a-way and then two blocks to the right."

The Bryan campaign gave rise to another story which he liked to repeat: The story was, on one occasion, William Jennings Bryan came to Fulton, Missouri. The only thing at that time worthy of showing to a distinguished visitor was the brand new building which housed the State Insane Asylum at Fulton. So the committee in charge of his reception took him out to visit the State Insane Asylum. While going through the halls, an inmate, who had the run of the place, rushed up to Bryan and said: "What's your hobby?"

He replied, "My friend, I have no hobby. But if you refer to what is the ruling passion of my life, it is the free and unlimited coinage of silver in the ratio of 16 to 1."

The inmate looked at him and said:

"You're not crazy."

"I should hope not," said Bryan.

"No," said the inmate, "you're not crazy, you're just a damn fool."

In due time, the wedding took place in Fulton, Missouri, September 23, 1896, and the two lived together happily from that time on until Burges' death in 1946.

On their arrival in El Paso, they took rooms at the home of Mr. and Mrs. W.W. Turney, whose house at the time was 816 North Oregon Street—the second house from the corner, on the east side of Oregon, south of Montana Street. Thereafter they moved to a house at 425 North El Paso Street, and then to 711 North El Paso Street. In 1907 they bought the house at 1302 Montana Street, principally because the basement was mostly one large room which would serve as his library. This was to be their home the rest of their lives, except for the twenty months in Chicago in 1917 and 1918.

Mrs. Burges was well-read, posted on current affairs (she could not have lived with Burges and have been otherwise), a lively conversationalist, and a gracious hostess. She was in her own way a tower of strength. She had the religious convictions of one brought up in the Presbyterian Church in the late 1800s, the rugged independence of Americans of that day and age, and unerring judgment in sizing people as to each one's character and innate worth. Her great handicap was her health, which was always bad. It was on this account that she spent a great deal of time at the old Virginia Hotel in Long Beach, California, back when that city was small and was a delightful resort for vacationers. Burges said he had paid the Virginia Hotel so much money he felt he should be entitled to a deed to it. They found it a delightful vacation spot, and enjoyed it.

She was not only a worthy mate for him, but was also an asset to the city of El Paso which was better, in many ways for her having lived in it.

IX

Turney & Burges

They lived and worked together as one.
—Anonymous

ON APRIL 1, 1897, the famed law firm of Turney & Burges came into existence. For forty-one years it was to be one of the principal institutions of El Paso in every way — a leader not only in the law, as it was throughout the Southwest, but also in business, civic and cultural areas. W.W. Turney, with whom W.H. Burges formed this great partnership, had lived in El Paso nearly five years at this time. He was born in Harrison County, near Marshall, Texas. His father owned a plantation, but the calamities of the Civil War and Reconstruction left the family in poor financial circumstances. Turney recalled that one winter the smokehouse on the farm was filled with hams, sides of bacon, and dry, unshelled peas, which were to be the mainstay of their food, but the smokehouse caught fire, and it, and all provisions in it were destroyed. This was a real calamity.

Sam Houston State Normal School opened in 1879, and the State of Texas paid the expenses of the students. Turney was one of the students that first year, following which he taught school in northeast Texas for two years. He was offered the job of school teacher at Ft. Davis for the school year of 1886-87, and accepted it. This was his introduction to Texas, west of the Pecos. He was a slender young man of average height, and found on arriving at Fort Davis a small frontier town and army post, boasting eleven saloons and a scholastic population of seventy-five, in the Davis mountain region of Texas. He soon

W.W. TURNEY

learned the older boys in the little one-room school were saying, "We threw the last teacher out, and we'll throw this one out, too."

One of the more troublesome students was a twelve-year-old redheaded boy, whose father, a saloon keeper, was one of the town's leading citizens. Not many days after school began, the redheaded boy, in the middle of the morning classes, jumped up on top of his desk, squatted down on all fours, let out a loud "baa-baa," like a goat, jumped to the top of the next desk, repeated the "baa-baa," and on to an open window through which he jumped.

But in spite of such disciplinary problems, he successfully taught the school through the year. He moved to Alpine, where he taught school, studied law, and was admitted to the Texas Bar. In 1892, he was elected to the legislature, and shortly thereafter moved to El Paso. He and his bride, the former Iva Guthrie, whose father owned the 101 Ranch near Alpine, soon established their home on North Oregon Street. He and M.W. Stanton formed a partnership, but it proved unsatisfactory, and after a few months, Turney dissolved it.

The press reported, during the legislative session of 1893, that Turney made an earnest and successful fight for the appropriation bill for the Texas Rangers, adding that he was always found on the right side of every question. In 1895, he introduced and secured passage of a bill to encourage irrigation, and to construct canals, ditches, flumes, dams, and reservoirs. In that same year, he endorsed the "Ranger Petition" in the antigambling effort of the reform group. He was elected to the Texas Senate in 1896, and in 1897 the local press reported he carried all his points in the Senate and every appropriation he supported was made.

Not long after coming to El Paso, Turney was employed as special prosecutor in *The State of Texas v. Oliver Lee,* at Pecos, Reeves County, Texas. Oliver Lee was a rancher in the Sacramento Mountains of New Mexico, a dead shot with a pistol, and a controversial character. He was indicted at Pecos for unlawful carrying of a gun in public. Turney had tried a number of cases before juries in Alpine, and that area, with uniform success. He had witnesses to Lee's carrying a gun in Pecos—typical Western fashion—and considered this an easy case. He had no doubt of getting a verdict of "guilty." On Sunday before the trial was to begin on Monday, he took the Texas & Pacific train to Pecos. On arrival there, he soon learned that Oliver Lee, and his retinue of cowboys, had ridden in a week earlier, pitched camp at the edge of town, and had been holding open house all week, serving drinks and barbecue and beans. It didn't take Turney long to see the case was already lost.

W.W. Turney was a man of forceful character, and high intelligence. His legal learning was sound, and he examined and analyzed minutely the facts of any public question or of any lawsuit in which he was involved, so that when he spoke on it, he knew intimately all its facets, and could speak with authority. He readily attracted clients, including those with substantial business interests. He brought with him into the Turney & Burges firm the Santa Fe Railroad as a client, and soon added the Southwest Telephone and Telegraph Co. Burges represented the First National Bank, and the firm represented the early-day entrepreneur, Zach T. White and others.

Turney was elected to the State Senate in 1896, after which he was prominently mentioned for various offices; in 1897 for commissioner of the General Land Office; in 1899 for Congress; and in 1900 for governor. He was nominated again for state senator in 1900, by acclamation, at the Senatorial Convention in Uvalde for the 25th Senatorial District. He was active in promoting the Midwinter Carnival, in the Chamber of Commerce, and in lobbying in Washington for the passage of an International Dam Bill. He bought the 02 Ranch, south of Alpine, and before he finished adding to it he had acquired 240,000 acres of land.

His business judgment—and good fortune—were proven by news items in 1901 that he had an interest in a quicksilver mine in Brewster County which was sold at a price that netted him over $75,000 and in 1902 that he sold 2,500 head of cattle on his ranch for $40,000. In that year he was elected president of the Texas Cattle Raisers Association, a position he held two terms. For his work in this office he received wide acclaim. In 1904 he was elected president of the El Paso Social Club, which had seventy-five members. Walter Arnold was elected secretary, and Julius Krakauer was treasurer. As president, he was ex-officio chairman of the Ball Committee, and appointed the committee to make the arrangements for the ball. In the same year, he was elected president of a group of businessmen whose goal was the organization of, and erection of, a building for a Y.M.C.A.

In 1906, he disclosed plans for a new residence he intended to build at a cost of $30,000. Later that year he was appointed to the State Democratic Executive Committee, succeeding John Nance Garner. In 1909, he and Mrs. Turney moved into their new residence at 1205 Montana Street, reported to have cost $40,000, then the finest residence in the Southwest. Thirty-odd years later his widow gave it to the city of El Paso to house the International Museum.

Such was the man with whom Burges entered into partnership in 1897. His character and ability, coupled with Burges' preeminent qualities as a legal scholar, his knowledge of how to apply it practically and the latter's own scintillating personality, made the success of this law firm a certainty.

They opened their office in quarters already occupied by Turney in the Bronson Block, at the northwest corner of the intersection of Oregon and San Antonio streets. This was a two-story building, and they had the corner offices on the second floor.

Burges represented Dr. S.T. Turner, a leading physician, and soon after Turney & Burges started, they were employed by Dr. Turner in a suit he brought against George Look. Shortly thereafter, he represented Dr. Turner in a suit brought against the G.H. & S.A. Railway Co., Dr. Amos Graves, and Dr. S.T. Turner for malpractice. Dr. Turner was reputed to be shrewd in making investments and either because of the property he owned, or because of professional matters, he was occasionally a party to lawsuits.

There were also suits in which Turney & Burges represented Zach T. White, mostly concerning the title to land. *J.F. Crosby v. Z.T. White; Z.T. White v. John Wesley;* and *Ernest Kohlberg v. Z.T. White* were some of the first ones. Some of their first cases were for the First National Bank, for which, first and last, they had a large amount of business. Burges was the bank's attorney over a long

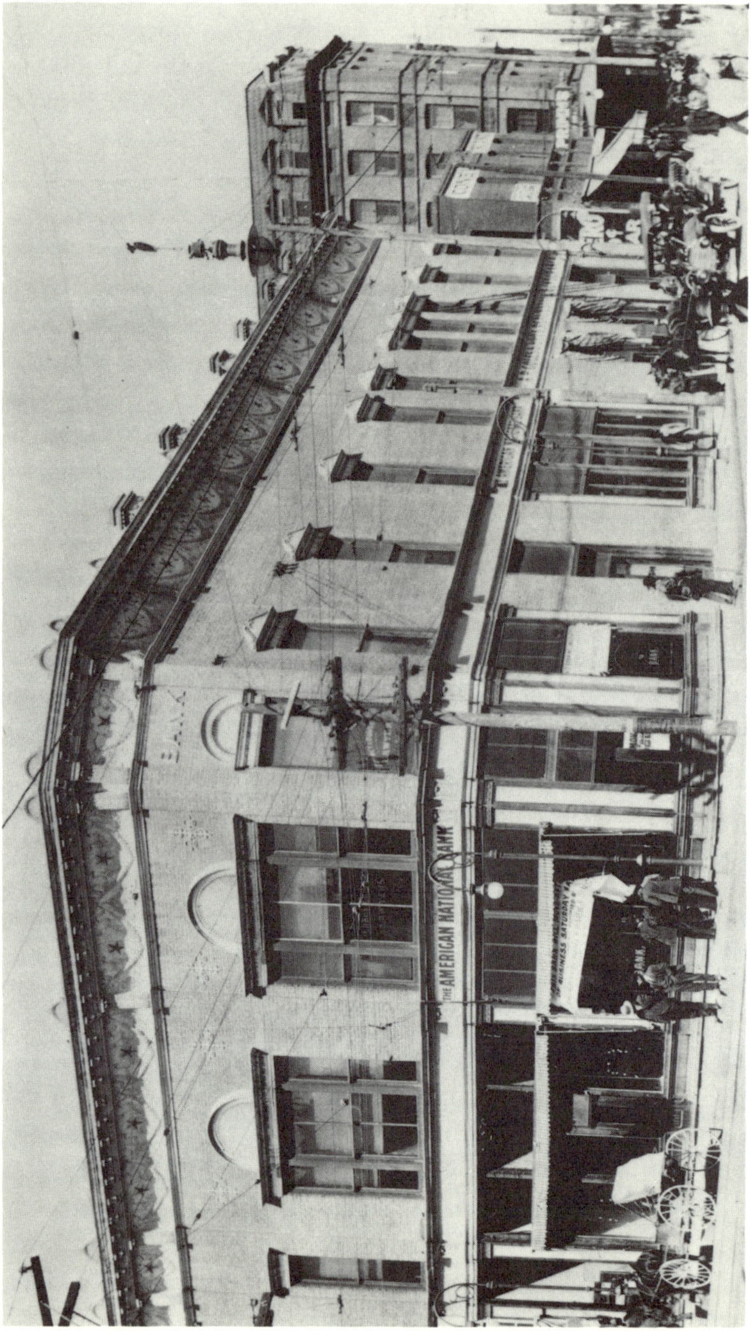

In 1897 Turney & Burges occupied corner offices on the second floor of this building at the northwest corner of the intersection of Oregon and San Antonio streets.

period of years; *Gypsy Davenport v. First National Bank,* and *First National Bank v. H.R. Hillebrand* were the earliest bank cases for Turney & Burges.

There were also suits for the Santa Fe Railway in 1897, and continuously thereafter. *Nestor Pacheco by Next Friend v. A.T.&S.F. Railway Co.,* and *El Paso County v. A.T.&S.F. Railway Co.* were the two first ones.

Then there were miscellaneous suits that first year; one for J.H. Nations, long a prominent El Pasoan, one for the Pullman Palace Car Co., and others for the Northwestern Life Assurance Co., John B. Tays, Brewster County, and one for A.S. Gage in the District Court of Brewster County. For years, Turney & Burges had one or more cases at nearly every term of court in Alpine, county seat of Brewster County.

Some of the difficulties of practicing law in a sparsely settled county was illustrated by their employment in the Carter Estate matter. They were employed by the widow, Anna C. Carter, to represent her. She and Mr. Carter lived on a ranch in Pecos County, and after his death she was fearful of living so far out and away by herself, so she left and went to Pass Christian, Mississippi, on the Gulf Coast. Much of the correspondence was with her father, who lived in New Orleans. Turney & Burges filed an application for her appointment as administratrix, but had some fears that County Judge O.W. Williams might refuse to appoint her on the grounds she was living out of the state, especially as there were local people in Pecos County opposing her appointment. She was appointed, but Judge Williams insisted she come to Fort Stockton to make the administratrix's bond. It was with difficulty Burges got her to come to San Antonio, where she stayed at the Menger Hotel. Eventually, a bond executed by her there, with a surety company on it, was accepted by Judge Williams. She was wholly unwilling to go to Fort Stockton for the purpose. It was a little frontier town she would have reached by taking the train to Alpine, and going from there to Fort Stockton, some sixty to seventy miles, by stagecoach or buckboard.

An item of interest is a letter written July 30, 1898, by Turney to C.H. Darkin, Elgin, Illinios, in answer to an inquiry, stating there is a demand for money on real estate seven to eight percent, or on cattle eight to nine percent, and that he regarded cattle as good a security as real estate.

And so it went – a busy law practice, examining abstracts, writing title opinions, writing wills and handling probate cases, advising clients about business matters, and trying all kinds of lawsuits. All this was interspersed with a leading role in civic affairs of the community, its politics and its social life.

It was during this era he had as a sometime client, Tillie Howard, one of the most notorious residents of El Paso during a part of the 1890s and into the early 1900s. She ran the plushest house in the El Paso red-light district, sometimes in those days, called the Tenderloin. It was the two-story red brick house which stood on the east side of Utah Street, now Mesa Street, about one-half block south of Overland Street. It was an imposing red brick residential-type house, and stood until torn down sometime in the late 1940s.

Burges, during the time he was city attorney, and during subsequent years, fought to have the city delineate a district or reservation to which the women in these houses would be confined. It irritated him greatly for them to have the run of the town, as they had without the establishment of a reservation. On many afternoons, they put on their finest clothes – some of the finest in town – long dresses made in the fashion of the times, with large hats decorated with ostrich plumes or other ostentatious decorations. They hired buggies or a rig from the livery stable and drove through the main parts of the city. Burges' proposal to establish a reservation for them shocked some of the supposedly good people of the city, who apparently wanted to ignore the fact that these women existed in El Paso. But since they were here, and were parading in their fine clothes through the center of town, he enthusiastically advocated a city ordinance of this kind.

He did, however, on occasion, represent Tillie Howard. Through this representation he learned her history. She was born in Wisconsin, but was left an orphan at an early age, and was taken by an aunt and uncle to live with them. There she lived until she was about thirteen years old, when, on a cold day, they told her they could no longer afford to keep her, and put her out of the house.

They lived in a rural area, and not far from their home ran a railroad track. A short distance down the track was a water tank, where steam engines could take on water, and a pond which supplied the water. She was destitute, had no one to whom she could turn for assistance, and in her dejection decided to go down to the pond and drown herself. She reached the bank of the pond, but the weather was so cold, and the water looked so frigid, that she could not muster up courage to jump into the pond. While she was sitting there in that condition and frame of mind, a train pulled up for water. The train crew asked her what was the matter, and she told them. They took her aboard the train, and for some two or three years she lived on the caboose of a train, riding up and down the road. Her relationship with some of the members of the train crews with whom she rode was only what might be expected under the circumstances. She met Willie Sells, of Sells Circus, and traveled with him for awhile, and later went with a Captain Nemmo to South Africa and lived there for a time, accumulating a small fortune. She returned to the United States, coming to El Paso where she bought the house on South Utah Street.

She came to Burges one day and said, "I have learned that my aunt and uncle who put me out of their home when I was thirteen years old, are destitute, and a bank is about to foreclose on their home. They are old, and unable to take care of themselves. In spite of their treatment of me, I do not wish to see them suffer, and I want to send them the money to pay off the mortgage. I don't want them to know where it came from. I don't want this money traced." She gave Burges the money—over five thousand dollars—and asked him to handle it through a bank so that the mortgage would be paid, but they would never know its source. This, he did, and always was of the opinion that it showed a fineness of spirit in her that one might not have expected to find in such a person. Somehow he managed to make use of this story in a lawsuit a little later on. She came to him again, with the citation in a case filed against her in the county court. George W. Emerson and others had filed a suit against her in the county court for $206.84. This, they alleged, was the agreed price of certain tiling which she had asked them to obtain for her, and which, they alleged had been delivered to her on April 20, 1899, but they said that she had not paid them. She told

THE LAW FIRM THROUGH THE YEARS

The Turney & Burges firm changed in personnel and name from time to time since 1897, due principally to additions or death. The firm has continued to the present time under the following names:

William Henry Burges, Jr.	1889
Turney and Burges	1897
Turney, Burges, Culwell, Holliday & Pollard	1918
Turney, Burges, Culwell & Pollard	1927
Burges, Burges & Scott	1938
Burges, Burges, Scott & Hulse	1941
Burges, Burges, Scott, Rasberry & Hulse	1942
Burges, Scott, Rasberry & Hulse	1945
Scott, Hulse, Marshall & Feuille	1957
Scott, Hulse, Marshall, Feuille, Finger & Thurmond	1980

Burges that she knew she owed the money, but for some reason, she felt she had been badly used by them, and she wanted to contest the case and make it as difficult for the plaintiffs to collect as possible. The plaintiffs obtained a judgment against her when the case first came up for trial, but was reversed by the Court of Civil Appeals at San Antonio. The opinion was written by Judge Fly and reflects that when the case was called for trial Burges was absent at the bedside of a sick relative, over six hundred miles from El Paso—no doubt at Seguin—and could not possibly be present at the trial and that his partner, W.W. Turney—who was not familiar with the case at all—was engaged in the trial of a suit in the district court. Judge Fly wrote that the judgment rendered by default against Tillie Howard was not due to any neglect on the part of her or her attorneys, and that the county court should have granted her motion for a new trial, and for failure to do so, the judgment for the plaintiffs was reversed and the cause remanded for further action in the county court. In due time, plaintiffs obtained a second judgment in the county court for $206.84. A second appeal was taken, attacking the judgment on the ground that interest had been improperly allowed in the judgment, but this point was overruled and the judgment was affirmed and payday for Tillie had come.

Somehow, in connection with the first appeal of the case, Burges was able to work in the story about Tillie's origin and the payment of the mortgage. It would not seem relevant to the issue before the court, but it certainly didn't hurt the attitude of the court to hear such an appealing story.

X

Chinese Exclusion Act Cases

With a smile that was childlike and bland.
—Bret Harte

THE CHINESE EXCLUSION ACT was in effect when Burges arrived in El Paso. Many Chinese had come to the United States after 1849, mostly entering through San Francisco, and by 1889 there was a considerable colony of them in El Paso. Estimates vary, but it appears there were somewhere between three or four hundred to possibly six or seven hundred Chinese in El Paso at that time. They were the subject of news items in the El Paso newspapers from time to time. The *Times* reported, January 17, 1886, opium dens were thick in El Paso, and many young men and women were seen going into them. A drive against them had been started, and Rev. Mr. Baines was leading it. Some three years later the *Herald* carried an editorial stating El Paso was the Chinese Mecca of the Southwest. They were liberally patronized, much to the detriment of the Americans. A year later it was reported that a Chinese laundryman had his picture taken, perhaps the first case of the kind on record in El Paso. On January 29, 1892, the papers reported it was the Chinese New Year and all labor had ceased. Old debts were cancelled if not paid that day. Open house or "wash house" was held by many, with incense burning to their gods, and gifts of food, cigars and liquor awaited friends. An article in February, 1893, stated there were about five hundred Chinese in El Paso, and that Lo Kay, a member of the big Chinese house of Kay, Dock Sing & Co. had been trying to smuggle Chinese across the border and was now under a $500 bond, signed by James Burns and Theodore Eggers, for him to appear before U.S. Commissioner Gibbs the next Monday.

Congress passed a Chinese registration law, and on March 9, 1893 this was covered by an article with the headline, Will The Chinese Register According To Law?, followed by one on March 18, reading, The Mongolians Register. At a later date it was reported the Chinese would be fingerprinted, as they all looked so much alike it was impossible to identify them.

Chinese New Year was in the news again February 5, 1894. It was said Chinese New Year, in the Celestial Kingdom, is the most important feast of the year. For the space of fifteen days all business is suspended, and the people give themselves up to merrymaking. In El Paso this day is celebrated in the peculiar manner of kiteflying, firecrackers, and other amusements.

Even the collector of customs could run afoul of the Chinese Exclusion Act, as on October 27, 1892, Collector Webster Flanagan and Ah Jake were tried in the United States District Court on the charge of illicitly assisting Chinese laborers to cross the river from Mexico into the United States. Jake's case was tried first, and there being practically no evidence against him, he was acquitted. He was represented by M.W. Stanton and Charles Patterson. The district attorney thereupon dismissed the case against Flanagan.

Many Chinese in El Paso had come in through the West Coast, but others had entered the United States illegally through Mexico, and all those who were not citizens, or who were not lawfully here prior to the passage of the Chinese Exclusion Act were subject to deportation to China. For more than twenty years after Burges' arrival in El Paso there were many Chinese Exclusion Act cases before the United States District Court, or before the U.S. commissioner, and in many of them he represented the defendant. Mar Ben Chew seems to have been the head of the Chinese colony in El Paso, and he was a staunch friend and client of Burges. Consequently, when any of his clan were in legal difficulties, Mar Ben Chew saw that Burges was employed to represent them.

The first of his many Chinese Exclusion Act cases was in 1890, when he represented Mah Mau, who had been arrested while working

This Chinese, from William Burges' files, was undoubtedly represented by Burges during the Chinese Exclusion Act cases.

as a cook in the hotel at Sanderson. The government charged he was illegally in the United States, and, after a hearing before Jas. D. McKie, U.S. commissioner at El Paso, obtained from the commissioner an order for Mah Mau to be deported to China. Burges filed a petition for a writ of habeas corpus in the United States District Court, for the Western District of Texas, and argued his case in that court, in San Antonio, Texas, based upon the record of the evidence before Commissioner McKie. His brief states there were but two witnesses for the government, one of whom testified only to finding the defendant working as a cook in the hotel at Sanderson, and to the defendant's stating, after his arrest and while on the way back to El Paso, he wanted to go back to China or San Francisco, but not to Mexico, as he did not like it there. The other witness he disposed of by saying the record showed his entire disregard for his oath, and nothing more need be said.

The testimony for the defense, from Hop Sing, C.M. Lincoln and James Burns, showed the defendant was living in San Francisco as early as 1881, then in Weaverville, California, then in El Paso, Texas from 1886 to 1890, when he went to Sanderson.

His brief is of interest particularly because it traces the history of the treaties between the United States and the Empire of China, the first treaty being dated July 3, 1844, 8 U.S. Stat. at Large 592, supplemented by one in June, 1858, 16 U.S. Stat. at Large 1023. The first one relating to immigration was the "Burlingame Treaty", dated July 28, 1868, 16 U.S. Stat. at Large 793, followed by one dated November 17, 1880, 22 U.S. Stat. at Large 826. Congress thereafter passed the "Restriction Act", 22 U.S. Stat at Large 60, and "Exclusion Act", 25 U.S. Stat. at Large 504. The net result was to declare Chinese who came in after the Exclusion Act illegal immigrants, and to order them deported to China. Available records do not show the outcome of the Mah Mau case, but on the basis of what is stated in Burges' brief, and the fact that he represented Chinese in Exclusion Act cases over the next twenty years, we must conclude that he won the Mah Mau case.

Turney & Burges office dockets show cases styled *U.S. v. U Pon Lin, Ex Parte Chin Ten, U.S. v. Mar Wing Kee,* and *U.S. v. Wong Chew.* Available briefs show charactertistic Chinese Exclusion Act cases in which he was engaged. In 1899 there was *The United States v. Mah Tuck* in which he argued that for one living in the United States, citizenship is presumed, and the government must prove the contrary; and the government having introduced a declaration by the defendant proving his American citizenship, and now showing the statements to be false, is bound by them. In 1902, it was the case of Mar Ying Yuen, who appeared to be a merchant in El Paso, and, with proper papers to show he was entitled to be here, went back to China on a visit. On his return, he was denied entry, and arranged to travel "in bond" from San Francisco to Eagle Pass, where he crossed into Mexico and came to Juarez, where he again attempted formal entry into the United States. The case was heard before W.D. Howe, U.S. Commissioner, and he held for the defendant. The case then went to the United States District Court at El Paso, where it is believed defendant again won his case.

In another early case, *The United States v. Ching Tung,* Burges filed a writ of habeas corpus in the United States District Court at El Paso, where an order was entered that defendant be released. Ching

Tung then left for San Antonio but at Marfa, Texas, the immigration officers again arrested him and held him as one illegally in the country. Burges went to Marfa and soon convinced the U.S. Commissioner there that the defendant could not then be held for any cause existing when the judgment of discharge was entered in the court at El Paso, and the defendant was again discharged from the custody of the officers.

The Turney & Burges letter press book for 1908 shows a long series of correspondence between Burges and O.P. Stidger, a lawyer in San Francisco. Burges had pending in the United States District Court at El Paso Exclusion Act cases for Wong Shee Nun, Yick Lae, Pon Dock Wah, Poon Sing Auk, Fong Fook Fooey, Maa Pak Ning, Wong Yee On, Ling Goey Fong, May Teng Yen and Wong Wah Kih. His letters to O.P. Stidger were requests for Stidger to attend to taking certain depositions in these cases. He wrote him in the Wong Shee Nun case, enclosing a picture of the defendant, with an affidavit of the defendant's mother, and an affidavit from the attendant at defendant's birth, stating he was born at No. 5 Prospect Place, San Francisco, giving the date, and asking Stidger to take the mother's and attendant's depositions. He also requested him to take the deposition of "a reputable white person." In event of any difficulty, he was to call on Wing Hong Guey, 753 Clay Street, San Francisco, for assistance. There were similar letters concerning the case of each defendant, and at one time Burges advised Stidger he would be at the St. Francis Hotel, in San Francisco, on the following Friday or Saturday. On July 15, 1908, he wrote Stidger he was just back from the Texas Bar Association Convention, and gave him instructions about these depositions, telling him, "our Court refuses to rely on Chinese testimony," and that "we must have a white witness." On another occasion he requested from Stidger a detailed statement of his account, "so the Chinese can see exactly what they are paying for. There is no problem with those who are represented by Mar Chew here, and Mah Yim Yen there," but the others wanted to see a detailed statement.

The government apparently determined to get at the head and fount of what it regarded as illegal entry by Chinese in the El Paso area, and in 1910 obtained an indictment against Mar Ben, along with Yee Yel, Toon Kate and others. They were charged with a conspiracy, in New Mexico, to bring Chinese aliens into the United States illegally. Mar Ben was in El Paso, and there were motions by the government to transfer the case to the United States District Court in New Mexico, but the motions were overruled and when Mar Ben was tried in 1912, the jury returned a verdict of "not guilty."

Sometime after Mr. and Mrs. Burges purchased the house at 1302 Montana Street for their home, Mar Ben came to it a few weeks before Christmas and asked Mrs. Burges to let him see the library. He looked it over including the doorway from the hallway at the foot of the stairs into the library, and at Christmas he sent out and had hung a pair of gorgeous red, brocaded portieres, which folded back against the facing on each side of the door. There they hung, always beautiful, during the rest of Burges' life.

In one of the Chinese Exclusion Act cases, Wu Li Chew was charged, in the usual language, with not being a citizen of the United States, and with being unlawfully in this country, and he was therefore subject to deportation. The government, acting through the United States district attorney, prayed for an order of the court to deport the defendant to China. The United States district attorney, Mr. Engleking, announced ready for trial, as did the defendant. The case proceeded to trial before the Honorable Judge Maxey, who was United States judge for the Western District of Texas for many years. The afternoon recess was taken on the first day of the trial about 3:15 P.M., and trial resumed at 3:30. The government had not produced a single witness since the trial had started at 9:30 A.M. that day who could testify either that the defendant was not born in the United States, or that he was born at any place outside the United States. The burden of proof was upon the government to prove that the defendant was not born in the United States, therefore was not a citizen, and subject to deportation. When the trial resumed at 3:30, the government had run out of witnesses and had nothing else to offer. An instructed verdict in favor of the defendant stared the district attorney in the face, so in desperation he called as his next witness, Wu Li Chew.

The defendant took the witness stand, was duly sworn to tell the truth, the whole truth, and nothing but the truth, so help me God, when the following examination of the witness took place:

District Attorney: "Please state your name."

Defendant: "Wu Li Chew."

District Attorney: "Where do you live?"

Defendant: "El Paso, Texas."

District Attorney: "How long have you lived in El Paso?"

Defendant: "Six years."

District Attorney: "How old are you?"

Defendant: "Fifty years."

District Attorney: "When were you born?"

Defendant: "1850."

District Attorney: "Where were you born?" (this was the crucial question.)

Defendant: "In San Francisco."

This answer rocked the district attorney back on his heels. Judge Maxey said, "Now Mr. Engleking, you have proved this defendant was born in the United States. He is therefore a citizen of the United States, and unless you have some other evidence to the contrary, I will have to enter judgment in his favor."

Engleking asked the court to give him until 9:30 the next morning to see what he could do. The court agreed, and recessed until the following day.

When court convened the next morning, the district attorney stood up, and the following exchange took place:

District Attorney: "If it please the Court, I have here a copy of the census of San Francisco for 1850, and I offer it in evidence."

Court: "What is the purpose of this, Mr. Engleking?"

District Attorney: "This census shows there were only four Chinese women in San Francisco in 1850, the year of the defendant's birth, and therefore, that it appears most improbable that he was born in San Francisco."

Court: "Mr. Engleking, it just took one Chinese woman to be the defendant's mother, and you have proved one of those four Chinese women was his mother. Now, unless you have something else to offer the court will enter judgment for the defendant."

And he did.

When telling this story, Burges always quoted from Bret Harte's "The Heathen Chinee," published under the title *Plain Language From Truthful James.* He quoted at length from the poem which tells of the inscrutable Chinese who, professing to know nothing of a card game, was winning, and turned out to have twenty-four packs of cards up his capacious oriental sleeves — it goes:

Which I wish to remark,
And my language is plain,
That for ways that are dark
And for tricks that are vain,
The heathen Chinee is peculiar,
Which the same I would rise to explain.

But he smiled as he sat by the table,
With the smile that was childlike and bland.

But the hands that were played
By that heathen Chinee
And the points that he made,
Were quite frightful to see,
Till at last he put down a right bower,
Which the same Nye had dealt unto me.

In his sleeves, which were long,
He had twenty-four packs,
Which was coming it strong,
Yet I state but the facts;
And we found on his nails, which were taper,
What is frequently in tapers — that's wax.

Which is why I remark,
And my language is plain
That for ways that are dark
And for tricks that are vain,
The heathen Chinee is peculiar,
Which the same I am free to maintain.

And then he would repeat with emphasis, "That for the ways that are dark, and for tricks that are vain, the heathen Chinee is peculiar . . . but he smiled as he sat by the table, with the smile that was childlike and bland.''

In another Chinese Exclusion Act case, Burges had obtained a favorable verdict from the jury. Judge Maxey, who was the United States District Judge for the Western District of Texas, lived in Austin, and had returned home before judgment was entered. In due time Burges prepared his judgment, and took it to Austin to get it signed by Judge Maxey. As he was walking down Congress Avenue he met his good friend R.E.L. Saner, a prominent Dallas lawyer.

''Hello, Bill,'' Mr. Saner said, ''what are you doing here?''

Burges stated briefly what brought him to Austin. Saner then said, ''I'm sure you'll get your judgment entered all right. I don't know of a better lawyer anywhere than you. But you'd better let me fix your fee. You don't have any sense about money, and if you will let me fix your fee, I'll make some money for you.''

''All right, Bob,'' he replied. ''How much fee do you think I have earned in this case?''

''Now let's see, you had to confer with your client, several times no doubt; probably interviewed several witnessess, tried the case in court to a jury, obtained a verdict for your client, and are now getting a judgment entered. I'd say you ought to be paid at least $300.''

''Well, Bob, no doubt you'll be interested to learn I have been paid already $750, and when I get back to El Paso with this judgment, I get another $750.''

The episode amused Burges greatly, for while his friends lauded his legal ability, some questioned his business and financial acumen. Yet he always collected top fees, and his clients were always happy with his services and his fees.

XI

Extradition

Revolutions are not made; they come.
—Wendell Phillips

OVER THE MANY years of his practice, Burges acquired one of the greatest law libraries in the Southwest. The library was in its infancy, however, July 3, 1892. On that date he acquired *Moore on Extradition,* a two-volume work, and numbered it 110. On June 14, 1897, he acquired a copy of Sir Edward Clarke's *A Treatise on the Law of Extradition.* It bore number 941. By June 14, 1897, he was counsel in a most interesting extradition case.

In August, 1896, in the little town of Ojinaga, situated in the state of Chihuahua, Mexico, just across the Rio Grande from Presidio, Texas, a small group of men undertook to lead a revolution against the government in power in Mexico. Some twenty-five or thirty men, armed with rifles and pistols, began their revolution by attempting to take over Ojinaga. They were expecting large reinforcements, which did not materialize. In the meantime, there was shooting back and forth between them and the government troops. The rebels confiscated guns, ammunition and food which they needed, and captured and held, for a while, several of the local citizens. They held captive one man named Ramon, and another named Rodriguez, and a courier of the Mexican government. On the afternoon of August 8, 1896, they turned Ramon loose, delivering to him his burros and wheat. They also set the courier at liberty, but without giving back the property taken from him—a horse—and they released Rodriguez and his family without taking anything from them. They took the courier's horse because he was an employee of the Mexican government, but private individuals who were captured were released without anything being taken from them.

The expected reinforcements did not come, and the little band of revolutionists, seeing that they were about to be overwhelmed by the government troops, fled across the river to the United States. Among them were Simon Rede and Epifanio Armendariz. Rede and Armendariz were arrested shortly thereafter, on a fugitive warrant, under the treaty between the United States of America and the United Mexican States for the extradition of criminals who were fugitives from justice. They were charged in the warrant with the offenses of murder, kidnapping, robbery and assault with intent to murder in the state of Chihuahua during the month of August, 1896. Burges was employed to represent them, and an interesting extradition case was on. Three other revolutionists were also arrested, and were charged with violating the neutrality laws of the United States in connection with this abortive revolution, and were convicted of this offense in the United States District Court at El Paso.

Rede and Armendariz were given a hearing before the extradition commissioner at El Paso, and the evidence in the extradition case consisted of a transcript of testimony taken before courts in Mexico, as well as the evidence reduced to writing and signed by the witnesses appearing before the extradition commissioner at El Paso.

The request for extradition being submitted through diplomatic channels, it rested with the Honorable John Sherman, secretary of state of the United States at Washington, D.C., for determination whether extradition should be granted or not. Burges prepared a brief on the question which he submitted to Secretary of State Sherman. Among other things, with reference to the facts of the matter, he referred to the evidence including the following matters:

> That when defendants were being prosecuted in the Mexican courts, Mexico proceeded upon the theory that the defendants and those with whom they associated were revolutionists, and that the purpose of their movement was the overthrow of the federal government of Mexico. When the defendants had escaped to the United States, however, and their extradition depended upon the nature of the offenses, the whole tone of the testimony changed and Mexico was urging upon the American officials that these men

were not revolutionists but that they were guilty of the ordinary crimes of murder, kidnapping, robbery and assault with intent to murder. These offenses would be extraditable, the other would not.

The tone of the brief was contained in the statement that prior cases of political refugees from Mexico demonstrated that the definition of Sir James FitzJames Stevens "that fugitive criminals are not to be surrendered for extradition crimes if those crimes were incidental to and formed a part of political disturbances" was applicable here, and on that basis these defendants were not to be extradited.

Many references to the testimony upon which the application was based were then made: that the testimony taken in Mexico from one witness was that a dispatch from an official in Ojinaga stated "their object is to revolt against the government and take this town (Ojinaga) as soon as they are joined by a large force they are awaiting." An officer at Ojinaga stated he was afraid "of an attack and destruction of the archives." It was significant that he was not afraid of injury to private property, nor to private individuals, but was afraid of an attack on and destruction of government property, the archives. The officer in command of the government troops with whom these revolutionists engaged, in his report referred to the revolutionists as the "enemy". It was pointed out this is not a term he would have used to refer to a small band of bandits as the Mexican government now contended these men were. A Mexican official at Ojinaga in a communication to his superior officer said, "We are badly situated with the flight of the revolutionists. In spite of the activity of the municipal president, we are desirous that the general government send sufficient forces to suppress a revolt that may otherwise gain in strength." The secretary of the Mexican consulate at El Paso called these men revolutionists. And this language was adopted by Governor Ahumada of the state of Chihuahua. District Judge D. Frias Camacho, of Chihuahua, stated, "There is not an intimation anywhere that these men are depredating upon private property; that they are threatening the peace of private individuals, but the matter is one that affects the public peace and may assume an international character."

Luciano Ontiveros testified to the capture and retention for a short time of Ramon Rodriguez and the courier of the Mexican government. It was he who testified that on the afternoon of the same day, August 8, they turned loose Ramon, delivering to him his burros and wheat; set the courier at liberty, but without giving back to him the property taken from him—his horse; and that they released Rodriguez and his family without taking anything from them. A number of other witnesses who testified before the Mexican courts, likewise referred to these men as "revolutionists" and some of them testified to the revolutionists telling them that their object was to overthrow the government of Mexico, and that they would begin by attacking the town of Ojinaga and deposing the authorities, and then march against Chihuahua or the city of Juarez. The general tenor of the testimony taken was to the effect that here was a small band of men whose stated purpose was to overthrow the government and that they would begin by taking over the town of Ojinaga. Their actions were thus motivated by and colored with political activities.

In the brief submitted to Secretary Sherman, before referring to this testimony, Burges referred, first, to the opinion of the United States District Judge Morrow of the Northern District of California *In Re Ezeta,* 62 F.972. Judge Morrow referred at length to the *Castioni* case, in England (First Queen's Bench 149), decided in 1891. Castioni was charged with the murder of one Rossi, by shooting him with a revolver in Bellinzona, in the Canton of Ticino, Switzerland. Rossi was a member of the State Council of Ticino. Castioni was a citizen of the same Canton. For some time previous to the murder much dissatisfaction had been felt and expressed by a large number of inhabitants of Ticino at the mode in which the political party in power was conducting the government.

The dissatisfaction reached such a point that a number of the citizens of Bellinzona, among them Castioni, seized the arsenal of the town, took rifles and ammunition from it, disarmed the gendarmes, arrested and bound or handcuffed several persons connected with the government, and forced them to march in front of the armed crowd to the municipal palace. Admission to the palace was demanded in the name of the people, and was refused by Rossi, and another member of the government, who were in the palace. The crowd then broke open the outer gate of the palace and rushed in, pushing before them the government officials whom they had arrested and bound. Castioni, who was armed with a revolver, was among the first to enter. A second door, which was locked, was broken open, and at this time, or immediately thereafter, Rossi, who was in the passage, was shot through the body with a revolver and died soon afterwards.

Castioni fled to England, and his extradition was requested by the Federal Council of Switzerland. He was arrested and taken before a police magistrate, who held him for extradition. His case came before the High Court of Justice of England on an application for a writ of habeas corpus. He was represented by some of the most eminent lawyers in England, as was the government. Judge Denman, of the High Court of Justice, said the question was whether it was clear from the facts that Castioni was acting as one of a number of persons engaged in acts of violence of a political character, with a political object, and as a part of the political movement and rising in which he was taking part. After a reference to the facts, and this rule, the prisoner was discharged upon the basis that his act, for which his extradition was sought, was a part of a political movement, and was therefore not extraditable.

The basis for this rule was referred to further in the brief as being "founded on the broad principle of humanity found everywhere in the criminal law, distinguishing its administration with respect to even the worst features of our civilization from the cruelties of barbarism."

Judge Morrow held in the case of General Ezeta that the latter and his companion were charged with crimes which were of a political character, and therefore discharged them from further confinement.

Reference was made at some length to the case of William Lyon McKenzie in the early part of the nineteenth century. He headed a revolt in Canada, which failed; whereupon he fled to the state of New York. His extradition was sought by Canada. He led a band of men from 600 to 1,500 in number.

His extradition was refused on the basis that this was a political movement.

Burges' brief then referred to the fact the defendants in this case were a member of a little group of some twenty-five or thirty men who tried to seize Ojinaga, as compared with McKenzie being at the head of a group of from 600 to 1,500 men. It pointed out the number of men in the group is not a controlling basis for decision, stating that when President Diaz crossed the Rio Grande from Texas into Mexico at Matamoros in March, 1876, he had with him just forty men; yet by November of that year, he had fought his way to the City of Mexico, entered it, and a few days later was installed as the provisional president of the Mexican Republic; that Diaz was waging war, and it was war no more when his last battle was fought with thousands on either side than it was when the first skirmish took place after he crossed from Texas into Mexico at Matamoros with only forty men under his banner, and that those who were killed in encounters at that time could not be said to have been murdered by Diaz.

The Mexican government's demand for extradition of these two men was based upon the claim that they were not revolutionists, but were local bandits and robbers who were pillaging in Ojinaga and merely violating local criminal laws. It was pointed out, however, that the demand for their surrender was based upon the very acts for which others of their group had already been convicted in the United States District Court at El Paso for the offense of violating the neutrality laws of the United States. The testimony on the subject given in proceedings in Mexico was reviewed at length, following which it was stated in the brief:

> From a careful perusal and study of the whole evidence in this case we think it quite clear — in fact, proven beyond a reasonable doubt—that while the acts for which these men are now demanded were in progress the Mexican government considered them political offenses.

The brief concluded:

> Therefore, we feel justified in urging upon the Secretary a careful review of this case, to the end that if these men are political offenders they may find an asylum in our country, founded, as the government of the United States is, upon the right of revolution, and extending, as it always has, a place of refuge to those who, mistaken though they may be, have sought to better their political condition by an appeal to that arbiter by virtue of whose judgment we exist today among the nations of the earth. Let them be punished for violating the neutrality laws of the United States, as their associates already have been, but do not do violence to that rule which, in the language

of Lord Palmerston, "has been observed in modern times by independent states, both great and small, of the civilized world, in refusing to deliver up political refugees. The laws of hospitality, the dictates of humanity, the general feelings of mankind, forbid such surrenders, and any independent government which, by its own free will, was to make any such surrender, would be universally stigmatized as dishonored, unless such is bound to extradition by the positive obligations of a treaty.

The point of the matter of course from the humanitarian standpoint is simply that a revolutionist, upon being returned to his own country, probably will be summarily shot. For this reason he was willing to be convicted of violating the neutrality laws of the United States, for anything was better than being returned to Mexico.

There is no available record of what the result in the case was. One can only presume from the facts stated, taken from the record, and from the law cited, that extradition was denied.

XII

The Twentieth Century: Early Years

And the great ages onward roll.
—Tennyson

THE FIRST DECADE of the twentieth century was a busy one for Turney & Burges. Besides the work done in their office, such as examining abstracts of title to real estate, preparing deeds, notes and mortgages, writing wills, preparation of various kinds of contracts, they had a busy trial docket. The Turney & Burges office dockets 2 and 3 cover this period, and they show the representation of a variety of clients. The Atchison, Topeka & Santa Fe Railway Company gave them the largest volume of trial work during this decade, averaging about fifteen lawsuits a year, mostly personal injury damage suits. Occasionally the docket bears a notation at the end of the case, "papers sent to Mr. Terry." The reference was to J.W. Terry of Galveston, general attorney in Texas of the Santa Fe railroad, and one of the giants among the lawyers of Texas in his day.

They had several land suits for Zeno B. Clardy, and after his death, had other cases for his widow, Allie D. Clardy. Mrs. Clardy was a fine looking woman, with dark eyes that flashed fire. She took one of their lawsuits to Turney, and lost in the trial court. Burges took over the appeal of the case. For some reason, this did not suit her, and on meeting him one day she said, "I didn't bring my case to you, and I don't want you to have anything to do with it." He replied, "Did anyone ever tell you I don't want any women clients, and you in particular?" But he won the appeal.

The Turney & Burges files show a wide range of correspondence during these early years, both as to subject matter and its geographic range. There was correspondence with Western Electric company, the Chatham National Bank of New York, Senator Charles A. Culberson, Kansas City Livestock Commission Company, J.J. Terrell, commissioner of the General Land Office, Austin, Texas; L.M. Crawford of St. Louis, who owned real estate in El Paso, and Lawler & Allen, attorneys of Los Angeles. Oscar Lawler was an outstanding lawyer of Los Angeles, and was long a great friend of Burges. The Mine & Smelter Supply Company shows to have been a Turney & Burges client, and there was considerable correspondence with Alexander & Green of New York relating to the Babicora Development Co., which was the Hearst Ranch Company in Mexico, as well as with the Sierra Madre Land and Lumber Co. and the Sierra Madre & Pacific Railroad Co., all doing business in Mexico.

H.J. Simmons, manager of the El Paso Union Depot Company, was advised the company's charter had been amended, increasing its capital stock from $120,000 to $240,000. Mrs. Charles S. Harle, Midland, Texas, was reminded she still owed them $100 on the fee she and her mother agreed to pay for the defense of Dr. Harle, and Mrs. Allie D. Clardy was billed $600 for one year's services and $500 for those in the succeeding year. There was an opinion to Nestor Armijo, Las Cruces, New Mexico, relating to the title of a lot in the Franklin Heights Addition, El Paso, and one to S.T. Turner relating to the title to a tract of land in the San Elizario Grant; and title opinions to Joshua S. Raynolds, El Paso and William H. Bucher, Hillsboro, New Mexico, among others.

Other correspondence at random was with Krakauer, Zork and Moye, E. Kohlberg, Phil Bargman, Randolph Parmly, New York, N.Y.; Mrs. J.F. Murphy, Bath, Maine; W. E. Blacksledge, Kokomo, Indiana; Houck & Dieter Co., El Paso; F.J. Hagenbarth, Salt Lake City; William Aubrey, San Antonio; F.Y.J. Gladney, St. Louis; W. Van Sickle, Alpine, Texas; J.F. Hess, Chicago; R.L.Young, Las Cruces, New Mexico; S. T. Turner, W.A. Hawkins, L.E. Booker,

First National Bank of El Paso, W.W. Varn, Postal Telephone & Telegraph Co., El Paso Foundry & Machine Co., U.S. & Mexican Trust Co., Kansas City, Missouri; Southwest Telephone & Telegraph Co., Dallas, Texas; and Royal Neighbors of America.

Their lawsuits included *Northwestern Life Insurnace Co. v. Sturdivant,* a hotly contested suit over a life insurance policy; *Crosby v. The First Presbyterian Church,* a land title suit in which they represented the church; *El Paso & Southwestern Ry. Co. v. Eichel & Weichel,* a suit by contractors for work done on the railroad; *Jayne v. Imperial Irrigation Co.,* one of the early water cases in Texas; *Tourtelot v. Booker,* a leading case on the question of limitations as applied to a foreign judgment; *Spence v. Fenchler,* 151 S.W. 1094, 180 S.W. 597 (Tex. Sup.) in which Spence was represented by Gunther Lessing, who later moved to Los Angeles and, for many years, was the attorney for Walt Disney and his enterprises.

Other clients for whom they had lawsuits included El Paso Union Passenger Depot Co., W.T. Hixson, Pomeroy's Transfer Co., Frank Powers, Postal Telegraph & Cable Co., the Colorado Fuel & Iron Co., A. Solomon, Krakauer, Zork & Moye, Phil Bargman, E. Kohberg, Sam Lapowski, Antoinette W. Davis, Jesus Ochoa, Herald News Co. and several insurance companies. The docket books also show garnishment suits, suits on notes, a few divorce suits, and a libel suit or two. In addition there were criminal cases which evidently were not carried in these docket books.

Burges was special prosecutor in Tombstone, Arizona, in the case of *The State of Arizona v. Andrews,* the defendant being charged with embezzling county funds. He always recalled that in Arizona you could cross-examine a witness only on the matters inquired into on direct examination (the rule being otherwise in Texas), and the defendant's counsel, while the defendant was testifying, made the mistake of asking his client, "Now have you ever in your life done anything that violates the laws of the state of Arizona?"

Burges glanced at the judge, and the expression on the latter's face showed he realized defendant's counsel "had opened the door," and Burges was enabled to go into previous violations of the law by defendant, to the latter's sorrow.

This and other cases here referred to, suffice to indicate the extensive and varied nature of the Turney & Burges law practice in these early years. The correspondence, and the lawsuits, show both Turney and Burges to have been most active. Turney was an excellent "business getter," and a large part of the firm's correspondence was carried on by him. He and Burges each tried numerous lawsuits, and often tried them as a team. One of their later partners said he never saw a more effective team of trial lawyers than W.W. Turney sitting in the front chair examining witnesses – which he did with the nth degree of thoroughness, and W.H. Burges sitting behind him, keeping the record of legal points, exceptions, etc., and arguing questions of law to the court.

Among the lawyers in El Paso during the early days was P.H. Clarke who was a graduate of Trinity University in Dublin, Ireland. He was an excellent scholar, but his effectiveness as a lawyer was dimmed by too close an association with John Barleycorn. Others were Edwards & Edwards–Peyton Edwards and Hayden Edwards–who were descendants of the Hayden Brothers. The latter were empresarios in the Nacogdoches area of Texas in the days of colonization under the Mexican government, and had been the leaders of the the "Freedonian Revolution." Patterson and Wallace were early-day leaders in the representation of plaintiffs in personal injury damage suits. One or the other of them periodically would go to San Francisco, and spend a few days in a park across the street from the Southern Pacific Hospital. On return to El Paso, they would have fifteen or twenty damage suits to file against the Southern Pacific Railroad. Waters Davis' father, E.J. Davis, had been a "Reconstruction" governor of Texas. This may have been a handicap in other parts of the state, but he was about six feet two inches tall, a fine athlete, and got along well in El Paso. T.A. Falvey, perhaps the greatest of them all, was a one-time district judge, and a long-time practitioner, whose reputation was he knew no fear, and that "he didn't have to read law, he thought law." The most eccentric, no doubt, was W.M. Coldwell, who subscribed to, and read, newspapers in several foreign languages, was quite well read, and whose conceit and peculiarities were legendary. From time to time he enlisted the aid of Burges in trying his cases. Typically, he came to Burges one day and said, "Burges, I want you to help me in a case I have before Goggin (J.M. Goggin, district judge, and a man of excellent ability). When I state my proposition of law to you, you'll think I am wrong. But you read my authorities, and after you have read them you'll agree with me. I want you to argue that proposition to Goggin, and give him the authorities. I can talk down to you, and make you see it, and you can talk down to Goggin and make him see it, but I can never bridge the gap between Goggin and me."

It was as Coldwell had stated it. Burges did not agree with him, until he read the authorities, and he then did agree; and he convinced Judge Goggin.

On another occasion, some years later, he enlisted Burges' aid in a case pending before District Judge Ballard Coldwell, who was his son. Waters Davis was on the other side of the case. As W.M. Coldwell and Burges walked to the courthouse on Monday morning to begin trial, the old gentleman said to Burges, "Between the animal cunning of Waters Davis and the abysmal ignorance of Ballard Coldwell, anything can happen in this case."

The general practice of law in those days was kaleidoscopic. Burges was one of three of four lawyers representing the defendant in a criminal case brought in the federal court against Webb Flanagan, the collector of customs at El Paso who was charged with being involved in a conspiracy to let a large number of sheep be imported from Mexico into the United States, and to classify them as lambs, there being a duty on sheep, but none on lambs. The chief prosecution witness testified the sheep were brought across the Rio Grande river from Mexico into the United States at a point near Ysleta early one morning just after daybreak, and he saw the defendant down on the river bank riding a white horse, while the crossing was being made. On cross examination, he was grilled on every aspect of his testimony, but he only reiterated what he had testified on direct examination. Finally, however, he was asked, "Do you see in the courtroom the man who was riding the white horse down on the river bank that morning?" "Yes," he anwered, "There he is right there."

All those in the courtroom nearly fell out of their chairs, for he had pointed to the closest juror sitting in the jury box. The district attorney took the witness on direct examination and tried to shake him loose from his identification, but without avail. The witness insisted the man he saw on the white horse, and about whom he had testified, was the closest man to him in the jury box—a juror. Burges always laughed a little about it and said, "To tell you the truth, there were several of us lawyers representing the defendant and he was sitting behind all of us where he could hardly have been seen by the witness."

Needless to say, under the circumstances, the defendant was acquitted.

On another occasion Burges received a telegram from the New York Life Insurance Company's home office in New York City. He had already heard about a fight between two men in a local hotel in El Paso, one of whom was the local agent for the New York Life Insurance Company, and who had been severely beaten. To his surprise the telegram from the New York Life Insurance Company requested him to look after the other man. The other man was charged with aggravated assault, and Burges represented him in the criminal case. The opening round was an examining trial in the justice court. The state had an eyeball witness, a Mexican maid who worked at the hotel where the fight had occurred. The loser in the fight had his face badly skinned and scarred, and there had been some previous testimony about the defendant having kicked the other man after he was down on the floor. Burges took the maid on cross-examination, and thought he was getting such good answers from her, he decided to see if he could get her to deny the story about the kicking taking place. He said he would not have asked the question upon a trial in the trial court, but since this was only a preliminary hearing he thought he had better find out all he could. So he asked, "Now, Maria, the defendant here didn't kick him, did he? "No," she answered, "He didn't kick him. He just took his heel and stomped him in the face." Then she proceeded to demonstrate with her own heel as she testified. The mystery about how the man's face got so badly skinned and scarred was immediately cleared up.

At another time, he met a rather pretty young woman who had

just come to town. She had lived somewhere on the Atlantic Coast and had moved to El Paso. She had some legal matters that she wanted to see about, and so she came into his office one day, in the summertime, wearing a white summery dress and with a large "Gibson Girl" hat, and was herself quite attractive. During her conference with Burges it developed that she had been married and divorced. He told her that before he could answer her questions, he would need to see a copy of the divorce decree, and asked her if she had one. She said she did, and came back into his office the next day with it. As she walked in, she lightly tossed her certified copy of the divorce decree on his desk in front of him and said, "There is my certificate of rejuvenated virginity."

Federal court was always busy when a term was held here. At one of the terms of federal court, Burges had twenty-seven cases on the docket. Before the term was over he tried all twenty-seven cases, and won them all. When the last was concluded, he went back to his office, telephoned Mrs. Burges, and said, "Pack up our suitcases. We are going to Chicago to see the opera."

Burges was active in bar association work, on the local, state and national levels. The El Paso Bar Association held its first annual banquet on January 13, 1902. Burges was in charge of the program. He asked W.M. Coldwell to be the principal speaker, and suggested the title of the speech: 'Law and Lawyers in the Sage Brush and Chaparral Days." Coldwell accepted the assignment, and a few days later he came into Burges' office with a written draft of his proposed speech.

"Please read this manuscript," he requested, "and tell me how you think it should be changed, in any respect."

Burges read it, and advised its author, "Don't change a word, Give it just as you have written it."

Its tone was set by the opening sentence: "With a natural modesty, so unobtrusive and retiring that it has never ventured to expose itself to the observation of my oldest acquaintances, and which has been increased by many years' connection with the most diffident of professions, I was at loss to conjecture the reason why I was elected to respond to any toast on this occasion, but at the last the truth dawned upon me—not at once—not with one burst of assuredness and splendor, as the tropic sun sweeps out of the mid-Pacific, but slowly, painfully, and with infinite reluctance, as dawns the consciousness of error upon an appellate court during the argument of a motion for a rehearing."

The banquet was a success, and has been held annually since 1902.

About May, 1906, Burges was elected a member of the General Council of the American Bar Association, and he later served, 1912-1915, on the Board of Governors of the American Bar Association. He attended the annual conventions of the assocation, where a comparatively small group of several hundred of the leading lawyers of the nation met together. He formed lasting friendships with many of the foremost lawyers of the country, who came from such widespread points as San Francisco and Los Angeles on the Pacific Coast, to New York and Philadelphia on the Eastern Seaboard, and Chicago, St. Louis, and other cities in between.

In the meantime, he served as president of the Texas Bar Association, 1909-1910. He presided at its annual convention, held July 5, 1910, in San Angelo, Texas, and began the president's annual address with these remarks:

For the first time in the twenty-nine years of its life, the Texas Bar Association meets west of San Antonio.

Here in the heart of the great West the people of this thriving city have opened to us their hearts and their homes. We have with us again many of those who, in the days that are no more, made the annual meetings of this association the most precious event of the year. We are glad to welcome so many new members, who we sincerely trust in the years to come will make the association an even greater power for good in the state we love.

The year that has passed since our last meeting has been one of peace and prosperity.

The seasons have returned in their courses; plenty has filled our garners and peace prevailed in our boundaries.

Our people have been spared from tempest and pestilence, and there has been no session of the legislature.

This has made impossible of performance the constitutional command to communicate the noteworthy changes in statutory law, and it has occurred to your president that it might not be unprofitable to take advantage of this fact and note the legislation of the past twenty years, and through this larger perspective endeavour to ascertain at least some of the deeper currents and more enduring tendencies of our statutory law.

He then launched into a discussion of bills passed by several legislatures, some constitutional, and some which had been unconstitutional. He also discussed, as a recent development, "platform demands", where the Democratic party platforms in Texas were demanding enactment of specific legislation, as compared with earlier platforms containing only declarations of general party principles and policies. Because all democratic nominees were admonished to support the enactment of such specific legislation, he quoted, as applicable, the phrase "embezzlement of power," cited Daniel Webster's refusal to follow such demands, and quoted Senator L.Q.C. Lamar's statement, in the United States Senate, his duty required him to follow the true and correct principles, as he saw them, and to be true and faithful to his constituents in so doing.

Several other pertinent matters were referred to briefly, and the address ended:

> Laws are enacted and annulled, but the law remains. Its fixed stars guide us. In spite of our every effort, shocking acts of injustice occur, but justice prevails and abides among men. Its mighty currents bear us on.
>
> The stars shine as of old. The unchanging river,
> Bent on its errand of immortal law,
> Works its appointed way to the immemorial sea,
> And the brave truth comes overwhelmingly home;
> That the law in us yet works and shines,
> Lives and fulfills itself,
> Unending as the river and the stars.

He had yet another service, in an appointed office, in which he was proud to serve. In 1911 the governor appointed him a member of the Board of Regents of the University of Texas. He was happy in the opportunity to serve his alma mater, which was growing and developing, and was already the leading educational institution of the Southwest. He served in this capacity until 1914, when the press of his law practice required him to give it up.

His greatest service to the University of Texas was yet to come, as is related in the chapter "Chicago Interlude."

The social life of El Paso was unique in many ways. The city had a population of about 10,000 in 1890, about 15,000 in 1900, and about 39,000 in 1910. It had one four-story building in 1890, the Sheldon Building, on Pioneer Plaza, where the Plaza Hotel now stands. Across Mills Street stood the three-story Grand Central Hotel, and at the southeast corner of Mills and Stanton was Bassett's Lumber Yard. The Southern Pacific (then G.H. & S.A. Railway Co.) depot was located at the corner of Main and Kansas streets, while at Kansas and Mills was the Pierson Hotel. There was little else east of Stanton Street. But the city grew rapidly, and soon Magoffin and East San Antonio streets were leading residential areas. When the mule cars—the original street car system—was inaugurated, there were two routes, one out to Cotton Avenue, through this residential area, and the other across the river, to make a circuit through Juarez.

The great center of entertainment was the Myar Opera House, until it burned November 4, 1905. The only proper place to go after a dance was the English Kitchen. This was the leading restaurant, operated by Dock Sing on East San Antonio Street, where the State Theater is now. Dinners in private homes were a main part of the social life. The dinners were formal and elegant, with the hosts and guests all wearing formal clothes. A typical dinner began with soup, followed by fish, with white wine. Then came the main course of roast turkey, or ham, squab—or whatever—with claret, peas and potatoes. The salad followed the main course; then came dessert, and afterwards, coffee. There were no cocktails before dinner. This was a later innovation.

No one excelled Burges in entertaining at dinner. He set out to lead the social life of El Paso, and succeeded well. His home had a semi-basement which he remodeled for his library. The house was admirably built for entertaining. Guests gathered in the living room, and then passed into the dining room, where a round top fitted over the dining table, at which sixteen people could be seated. He was a great singlehanded conversationalist, and the conversation flowed, dominated by him with appropriate quotations from plays and poems, interspersed with anecdotes about great figures of history, or from his own personal experiences. A goodly portion of the time they had a Chinese man for a cook, first "Yee" and later, for many years, Tom Simpson.

After dinner, everyone went downstairs to the library, for an evening of conversation and relaxation. At the foot of the stairs they were face to face with busts of Napoleon and Beethoven, and a group of autographed pictures, one of which was a picture of General John J. Pershing. These dinners were leading social affairs for many years in the life of El Paso.

Of interest is the fact that El Paso in its early days, after the coming of the railroad, had a sizable Jewish community, the members of which were prominent in the business life of the city. Burges represented many of them. Early Turney & Burges office dockets show representation in lawsuits of Phil Bargman, Krakauer, Zork & Moye, and Ernest Kolhberg. Others were represented in office practice, not shown by dockets listing lawsuits. He remarked in later years that he and Mrs. Burges, in the early days, often went to very elegant parties where they were the only gentiles present.

Juarez has always played a major part in the life of El Paso. As the two cities are separated only by the Rio Grande, this was inevitable.

Juarez figured prominently in the social affairs of El Paso citizens. Not only did they attend the bullfights in Juarez, but any large social functions on either side of the river were attended by people from both El Paso and Juarez. In Juarez, a favorite place of the El Pasoans was the Juarez Customs House, where dances were held. These were often lavish affairs. On occasions, Governor Ahumada came to Juarez, bringing the Chihuahua band, and gave parties that lasted until dawn. The oldtimers always mentioned the social functions at the home of the German consul, Max Weber who lived in the valley just below Juarez, and whose parties often were social extravaganzas.

El Paso's most elegant club was the Toltec Club. It was preeminent in the social life of El Paso during the period. After the turn of the century the city was growing rapidly, and many of the social activities were carried on with a grace and formality that no longer obtains, generally, in this country.

Burges and others wanted a club where dinners, balls and parties could be held. Their efforts resulted in the organization of the Toltec Club. It was incorporated, the incorporators being Britton Davis, J.A. Eddy, A.P. Coles, W.W. Turney, C.N. Tibbitts, U.S. Stewart, Felix Martinez, Jr., C.W. Kendrick, W.G. Choates, T.M. Wingo, J.G. Hunzinger and William H. Burges. The articles of incorporation were signed by J.A. Eddy, W.H. Burges and A.P. Coles, dated November 18, 1902, and filed in the office of the secretary of state at Austin on November 19, 1902.

For a time the club rooms were on the second floor over 207-209 Texas Street. On March 16, 1906, the *Herald* reported plans for a permanent home for the Toltec Club were under way. The lease on the Texas Street property still had two years to run, but it was hoped a new clubhouse would be ready by the expiration of the lease. The estimated cost of it was $25,000.

The new clubhouse was not built that soon. On July 23, 1908, the *Herald* reported the Toltec Club was to build a home that would cost $65,000 and on December 12, 1908, the *Times* reported the Toltec Club bought a site at San Antonio and Magoffin streets, where it would build a clubhouse to cost $80,000. The building permit was taken out in February, 1909, for $75,000, and a few months later a contract was let to build "a handsome five-story building" for $82,000. The formal opening was held October 14, 1910, with an open house and reception. For many years thereafter the Toltec Club was the scene of the leading banquets and balls held in El Paso, and was the brightest spot of its time in the life of El Paso.

As for politics, since the 1895 effort, the Reform group continued to work to eliminate open gambling, but no major moves were made for several years, as the time did not seem to be quite ripe. El Paso was still an open town in 1903, however the Reform group mustered enough strength to take on the opposition in the city election of that year. But the elections of 1903 and 1905, and Burges' part in them deserve separate chapters.

XIII

The Henry Ward Beecher Episode

President of Heaven and Hell Amalgamation Society.
—Carlyle

DURING THE EARLY 1900s, Henry T. Moore was the minister at the First Presbyterian Church in El Paso. Moore, who had come from "up north," was a man of fine ability, including the fact that he had excellent oratorical abilities. Mrs. Burges was, as she put it, "a blue-stocking Presbyterian," while Burges was not a member of the church. However, he liked going to Sunday evening services with her, as he enjoyed hearing Moore preach.

In late 1902, Rev. Moore announced that his sermon for the evening would be on Henry Ward Beecher, the great abolitionist preacher. Beecher was no favorite of Burges', and you may be sure that he listened intently to Moore's eulogy of Beecher.

Moore opened with the statement, "Henry Ward Beecher had his Gethsemane, and if Tilton had had his way, would have had his Calvary." He went on to extol the virtues of Beecher, and the further he went, the more Burges fumed. He had much to say to friends and acquaintances immediately afterwards about what he thought about Henry Ward Beecher. In fact, it was the main topic of conversation in the town at the time.

His brother Richard said, "Will, are you going to answer Mr. Moore? Because if you don't, I will." The editor of *The Times* heard reports of what Burges had said about the Moore sermon and asked him if he wouldn't like to put his statements about it in writing, for publicaton in *The Times.* Burges answered, "I don't think *The Times* would be willing to publish what I would say, if I wrote about it." The editor replied, "Anything you write about it, I will publish."

He had read the verbatim report of the trial of *Theodore Tilton v. Henry Ward Beecher,* the cause celebre of 1875 tried in Brooklyn, wherein Tilton, whose wife had confessed to him an adulterous relationship with Beecher, sued the preacher for criminal conversation, as the legal language put it. He remarked on Beecher, who made a poor witness for himself, having admitted that he committed perjury, in his attempt to clear himself. Burges, having read the report of this sordid trial, was ready to expound on Beecher.

So he sat down and wrote an article which was published in the *Times.* He castigated Henry Ward Beecher from beginning to end, but better than characterizing the article is to reprint it. It read:

GARB OF LAMB AND SOUL OF WOLF

The life and character of Henry Ward Beecher were made the subject of a eulogistic sermon in one of the churches of El Paso last night. The speaker is a man of the purest character for whom the writer has a high regard and what is said here is not said in any malice toward him.

The writer is a Southerner. Almost without exception his people were participants on the Southern side in the War of Secession, and the establishment of truth and justice to them and those who sacrificed their lives with them in that most momentous episode in our national history is a matter of much importance.

As Henry Ward Beecher is one of those who has most freely expressed his opinion, and in most enduring form, of our people, it is due to impartial history that his testimony should be given its proper weight and no more, and to this end that his true character be known.

I do not want Mr. Moore's good character interposed between Mr. Beecher and his judges. A very good man can defend a very bad man. Mr. Beecher alone is the subject of this article, and his very great abilities are freely conceded. It is the deliberate judgment of the writer that Henry Ward Beecher possessed more of the qualities that make a character loathsome than any man of great or little note in our history.

Cowardice, lying, and malevolence are the predominating traits.

Mr. Beecher, by his preaching and lecturing, as much as anyone contributed to bringing on the War of Secession. For this I find no fault with him, but when the issue was joined, when the call to arms came, when brave men and true on both sides, north as well as south, were laying down their lives for the right as they were given to see it, Mr. Beecher took good pains to see that his precious person was kept from harm's way. He waged a Chinese warfare—that is, with the stink pots of his malignant speech, but he never risked himself within the range of Confederate bullets. All he ever knew of a war he helped to bring on, and which called for the service of every able-bodied man in his state, he learned from hearsay. However, maybe we ought not to be too severe on him. His time probably too completely occupied by ministering to the spiritual wants of his 'dear flock' of Plymouth Church—Mrs. Theodore Tilton not excepted. So much for his contemptible cowardice.

No less remarkable was his capacity for lying. It was multiform and various. His testimony in the Tilton-Beecher trial abounds in the lie circumstantial and the lie direct.

I have in my library, in three large volumes, the verbatim report of that trial, and with it I have reasonably familiarized myself. I commend it to anyone who would see and study a true picture of the character of Henry Ward Beecher.

It may not convince every reader that he debauched a member of his congregation, the wife of his associate and friend, and the playmate of his own daughter, though it is in my settled conviction that the testimony shows he did. But, whether like the jury that tried him, all readers cannot agree on this (and the jury, in the report of the proceeding, states that their inability to agree was due to the irreconcilable conflict in the testimony, and differences as to the credibility of the witnesses). One conclusion is irresistibly forced on the student of that case, and that is that Henry Ward Beecher is one of the greatest liars that ever testified in a court of justice. On vital points in the case he was contradicted by persons whose reputation for truthfulness was as good as his own, and in whom no motive to commit perjury was shown; and again and again in the course of the cross-examination he took refuge behind the assertion that he could not remember whether he did or did not certain things about which no sane man's memory could be in doubt.

Then, too, how pitiful is his explanation of the ruin of this home 'Mrs. Tilton was madly in love with him,' and he was a second Joseph. The first Joseph saved his virtue at the expense of his garment. The second Joseph saved his coat (probably the more valuable asset in his case) and hasn't been able to convince his sinful minded fellowmen that his character came through uninjured.

A brave man would have shielded that woman at the cost of ruin to himself. Moved by cowardice and resorting to lying, Beecher ruined both.

We are told that Charles Maddon Spurgeon, one of the greatest preachers of our language and one of the best of men—a man who did things, a man who did something beside defaming the dead and debauching members of his church—said he would not preach in a pulpit that had been polluted by the presence of Henry Ward Beecher. I think he was right about it. In truth, I think that if Beecher's long-cherished belief in and hope for a future life of punishment for his weak and erring fellowmen who have not suffered enough here, as he confidently assures us he did, is with him a realized fact, then hell itself is viler for his entrance into that choice circle of 'dogs and sorcerers, and whoremongers and murderers, and idolators and whosoever loveth and maketh a lie.' (*Revelations* 22:15)

Now just a word as to his malevolence. Mr. Beecher took no part in the actual warfare of the War of Secession. Like a few others, his valor rose as danger diminished. When the brave men who had fought on both sides returned to the ways of peace, and undertook the task of healing the wounds in the hearts of the people and uniting all again in a common patriotism as in a common destiny, this human hyena, in a church dedicated, professedly, to the worship of One who we are taught came to teach the gospel of peace on earth and good will to men, found it in his craven heart to say: 'It (referring to the war between the states) was the worst work that Satan and sin ever undertook in this world, and they that suffered in it were not martyrs in a good cause, but convicts in a bad one. Who shall comfort them that sit by dishonored graves?'

Measure if you can the measureless infamy of those words! 'Convicts in a bad cause.' Most of the young men and young women of this State are the sons and daughters of those 'convicts' as the writer is, and they are proud of it. They are loyal to this Union today. They are part of its bone and sinew, but they never expect to hear, without resenting, praise of this maligner of their fathers. We never expect to hear his truthfulness asserted without entering our protest.

Language such as Beecher used has found no place in the vocabulary of the brave men who fought the war for the Union. Being brave men, with convictions, and the courage of their convictions, they respect the convictions and the courage of others.

The proper sewer for the discharge of such a sentiment is the mouth of Henry Ward Beecher, a coward in war and a perjured miscreant in peace.

'Dishonored graves!' Hear the ghoul! Who are filling those graves? The flower of the young manhood of thirteen states of this Union.

Permit me to present in striking contrast to this libeler and defamer of the dead, one of those who now sleeps in what Mr. Beecher is pleased to term a 'dishonored grave.' Stonewall Jackson was one of the foremost soldiers of our race, and one of the most conspicuous members of the Presbyterian Church in America. He commanded the troops present to preserve order when John Brown was hung at Harper's Ferry. On his scaffold, Brown called for someone to pray for him. Mr. Beecher, instead of being present to strengthen and console this first victim of his eloquence, was busy with his "dear flock" (probably not excepting Mrs. Tilton), and Stonewall Jackson mounted the scaffold and offered up that prayer. I commend to the consideration of the impartial student the occupants of Stonewall Jackson's grave and the pulpit of Plymouth Church. Henry Ward Beecher—Stonewall Jackson; dirt to diamond; darkness to light; malignity to charity; a poor, pitiful contemptible loathsome lie to an eternal truth.

I again repeat, nothing I have said is intended to offend my friend who pronounced Beecher's eulogy last night, but sincerely entertaining the opinion, as I do, that it is the duty of every self-respecting Southerner, as far as lies in his power, to make Henry Ward Beecher's memory hideous, I have, in the truth as I am given to see it, presented the other side of that many-sided man who combined in his character every attribute, except stupidity, that is the proper object either of hatred or contempt.

His portrait has been unconsciously drawn by one of the greatest masters of our language, in which no lineament of cowardice, falsehood, treachery, hypocrisy, sensuality or malignity has been unduly darkened.

Look on the picture of Henry Ward Beecher and see him—

> 'With all his conscience and one eye askew,
> So false, he partly took himself for true;
> Whose pious talk, when most his heart was dry,
> Made wet the crafty crowsfoot around his eye;
> Who, never naming God except for gain,
> So never took that useful name in vain,
> Made Him his catspaw and the Cross his tool,
> And Christ the bait to trap his dupe and fool;
> Her deeds of gift, but gifts of grace he forged,
> And snake-like slimed his victim ere he gorged.'

We are told then that Mr. Beecher had his Gethsemane, but not his Calvary. He ought to have had that too, for no man ever born of woman was more richly endowed by nature, training and inclination for the role of the thief who died unrepentant on the Cross.

Very respectfully,
Wm. H. Burges

XIV

Gambling and the Election of 1903

So politicians thrive . . . With their crabbed faces, and sly tricks.
—John Ford

IN THE 1890s and the early 1900s, El Paso was a wide-open town. It had a population of only 10,000 in 1890, growing to 15,000 in the following ten years. The downtown area was saturated with saloons, gambling halls and "dance halls." It was still a frontier town, until recently surrounded by areas where the war whoop of the Apaches resounded. It was also the main southern thoroughfare "through the pass" for east-west traffic, as well as for the north-south traffic which had existed from early Spanish days, from Santa Fe to Chihuahua and Mexico City. It was as rough as any frontier western town, and its saloons, gambling halls and dance halls were a dominating characteristic of the community.

The growth of the city made inevitable the emergence of a "reform" party, and in 1893 reform was beginning to raise its head. But, as we have seen, it was not to triumph in the 1890s.

Texas had a state law against gambling, but enforcement at the time seemed out of the question. The overwhelming sentiment in the town was in favor of the gamblers. To a considerable part of the business community, they represented money and business. They brought additional people to town. If closed up, it would result in many persons leaving El Paso.

Not all of the opposition to gambling was on moral grounds. A sizable, and growing element among the El Paso citizens were opposed to open gambling, and, while these citizens were against it on moral grounds, many of them were motivated also by the realization it was hurting the business of shopkeepers and professional men. Money which should have gone to pay bills for necessities for the support of families was being lost at the gaming tables of the professionals. So, the thought that open gambling must go crystallized in the minds of a number of the town's leaders. The fight was renewed in the early 1900s.

The opening round began May 3, 1902. Mayor B.F. Hammett published a "gambling proclamation." It stated saloons must close all day Sunday, and all gambling must be taken out of saloons, i.e., moved either upstairs or into basements. The matter had been discussed at several city council meetings, sometimes heatedly, with some aldermen declaring the city should run the gamblers out of town. Legally, they were on sound ground, in view of the state laws prohibiting gambling, for the open gambling in El Paso was in notorious violation of those laws. One deterrent to the complete abolition of open gambling, at least in the eyes of the mayor and some of the city's leaders, was its direct effect on city finances. Each gambling house paid a weekly assessment to the city. In effect, though not in name, the city licensed these illegal businesses. Indeed, it did the same thing with houses of prostitution. Payment by gambling houses and the so-called "dance halls" and "cribs" varied, but they provided a substantial part of the city's revenue; and, it was rumored a part of the collections remained in the collector's pockets. So someone connected with city politics had a vested interest in seeing there was no change. Mayor Hammett did not propose to outlaw these revenue-producing occupations, but only to clean them up somewhat, and to keep the Sabbath clean. So, his order was published.

The saloon keepers closed on Sunday, but soon they began to complain. The loss of Sunday business, they said, was irretrievable; loss of profits could not be made up other days of the week. In short, they claimed they were going broke. The complaint soon broadened to say other businesses were also being hurt. A petition bearing the signature of a majority of the leading businessmen was presented to the mayor, seeking the recession of his order, and permitting the city to be wide open Sunday, as well as other days. The mayor modified his order. On June 19, 1902, he issued an order that saloons need only be closed from 9:00 A.M. to 4:00 P.M on Sunday, and he would "leave enforcement to state officers." With this, saloons were again open on Sunday.

But the fight against open gambling was not over. It was led by W.H. Burges, Felix Martinez, then publisher of the *El Paso Evening News,* and Richard F. Burges.

The "reform" group put a ticket in field in the city election of 1903. It was headed by James H. White, a candidate for mayor. He was a former sheriff, and a man of highest integrity and standing in the community. The opposition's ticket was headed by C.R. Morehead, president of The State National Bank.

The White-Morehead election was long remembered as one of the hottest El Paso, or any town, had ever seen. The spark plug of the White campaign was W.H. Burges. He pulled no punches, and said whatever the facts would justify. The election heat and hatred centered on him. Almost daily Mrs. Burges received anonymous telephone calls, "Better make your husband quit talking the way he does, or he'll be dead before tomorrow night."

Prior to 1903 there was no secret ballot in El Paso elections. Each side lined up its followers, including, it is reported, all the Juarez residents they could corral for the purpose, and lead them to the polls. In an attempt to achieve an honest election, the city council passed an ordinance providing for the "Australian" ballot—a secret ballot not then generally in use in this country. It also provided for a registration of all voters prior to the election. To implement this, the ordinance created the office of "registrar," whose duty it was to take all lawful registrations, and keep the list of registered voters. Come election day, anyone whose name was not on the list would not be permitted to vote. W.M. Peticolas, a lawyer, and later chief justice of the Court of Civil Appeals at El Paso, was appointed registrar. The fight, to a large degree, centered around the attack by the Morehead forces on both the ordinance and on W.M. Peticolas as the registrar.

No sooner had New Year's Day of 1903 passed, than the campaign of the city election was on. The newspapers kept the issues and the arguments going almost from day to day. *The El Paso Times* backed the Morehead ticket, while the *El Paso Herald* was the enthusiastic supporter of the White ticket.

On Sunday, January 4, 1903, *The Times* had an editorial entitled "The Issues Are The Thing", and proceeded to belabor the Hammett-Turney-Martinez Trust. Hammett was then mayor, Felix Martinez was one of those actively supporting James H. White, and W.W. Turney we have met. The editorial stated there was an agreement to reelect Hammett mayor, otherwise Hammett would not have appointed W. Cooley, an employee of the First National Bank, W.H. Burges, its attorney, and W.D. Howe, brother-in-law of one of the Burgeses (Richard) as judges of the election. *The Times* went on to refer to some campaign poetry that appeared in the *Herald,* and offered its own variation, which read:

When Felix Turney pulls the string—
Not strangers in El Paso,
I've got a little toy, I bought it on
the street,
And any little girl or boy would think
it just too sweet,
I play with it a lot of times, it's such
a funny thing -
A monkey that will jump and climb,
When
Felix Turney
Pulls
The
Strings.

The Times also asked, if the "trust" was friendly to the poor man, why did it levy a dollar poll tax, when it could have been twenty-five cents. "Was it to disenfranchise Americans, Mexicans, or the colored man?"

On the same date there was a news item stating Joseph Escajeda, of the Turney-Hammett faction, paid five hundred poll taxes with $500 cold cash.

Two days later *The Times* had another article on poll tax payments, stating the "Dwyer boys" were paying poll taxes for the

Morehead ticket, and Joe Escajeda was paying them for the Turney-Hammett-Martinez group. The next day the same paper reported politics were growing warmer daily, and the parties were herding Mexican voters and paying their poll taxes.

The tenor of things can be seen from *The Times* editorial on the following day headed "Felix Soliloquizes to the Rich."

The *Herald,* on Monday, carried a statement by Felix Martinez stating he was replying to Juan S. Hart, editor of *The Times.* Martinez referred to the assault on him by the opposition, and referred to Juan Hart as the Captain of the Artillery. He then said Hart had referred to him as "a little Mexican." He went on to say that he was proud of being a Mexican, as much so as proud of being an American citizen, and referred to Hart as "a half-breed in whose mongrel composition one-half is Mexican blood" . . . and to one who undertakes to belittle his own race by thus characterizing another . . . and to Hart as one whose brain is loaded with alcohol, and who is inspired by jealous hatred.

Ten days later *The Times* carried an article reporting the meeting of the "Young Democratic Club of El Paso," stating that Judge Wyndham Kemp spoke, as did "Give-a-Damn" Jones, Zach L. Cobb, and M.W. Stanton.

A week thereafter *The Times* reported a Grand Rally for White, and on Sunday it reported a big political rally at the opera house the previous night, stating there was a large crowd present, with many ladies among them, and people on both sides of the campaign were there in the crowd. Judge Peyton Edwards presided, and he introduced W.H. Burges. The crowd called for Howe (W.D. Howe), and among the speakers were D. Storms, W.M. Coldwell, who the opposition *Times* said, "spoke in his usual conceited manner," and S.H. Newman.

Meanwhile, the news related to the question of which candidate would get the support of the labor unions. The *Herald* reported the Labor Party would hold its convention that night. It was anti-Morehead, and they expected "hooliganism" at the convention, by which they meant a noisy mob in the gallery. The next day it reported a big occasion the night before at the Labor Party Convention at the

Myar Opera House. There was a brass band to give a lively air to the occasion. A ticket was named—the same as the J.H. White ticket—including J.H. White for mayor and R.F. Burges for recorder. But the opposition would not concede it, and *The Times* carried an article headed "Labor Will Be For Morehead," and the next day it carried "Give-a-Damn" Jones' reply. This recalls two colorful characters in the early day legal ranks of El Paso, "Give-a-Damn" Jones and "God-Almighty" Jones.

The next day the *Herald* carried Felix Martinez' reply to Juan S. Hart. He said, "They will certainly get as good as they send. This city is not going to be dominated by the methods of vice and depravity, nor its citizens swayed by the low and cheap tactics of working prejudice only to flatter the ambitions of a political tyrant who sets his hounds on any citizen who undertakes to exercise the rights that his Constitution guarantees him."

The Times, on its editorial page, carried a headline, "Burges' Bluff," and belabored him; and in a later issue, it reported a meeting of the Morehead crowd. The Morehead forces lashed out savagely at the ordinance setting up a secret ballot, and filed suit for an injunction to enjoin the enforcement of the ordinance and to prevent Peticolas from acting as city registrar. It was heard at 9:00 A.M. on Saturday, March 14, 1903, before District Judge Walthall. A large crowd was present. Arguments on behalf of the plaintiffs were presented by Judge Beall, with Judge Peyton Edwards replying for the defendants. Judge Walthall took the case under advisement, and on the following Monday announced his decision. He held Peticolas was duly empowered by city ordinances to act as registrar, and that this did not contravene the Constitution and statutes of the State of Texas.

The time for registration of voters ended at 8:00 P.M., March 25, 1903. The *Herald* reported that Pat Dwyer and Ike Alderete were busy right up to 8:00 P.M., hauling in persons to be registered. When the registrar's book closed, 3,251 voters had registered.

But the biggest day of the campaign was April 1, 1903. The Lowdon National Bank stood at the northwest corner of the intersection of Oregon and San Antonio Streets. The Herald dubbed it "The

Famous Fighting Corner." And well it might have been so named, as three fights took place on that corner on April 1. The first one, just after noon, reportedly involved an attack on N.L. Griest, publisher of the *Labor Advocate,* by Dr. I.J. Bush and W.H. Demain. But the details of this affray have not survived the intervening span of years.

The second fight occurred about 5:30 P.M. S.P. Weisiger and W.M. Peticolas, the city registrar, both El Paso lawyers, were standing on the corner talking when Jim Dwyer came up. He engaged them in a conversation, which was marked by considerable jocularity and sarcasm, and then finally drifted to the subject of the registration of the voters.

Dwyer said to Peticolas, "You know your registration office was not fair."

Peticolas replied, "You know our office was fair."

Jim Dwyer kept insisting Peticolas' office was not fair, when Peticolas said Jim was not telling the truth. The lie was exchanged, and just then Pat Dwyer drove up in a buggy with his brother Sam, and called out to Jim:

"Why don't you take that up, Jim?"

Jim hesitated. Pat jumped out of the buggy and started for Peticolas, saying,

"No man can call my brother a liar."

Pat struck Peticolas a glancing blow on the side of the face, and then Dr. Bush, a very large man, who was standing nearby, jumped in between the two. He put his arm partly around Peticolas, and warded off Dwyer with his other arm. He was busily engaged in trying to stop the incipient fight, but Mr. Weisiger, father of attorney Weisiger, mistook his actions. Weisiger, Sr. was a slightly built man, past seventy years of age, who had recently come to El Paso for his health. Believing Dr. Bush was attacking Peticolas, he let Dr. Bush have a heavy blow on the head with a walking cane. Bush went to his knees, but quickly regained his feet, and said to Weisiger, Sr., "You have struck me by mistake. I was not going to interfere with Peticolas. I was simply going to try to keep him and Pat from fighting."

Weisiger, Sr., and Dr. Bush readily saw the blow was given by mistake, and quickly adjusted the matter between themselves, and

Weisiger, Sr. said, "I thought they were going to kill Peticolas. The doctor explained the matter to me, and now I see he really was trying to prevent the pending trouble. I cannot recall the blow that was struck; I can only say that I am sorry."

But the fighting was not over for the day. About 11:30 P.M. Harry Norman, who was on the staff of the *Herald,* walked along the street, and reached the Lowdon National Bank corner. Just as he reached the corner Jim Dwyer jumped out at him, and said, "Are you going to make any more cartoons?"

"I will make as many cartoons as I want to," he replied, at the same time gracefully responding to Jim's blow by landing a good one on Jim's nose, and following it up fast and furiously until after about twenty-five blows by each had been struck. At this juncture a policeman appeared. His first act was to take Jim Dwyer's gun away from him.

Jim was accompanied by his brothers Pat and Sam, Ike Alderete and others. In the midst of the row the Dwyer boys swore vengeance against Frank Alderete, Ike's brother, and Ike said to the Dwyers, "Boys, whenever you harm my brother Frank, I will forget politics, and stay by him."

There had been a loud clamor by the Morehead crowd to get hold of the much-looked-for Felix Martinez when all of a sudden, following the third fight of the day, Felix appeared and said to the crowd present, "Here is Felix Martinez. You have wanted him. Now what do you want? I will stand out here and meet any one of you in any way you want to come."

Luckily, further trouble was averted, and the men left for their respective homes.

The day's activities resulted in a busy time for the recorder's (municipal) court. Dr. Bush was fined $50 for displaying a pistol, W.H. Dunman and Jim Dwyer were fined $100 each for displaying pistols, and Jim Dwyer was fined an additional $5 for assaulting Harry Norman. The judge said he fined Dr. Bush less than the fine assessed against Dunman and Dwyer "because of extenuating circumstances." This, no doubt, was because of Bush's effort to keep the peace between Peticolas and Dwyer.

Not long after the above events occurred, the Morehead ticket held a rally at the Myar Opera House. Before it opened, a brass band paraded the streets to whip up enthusiasm and help collect a crowd. Judge A.S. Eylar spoke to the meeting, then a Mexican orchestra played, following which Zach Cobb was introduced as a gallant young Georgian. He said, among other things: "The Democratic and Republican parties of El Paso are united for C.R. Morehead. We will not descend to the dirty and low work practiced by our opponents." He then said Will Burges had tried to ridicule him, and stated that he (Cobb) intended to roast him. "I don't intend to do it, for there is not enough meat on Mr. Burges to roast. He's a half-fry. He's better known as the junior partner of Senator Turney." He added, "I am just a young lawyer, trying to get started, but ask no sympathy of Mr. Will Burges. I have made more money fighting him than I could have made serving him."

The climax of the campaign came on the night of April 2, 1903. The Young Men's White Club scheduled a rally at the Myar Opera House, on South El Paso Street. It was talked up all over town, a substantial part of the talk by the White supporters being W.H. Burges would make a principal speech, and that he'd take the hide off Morehead. The more hotheaded ones among the Morehead supporters, for their part, stated publicly over town that if Burges said one word derogatory to Morehead, he would be shot dead on the stage of the opera house; and many were the telephone calls received by Mrs. Burges at home, from anonymous callers, who said, "You'd better keep your husband at home. If he makes a speech against Mr. Morehead, he's going to be killed."

Came the night of April 2, 1903. The opera house was full, about eight hundred persons being present, including two hundred women. Those present were from both factions, the White supporters to cheer their speakers and candidates; the Morehead people to heckle and discourage the opposition.

The meeting opened with music by the Wilson Band followed by select numbers of the Mexican orchestra. Even before the meeting was started trouble developed. N.L. Griest, editor of the *Labor Advocate,* and a White supporter, started to enter the opera house, but was arrested at the door. He was taken to the police station, where he made bond, and returned to the meeting. When he entered, he was received with cheers, and made a speech to the assembled group. He was followed by Jose Escajeda, also a White backer.

Then Burges was introduced. He began by referring to the arrest. "The opposition has seen fit to arrest Mr. Griest," he said, "They have threatened bloodshed. This country was won with the shedding of blood, and we have as much blood to risk as they have." Zach Lamar Cobb, a Morehead supporter, was present with his fiancee, sitting near the front of the opera house. Cobb had tried to attract attention to himself by slinging his darts and arrows at Burges, and he had, in fact, at a little earlier date, invited Burges to come to a Morehead meeting to hear him roast Burges.

On this night Burges referred to Cobb, who was less than an average size, and said he felt kindly toward Cobb, as he did toward all young lawyers trying to get up in the world. But he did not go to hear him, as he had no quarrel with Cobb and, he said, "Besides, I've no time to shuck a nubbin." The crowd cheered, and Cobb's fiancee, enjoying the performance, half rose out of her seat and clapped her hands.

The Morehead ticket was running as the regular Democratic ticket, so Burges next said, "I am a Democrat and always have been one, while Mr. Morehead, who now runs as a Democrat, bolted the party in 1893. He bolted it again in 1895, and again in 1897, and again in 1900, and he then quit the Democratic Party. He flops easily and often. He bought his nomination for mayor this year, but he couldn't buy up the registration market." He then said, "Morehead says he is for the laboring man. Has any man in the audience been favored with one of Mr. Morehead's *cheap* loans? If so, hold up your hand." There was no response.

"Now, when Mr. Morehead was mayor of Leavenworth (Kansas), he used his office for private gain. Cannot we expect that he will do the same thing in El Paso if elected mayor here? Mr. Morehead is of the adobe age. El Paso is ahead of him. Show me one brick building or improvement this man has made in El Paso! He has made none. He doesn't want the city to advance, a little village is easier to boss than a big busy city. Morehead is a politician first, last and all the time, and if he has anything to do with the management of the present campaign, he's the worst that ever crossed the Pecos River. Morehead has lost the respect of more decent people when he attempted to thwart the registration law than by anything else he ever did. He—if he ever gets in and can hurt you—is going to do it. He has fought me, and I have fought him, and I am going to give him some more.

"If Morehead sold out in Leavenworth when he was mayor there, he certainly will treat El Paso likewise in his endeavor to get back that campaign fund which he has spent like water."

Such was the tenor of his speech, which was applauded enthusiastically by the audience.

Owen P. White who was present at the rally at the Myar Opera House as well as living through the campaign, wrote in his *Out Of The Desert:*

For several weeks prior to the date of the election the people of the town did nothing but breathe, eat and sleep politics. It was early a foregone conclusion that all previous elections which had been held in the town were destined to become tame and uninteresting by comparison.

The air was filled with rumors in regard to the presence in the city of paid gunmen brought here for the purpose of assassinating prominent citizens. Feeling immensely important, the citizens whose lives were said to be sought went about the streets escorted by bodyguards of their friends. A dozen fistic battles a day were indulged in by supporters of contending factions, and, as the campaign funds were large and candidates were liberal, an unusual amount of liquor, even for El Paso, was consumed.

During this campaign the women, and even the children, became deeply interested, and on the night preceding the election, when a mass meeting was held in the Myar Opera House by the White forces, the building could not contain one-half of the people who tried to gain admittance. It was just possible, however, that the enormous attendance on this occasion can be attributed as much to morbid curiosity as it can to political feeling. During the preceding two weeks of the campaign a young, fearless and eloquent attorney had been making speeches in which he bitterly and unfeelingly assailed Morehead. Whether or not Morehead took the remarks of the attorney deeply to heart is a question. During the entire fight, the 'ring' candidate preserved a grave and quiet demeanor, but some of his friends were not equally self-contained. Some of the younger men were especially resentful, and when the call for the mass meeting at the opera house was published, a warning was sent to the young attorney, who was advertised as one of the speakers of the occasion. This warning was to the effect that if he, the young attorney, dared utter a word that was critical of, or derogatory to, the character of C.R. Morehead, he would be shot down on the platform.

The public knew all about this warning, in fact the public knew all about everything pertaining to the campaign and the result was that a capacity house greeted the young attorney when he arose to speak. As far as it was in his power to do so this young lawyer justified the people for the trouble they had taken in coming out to hear him.

A good many years have passed since that occasion, and in those years it has often been our privilege to hear various public characters vindictively and mercilessly attacked. But never have we listened to public utterances which carried with them as severe an indictment as was poured forth into the ears of his audience that night by Mr. W.H. Burges. His part of the performance was carried off creditably and to the entire satisfaction of all his friends, but the part which the other young men had scheduled themselves to play failed to materialize. No shot, fired to vindicate the character of the 'ring' candidate, rang out from the gallery; no young attorney lay sweltering in his own blood on the stage of the opera house, and those of the audience who, filled with gory anticipation and hoping to see a tragedy, had attended the meeting, went home disappointed and sore.

But the Reform movement had not come to fruition, and on election day Morehead was elected. Reform would have to await another election day.

XV

The Case of the Lost Record

I can only look at the evidence.
—Lord Selborne

THE CAUSE CELEBRE in late 1902 and early 1903 was the Richardson-Mason-Harle extradition case. It broke on public view with the newspapers of November 3, 1902. This was the same date the newspapers carried the news item that a hot fight was going on in the Fifteenth Congressional District in the race for Congress between John N. Garner, the Democratic nominee and John C. Scott, the Republican candidate, and the Honorable William H. Burges had been down in the Fifteenth District speaking for Garner. Burges, in fact, had gone to Garner's aid, in his first race for Congress, and had campaigned for him particularly in those areas of the Fifteenth District where either Burges or members of his family were best known.

Other prominent news in the El Paso newspapers of this date was that about dusk, just outside the Sheldon Building (where the Plaza Hotel now stands), Deputy Sheriff Comstock, Constable Bryant and Deputy Franco made a sensational arrest of T.C. Richardson, W. Mason, and a Mr. Gray, who were charged with being conspirators in a gigantic scheme to swindle the New York Life Insurance Company. The three men arrested were just in from Mexico, and at the time of their arrest their attention was attracted by Constable Bryant, while Comstock caught Gray and Richardson unawares from behind a large telephone pole on the Sheldon corner. These two men were unarmed, but when Comstock made a move toward Mason, the latter reached for his gun, but the deputy was too quick for him. They bitterly resented the arrest, Gray declaring he would not go to jail until the warrant was read to him, but he was given to understand he could take his choice between the undertaker or the jail, and he went along peaceably.

The New York Life Insurance Company, for a period of several months, had been investigating a series of gigantic swindles which had been perpetrated upon it. The modus operandi appeared to be for the swindlers to insure the life of some poor consumptive or other invalid, who was not expected to live very long. In order to obtain the insurance, they would send a strong, well man to the examining doctor. He would give the doctor the name of the consumptive, as being his own name, and in that way a good medical report was obtained. When the consumptive died, however, a death report was made to the insurance company resulting in the conspirators collecting over $20,000 in several such swindles the previous year. Richardson was a duly authorized agent of the Company, while the others were simple members of the conspiracy. There was another facet to the method used by the conspirators to swindle the insurance company, and these cases appeared to have occurred in or around the city of Chihuahua, Mexico. It seems the conspirators in some cases had insured the life of a person who was in good enough health to get insurance, and then by poison or other means killed the insured and collected the proceeds of the policy from the insurance company.

The defendants engaged Patterson & Wallace, a well-known law firm in El Paso to represent them, particularly Richardson, in the preliminary hearing, where the defendants were charged with conspiracy to swindle the New York Life Insurance Company out of $100,000.

The matter was scheduled to come on before Justice of the Peace Spencer at 2:30 P.M. on Saturday, November 8, 1902. Richardson was thought to be getting ready for a suicide attempt, as he sent all of his personal effects, jewelry, watch, and $20 in cash to his wife in Dallas by a Dallas banker who had been in El Paso. The banker had identified Mason as the beneficiary of the Evans policy (which had been written in Dallas), to whom the banker's bank paid $10,000 on the death of the supposed Evans. The physician, who examined Evans in Dallas for the policy, identified defendant Mason as the man he examined, but who identified himself to the doctor as Evans. Mason claimed to be too ill to appear in court. He was in the jail unconscious, or pretended to be unconscious. Dr. Vilas, however, stated in court he had examined Mason that morning and there was nothing wrong with him. Mason was hauled into court in the middle of the afternoon by Constable Bryant, being practically dragged along by two Mexicans. He was set in a chair, appeared to be in a dazed condition, and did not seem to be conscious of anything. Richardson on the other hand, at the same time was in court and appeared to be cool but worried. It was 3:30 P.M. before they were ready to proceed with the hearing.

Gray, it turned out, was a famous detective who had been employed by the New York Life Insurance Company to investigate these frauds. The company became suspicious from noticing a substantial part of the proceeds of policies which it paid had gone, in several instances, to its agent, Richardson. A part of Gray's fame rested upon the fact that he investigated the murder of William Morris Rice in New York, the benefactor of Rice Institute, and brought the murderer to justice.

Judge Thurmond appeared for the prosecution and produced as witnesses Drs. Vilas, Wright, and Thornhill, Mr. Adams, (cashier of the Dallas Exchange Bank), and H. Cook, state agent for the New York Life Insurance Company. Dr. Vilas testified that Gray was the man brought to him for examination for the $100,000 policy taken out in the name of Marshal Sanguinet. He was introduced to Dr. Vilas by Richardson. Dr. M.O. Wright testified he had examined Sanguinet for a $100,000 policy, and went to the Sheldon Hotel for that purpose at the request of Richardson, who told him that in a matter of so large a policy it required two physicians to make the examination. He stated the applicant's shirt was pulled up at the time of the examination and he could see the name "Gray" tatooed on the man's back. Dr. Thornhill, of Dallas, identified Mason as the man he had seen in Dallas, and that he had examined him there for an insurance policy under the name of J.H. Evans. Mason was introduced to Dr. Thornhill by Richardson. Cashier Adams testified he had known Richardson and Mason since the previous summer and he knew Mason under the name of William Meredith and the introduction was made by Richardson. Richardson told Adams that Meredith had a deal on in Mexico and wanted a loan of $8,000, giving an insurance policy as security, and explained that Meredith was the half-brother of the deceased policy holder.

Gray learned enough of the conspirators' operations in Chihuahua City for the New York Life Insurance Company to send a man from its law department to Mexico City to familiarize himself with criminal proceedings, to learn who were the best lawyers in Chihuahua, and to get proper letters of introduction to authorities in that city. Then, if they could catch Richardson and Meredith in Mexico, they would have them in the toils of the law there.

Detective Gray, in fact, had wormed himself into the confidence of Richardson and Meredith, and learned that Richardson's real name was Charles E. Hurlbert, born in Fairport, New York, and was a graduate of the Cornell Law School either in 1894 or 1895. He had been in various difficulties, and sometime prior to these extradition proceedings became an agent in some parts of Texas, apparently including El Paso, as well as also operating in Chihuahua City for the New York Life Insurance Company. The New York Life's legal representative who went to Mexico came to Chihuahua, but there he was told the company had no case against Richardson and Meredith. Apparently this was based upon lack of concrete evidence they had murdered Mitchell and Devers.

Sometime after the preliminary hearing before Justice of the Peace Spencer, an application was made for a writ of habeas corpus to the District Court in El Paso, but after a hearing, the application was refused. The prisoners were held, as Mexico had decided to file an application to extradite the prisoners to Chihuahua for the purpose of trying them on the charge of murder.

Mason, who it developed was also known as Meredith, had either been non compos mentis, or had pretended to be, since the time of his arrest, lying on the bed or slumped over in a chair as though he was not paying any attention to what was going on, and appearing to be out of his mind. The extradition case was set for hearing before W.D. Howe, the United States Commissioner, who later, for many years, was judge of the Thirty-Fourth District Court. A few days before the hearing it was reported Mason had been plied with liquor, and had begun to talk. Apparently, he said nothing inimical to his position in the case, but had a great deal to say about who he was, where he came from, and his personal history.

The extradition case came on to be heard before U.S. Commissioner Howe on February 3, 1903. Burges, Judge Smallwood, and Harris Walthall appeared for the defendants. Judge Howe opened court with a statement he had information someone was threatening that if various people came to El Paso and appeared as witnesses on behalf of the defendant, they would likewise be charged with these crimes, and that someone was trying to scare witnesses for the defense away. He stated the defendants themselves were in the custody of the United States government and would be fully protected, as would any witnesses who appeared for them. The attorneys for the prosecution disclaimed having any knowledge of any such threats being made. The hearing then began with the taking of evidence. The prosecution, represented by Captain Beall, offered in evidence the record from Mexico, which consisted of the complaint, the application for extradition, and the certification of the legal officials who signed the official documents, together with other documents. The complaint showed the defendants Mason, Richardson, or Meredith and Harle were charged with murder, and their surrender was asked for, based on the evidence submitted in the record.

A record of this kind had to be signed by the proper officials of the state of Chihuahua, whose signatures and position were certified to by the governor of Chihuahua, in turn certified to by the proper officials of the Mexican Government at Mexico City, and submitted to the United States through diplomatic channels in Washington. It was quite official looking, bound with ribbons, and having red seals made with sealing wax, and without which record there was no basis for the extradition hearing. The testimony in this record from Chihuahua was to the effect that two men, Mitchell and Devers, had died suddenly and mysteriously in Chihuahua; their death was caused by poison, their bodies had beeen exhumed and identified, a chemist report on an analysis from the caskets showed poison, and testimony of doctors that their death must have been the result of the administration of poison to the deceased. It included a confession by Dr. Harle to the effect that he had been called to attend these two men, who apparently were sick, and he had given them the proper medicine for what their ailments appeared to be, and he did not know until just before their deaths that there seemed to have been any untoward incidents, such as the administration of strychnine, or of whiskey to the deceased by the other defendants in an effort to kill them. It did show, however, he knew a short time before their deaths these things had been done.

The attorneys for the defendants objected to the introduction of all this evidence on the ground that it was immaterial, irrelevant, and was hearsay. It was Richardson's position Harle's testimony given in Chihuahua was not only false, but was given under threats and duress. It developed Harle's position was that the statement was made under a promise to him by H.H. Battome, an attorney for New York Life Insurance Company, and that if he would make such a statement—the confession—he would be held harmless, and no action would be taken against him.

This testimony was partly given on February 3 and was continued on February 4. When the hearing before the commissioner resumed at 2:00 P.M. on February 4, it was at once discovered the record from Mexico, on which the extradition was based, and which had been lying on a table in the Commissioner's Courtroom, had disappeared. An immediate search was instituted for it, for without the record, the case could not go forward. Amidst the intensive efforts to find the Mexican record, in came Deputy U.S. Marshal Hildebrand carrying a large bucket. He told Judge Howe he thought he had the Mexican record in the bucket. And indeed he did. It developed the sewer from the jail had been stopped somewhere along the line, and the sewer line had been cut while the line was being cleared. At the point where it was cut, a bucket had been hung on the end of the sewer line. Deputy Marshal Hildebrand said when Court adjourned at twelve, for about ten minutes he and jailer Molina, and defendants Richardson and Mason were left in the courtroom alone, while Harle, in an adjacent room, conferred with his wife and mother. He felt reasonably certain Richardson used this opportunity surreptitiously to pick up the record, hide it under his coat or shirt, and take it with him to the jail, where he evidently tore it into small pieces and flushed it down the toilet. Under ordinary circumstances it would have been long gone, with no trace of it to be found. It was only the fortuitous circumstance the sewer line was being worked on, and a bucket hung on the line, that resulted in the torn record being found, instead of winding up in the waters of the Rio Grande.

Not only was this the most unusual case ever heard in El Paso up to that date, but it had national prominence in newspapers throughout the country, and this incident made it unique in the annals of legal history.

A translated copy of the Mexican records was available, however, and Judge Howe ruled the hearing would proceed on the basis of the translated copy, and defendants' attorney did not object. All of the attorneys in the case had disclaimed having any knowledge of what happened to the Mexican record, and it was felt by everyone familiar with the case the responsibility for its disappearance rested upon Richardson, and upon Richardson alone.

On resumption of the hearing, Burges engaged in the cross-examination of Battome, whom he had already denounced as a perjurer. Among other things that developed on the cross-examination, he asked if he did not tell Dr. Harle that if he would testify against Richardson and Mason, he would go unharmed. Battome at first denied it, but finally did admit he had promised Harle he would not be harmed. He was asked if he had not furnished Dr. Harle with money to buy meals for twenty days after being taken to jail, and he at first denied it, but jailer Molina was present to swear the money left with him for Harle was given him by Battome, and he then admitted it. Burges asked him a continuous chain of questions, and before Battome was aware of it, he had told the court that instead of one detective assisting him, there were four. He at first denied he had induced Dr. Harle to make a statement, but then conceded that he had paid Harle's expenses while in the city and had showed him in other ways he was footing all his expenses. Burges then said to Battome, "Tell the Court, Mr. Battome, the nature of the telegram you sent to Dr. Harle at Chihuahua." Battome told them what was in the telegram, whereupon Burges produced the original telegram, and it read quite the contrary to what Battome had just said. The cross-examination completely discredited Battome.

On application by Burges, the hearing was postponed to give him the opportunity to bring in additional evidence on behalf of Dr. Harle. Testimony was again taken March 4, 1903 and was concluded by noon of that day. Judge Howe had already ruled the confession of Harle was admissible against him, but it was not admissible against Richardson and Mason. On behalf of Harle it was contended the confession was made under duress or promises of protection, and it could not be considered as a voluntary statement, admissible in evidence. It was also urged the testimony presented established the fact that Harle did not possibly know the men had been poisoned until they were beyond earthly help, so he could not be charged with being a principal in the crime, and even if the evidence supported an allegation that he was an accomplice, still the existing treaty does not include an offense of this nature. The argument was also advanced on his behalf that the testimony showed Mitchell committed suicide, while in Dever's case, Harle prescribed the proper course of treatment. It was also urged the complaint upon which the warrants were issued did come from the proper source. Burges' trial brief contained citations of legal authorities for, among others, the following propositions:

To support extradition proceedings there must be an affidavit of one having personal knowledge of the facts setting forth the facts and circumstances relied upon to prove the crime and an affidavit based on information and belief is insufficient.

Complaint can only be made by the duly accredited representative of the executive of the foreign government demanding extradition.

The existence of a legally sufficient complaint is a prerequisite to lawful extradition proceedings, and if the complaint is insufficient the entire case falls with it.

The government having introduced in evidence the declaration of defendant and not having shown them false and they not being in themselves improbable or unreasonable, is bound by them.

The commissioner should refuse to surrender unless evidence would justify conviction if the case were on trial before him.

Governor Ahumada's signature and capacity should be certified to by the American ambassador to Mexico.

Burges argued from the facts in the record that, (1) it showed Harle testified he gave Devers strychnine and nitroglycerine just before his death; (2) Dr. Harle did not suspect Mitchell and Devers of taking poison; (3) the Mexican death certificate, Dr. Harle recited Mitchell was a native of the state of New York; (4) before making a clinical examination, the chemists were told of the testimony of Dr. Harle; (5) Mr. Gandara undertook to tell what Harle said before Judge Spencer, but the prosecution does not introduce that testimony, although they have a stenographic copy of it; (6) Harle was only to furnish the necessary certificate of death; (7) the official doctors state they cannot say positively that Mitchell and Devers died from strychnine and bichloride of mercury, respectively, but only that the symptoms indicate they did.

Captain Beall argued at some length on behalf of the prosecution. Judge Smallwood and Harris Walthall also argued on behalf of the defendants. At the conclusion of the arguments, the commissioner ruled since the confession of Harle was not admitted as against Richardson and Mason, the evidence against them was insufficient and they were released. He held, on the other hand, based on the confession of Harle, there was enough evidence to hold him, and ruled he should surrender to the Mexican authorities.

The information available is to the effect the fight on behalf of Dr. Harle was then transferred to the secretary of states's office at Washington, D.C. from which the extradition order would have to come. No records have been found as to what happened with respect to this, and at the present sitting, we do not know what finally happened to Dr. Harle.

XVI

1905: Reform Triumphs

O, reform it altogether.
—Shakespeare

POLITICS CONTINUED to boil, and took a different form in 1905 for the crowd with which Burges worked. The biennial city election came on again, and this one proved to be a three-way race.

On January 10, 1905, Juan Hart, publisher of *The El Paso Times,* announced a "Municipal Waterworks League." His goal was municipal ownership of the city waterworks system, and he announced a full slate of candidates. J.J. Stewart for mayor headed the list, followed by J.W. Magoffin for tax assessor and collector, John Brunner for treasurer, S.H. London for recorder, and a full aldermanic slate.

The *El Paso Herald* of March 3, 1905, came out with a list of the Republican Party candidates, which ticket it supported. The leadoff man was J.A. Smith for mayor, then came H.C. Myles for treasurer, U.S. Goen for recorder, John Wilson for engineer. They also had a complete aldermanic slate.

Shortly, the official Democratic ticket was announced in the *El Paso Evening News.* It was Capt. Charles Davis, Sr. for mayor, B.F. Jenkins for tax assessor and collector, George A. Wimberly for city engineer, L.M. Turner for treasurer, A.S.J. Eyler for recorder, and eight candidates for aldermen.

The Stewart ticket ran strictly on a municipal ownership of the waterworks platform. It demanded mesa water (as distinguished from river water), and insisted no more franchises for waterworks be granted, and that the city take over the ownership and operation of the waterworks as soon as possible.

The Republican party tried to revive the gambling issue, throwing its darts in the direction of Capt. Davis, but it was hard to put the gambling issue on a ticket whose chief supporters were the very people who had led the antigambling, "reform" ticket in the election of 1903.

The Davis ticket came out for mesa water too, but proposed to require the International Water Co. to provide it, in compliance with its obligations. Its biggest thrust, however, was for paved streets and improved sidewalks. There were no paved streets in town, and sidewalks were largely unimproved. This, together with a plank in favor of new parks, and beautifying the existing parks, gave them their points of appeal to the public. The campaign was still young when it became evident the Municipal Ownership League had about faded away. The regular Democrats were active for their ticket—good men, in whom the public had confidence. Typical was the meeting of the International Athletic Club on March 24, at which 325 members of the club were present. Captain Davis and others, including R.F. Burges, addressed the club. Enthusiasm ran high. The Republicans, on the other hand, were reported to have engaged in a fist fight among themselves at one of their meetings.

Came election day, and when the votes were tallied, it stood:

Davis — 1,734
Smith — 723
Stewart — 135

The *El Paso Evening News* of April 12, 1905, carried a telegram, sent from San Antonio, reading:

> The splendid majority for Davis is a merited accomplishment to a just man and a fitting rebuke to a horde of time servers and soreheads, who, while proclaiming their own virtues publicly, were always secretly awaiting the time when grafting would begin. Municipal ownership for them was only the cloak for vengeance and spoils.
>
> The News did much to secure this happy result. Honest investors may now feel safe. W.W. Turney.

The newspaper accounts of the election made no reference to

W.H. Burges. There was no speech making by him at the Myar Opera House, or in San Jacinto Plaza. But the election was won by his crowd, and many people ascribed to him the role of quarterbacking the team from behind the scenes. This was the beginning of what the opposition for the next ten years called "the ring," insinuating it was something sinister in politics. And it operated successfully for ten years, 1905-1915, during all of which time W.H. Burges was widely said to be the architect of the political edifice built and controlled by "the ring."

The man actually holding a municipal office and putting together "the ring" from the inside was C.E. Kelly. He had joined J.H. Pollard in a retail drug store in 1893. Pollard was the brother-in-law of W.H. Burges. In 1902 Kelly became city treasurer, and started work on the political machine with which he was associated until 1915. He worked in the Democratic party, but it soon split, with Morehead and the Dwyers on one side, and Kelly and his group on the other side. The Kelly group elected Joseph U. Sweeney mayor in 1907, and when he resigned in 1910, the council appointed W.F. Robinson mayor. He was killed by a falling wall in a downtown fire, and the council then appointed C.E. Kelly mayor. He continued in this office until 1915 when Tom Lea, running on an "anti-ring" platform, defeated him. Burges, who was a key figure in the Kelly group, realized times, things, or voters had changed, and tried to persuade Mayor Kelly not to run in 1915. "You can't win this time," he told Kelly, but the mayor insisted he could be re-elected, and Burges, ever loyal to a friend, said, in effect, "so be it," and gave him his fullest support. But Burges' appraisal had been correct. Lea was elected, and "the ring" was out.

The chief effect of the election of 1905 on the material well-being of the city of El Paso was that the Davis administration paved the streets. There were no paved streets in El Paso until 1906, and the Davis paving program was a giant leap forward for the city.

XVII

The Case of the Ticket Scalpers

Out of the facts arises the law.
—Ancient Maxim of the Law

JUST BEFORE, and after, the turn of the century, it was common practice for railroads to put on "excursions" with special rates to various points which were vacation resorts or to cities where conventions or other meetings were being held. The excursion tickets were always round trip and were designed to attract crowds by low, round trip rates. The profit for the railroad was in the volume of passengers carried to and from a given place at a particular time.

Excursions were put on from various points, both in and out of Texas. For example, to San Antonio for the San Jacinto Day festivities, for the Battle of Flowers, for the International Fair, the Roughriders' Reunion, and for various conventions such as teachers' conventions, medical association conventions, Labor Day celebrations, and meetings of various fraternal orders. They were put on to Galveston, as a vacation resort city, and from other cities to El Paso, as a place of interest that drew many visitors, especially for its salubrious winter climate. These round trip tickets, which were stamped, "non-transferable," sold at such a low price that the round trip ticket often was less than a one way ticket at the regular fare. This resulted in many people buying an excursion ticket to Galveston, San Antonio, or El Paso, or other points to which excursions were run, and using it only one way. Such persons had the return portion of their tickets left, and shortly, enterprising people in each of the cities to which such excursions were run got into the business of buying up the unused portion of the ticket for small sums, and selling the ticket at less than the regular fare to persons who could use the return portion.

The railroads complained about "ticket scalping," and tried in vain, to get law passed against it. After much furor, and consultation with their attorneys, they decided to sue for an injunction to stop the "ticket scalping."

The test case was filed in San Antonio. The several railroads running into San Antonio joined as plaintiffs, filing the case known as *G.H. & S.A. Railway Company, et al. v. Lytle,* No. 17,124 on the docket of the District Court of Bexar County. Turney & Burges represented the Santa Fe in El Paso, but the line did not run into San Antonio. The railroads wanted Burges in the case, so he joined with W.A. Hawkins, also of El Paso, in representing the G.H. & S.A. Railway Company in the case filed in San Antonio. Judgment in favor of the railroads was entered on June 28, 1905, enjoining Defendant Lytle and others from buying and selling excursion tickets at less than the fixed price for regular tickets.

The defendants could see a flourishing business going down the drain under this injunction, and hired able attorneys to represent them. They appealed the case to the Court of Civil Appeals, which certified questions relating to it to the Supreme Court of Texas. The defendants contended that a railroad ticket is a nonnegotiable instrument, and as such, may be assigned by the owner of it, any stipulation in the ticket to the contrary notwithstanding. But they principally urged their defense upon the proposition that the railroads had formed a combination or entered into an agreement, express or implied, to fix the cost of transporting passengers, and this was in violation of the antitrust laws and therefore that the railroads had no standing in court to obtain an injunction relating to rates so fixed. On January 23, 1907, in *Lytle v. G.H. & S.A. Ry. Co.* the Supreme Court of Texas handed down an opinion, written by Chief Justice Gaines, one of the great judges in the history of the Supreme Court of Texas, affirming the judgment issuing the injunction.

The court held that the railroads had a right to sell tickets at the reduced rate, and to make them nontransferable, stamping this on the ticket; and it overruled the contention about the antitrust laws. It quoted from the certificate from the Court of Civil Appeals to the Supreme Court, with reference to the facts, to the effect that these special low rates were made to San Antonio by the railroads at the request of various associations and various citizens of San Antonio asking for special rates to and from San Antonio for the Spring Carnival and other occasions in that city. This admitted the reasonable inference that the railroads simply acceded to the request of the citizens and the association in San Antonio making the request, but that there was nothing to indicate any violation of the antitrust laws.

In the meantime, the defendants had been made to see that the injunction meant just what it said. While the case was on appeal to the Court of Civil Appeals at San Antonio, the defendants continued to sell the return portion of excursion tickets in violation of the injunction, and the railroads promptly instituted in the Court of Civil Appeals a proceeding praying the court to punish the defendants for contempt of court by violating the injunction. In an opinion dated December 6, 1905, Judge Neill of the San Antonio Court of Civil Appeals held the defendants in contempt, saying that whether the judgment of the district court was right or wrong, the injunction had been issued and must be obeyed while on appeal until the appellate courts could decide the issue; and it assessed a fine of $350 against W.J. Lytle, and a fine of $200 against Robert Reid for contempt of court in this connection.

There was a further contempt case, Ex Parte Testarde with an opinion from the Supreme Court on January 8, 1908, upholding an injunction against the "ticket scalpers."

With these cases, the railroad had won its fight against "ticket scalping," and Burges had helped carry to a successful conclusion a lawsuit involving one of the most colorful questions of that day.

XVIII

Appomattox: Laying a Trap for The Distict Attorney

Try if you can trap him in any question.
—Dolben, J.

It was in one of the early years of the twentieth century. The October term of the federal court opened at 9:30 A.M., Judge Maxey presiding. There were a number of criminal cases scheduled for trial that term. Engleking, the United States district attorney, who lived in San Antonio, was present to handle the criminal cases for the government.

The case of John Robertson was called. A man in his sixties stood up. He was in custody of the United States marshal, with a deputy marshal sitting at his side. When he stood up the court asked him:

"How do you plead, guilty or not guilty?"

"Not guilty, Your Honor," came the reply in a strong and steady voice.

"Do you have a lawyer to represent you?"

"No, Your Honor, I do not. I have no money with which to employ a lawyer."

"Would you like for the court to appoint a lawyer to represent you if you desire it."

"Yes, Your Honor, I would like to have a lawyer."

Judge Maxey looked out among the several lawyers who were assembled in the courtoom for the purpose of appearing with their clients when the docket was called. His gaze lighted on Burges, and he said:

"I will appoint Mr. W.H. Burges as your attorney to represent you. Mr. Burges, you are appointed by the court to represent Mr. Robertson in this case."

"If the court please, I would like an opportunity to confer with my client," Burges said.

"Mr. Marshal," Judge Maxey said to the deputy marshal in whose custody Robertson was, "take Mr. Robertson and Mr. Burges into your office and give them a place where Mr. Burges can talk privately with the defendant."

Burges obtained a copy of the indictment from the clerk. It appeared that the defendant was indicted on a charge of counterfeiting $1, $5 and $10 bills in United States currency. In a private room in the marshal's office, Burges read to Robertson the indictment and said:

"Mr. Robertson if I am going to defend you I have to know the truth. I have just read to you the indictment in which you are charged with counterfeiting. Are you guilty or not guilty?"

The old man looked him straight in the eye with a steady gaze and said in a clear, vibrant voice, "I am not guilty."

It appeared from his further statement it likely was true that some friends, or at least acquaintances, with whom he had been living the last few weeks were probably engaged in the business of counterfeiting, but the old gentleman stoutly denied he had any connection with it, or any knowledge of it prior to the time of his arrest. After reviewing the facts relating to his life in El Paso, where he had been for only a few months, and what he knew about the counterfeiting, Burges then proceeded to take from him a short statement relative to this life history.

"Where were you born?"

"Gallatin, Tennessee."

"When?"

"October 12th, 1835."

"How long did you live in Gallatin, Tennessee?"

"I lived there with my family until I was five years old. In 1841 my family moved to Clarksville, Tennessee."

"Just tell me where you lived the rest of the time after you left Clarksville until you came to El Paso."

"We left Clarksville in 1848, and moved to Paris, Tennessee where I lived until 1861. In 1865 I moved to Jonesboro, Arkansas, and lived there until 1886, when I moved to Pine Bluff, Arkansas. I lived in Pine Bluff from 1886 to 1899, then I moved to Texarkana, and since then have been on the move from place to place in Texas, until I came to El Paso about three months ago.

"Where were you between 1861 and 1865?"

The old gentlemen drew himself erect and said:

"Anywhere I was ordered in the Army of Northern Virginia. I went in with the first call for troops and I was actually at Appomattox."

Burges said, "I'll try your case all right. I'm going to put you on the witness stand and I'll ask you about where you have lived at different times in your life and I want you to answer just in the way you have answered me here this morning. Now, did you know any public official such as the sheriff or the mayor or the county judge in Pine Bluff or in Texarkana?"

"Yes, I know both the county judge and the sheriff in Pine Bluff very well."

"Will they state that your reputation for truth and veracity is good, and for being a law-abiding citizen or not?"

"I am sure they will say that my reputation for truth is good. I've always been an honest man and have never been given to telling lies about anybody. I'm sure that they would give me a good statement about it."

Burges obtained from the old gentleman the name of the county judge and the sheriff and went into the district attorney's office.

"Mr. Engleking," he said, "Mr. Robertson, whom the court has appointed me to defend is an indigent. He is completely without funds and has no relatives or friends on whom he can call. He tells me that the county judge and sheriff back in Pine Bluff, Arkansas, where he once lived, will vouch for his reputation for truth and veracity, and for being a law-abiding citizen. I have no personal knowledge of it myself, but if you will agree to its admissibility in evidence, I want to send a telegram to the county judge and to the sheriff in Pine Bluff, Arkansas and ask them whether or not his reputation there for truth and veracity and for being a law-abiding citizen is good. I will agree that whatever their answer is will be put in evidence."

Engleking agreed to this propostion, and Burges sent the telegrams. The following day the answers came back, stating that John Robertson's reputation for truth and veracity and for being a law-abiding citizen in Pine Bluff, Arkansas was good.

In due time his case was called for trial. Engleking put on the witnesses for the prosecution, undertaking to show that Robertson had lived in a house where others lived who were engaged in counterfeiting, and trying to draw from this the conclusion that he was part of a conspiracy engaged in the making and passing of counterfeit money. When the government rested, Burges placed Robertson on the stand to testify.

He now repeated, in open court, the questions he had asked the defendant in private the previous Monday.

"Where were you born?"

"Gallatin, Tennessee."

"When?"

"October 12, 1835."

"How long did you live in Gallatin?"

"Until I was five years old. My family moved to Clarksville, Tennessee in 1841."

"How long did you live in Clarksville?"

"I lived in Clarksville, Tennessee from 1841 to 1848."

"Just tell the jury where you have lived from the time you left Clarksville until you came to El Paso."

"We left Clarksville in 1848 and moved to Paris, Tennessee, where I lived until 1861. In 1865 I moved to Jonesboro, Arkansas and lived there until 1886, when I moved to Pine Bluff, Arkansas. I lived in Pine Bluff, Arkansas from 1886 to 1899 when I moved to Texarkana, and since then I have been on the move from place to place in Texas until I came to El Paso about three months ago."

Burges proceeded with questions about the alleged crime. The defendant testified he was not connected with any counterfeiting, and he had not had any part in it, and no knowledge of the counterfeiting with which he was charged.

It was obvious the United States District Attorney, Engleking, was champing at the bit to "get at" the defendant on cross-examination. As soon as Burges had finished, and said, "Your witness," Engleking leaned forward in his chair and said, "Mr. Robertson, where were you from 1861 to 1865?"

The old gentleman drew himself erect in the witness chair, and answered, "Anywhere I was ordered in the Army of Northern Virginia. I went in with the first call for troops, and I was actually at Appomattox."

This was a body blow. The district attorney had taken the bait, and court and jury got the full effect of it. Engleking looked at the jury out of the corner of his eye, saw he had been taken in, and leaned across the counsel table and said to Burges, in a whisper,

"Damn you, how many Confederate soldiers do you have on the jury?"

"Major Fewel and eleven others," was the reply.

In due time the jury retired to deliberate on their verdict, and in a short time was back with a verdict of "not guilty" and $15 they had taken up among themselves to give the defendant in view of the fact that he was financially strapped.

XIX

A Hat Full of Diamonds

Diamond me no diamonds!
—Tennyson

IN 1908 Abraham Rosenthal and Max Rosenthal, both strangers to the El Paso area, crossed the Rio Grande from Juarez into the United States at El Paso. The Immigration and Customs Services were housed on the north bank of the river, and all persons entering the United States at this point went through both the Immigration Service Station and the Customs Service Station. The person coming in reached the Immigration Service Station first, where he declared his citizenship and where his right to enter the United States was checked. He then proceeded on some fifteen feet to the Customs Service Station where he declared any goods, wares, merchandise, or other items of value which he was bringing in with him. If items of value which he might have were subject to the payment of import duties—tariff—he was required to fill out a form listing them and the value of each item, and the duty would have to be paid before he could take the merchandise any further with him.

Abraham Rosenthal and Max Rosenthal were arrested and charged with an attempt to smuggle a large number of diamonds into the United States. There was a duty on the importation of diamonds, and the duty had not been paid.

The defendants employed Burges as their counsel. He conferred with them, and it appeared they had in their possession, at the time of their arrest, a large number of diamonds. Burges described it as being "a hat full." They had cleared the Immigration Service Station, and had reached the Customs Service Station. Here the customs officer inquired if they had brought anything in with them, to which they answered "no." As they started to proceed, they were arrested, searched and the diamonds brought to light. It was about fifteen feet further from this point to an office with a window and a counter at which the forms for declaring goods and merchandise being imported into the country could be made out and signed by the importer, and the duty paid. This point had not been reached by Rosenberg and his companions at the time of their arrest.

The case came on for trial before Judge Maxey, the defendants pled "not guilty," and the trial proceeded. Burges stated to the court and jury the defense, which was, under the law these defendants had the right to proceed until they had reached the window where the forms for making the declaration were available, and where such declarations customarily were made, before it could be said they had imported the diamonds, and failed and refused to declare them, i.e., they were not smugglers until they had passed the point where the declaration either would or would not be made by them. It turned out the facts were not in dispute. The witnesses for the prosecution, who were the customs officers, testified that at the Customs Agent's Station where the defendants were asked if they had brought any goods or merchandise or items with them, and they answered "no," and having wrongfully stated they did not have anything with them, were thereupon arrested and the presence of the diamonds brought to light. A sketch of the area was introduced clearly showing the location of the Immigration Agent's Station, the Customs Agent's Station and the window and counter.

The defendants testified they did not understand what the customs agent had asked them, and they were looking for the printed forms on which to make the declaration, and intended to make the declaration as soon as they reached the place where the forms were available.

Burges requested the court to charge the jury in the language of the statute which provided, in effect, every person entering the United States, and bringing with him any goods, wares, merchandise or items subject to the tariff or import duty must declare the same at the place provided by the government at the Port of Entry for making such declaration, and under the law the defendants had until they reached the point where the forms for making the declaration were available on which to make the same, and failure to do so before reaching such point would not constitute a violation of the law.

The case was strongly argued to the jury on behalf of the government that it was plain the defendants intended to smuggle these diamonds into the United States; they denied to the customs agent who interrogated them that they had any such goods, wares or merchandise with them, and if permitted to proceed, within another half dozen steps they would be beyond the area in which the customs agents had their post and would be loose in this country with their hat full of diamonds.

Burges, on the other hand, argued that under the law, as set out in the statutes, and as would be charged to them by the court, the defendants were not required by law to make a declaration of what they had with them subject to the tariff or import duties until they reached the station at which the printed forms for making such declaration were available, and they were still some fifteen feet short of that point at the time of their arrest.

After the judge had charged the jury, including the charge which Burges had requested, they retired for their deliberations, and were out for approximately an hour. At the end of this time the jury came in with the verdict, which upon being handed by the foreman to the clerk and announced by him, read "not guilty." While the defendants and Burges stood in the courtoom congratulating each other after the judge had retired from the bench, the marshal came in and said he had something of interest to show Burges. He had gone into the jury room after the jury had returned its verdict and had been discharged by the court, and there on the table in the jury room he found a sheet of paper upon which one of the jurors had drawn a diagram. It was similar to the way one would diagram a sentence in a grammar class, marking on it, pursuant to the charge of the court, the point to which the defendants could proceed without declaring what they had with them and not violate the law, but beyond which, if they went without declaring what they had, they would be in violation of the law. The diagram also marked the point where the defendants had been arrested, and it was clear, on a comparison of these points on the diagram, the defendants had not reached the "point of no return." This is one case in which the jury, following the charge of the court, diagrammed the defendants right into a verdict of "not guilty."

The case had a sequel. The government had levied an attachment upon the diamonds, and the district attorney then sought to proceed with an action for a judicial declaration that the diamonds had been smuggled into this country, and that they were forfeited to the United States. Other counsel had been engaged to represent the defendants in connection with the claim of forfeiture of the diamonds. Hearing the district attorney was going to proceed with the forfeiture case, they hastily sent for Burges. They told him in view of the fact he had obtained a verdict of "not guilty" in the smuggling trial, they wanted him to help them in the trial of the forfeiture case, because, if after he had gotten the defendants off on the smuggling charge, they should lose the forfeiture case of the diamonds, they would be laughed out of town.

He went to work hastily to formulate his theory of the defense in the forfeiture case, and to get his legal authorities to sustain the defense. When they appeared in court at 2:00 on the afternoon of the date set, he stated the defense, which was that the Constitution prohibited putting a person twice in jeopardy of life, limb or property. And since the defendants in the smuggling case had been in jeopardy of their liberty, their acquittal in that case also inured to the protection of their property. Their property could not now be put in jeopardy for the same set of facts out of which the smuggling case grew, and in which they had been acquitted. He cited the authorities, argued the point to the court, and Judge Maxey held that his position was correct. The result was that judgment was entered against the government in its forfeiture case, and the defendants and their counsel went off with a hat full of diamonds.

XX

The International Water Co. Case

Water, water everywhere, nor any drop to drink.
—Coleridge

IN DECEMBER , 1909, a suit was filed, the issues and outcome of which were uppermost in the minds of people of El Paso for many months thereafter. For several years Burges had represented the International Water Co., which was engaged in supplying water to the people of El Paso, which at that time, comprised approximately 39,000 souls. On December 24, 1909, the city filed a suit in the United States District Court, at El Paso, praying for an injunction to compel the water company to comply with its obligation to supply an adequate amount of "mesa" water.

The background of the case was long, with an unhappy history concerning efforts to obtain an adequate supply of good water for this city. From the days of water taken from the acequias to the time of the Watts franchise of 1882, and the Watts plant and thereafter there were constant complaints about the inadequate supply of water and its poor quality; that it was muddy, dirty, unpalatable and unsafe. As early as 1893 Burges, in speeches in city elections, was remarking on the crying need for pure water. Juan Hart, publisher of *The El Paso Times,* had been crusading since 1889 for municipal ownership of the waterworks as the only solution. In 1890 there was a $75,000 bond election to raise money to buy the waterworks, but the bonds lost.

On November 3, 1902, the city granted the water franchise to W.J. Davis, who promised to furnish pure mesa water from wells near Fort Bliss, rather than from the "Watts" wells near the river. He agreed to charge not over twenty cents per 1,000 gallons, and when the population reached 35,000, to charge not more than eighteen cents per 1,000 gallons, and not over fifteen cents when the population reached 50,000. In February, 1905, the International Water Co. acquired the Watts property, and soon acquired the Davis franchise, and began supplying El Paso with water in October, 1905. In the meantime Juan Hart had again raised the banner of municipal ownership in the election of 1905, only to have the candidates espoused by him go down to ignominous defeat.

By the Spring of 1907, the city had grown so much the plant was inadequate, and it was necessary to begin using water from the Watts wells near the river, which had been the source of the entire water supply prior to the International Water Co. putting in mesa wells. There were constant demands for more mains and larger mains, and all receipts, over and above those required for operations, had been used to increase the plant, with no dividends being paid, except for one 3 percent dividend in May of 1906. Nevertheless, the funds generated were inadequate to increase the mains and improve the plant, and they were also insufficient to enable the company to borrow money for that purpose.

When the suit was filed December 24, 1909, a receiver was appointed for the company, and Judge Maxey appointed former Govenor Joseph D. Sayers as Master in Chancery to take testimony in the case, and report his findings and recommendations to the court. He was directed to inquire into the report on (1) the justice of the minimum charges fixed by the court, and (2) the improvements necessary to supply mesa water. Governor Sayers took testimony, and Turney & Burges filed a printed brief with him in which they stated the evidence showed it would take $442,736 to make necessary improvements to the plant of the water company. They further stated the value of the plant to be $908,639.37. They also told the Master in Chancery it was necessary the company be permitted to charge rates which would produce enough revenue to pay necessary operating expenses, fixed charges, set aside a reasonable fund to cover extraordinary replacement, cover depreciation and pay a fair dividend, citing cases from the United States Supreme Court. They also urged the basis for valuation of the company property as being the replacement costs, less depreciation, citing many cases.

In concluding their brief, they urged the need for a fair result for the city, consumers, the company and its stockholders and quoted from the *Knoxville Waterworks Company case,* 212 U.S. 1 at 18:

> The slight gain to the consumer, which he would obtain from a reduction in the rates charged by public service corporations, is as nothing compared with his share in the ruin which would be brought about by denying to private property its just reward, thus unsettling value and destroying confidence. On the other hand, the companies to be regulated will find it to their lasting interest to furnish freely the information upon which a just regulation can be based.

Governor Sayers filed his report in due time, in which he found the company was not furnishing the water required; the company's earnings were not sufficient to enable it to borrow the money necessary to make the necessary improvements; $442,736 was the sum needed to make said improvements; that the company had expended on the plant, including its purchase of the Watt's plant, the sum of $936,215. He also reported the experts agreed there was a sufficient quantity of mesa water to supply a city of 150,000 people, more than three times the then population of the city. He concluded with expressing the hope the parties would reach a settlement beneficial to all.

Actually, the International Water Co. and Burges were fighting the lawsuit on one hand, and were looking forward to a settlement on the other hand. H.J. Simmons, who headed the management of the company, had long since concluded the company could not operate successfully, and that the best its stockholders could do was to sell out to the city at a reasonable price. They were in negotiations with the city in the early part of 1909, and on April 21, 1909, *The El Paso Times* ran a five column story giving the company's side of the matter. They quoted the figures the company took to the city council as requiring an increase in rates, and an extension of the term of its franchise, so it could borrow the money to make the necessary improvments and additions. Mayor Sweeney appointed a commission "to confer with the city council and probably act as a board of arbitrators in the waterworks question,'' consisting of Juan Hart, James R. Harper, C.E. Kelly, Felix Martinez, Beverly Thomas, H.D. Slater and C.R. Morehead. They inquired into the value of the waterworks, and reported the $977,000 claimed by the company was too high, giving their opinion it should be $927,000. Thomas, editor of the *Times,* filed a minority report, stating it should be $714,000. Juan Hart, publisher of the *Times,* had been the great proponent of municipal ownership of the waterworks, and an implacable foe of the International Water Co., so it was easy to see from whence the minority report came. It was the opposition of Juan Hart and the *Times* that was making it hard for the International Water Co.

It occurred to Burges and Simmons the way out of the imbroglio was to buy *The El Paso Times.* They secured Thomas O'Keefe, a former newspaper man, to negotiate the purchase, and on April 22, 1910, the *Times* announced its management changed on April 21 into the hands of Thomas O'Keefe representing the purchasers. It had cost $150,000, of which $50,000 was paid in cash, the rest being represented by five notes each for $20,000 payable over thirty months.

Soon thereafter they were able to bring the International Water Co. case to a close. An election on May 12, 1910 voted in favor of municipal ownership as opposed to allowing the company to raise its rates, and August 13, 1910, the city agreed on a purchase price of $927,000. The long fight over ''pure mesa water,'' an adequate supply of water, and municipal ownership was over.

XXI

Intertwined with Mexico

A mystic bond of brotherhood makes all men one.
—Carlyle

EL PASO, TEXAS and Juarez, Chihuahua are twin cities, separated only by the Rio Grande. The warp of one inevitably is intertwined with the woof of the other, and it was to be expected that Burges would have matters of interest, as well as business, which had their roots in Mexico. Not only did social affairs on both sides of the river bring people from El Paso and Juarez together, there were other matters in Mexico of interest to El Pasoans. On July 13, 1905, Burges read a paper before the Texas Bar Association, entitled "A Comparative Study of the Constitutions of the United States of Mexico and the United States of America." This was at a time when Porfirio Diaz, who had become President of Mexico in 1876, was still head of the government, a dictator, and whether referred to as a "benevolent" despot or not depended on whose opinion was being aired. The Constitution of the United States of Mexico in 1905 was the one adopted in 1857. After analyzing various provisions, and discussing how they compared with the Constitution of the United States of America, including the absence from the Mexican Constitution of a guarantee—or any provision for—a trial by jury, or a writ of habeas corpus, he said:

Bearing all these in mind, the Mexican Constitution is entitled to our respectful consideration and study, though it is not equal to our own, nor could that be expected.

They had our example, but we had what was even more valuable, a training in self-government. Every principle in our bill of rights was vital in our history before it was moulded into the Constitution. The light in the council chamber wherein was framed our Constitution came in an unbroken stream from Runnymede. Back of the Constitution were the Declaration of Independence, the Habeas Corpus Act, the Bill of Rights, the Petition of Right and Magna Charta. The framers of the Constitution of the United States of Mexico had no such heritage, no treasure house of precedents recording the triumphant struggles of the individual with the government, which are the crowning glory of our profession. While the present Constitution of Mexico was adopted in 1857, constitutional liberty in the sense which we know it, is to all intents and purposes contemporaneous with the ascendency of General Diaz, in my judgment the greatest of living men. In short, constitutional government, orderly liberty, is largely the gift of Diaz to Mexico.

It was the boast of Augustus that he found Rome brick and left it marble. How vastly nobler than this must be the judgment on Diaz when the Final Decree has been entered.

It will be that he found his country threatened from without and lifted her to an exalted station among the nations of the earth, bringing her a lasting and an honorable peace. He found her rent with civil strife, and torn by warring factions. Her people are united, prosperous and happy.

He found her treasury exhausted, her credit gone, her industries paralyzed, her commerce shackled.

Now her debt is secured, her credit established, every industry vital with the energies of an upward moving people, 'while through a thousand arteries in strengthening tides flows trade, the calm health of nations.'

Out of strife and discord has come a sober reverence for the law, in which life is as safe as in our own country, and in which the title of private property is as secure.

Almost the four score years alloted to those of great strength have come to Mexico's Grand Old Man. A long and useful life lies behind him—a life single in its devotion to the welfare of the people he has been chosen to lead. Let us, as members of the Texas Bar, accord to him the full measure of our admiration. Let us remember with professional pride the years of his young manhood as a lawyer; his years of usefulness as professor of Roman Law in the National Institute of Mexico; his pre-eminent services to his race as a defender of liberty and law; and let us unite in the hope that he may be spared many years for the accomplishment of the work he has done so much to advance.

Nor was Burges alone in his praise of Don Porfirio, as Diaz was widely known. Elihu Root offered a toast in 1907, in which he said:

If I were a poet I should write eulogies; if I were a musician I should compose triumphal marches; if I were a Mexican I should feel that that steadfast loyalty of a lifetime would not be too much to give in return for the blessing he has brought to my country. But as I am neither poet, musician, nor Mexican, but only an American who loves justice and liberty, and hopes to see their reign among mankind progress and strengthen and become perpetual, I look to Porfirio Diaz, the President of Mexico, as one of the great men to be held up for the hero worship of mankind!

The Encyclopaedia Britannica (11th edition) said of Porfirio Diaz:

> His term of office marks a prominent change in the history of Mexico; from that date he at once forged ahead with financial and political reform, the scrupulous settlement of all national debts, the welding together of the peoples and tribes (there are 150 different Indian tribes) of his country, the establishment of railroads and telegraphs, and all of this in a land which had been upheaved for a century with revolutions and bloodshed, and which had had fifty-two dictators, presidents and rulers in fifty-nine years.

Four years later, in 1909, Porfirio Diaz was prominent in the news of El Paso. As early as April, the press reported plans for President William Howard Taft and President Porfirio Diaz to meet in El Paso on or about November 1. This was to be called "President's Day," and it was expected the two presidents would meet right at the border, as it was against custom for a president to leave his nation while in office. President Taft was officially invited by John A. Happer, president of the Chamber of Commerce; Joseph U. Sweeney, mayor; A.S.J. Eyler, county judge, John M. Wyatt, president of the El Paso Fair Association. Later there was a committee to invite President Taft formally, the committee being Horace B. Stevens, Senator Charles A. Culberson, Congressman W.R. Smith, General Anson Mills, and G.F. Hawks.

A little later it was reported President Taft had invited President Diaz to meet him in El Paso on October 15, and Diaz had accepted the invitation; but Diaz would come only to the border, and would not cross the river. An El Paso committee of Mayor Sweeney, John M. Wyatt, Felix Martinez, W.C. Davis, and Park Pittman, went to Mexico City to extend the invitation to Diaz on behalf of the city of El Paso.

The impending meeting of the presidents gave rise to great expectations. The press was full of it: Juarez making preparations for the coming of Diaz—will spend $25,000 to put Custom House in order—President Diaz will stay in Custom House—Juarez Avenue will be paved—arches along Juarez Avenue will show the president that all of the counties of Chihuahua heartily join in the reception—the arches will continue in El Paso up Santa Fe Street—Taft and Diaz exchange visits over river at El Paso—Diaz will cross into El Paso and Taft will cross into Juarez—this will be the first time a U.S. president has left the United States while president—Diaz to be guest at President Taft's luncheon in El Paso on October 16, at eleven o'clock—Taft will visit Juarez at twelve o'clock—Taft has accepted a six o'clock dinner date in Juarez.

The historic event occured October 16, 1909. Diaz had arrived in Juarez at 2:00 P.M. the day before. He was greeted by three bands, bugle corps, and the roar of brass-throated cannons just south of the Customs House, where several regiments of soldiers were drawn up, and he was given a twenty-one gun salute. Twenty thousand people crowded the street of Juarez, shouting "Viva Diaz! Viva Mexico!"

Taft's train arrived in the El Paso Union Passenger Depot yards shortly after 9:00 A.M. on the 16th, and then pulled down Main Street to the Oregon Street crossing. President Taft and his party, which included two cabinet members, Secretary of War Dickinson and Secretary Hitchcock alighted from the train, and were escorted into the St. Regis Hotel by Governor Campbell, Mayor Sweeney and General Myer. Here, in the hotel dining room, an elaborate breakfast was served to 150 guests. The dining room had been closed for a week while being decorated for the occasion. Garlands of flowers with light bulbs under them snaked down the tables. Gold match boxes were given as souvenirs at the head table, and silver ones were given out at the other tables. At 11:00 A.M., after the breakfast was finished, President Taft was in a parade that took him by carriage around San Jacinto Plaza, where four thousand massed school children sang "America" for him, and on to San Francisco Street, to the Chamber of Commerce Building.

But it was not President Taft's route that concerned Burges. He knew there were anti-Diaz persons in both Juarez and El Paso, and he was concerned lest an attempt to assassinate President Diaz be made

The meeting of presidents Taft and Diaz in 1909.
[Aultman Collection]

on him in El Paso. The two presidents originally had planned to meet in the middle of Santa Fe Street bridge over the Rio Grande, as tradition and existing opinion was the president should not leave his own country. But they worked it out differently and shortly before 11:00 A.M., President Diaz left the Juarez Customhouse for El Paso. His carriage, acccompanied by a troop of cavalry, of which there was a double line on each side of his carriage, alternating back and forth to form a screen, drove as rapidly as possible down Juarez Avenue, which was lined by regiments of the Zaparotes, the Eleventh Cavalry and the Twelfth Infantry, Mexican Army. The cavalcade included other carriages carrying the rest of his official staff.

President Diaz's carriage stopped at a reception platform at Seventh Street over which a handsome arch had been built. He alighted from his carriage and was escorted into a carriage provided by the United States. He was received by a party headed by Secretary of War J.M. Dickinson, Governor Campbell and Mayor Sweeney. Thousands of onlookers massed in the area gave President Diaz a tremendous ovation, which visibly moved him. The Mexican troops accompanying him stopped at Seventh Street, and the security duty was taken over by a squadron of United States Army Cavalry, which together with the Third Cavalry Band, and carriages containing General Myer and staff, Governor Campbell and staff, and Mayor Sweeney, proceeded to the Chamber of Commerce Building, by way of Mesa, East San Antonio, Campbell, Myrtle, Stanton, Texas, Mills and San Francisco streets. It was this parade that worried Burges, for it could offer many points of vantage to a determined assassin. The security measures had been taken by the proper authorities, but not being satisfied with this, Burges the day before walked the entire distance of the parade route, noting possible danger points, and checking to see all were well guarded. He wanted no international incident, no tragedy, and no recriminations which might flow from it, that would result from the assassination of the president of Mexico in El Paso.

Any account of the Taft-Diaz meeting requires at least a brief statement of the banquet on the evening of October 16, 1909. President Diaz was host at a dinner in the Custom House in Juarez, where places were set for one hundred fifty. That it was elaborate is attested by the report the decorations in the banquet room alone cost $20,000. The chef, who was once chef for King Alfonso XII of Spain, worked a month preparing for the banquet. The menu was:

Consomme Regence
Chablis Moutonne 1898
Paupiettes de Brochet a la Olga
Chateau Bon Air 1893
Timbales a la Palermitaine
Filets de Boeuf a La Varin
Corton clos du Rois 1893
Chaud Froid de Voibalile a la Estragon
Quartiers de Chevrouil
Aux Deux Sauces
Champagne Veuve Cliquot Brut
Salade Charboniere
Liqueurs
Asperges Lance Suedoise
Chateux Napolitains
Cafe

It was served on the famous banquet service of Maximilian, which was brought under guard from Mexico City, shipped in twenty-four specially made boxes. It was reportedly valued at $1,200,000, two of the most valuable items being the solid gold coffee and tea service. The banquet service was used only on the presidents' table, where fifty covers were laid, but the service used on the other tables was also special, having been shipped from Mexico City.

President Taft went to the banquet in the same style that President Diaz had come to El Paso that morning, driving down Juarez Avenue in President Diaz's carriage between rows of Mexican soldiers, both infantry and cavalry. It was a precedent-breaking occasion, for never before had a president of the United States left this country while in office.

The meeting closed with Taft saying, "What is it I say? Hasta la vista? Hasta la vista!"

President Diaz replied, "Ah, si, si. Hasta la vista, es muy buena, muy expresiva; Hasta la vista," and they parted.

Twenty thousand people had stood in the streets of Juarez, and shouted "Viva Diaz." But the plaudits of the multitude are notoriously fickle, and the very next year—1910—Francisco I. Madero launched his revolution with the slogan "Effective Suffrage—No Re-election," augmented by Emiliano Zapata's cry in Morelos, "Land and Liberty, and Death to the Hacendados." Diaz was reelected president September 30, 1910, but the revolution smouldered and flamed, and under pressure of impending defeat, Diaz resigned May 25, 1911. On the 30th, he and his family left Mexico for exile, he never to return.

The revolution had moved with considerable speed across the river from El Paso. The revolutionists gathered an army which assaulted and took Juarez on May 10, 1911. Their two military leaders, Pascual Orozco and Francisco (Pancho) Villa, planned to cut off the head of General Juan Navarro, the defeated Federal general, but they were foiled by Madero, who sneaked his captive away and sent him across the river to El Paso.

On May 31, 1911, a group of El Paso citizens gave a dinner for Madero at the Toltec Club. General Navarro was also a guest. Burges spoke at the dinner, and said:

Mr. Toastmaster:

That "grim visag'd war hath smoothed his wrinkled front" is abundantly proven by the friendly faces we see around this board, and here tonight we all find a common pleasure in wishing our distinguished guest of honor God-speed on his pathway to the high station and a fair count, to the chief of magistracy of a great republic and of a liberty-loving people.

Now, Mr. Madero, we do not want you to take that expression "a free ballot" too literally. In this country we have never been quite able to attain that ideal. The fact is, if we can hold them down to the market value, we are satisfied; and if, when you join issue with your adversaries at the polls and you find you need a few extra votes, not free but at the market price, and you will let us know, we'll endeavor to reciprocate past favors and supply the needful majority as rumor, (unfounded and malicious, of course,) says our El Paso Democratic majority has so frequently been supplied in other times by your constituents.

We want you carry away with you, if you have determined you can not remain with us and make Juarez the permanent capital of Mexico, an accurate idea of our strong desire for the closest reciprocal relations, trade and other, with our neighbors across the narrow river, soon destined to be, under the beneficient work of the Reclamation Service, more bond than boundary, between the two great republics of this western world.

Now, Mr. Madero, I said a few moments ago we were glad to have this opportunity to cheer you on to the high office you are soon to attain, and it is a high station. Not only it is a high station because it is the chief magistracy of a great republic, but also because of the great men who have held that exalted position in past, greatest and foremost of whom is that man, exile from his native land though now he be, who was lifted up by brain and heart in an hour of your supremest national trial, to take into his hand, his iron hand, if you please, the hand of a weak and struggling people, unaccustomed to the powers and responsibilities of self-government, unrestrained by the traditions and the exercise of individual rights and individual duties, and to lead you through years of strain on heart and nerve and brain, years of unfailing loyalty to himself, his duty and his people, to the honored position you now hold among the nations of the world. (A Mexican cried out "Shut Up"). No, I am not going to shut up. You have been demanding free speech and I am giving you your first lesson in it.

You tell us you overthrew him because he was not in sympathy with modern Mexico. We admit it, but we tell you that he made modern Mexico.

The Mexico in which order is preserved, the laws enforced, property held inviolate and life secure, is the gift of General Diaz to you and to the world, and you as Mexicans should be proud to know that he carries with him in his exile the respect and the admiration of all men who know that the only liberty worth having is liberty regulated by law; and, Mr. Madero, I beg leave to say to you that success in your high undertaking can only be had by making your own the great truth he taught both by precept and example, that a government's first duty is to govern; that peace, prosperity and progress go hand in hand in the modern world, and if you come back to us "El Presidente" in fact, as we hope you will and at no distant day, and you bring with you the record of juster laws, better administered; of more schools and better schools; of more factories and better factories; more railroads and better railroads, and railroads that run and are not mere streaks of rust across the face of the desert, you will, in very fact, have earned the right to the proud title of the Liberator, and you may rest assured of that welcome justly due to those who extend the bounds of freedom from those who have struggled upward through the long gorge, up with the toils of heart and head and hands to the shining table-land where liberty itself is sun and stars.

You start on your long journey with our sincerest good wishes. You have had our sympathies in your every effort to better the condition of the

Mexican people. Some of us in this country naturally sympathize with a revolution. Just before my arrival in the United States some forty odd years ago, my people were indulging in the inalienable right of revolting and we can therefore extend you an assurance of a fellow feeling—an inherited fellow feeling only—it is true, but nevertheless a fellow feeling.

I feel sure you will agree that we gave the best evidence of our sympathy with the revolution. We were in favor of it from the beginning, and perfect candor compels me to say we shall be just as much in favor of the next one.

We have heard much said this evening in praise of Mr. Madero for not having shot Gen. Navarro. Of couse he did not kill Gen. Navarro and it was well he did not, as it would have cost him the good will of his neighbors to the north. Gen. Navarro was a prisoner of war, and among civilized nations, prisoners of war are protected, not murdered. It would have dishonored your victory. We of the English speaking world have learned that "grass soon grows green over blood shed on battle field, but never over blood shed on the scaffold."

Your battle has been won but your task is not yet accomplished. We learned in our own case that it takes years to bind up a nation's wounds. An old order does not change, yielding place to new, without birth pains. The task is honorable but exacting; the reward certain and commensurate when the task is done.

Here tonight, in this

"Land of settled government,
A land of fair and just renown,
When freedom slowly broadens down
From precedent to precedent,"

from which you go to your high calling, we beg you to bear with you the assurances of our high personal regard, of our abiding goodwill.

"Our hearts, our hopes, are all with thee;
Our hearts, our hopes, our prayers, our tears,
Our faith triumphant o'er our fears,
Are all with thee, are all with thee."

Burges made a speech a few days before in which references to Mexico figured prominently. On May 25, 1911, he delivered an address before the Missouri Bankers Association at Kansas City, Missouri entitled "International Commerce." There were numerous references to decisions by the United States Supreme Court on the matter of commerce, and after stating that just and efficient treaties of commerce should exist between countries whose people are engaged largely in reciprocal commercial transactions, and the public sentiment of both should demand an enlightened comity between such countries, in the recognition of the laws of each country by the courts of the other, he said:

> Take, for example, our relations with the Republic of Mexico: Our exports to Mexico for the year ending June 30, 1910, fell but a little short of sixty million dollars. We have no commercial treaty with that country. The treaty of Amity, Commerce and Navigation, entered into in 1831, was denounced by Mexico on the 30th day of November, 1881, and thereby ceased to be effective for any purpose.
>
> As a result of this state of affairs the Mexican courts now refuse to enforce contracts made in this country, unless in the very forms of their laws. Bills of exchange and other negotiable instruments are not enforceable in their country, unless made in accordance with their usages and expressly made payable in Mexico, and even the judgments of our courts are refused recognition or enforcement in theirs.

After a discussion of international commerce, commercially, legally and philosophically, he said:

> A great army and a great navy may be objects of great pride, but a vast foreign trade in articles of prime necessity, is a source of supreme power in the affairs of nations.
>
> The power of an enlightened public sentiment, such as would make you, as bankers, refuse capital or credit to enterprises wanting in honesty and fair dealing; such as makes the bankers of a country refuse credit to another nation in a war of conquest or oppression, is a power never to be denied or underrated. You have that power, and you use it. America has that power and has used it wisely and well. It was that power that brought peace to Russia and Japan; that brought Russia to realize that the further maintenance of a war entailing such sacrifices would place her beyond the pale of the benefit of our friendship; that made Japan realize that the further conduct of war to secure indemnity could not be financed in this country. This enlightened opinion of the world, and especially of America, was the dove that carried the blessing of peace to the warring nations and their sorely stricken people.

A few minutes later he said:

> Lord Russell, of Killowen, in his memorable address to the American Bar Association, declared that the fact that we had found no way to settle in-

ternational disputes except through the horrors of war, its waste, its suffering, its brutality, is a standing disgrace to our civilization. War, with its harvest of "cities sacked, fields ravaged, hearths profaned, men butchered." Do you say I speak with feeling? I do. I feel strongly. This address was prepared in the red glare of a burning city, into which no railroad train has run in more than four months; whose prostrate commerce, whose paralyzed industries, blackened ruins and desolated homes plead in language stronger than I can command, for the coming of that time,

'When the war drums shall throb no longer and the
battle flags be furled,
In the Parliament of man, the Federation of a world.'

What is the remedy? International arbitration; the substitution of reason and justice for brute force between nations as between men.

In this, as in many other things, the United States has furnished the world a great precedent. The Constitution of the United States provides in the second section of its third article, that the Supreme Court of the United States shall have original jurisdiction to hear and determine all controversies between two or more states.

By virtue of the power granted, as above stated, many and important controversies between states of this Union have been settled, settled amicably and settled honorably, when, without such a tribunal with such a power, an appeal to arms must almost of necessity have resulted.

He then cited a number of cases from the United States Supreme Court where boundary disputes between states of the United States had been decided peaceably at law, and stated this was the American way which could be followed in disputes between nations saying:

As I speak an International Court of Arbitration sits in the City of El Paso to decide the dispute between the United States and Mexico as to the location of the boundary line between them, in the City of El Paso. Immense property rights and titles to homes of thousands of people will be conclusively decided by that award, but we know it will be honestly and intelligently made and all concerned, the high contracting parties and their citizens whose interests depend on it, will accept the result and carry out the judgment without question and without appeal.

He concluded with an appeal to the bankers to whom he was talking to prevent war by refusing to finance a war between foreign countries, being careful to say however that this did not apply to our own country should war be made upon it, and he looked forward to that day:

> 'When the common sense of most shall hold a
> fretful realm in awe,
> And the kindly earth shall slumber, lapt in
> universal law.'

Even though the revolution had begun in Mexico, a historic step in peaceful relations between the United States of America and the United Mexican States had occurred in the Federal Courthouse at El Paso on May 15, 1911. On that date the Arbitration Commission held its opening meeting for the purpose of hearing matters relevant to, and deciding, the issue submitted to it by the two countries. It related to the international ownership of a strip of land in South El Paso known as the "Chamizal." The issue submitted read:

> The Commission shall decide solely and exclusively as to whether the international title to the Chamizal tract is in the United States of America or Mexico. The decision of the Commission, whether rendered unanimously or by majority vote of the Commissioners, shall be final and conclusive upon both governments, and without appeal. The decision shall be in writing and shall state the reasons upon which it is based. It shall be rendered within thirty days after the close of the hearings.

The tract in dispute was defined by metes and bounds in Article I of the Convention in which this arbitration had been provided for. The issue for decision by the arbitrators, therefore, was whether the Chamizal tract, as described by metes and bounds, belongs to the United States or to Mexico.

The matter in dispute had a long history, but its background, succinctly stated is as follows:

When the Republic of Texas was established in 1836, it decreed its southwesterly, and westerly boundary to be from the mouth of the Rio Grande, and up the middle of that river, following the deepest channel, to its headwaters. The treaty of Guadalupe-Hidalgo in 1848 between the United States and Mexico, likewise provided for the boundary to run up the Rio Grande "up the middle of that river, following the deepest channel" to the southern boundary of New

Triumphant Rebel troops enter Juarez in 1911.
[Aultman Collection]

Mexico. It provided for a commissioner from each country to run the line on the ground. The treaty of Mesilla in 1853 referred to the line so fixed by commissioners, and stated the line so fixed should remain the boundary. Necessarily woven into this was the rule of international law that where the boundary between two countries is a river, and there is a change in the location of the channel of the river, the boundary follows the river channel if the change is due to erosion and accretion, but the boundary remains where it was if the change was due to avulsion.

The Rio Grande was moody, varying from a western stream with little water in dry periods, to a swollen river with rampaging floods on occasion. The river had a wide, sandy bed, and floods changed its channel from time to time, eating away soil from one bank, and depositing it on the other bank, as in accretion, or cutting across the neck of a horseshoe bend, as in the case of avulsion. There were floods and channel changes from time to time. The worst flood at El Paso occurred in 1864, and in 1884 Mexico claimed a southward shift in the channel of the river in 1864 was due to avulsion, and asserted title to a strip of land that by then had become a material part of South El Paso. The two countries entered into a treaty in 1884 with respect to the boundary, providing:

> The dividing line shall forever be that described in the aforesaid Treaty and follow the center of the normal channels of the river named, provided that such alterations be effected by natural causes through the slow and gradual erosion and deposit of alluvium and not by the abandonment of the existing river bed and the opening of a new one.
>
> Any other change wrought by the forces of the current . . . shall produce no change in the dividing line as fixed by the survey of the International Boundary Commission of 1852.

Floods on the Rio Grande continued to come from time to time, and by the Convention of March 1, 1889, the two countries established the International Boundary Commission to solve the boundary problems arising from the floods, and the changes in the river channel. That such a commission was needed was emphasized by another bad flood in 1897. The International Boundary Commission held a hearing on the Chamizal in 1895, taking testimony about changes in the river channel as far back as old-time residents could remember, and this was the testimony used by the Arbitration Commission in 1911.

In 1910 the United States of America and Mexico agreed to binding arbitration, and selected as arbitrators, Anson Mills of the United States, Fernando Beltran y Puga of Mexico, and Eugene LaFleur of Canada. LaFleur was Presiding Commissioner and had the deciding vote.

Burges had no official part in the arbitration, but he was deeply interested in it not only because it involved a public matter, but also because he had clients who owned property in the Chamizal area. He no doubt conveyed his thoughts and ideas about it to the United States representatives, as counsel for this country was Judge Walter B. Grant of Boston, his good friend and client, and the U.S. assistant counsel was Richard F. Burges, and he kept a complete file of all the official proceedings of the arbitration.

There was no evidence of avulsion in the changes of the river channel in the Chamizal area. The most the evidence showed was, on certain occasions, flood waters eating into sandbanks on the Mexican side, with a yard or two of sand falling into the water with some frequency, and a building up of soil along the riverbank on the American side. It was the contention of the Mexican counsel that the treaties provided for a fixed line, as established in 1852, but Anson Mills and Eugene LaFleur voted against Mexico on this. The United States contended that the treaties and international law provided the boundary shifted with the river in the case of erosion and accretion, and remained where it originally was only in cases of avulsion. Both countries claimed the entire Chamizal area, as described by metes and bounds in the arbitration agreement. One notable fact stood: there was no evidence from which anyone could draw a line on the ground where the river ran prior to the 1864 floods. There had been so many floods, and so many changes, the pre-1864 river channel simply could not be established on the ground.

LaFleur came up with a compromise decision as arbitrators are sometimes prone to do. He held the changes made between 1852 and 1864 were by "gradual" erosion and accretion, and the land thus formed on the north bank belonged to the United States. He further

The Chamizal Arbitration hearings were held in El Paso in 1911. Seated at the bench in background are, from left, Anson Mills of the United States, Eugene LaFleur of Canada, and Fernando Beltran y Puga of Mexico.

held the changes made by the 1864 flood were by "rapid erosion", a term unknown to International law, and the boundary was the river channel as it ran prior to the 1864 flood. Puga reluctantly agreed with LaFleur, as this decision would, at best, give Mexico only part of the Chamizal.

Anson Mills dissented, on the grounds (1) the Arbitration Commission was authorized under the issue submitted to them only to decide the international title to the entire Chamizal area, and had no right or authority to divide the Chamizal, and award part to the United States and part to Mexico; (2) the commission was authorized to decide only whether the change in the river channel was due to erosion and accretion, or to avulsion, and there was no authority or right on the part of LaFleur to inject a new idea, i.e., rapid erosion, as the basis for the decision; and (3) since the river channel of pre-flood 1864 could not be located on the ground, the award was vague, indeterminate and uncertain in its terms and impossible of execution. There were also ugly rumors afloat in El Paso of undue influence used on LaFleur, but they, no doubt, could not be substantiated, and were never mentioned officially.

The Department of State and President Taft sustained Anson Mills' dissenting opinion, and refused to recognize or abide by LaFleur's decision. Under generally recognized rules relating to arbitration, LaFleur's award was void, and the United States was right in repudiating it. The ballyhoo raised in 1963 by those supporting President Kennedy's Chamizal settlement, in which they loudly proclaimed, and denounced, the United States' repudiation of the LaFleur award showed either gross ignorance on their part, or a willful perversion of the facts.

The Mexican Revolution had many repercussions in El Paso. The City was full of refugees from the northern part of Mexico, especially in the state of Chihuahua, where Villa's activities chiefly centered, and there were spies, counterspies, cabals, gunrunners, and all the activity concomitant to an active revolution across the border. The Mexico Northwestern Railway, which ran from El Paso southwesterly through Madera, in the mountains, on down to Chihuahua, was a pawn in the revolutionary game, and had its tracks, bridges and tunnels destroyed.

It was a client of Turney & Burges, and they got the news of this destruction firsthand. Many clients either American citizens, or refugee Mexican citizens came to them for advice and assistance, and Burges soon acquired a sizable library on international law.

One group of refugees were the owners of large cotton farms near Torreon. They left thousands of bales of cotton behind when they fled to El Paso. Villa, then in control of that part of Mexico, and with a de facto government running it, published a confiscation decree, and declared the cotton transferred to it. He was desperate for funds, and the cotton bid fair to be a source of revenue. He sent it to Juarez, and crossed it into El Paso, where it was put on a train for New York, for export to Europe. The original owners of the cotton watched all this from the Hotel Paso del Norte in El Paso where they were staying. They called on Burges for help. The cotton, worth $3 million was en route to New York via Texarkana, and he knew he had to act fast, before the cotton passed out of the jurisdiction of the Texas courts. He filed suit for an injunction, to prevent the cotton leaving Texas, and attacked the validity of the confiscation decree. As the act of a de facto government, during a state of war, the decree stood a good chance of being held valid. The cotton was caught by the injunction before it passed through Texarkana. Villa could not wait. He needed money. So a compromise settlement was reached, and Burges collected a large sum of money for his clients.

At a later time he had a suit over a contract of sale of cattle. On the other side of the case was Don Luis Terrazas, former governor of Chihuahua, and who, before the revolution, had large properties in Chihuahua. Burges briefed the legal questions, and the law, applied to the facts as he knew them, were in favor of his client. He never doubted winning the case, for he said he knew Don Luis would tell the truth when he testified. He was right. Don Luis testified to the facts just as they were, and Burges' client won the case.

On another occasion, two prominent El Pasoans came to Burges, and wanted him to write a confiscation decree. They said they knew where a large cache of gold was buried in Mexico, hidden from the dangers of the war. If he would write a confiscation decree, to be issued in Mexico, that would hold up in the courts in Texas, they could come into possession of a fortune in gold, and he would receive a large fee. Burges looked at them in cool contempt, and said, "Gentlemen, I never wanted money bad enough to steal it."

The Mexican revolution was in full swing, and Villa's murderous assault on Columbus, New Mexico resulted in the United States sending an expeditionary force, under General John J. Pershing. General Pershing had been in El Paso on occasions, but was transferred to Fort Bliss early in 1916. He had known Burges and they were great personal friends.

General Pershing's phone in his office rang one day. He answered it and said, "What's that—how's that?" And after listening again for a moment, handed his phone to his aide and said, "You take the message."

When the aide had finished talking, he turned and confirmed what had already been said to General Pershing on the phone, that there had been a fire at the Presidio in San Francisco and that his wife and two daughters had perished in the fire. It left his only remaining member of the family, his son.

General Pershing turned to his aide and said, "Call Burges." The aide called Burges who went out immediately to General Pershing's office to render such assistance and consolation as he could.

Villa proved to be elusive, and the chase of him was ineffective. It was soon called off, and General Pershing was made commander of the American Army sent to France in World War I, after the declaration of war on April 6, 1917, which followed the sinking of the Lusitania and Germany's institution of its policy of unrestricted submarine warfare.

XXII

Chicago Interlude

The great city is that which has the greatest man or woman.
—*Whitman*

DURING THE EARLY part of the twentieth century, the annual meeting of the American Bar Association was attended by only a few hundred lawyers. Burges, early in his career, joined the American Bar Association and soon began attending the annual meetings. The early ones he attended would have some 300 to 400, or perhaps 500 persons in attendance at the meeting, with the result that it was easy for all of them to get to know each other well. In this way he made friends with several hundred of the leading lawyers in the United States, who lived in cities scattered all over the country.

One of the great lawyers of the country, with whom he formed a fast friendship, was S.S. Gregory of Chicago, Illinois. Gregory was one of the leaders of the Bar in Chicago and had a topnotch legal practice, with far above the average income from it. In 1916 he suggested to Burges that he come to Chicago and join his firm, then known as Gregory and McNabb. The result was that in December of 1916, Burges announced his decision to move from El Paso to Chicago and to go into practice with S.S. Gregory, under the firm name of Gregory, Burges and McNabb. The new Chicago partnership was to be effective March 1, 1917. The newspapers, in carrying the story, at one time ran pictures both of Mr. Burges and Mrs. Burges. On the morning that Mrs. Burges' picture appeared in *The El Paso Times,* Victoria, her Negro cook having seen the newspaper before she served Mrs. Burges' breakfast, said the first thing when she saw her, "I seed your ad in the paper this morning."

During the first two months of 1917, they were busy getting everything shipshape with their business, social and personal affairs in El Paso, so as to be ready to move to Chicago. While it necessarily was quite a change for them, it was not like going to an entirely new locale, for over prior years they had made frequent trips to Chicago, some on business, but many merely for relaxation. Burges loved to take the train to Chicago, where a number of theatres with plays or operas were performing, and to attend musicals, the operas, the plays, or whatever there was to be seen in the theater. In addition to visiting friends at the same time, he loved to browse in bookstores, particularly those carrying secondhand books. He examined all items of interest to him, noting their physical condition, which edition each of them was, and its price.

Beside smaller personal dinners, two large dinners were given for Burges as farewell parties, one by the El Paso Bar Association and another by a group of 115 of the leading citizens of the town. The El Paso Bar Association dinner was given on February 19, 1917, at Hotel Paso del Norte. At the top of the cover of the printed menu and program appeared a quotation from Lord Byron:

> "Farewell! A word that must be and hath been—
> a sound that makes us linger; yet farewell."

The toastmaster was Judge F.E. Hunter, and five members of the Bar were on the program to speak on various subjects related to his moving away from El Paso, while the last item on the program being given as "Adios . . . William H. Burges."

The other dinner, given on February 22, was held in the Toltec Club, and at the top of the cover to the printed menu and program was the quotation from Shakespeare:

> "I am wealthy in my friends."

There also appeared at the bottom of the menu the quote:

> "He done his damndest,
> Angels can do no more."

And so at the end of February it was on to Chicago. He and Mrs. Burges went to the Congress Hotel, where they made their home for the next twenty months, the period of time he lived in Chicago. They had been there less than six weeks when on April 6, 1917, Congress declared war against Germany and the Central Powers. Shortly thereafter, Gregory called for a firm meeting of himself, Burges and McNabb. He had a legal problem. One of his clients, the Continental Can Company, had contracts for supplies to be furnished it from overseas, and which contracts might be incapable of fulfillment on account of the war. Questions had been raised by the client as to its legal rights and its legal position under the circumstances.

Gregory laid the problem before his two partners, with the remark he would like to have any suggestions they had about it, as this was an entirely new field of the law to him, and he did not know where to turn to get the answer quickly. Neither did McNabb. Burges said, "I haven't been here long enough to get my card to the County Law Library. If you will give me a card of introduction, so that I can get in the County Law Library, I will write the opinion for you."

The card was given him, and he went to the library and spent the day. At the end of the day he returned with an opinion written out, citing appropriate authorities in the field of international law. Gregory took it and read it with great interest and said, "Excellent. This is just what I need. But I would never have known where to look for this law. I never heard of these books before. How did you know where to look for it?"

"I haven't lived on the Mexican border during a Revolutionary period some years for nothing. I've had many questions, and some lawsuits, arising out of matters controlled by international law, due to the fighting in the Mexican Revolution, and I have necessarily had to be familiar with these books for some years," was the reply.

As the new man in the office, he was given a large stack of files that had been accumulating over a period of a few years, and which the other men in the office had either not kept moving because of the press of other matters, or had lost interest in because they doubted the client's position had merit. They were mostly lawsuits, and he was to review these files and see if there was anything there he wanted to take charge of and handle. As might be expected, he found several of them which he thought worth his efforts, and so he took over these cases. One of the typical things he did in this connection was to take over a plaintiff's patent suit. Gregory and McNabb had filed an action on behalf of the holder of a patent against a defendant whom plaintiff claimed was infringing his patent, and therefore owed him damages. Gregory and McNabb had not seemed to think too much of the case, and it had not been pushed. It looked to Burges like this was a meritorious case, and that there were enough damages involved in it to make it worthwhile to pursue. Accordingly, he began to work on it and through his preliminary action in it, the defendant's lawyers learned the case was being made ready for trial. Settlement negotiations followed, and shortly Burges had settled the case for $50,000 -worth, in comparison to the present value of money, four or five times what that sum is worth today. The client was not only happy, but was grateful to Burges for having picked up a dead file and breathed life into it, and for having obtained a $50,000 settlement. Burges then broached to Gregory and McNabb the questions of what would be a reasonable fee to charge their client. Burges later said that McNabb usually thought in much smaller figures than he did, and after a brief discussion, McNabb ventured the opinion that $500 might be a proper fee. After a little further discussion, Burges said to his two partners, "It might interest you to know that I have already collected the fee in this case. The fee is $15,000 and your client was most happy with it."

The practice in this office was lucrative by almost any standard, and Burges enjoyed his association with Gregory and McNabb, and he enjoyed Chicago. The most important thing he did while there, however, was not in the field of law, but was in the acquisition of the Wrenn Library for the University of Texas.

John Henry Wrenn, of Chicago, was a paper manufacturer and a banker who amassed a fortune. But he was also a lover of books, and had a propensity for collecting them. He had his favorite authors and had obtained copies in England of their works, when copies of them could be not found in this country. The result was a library of about 5,300 volumes, collected by Wrenn between 1885 and 1911. It was his ambition to make it, as nearly as possible, a complete history of the development of English literature from the sixteenth to the twentieth century. A description of the library states:

Within the collection as a whole are several outstanding groups of books; e.g., more than 1,100 plays ranging from 1560 to 1900; an extraordinary collection of pamphlets relating to the struggle for constitutional liberty in England; and almost complete representations of Seventeenth Century poetry — Daniel, Drayton, Milton, Cleveland, Suckling, Lovelace, Herrick, Roscommon, Rochester, Waller, Dryden, etc.; a surprisingly full array of Eighteenth Century prose and poetry — Addison, Steele, Swift, Pope, Defoe, Prior, etc; an enviable collection of the Romantic poets — Wordsworth, Coleridge, Scott, Keats, Shelley and Byron; almost complete lists of the Victorian poets — Tennyson, Matthew Arnold, the Brownings, Rosetti and Swinburne; and a fair showing of American writers — Washington Irving, Hawthorne, Longfellow, Lowell, Poe, Holmes, etc.

Wrenn died in 1911, leaving his collection of books to his son, Harold B. Wrenn, and his daughter, Mrs. F.F. Norcross. Dr. R.H. Griffith, Professor of English at the University of Texas, visited Chicago during the Christmas holidays of 1917 for the purpose of examining certain rare works of Alexander Pope in the Wrenn Library. While there he learned the library would be sold, and that if sold so that the library would remain intact, the heirs would sell at a price substantially below the market value of the books. He relayed this information to Dr. R.E. Vinson, president of the university, who enlisted the support of Major George W. Littlefield, a wealthy cattleman and banker, a member of the Board of Regents, and a strong supporter of the university. Major Littlefield agreed to give $225,000 if the library could be purchased for that amount.

It was here that Burges came into the picture. He was a connoisseur of fine books, and had a good acquaintance with many of them, i.e., knew the various editions of the works of well-known authors, their peculiarities, if any, and had considerable knowledge as to their monetary value. He had obtained this knowledge from the purchase of many books and the examination of others, as well as from examining book catalogues and lists which he received from booksellers in New York, Chicago, and other cities.

Dr. Vinson contacted Burges, and asked him to handle the negotiations for the purchase of the Wrenn Library. The university could not have made a happier choice of a negotiator, nor could Burges have had a more pleasurable assignment. He talked with

Harold B. Wrenn immediately, who not only was one of the heirs, but was also executor of his father's estate. Although the library was appraised at a sum in excess of $300,000—some thought it was worth $500,000—if sold book by book, or set by set at auction, he and his sister agreed they would sell it for a much smaller sum if it were bought by an institution of good standing, which would agree to keep the library intact, provide suitable housing for it, and name it the "Wrenn Library." Negotiations were conducted quietly, as it was feared there might be rival offers from other educational institutions or private collectors, and Major Littlefield had indicated his proffered gift was as high as he would go. Burges, on behalf of the university, agreed to the terms stipulated by Harold B. Wrenn, and the latter accepted the $225,000 offered through the generosity of Major Littlefield.

Burges wrote Dr. Vinson about the library:

> To begin with the collection of about 5,300 volumes contains a great many of the most extremely rare books in our literature.
>
> There is no first folio of Shakespeare, but there are superior copies of the second, third and fourth folios.
>
> There are practically complete collections of the first editions of Fielding, Swift, Dryden, Pope and countless others.
>
> There is a collection of the royal decrees and proclamations of the times of Charles I and Charles II that is beyond price.
>
> The collection of political and other broadsides of the time of Charles I and II and Queen Anne and other times is perfectly wonderful.
>
> In almost every case I am assured, and my observation leads me to believe the assurance is well-founded, the copy of the book is perfect and it is so bound as to keep it in perfect condition practically forever.
>
> I have seen some fine books in good condition in my time, but I have never seen anything that as a whole was anything comparable with this collection.
>
> With it the university would have the nucleus of one of the greatest collections possibly to be had.
>
> In fact, I should say the collection itself alone would place the university among the world's great libraries that had to be reckoned with in looking to original sources of English political history.

On February 21, 1918, Major Littlefield signed his check for $225,000 drawn on the American National Bank of Austin, Texas, payable to the order of Robert E. Vinson, president of the University of Texas, with the notation on the check, "For the purchase of the Wrenn Library." Vinson took the train to Chicago, where he met Burges, and the purchase was closed on February 27, 1918. The books were packed with the greatest of care, and were sent to Austin by special express car, with every provision for security of the books being taken.

Burges later said that the metropolitan papers across the country carried as a front-page story the sale of the Wrenn Library of Chicago to the University of Texas at Austin. Not too long afterward, he had occasion to be in Boston, and after having finished his business, had a few hours to spend before train time to leave, and spent it by going to a comparable library at Harvard University. The curator, or the curator's employee, was a very nice appearing and talking middle-aged woman. She graciously gave him permission to look at the books on the stacks in the library, but in following him as he looked at them, she engaged in conversation, and said, "Wasn't it a shame about those barbarians down in Texas getting that wonderful Wrenn Library?"

"I don't know about that," he said, "I purchased the Wrenn Library for the University of Texas myself."

"Oh, then you are Major Littlefield?"

"No, I am W.H. Burges. Major Littlefield put up the money and I negotiated the purchase."

He said thereafter as he went through the Widner Library and saw other copies of some of the same books that were in the Wrenn Library—but in some instances not as good—he took pleasure in taking such books off the shelf and saying, "Well, this is a very nice copy of this book, but it's not nearly as good as we have in the Wrenn Library in Austin."

His life-long enemy, asthma, was not to be denied. The cold, damp climate of Chicago aggravated his asthma, to where, after having lived there for a year and a half or so, he finally realized he would not be able to continue to do so. And there is the possibility the speed at which things moved in a city like Chicago were not altogether pleasing. He said they had to keep two clerks in the courthouse to keep track of cases that were called to trial, and be ready to run to court on short notice. He had already decided in late 1918 to return to El Paso to live

Wrenn Library at the University of Texas.

and practice law, when into his office walked Walter Douglas, vice president and general manager of Phelps Dodge Corporation, whom he had long known. The Phelps Dodge Corporation had copper mines in Arizona, and the purpose of Douglas' visit was to ask Burges to take over the defense of what was known as the Bisbee I.W.W. Deportation cases. Douglas told him that their New York and Arizona lawyers had said the cases could not be won, and he wanted Burges to take over the defense. He agreed to do so, and returned to El Paso and resumed his place in the firm of Turney, Burges, Culwell, Holliday & Pollard.

XXIII

The I.W.W. Calls a Strike

Onward, Christian soldiers! Duty's way is plain:
Slay your Christian neighbors, or by them be slain,
Pulpiteers are shouting effervescent swill,
God above is calling you to rob and rape and kill,
All your acts are sanctified by the Lamb on high;
If you love the Holy Ghost, go murder, pray and die.

—*I.W.W. Songs to Fan the Flames of Discontent*

IT WAS THE SUMMER of 1917. World War I had been raging across Europe and upon the high seas for nearly three years. On the Western Front the Allies were on the defensive, clinging tenaciously to the long line of trenches they had dug from the North Sea, across the southern corner of Belgium, and northern France. The River Somme ran with the blood of its British defenders, while Frenchmen died by tens of thousands before Verdun, to make good the heroic declaration, protecting the remainder of France, "They shall not pass." Tenuous as were the Allies' lines of defense in the West, they were strongly supportable when compared to those in the East, for Russia had been dealt a destructive blow in the battles of Tannenburg and the Masurian Lakes of East Prussia, driven back into what actually was Poland, and, to the south of that, had lost all of her earlier gains in the Carpathian mountains, which formed a barrier between Russia and the old Austro-Hungarian Empire. Russia's help was vital to Britain and to France; but it was not merely that Russia's armies were being defeated by Germany. Russia, the government of which was rotten to the core under the last of the Romanoffs, was falling apart. Any serious opposition by Russia to the German army was nearing an end, and in Russia Socialist–Communist exiles were busy furthering their conspiracy to return in a bold scheme to seize the governmental power in the confusion and strife that must inevitably follow the defeat of Russia, and the upset of the monarchy.

Dark though this picture was for the Allies, barely holding on the Western Front, and faced with the probability of German troops in the East soon being transferred to the West, it had another angle from which burst forth a strong ray of hope. Von Tirpitz, early in 1915 embarked on a policy of unrestricted submarine warfare. On May 7, 1915, the Lusitania, a British passenger vessel carrying a large number of Americans, was torpedoed, with great loss of life among the passengers. Despite negotiations by the United States with Germany to rid the seas of this menace, Germany persisted in it, and many more ships were sunk. President Wilson called for a declaration of war, and Congress responded on April 6, 1917, with a declaration of war against Germany, as well as against its two allies, Austro-Hungary and Turkey.

America was largely, but not entirely, united in the war. There were in the country a few pacifists and some German sympathizers; but worse than either of these were the revolutionary radicals among us who looked upon the strain and crises of war as a propitious time for destroying our democractic system of government, and erecting upon the ruins that most baleful of despotisms, which they called "the Dictatorship of the Proletariat." Foremost among these radicals in 1917 was the I.W.W.

Their name of the organization was "Industrial Workers of the World," but the initials I.W.W. were more widely translated as meaning "I Won't Work," and the individual members were commonly referred to by the name "Wobbly."

The I.W.W., organized in 1905, had either instigated, fomented, or fanned the flames of strikes, violence and sabotage over the country. There was the Lawrence, Massachusetts strike in 1912, with great violence, so that the I.W.W. called it the greatest of the I.W.W. strikes. During the years that followed, and prior to World War I there were strikes at Paterson, New Jersey—led by W.W. "Big Bill" Haywood; and in Akron, Ohio; Spokane, Washington; Denver, Colorado; San Diego, California; and Shreveport, Louisiana. There were riots in the California hop fields, fires in the wheat fields of the Midwest, and sabotage in the lumbering and sawmill areas of the West. They proclaimed it as "we few against the World" and "there is eternal enmity between the *haves* and *have-nots.*" Their position is nowhere better stated than in the I.W.W. "Preamble" which read:

> The working class and the employing class have nothing in common. There can be no peace so long as hunger and want are found among millions of working people and the few, who make up the employing class, have all the good things of life.
>
> Between these two classes a struggle must go on until the workers of the world organize as a class, take possession of the earth and machinery of production, and abolish the wage system.
>
> We find that the centering of the management of industries into fewer and fewer hands makes the trade-unions unable to cope with the ever growing power of the employing class. The trade-unions foster a state of affairs which allows one set of workers to be pitted against another set of workers in the same industry, thereby helping defeat one another in wage wars. Moreover, the trade-unions aid the employing class to mislead the workers into the belief that the working class have interests in common with their employers.
>
> The conditions can be changed and the interest of the working class upheld only by an organization formed in such a way that all its members in any one industry, or in all industries, if necessary, cease work whenever a strike or lockout is on in any department thereof, thus making an injury to one an injury to all.
>
> Instead of the conservative motto, 'A fair day's wages for a fair day's work' we must inscribe on our banner the revolutionary watchword, 'Abolition of the wage system.'
>
> It is the historic mission of the working class to do away with capitalism. The army of production must be organized, not only for the every day struggle with capitalists, but also to carry on production when capitalism shall have been overthrown. By organizing industrially we are forming the structure of the new society within the shell of the old.
>
> Knowing, therefore, that such an organization is absolutely necessary for our emancipation, we unite under the following constitution . . .

One of the focal meeting points of the central figures of the

The I.W.W., organized in 1905, had either instigated, fomented, or fanned the flames of strikes, violence and sabotage in the U.S. This song book was used as a rallying cry by the radicals and was published a hundred thousand at a time.

I.W.W. organization was the Radical Book Shop at 817 1/2 North Clark Street in Chicago. Big Bill Haywood and a small group of friends and kindred spirits used to spend evenings there, sitting around an old round-bellied stove in back of the book counter in the rear of the store. Among those who dropped in was Carl Sandburg, who was looking for bits of labor news for the *Day Book*. He had moved to Chicago recently from Milwaukee, where he had worked on Victor Berger's *Socialist Leader*.

The I.W.W. raised an agitation every time it could find a cause, no matter how specious, on which to foment a riot. Joe Hill, a Wobbly who was caught in an armed robbery in Utah, and was executed for it, was the excuse for some agitations. Mooney and Billings, who were arrested, and later convicted of the bombings and murders in the San Francisco Preparedness Day parade in 1916 gave an excuse for additional demonstrations. Labor unrest served as a focal point for revolutionary agitations. Once the I.W.W. had located an industry where there was employee dissatisfaction, it moved in and began magnifying minor complaints into major grievances. It sowed the seeds of discontent, and then followed a regular procedure. This consisted of handbills enlarging on the grievances, and demanding radical corrective action by the employer, talking to employees as they left work, holding mass meetings in public parks or other available places, working up a "strike" atmosphere, soliciting members, and eventually calling a strike, with pickets at the plant gates, and inevitably, violence.

The I.W.W. Publishing Bureau was turning out the *Little Red Song Book* bearing the subtitle "To Fan The Flames of Discontent" a hundred thousand at a time. It was full of revolutionary songs, many sung to the tune of popular Christian hymns, and was used as a rallying cry by the radicals. It illustrated typically the agitation for revolution and violence carried on by the I.W.W.

Germany's announcement of a policy of unrestricted submarine warfare was an obvious threat against the United States, and it constituted a signal for the I.W.W. to redouble its propaganda efforts against the nation's preparedness, and to engage in sabotage against the war effort. Just two months after the United States declared war on Germany and the Central powers, the Metal Mine Workers Industrial Union, a branch of the I.W.W., called a strike in the Butte, Montana District. Shortly thereafter the I.W.W. called strikes in the various copper mining camps throughout Arizona. This included the mines at Globe, Miami, Morenci, Ray, Clifton and many smaller communities. The demands made by the I.W.W. strike committee in each camp were practically the same. It was the strike at Bisbee, Arizona, occurring against the background here briefly alluded to, that gave rise to the celebrated Bisbee Deportation Case.

In late spring and early summer of 1917 many strangers had come into the Warren District of Arizona, which includes Bisbee, a large part of whom were of foreign birth or extraction. There was a period when every train brought in fifteen to twenty of them, wearing I.W.W. buttons, and carrying red cards in their shirt pockets. On June 26, 1917, at 1:30 P.M. demands were made by the I.W.W. on the three big copper producing companies in the Warren District. Their employees numbered about five thousand and their output of copper was approximately a tenth of the world production. The demands were chiefly for higher wages and shorter hours – made under a plan to demand ever higher wages and ever shorter hours – although the miners were earning high wages. The mining companies were given until 5:00 P.M. to accept or reject the demands, the I.W.W. leaders having stated among their own people the object was not only to oust the owners from control of their properties, but also to embarrass and defeat the United States in the war with Germany.

The companies flatly refused to accept the demands or deal with the I.W.W. The Metal Mine Workers Industrial Union No. 800, of the Warren District, immediately called a strike. Picket lines were established at the approaches to the mine shafts, and employees who continued to work were forced to pass between lines of pickets, enduring jeers, epithets and threats. Some employees who wore American flag pins were derided for their patriotism, with reference to the flag as "that rag," with open expression of hope the United States would lose the war. Some employees were caught by their arms as they ran the gauntlet of pickets, their lunch buckets were jerked away from them and kicked down the street and all the while profane threats of greater violence were hurled at them. Daily meetings were held in the city park by the strikers, where I.W.W. speakers proclaimed the victory of the I.W.W. Their speakers declared, "We demand six dollars per day and eight hours, but that is not what we want. We want eight dollars and six hours, but that is not what we want. We want the mines, they are ours." Presently their boasts of winning the strike appeared to be unfounded, as the mines continued to operate, and the chances of the strike succeeding began to fade. The inevitable sequence followed—an ever increasing crescendo of threats of violence to stop the miners who continued to work and to shut down the mines, and to take vengeance by beatings, dynamiting and arson on all the townspeople who did not support the strike.

On the afternoon of July 11, a conference was held between the city marshal, the mayor, I.W.W. strike leaders and the sheriff. At this meeting Mayor Jacob Erickson, himself a hard rock miner, incensed at the disloyal speeches made in the park by I.W.W. agitators, informed A.S. Embree, one of the striker leaders, the strikers were forbidden to use the park for meeting without a permit. He also called Embree's attention to city ordinances forbidding troublesome congregations on the streets. Embree replied he and the strikers were tired of "being deprived of our rights" and declared he could no longer be responsible for the conduct of the I.W.W. strikers as he could "no longer control them."

Sheriff Harry Wheeler, a former Arizona Ranger, and known as "the fighting Captain," replied, "If you can't control them, I can."

There was open talk that the "takeover" by violence was set to take place July 13. Sheriff Wheeler kept abreast of the situation, and he sent telegrams to President Wilson and Governor Campbell asking for help to keep the peace, but they did nothing. Finally, Sheriff Wheeler, seeing the threats were intensified as July 13 approached, and that the strikers were threatening an immediate takeover, determined to strike first to preserve peace and order, and avert violence and rebellion. On the night of July 11, he deputized twelve hundred citizens, and published a proclamation in the Bisbee paper on the morning of July 12 describing the situation, and calling on loyal citizens for support.

Early on the morning of July 12, 1917, Sheriff Wheeler and his posse comitatus rounded up the I.W.W. members and those who were their active sympathizers in the Warren District. The deputies identified themselves by each tying a white handkerchief around his arm. As the I.W.W.s and sympathizers came out onto the streets, they were arrested. Most of them were arrested on the picket line, or at their favorite "hangouts," but some others were arrested at their homes. They were marched to the ball park at Warren, for the lack of any other place large enough to hold them, a total of 1,188 having been arrested. When the roundup was completed, they were placed aboard a train of empty freight cars, and were taken to Columbus, New Mexico. A great cry went up from the I.W.W., their sympathizers, and others whose sympathies can be aroused, it seems, in favor of radicals, although done on the basis of false idealism.

President Wilson, who had not responded to Sheriff Wheeler's appeal for help, appointed Felix Frankfurter, a Harvard Law School professor, to go to Arizona and make an investigation of the deportation. The governor, who had not responded either, made strong statements about it. Some religious leaders made strong complaints about it, and shortly criminal complaints were filed by the county attorney of Cochise County against 403 individuals charging each of them with violating the kidnapping laws of the of the state of Arizona in removing by force, and against their will, the deportees from the state of Arizona into the state of New Mexico. There was considerable legal opinion to the effect that the facts were open and shut. In fact they were notorious, and regardless of the good motives of Sheriff Wheeler and his deputies for their own self-preservation and the preservation of the community of Bisbee, and regardless of their moral right, the law nevertheless had been violated and there was no legal defense to these criminal complaints.

During all of the matters above recited, Burges was living in Chicago. These events, which occurred while he lived on the shores of Lake Michigan, were to give him perhaps the greatest, and certainly the most unique case of his legal career. Upon his return to El Paso, the Bisbee case was to consume all of his time until the trial of the case of *The State of Arizona v. Harry E. Wootton* had been finished.

Twelve hundred citizens in Bisbee, Arizona were deputized to arrest I.W.W. members. Above, I.W.W.s are rounded up at the post office in Bisbee on July 12, 1917. Deportation begins (below) at the ball park in Warren.

When the I.W.W. roundup was completed (above and below), a total of 1,188 were arrested and placed aboard a train of empty freight cars and were taken to Columbus, New Mexico.

XXIV

Gathering the Evidence: From Bisbee to Chicago

He is well armed who is well prepared.
—Anonymous

BURGES SOON HAD a general description of the facts leading to the deportation. He obtained them first and foremost from his client, Sheriff Harry C. Wheeler, who was one of the defendants in the case. But there were several hundred other defendants and other witnesses to interview. One of his first acts was to walk over all of Bisbee, and firmly fix in his mind the location of all the streets and places of importance to the case, as he realized he might not be able to do this as they approached the trial date.

Once he had the picture of the facts which caused Wheeler to move into action that July 12, 1917 day, he had to determine the theory of the defense, i.e., the justification for the deportation. He had it from Sheriff Wheeler in the latter's own words, that he acted because of the necessity to do so in order to forestall violence and rebellion, and to preserve the peace, protect the people of Bisbee, and keep the war effort from being impaired by hostile forces in the persons of the I.W.W. The first thought that occurred to Burges was that this obviously was a case of self-defense on the part of a community that was on the verge of destruction by the I.W.W. His extensive reading in legal books and periodicals included various law reviews, many of which are no longer published, such as the *American Law Review, The Southern Law Review* and *The Law Times.* There came back to his mind at this time an article which had discussed "the law of necessity." It was based upon the theory that when a community finds itself threatened with destruction, it is justified in taking whatever reasonable steps may be necessary to protect itself. It is akin to the law of self-defense where an individual is assaulted or threatened and must defend himself in order to protect his life.

It is best and most frequently illustrated by the cases in which a town or city is threatened by a disastrous fire, and its officials and leader find it necessary to destroy property in the path of the fire. He spent many weeks briefing the case and particularly briefing "the law of necessity." When he had finished he had an extensive brief which was full of legal authorities on the right of the officials and leaders of a community to do that which is reasonably necessary when there is a reasonable appearance of threats, which might be carried out, to destroy the community.

Equally important was the interviewing of witnesses and gathering of information and documentary evidence about the I.W.W. which would prove its revolutionary nature and its purpose to handicap the nation's war effort. He went to Chicago, where he examined the file of evidence which had been accumulated by the United States government and used in the Big Bill Haywood trial; he went to Salt Lake City where additional material was to be obtained. He visited Los Angeles, San Francisco, Denver, Spokane, Butte and other western cities where the I.W.W. had left their tracks, and where testimony, mostly with respect to identifying I.W.W. documents could be secured.

He thereafter returned to several of these cities to take depositions, primarily to prove up documentary evidence about the I.W.W. When he called on the United States district attorney in Chicago for the purpose of examining the evidence used in the government's case against Big Bill Haywood (I.W.W. revolutionary publications, etc.) it developed that the evidence, already used in that case, was held in a separate room used for that purpose, with a guard there to see it was not lost or damaged. But when the guard heard why Burges was interested in it, he said, "What I don't see, I don't know," and deliberately turned his back, whereupon Burges carefully examined the many documents used as evidence in the Haywood case. He had found what he wanted, and thereafter proceeded to take many depositions to identify these documents and tie them in with the I.W.W. He took the depositions of men in the U.S. Department of Justice, the deputy clerk of the U.S. Court of Appeals and deputy U.S. marshals in Chicago. He also took the depositions of a U.S. marshal and a clerk in the U.S. Attorney's Office in Salt Lake City, where some of the documents identified included the Preamble to the I.W.W. Constitution, "The I.W.W., Its History, Structure and Methods," by Vincent St. John; "Patriotism and the Worker," by Gustave Herve; "The General Strike," by William D. Haywood; "I.W.W. Songs to Fan the Flames of Discontent," otherwise known as the Little Red Songbook; "Proletarian and Petit Burgeois," by Austin Lewis; "Sabotage, Its History, Philosophy and Function," by Walker C. Smith; "Sabotage," by Pouget; and the "Revolutionary I.W.W.," by Grover H. Perry. He had them legally ready to be put into evidence, provided the judge presiding at the trial would hold them admissible in evidence.

While all the other preparation for trial was going on, Burges employed several men to compile all possible biographical material about every man in Cochise County who was subject to jury service. There were 8,500 qualified electors in the county, which meant the men employed on this job had their work cut out for them. They busily engaged in assembling all available information and in typing it up on looseleaf sheets. When they finished, they had four black books containing all of the information they could find or ferret out with respect to each possible juror. These were known as the "Black Books," and proved of inestimable value to Burges and those associated with him on the defense side of the case. These books were so important, in fact, that two men, Biddy Doyle and another, were assigned the job of guarding them. They were to come into good use later.

Meanwhile several preliminary hearings were held in the justice court in Douglas, Arizona in the summer of 1919. They were important because they gave the defense an opportunity to cross-examine some of the prosecution witnesses and make a record of their testimony. They were of interest because they were a preview of what was to come.

On August 27, during the cross-examination of one of the witnesses for the state, Burges asked him if he had ever heard of any person being deported from the United States or being refused citizenship papers on the grounds that he was an I.W.W. The county attorney objected on the grounds he had never heard of such a case and declared he believed there never had been such a case and challenged Burges to produce evidence of any such incident if he could.

Burges accepted the challenge and promised he would produce the evidence.

When the afternoon session opened, Burges arose, with the latest issue of the *Federal Reporter* in his hands. He read from two cases where the findings of the Department of Labor for the deportation of aliens for the reason that they were I.W.W. agitators had been upheld in a United States court. A third case was cited in which a man of German birth had been denied citizenship papers for being a member of the I.W.W. and having such anarchistic views as to make it impossible, in the opinion of the federal court judge, for him to respect any oath to obey the Constitution of the United States.

The county attorney was not convinced. He arose and wanted to know what the federal court cases had to do with the preliminary hearing. Burges replied that the defense had produced the cases only after Robert N. French had challenged him to produce them, because he didn't believe they existed.

Mr. French answered in strident tones. In a voice that almost shook the plaster off the ceiling, he declared, "I have no sympathy for the I.W.W. or its doctrines." In thunderous tones he attempted to convince the attorneys and the defendants the I.W.W. had nothing to do with the issue and objected to the defense's question. He declared he was not a Socialist, but stated there was no connection between a Socialist and an I.W.W. Mr. French said he was a reactionary Democrat, so much so, in fact, he was "often accused of being a Republican." He added he was determined to do his duty as county attorney regardless of party.

Since the matter under discussion had no particular bearing upon the main issue, the bout was a no-decision affair, although "ringside" fans gave a "paper" decision to Burges for proving his claims which the county attorney had challenged. The prosecution next raised an objection to the defense questioning witnesses about the action of any men who had previously been given preliminary hearings in the deportation cases. The verbal barrages fell hot and fast on both sides, but the contest was a good-natured one, although both sides fired their best ammunition. The law was argued at length, following which the court took a recess. When court resumed, the county attorney withdrew his objections, and the court announced that counsel for the defendant would be allowed to ask the questions, and the same privilege would be extended to the county attorney. The state thereupon called to the witness stand Dominic Catero, who had taken the stand prior to the beginning of the argument, but had been excused while the legal arguments took place.

Dominic turned to Justice of the Peace Jacks, and asked the court for permission to make a little speech. He then proceeded with the statement that with his knowledge of things, he was confident he would be able to impart some valuable information to the court concerning the Warren District situation on July 12, 1917. He started to make references to John Greenway, Lem Shattuck and Bassett Watkins, but he was interrupted at this point, and was informed he had been called as a witness, and not to deliver an address. Upon being questioned, he testified to seeing E.L. Crook in Brewery Gulch on the day of the deportation, but saw him molest no one. He said he saw E.A. Tovrea in the Johnson Addition, with a rifle in an auto, but did not see him otherwise. He saw two mine shift bosses at the Warren baseball park on the left-hand side of the "gunmen," armed with guns, and added he saw another defendant, A.A. Finotti, at the ball park. Dominic turned to two hundred defendants in the courtroom and asked Finotti to stand up. This was objected to, however, and Dominic was directed, if he wanted to make sure of him, he could go among the defendants and identify him. He did so, but said he guessed he was mistaken about Finotti when the latter stood up and turned out to be the wrong man.

William Curnow, an avowed I.W.W., was the next witness called by the county attorney. He said he was arrested in his room in the El Paso House at Bisbee on the morning of the deportations by a man named Kelley who, he said, was working under the orders of Lew Supplee, one of the defendants. Curnow expounded many I.W.W. doctrines while testifying in the trial of Harry Anderson, a Bisbee mine-shift boss, and he was asked if he were still an I.W.W., and he said he was. He backed up his claim by showing a late date I.W.W. pamphlet and handed it to Burges.

Curnow said he believed a struggle should go on between capital and labor until the workers had organized sufficiently to take possession of the "earth and its machinery."

He was asked if it were not true he was deriving a living mainly from income from some property, instead of working. He attempted to evade the question, but at last the court, who had listened patiently to the questions repeated by Burges several times without direct answers from Curnow, informed Curnow that the time had come for him to cease being impertinent, stop endeavouring to argue with the attorneys and answer questions put to him as a witness.

With a gesture of surrender, Curnow then admitted it was true he was doing very little work. He was asked if, in line with his doctrines, he did not think the workers should take his own property and make him work for a living. Shrugging his shoulder, he said he guessed they should. He was not willing to voluntarily turn over his property to the workers though, he said, but if they organized sufficiently to take it by force, he would yield to the principle that "might is right."

The last state witness called during the afternoon, Alfred P. Hendrick, said he did not know whether he still belonged to the I.W.W. or not as he had not paid dues since last March, and he then testified to having seen R.A. Clampitt, former assistant postmaster at Bisbee, and Harry Jacobs, a Warren District insurance man, on the day of the deportations. He said he saw Clampitt armed in front of the post office, but did not remember seeing Clampitt put anybody in line or speak to any of the men in line, and did not see him again that day to the best of his knowledge. Hendrick said he saw Jacobs when the latter, with a rifle in his hand, ran by the line of deported men while they were being marched from the post office in Bisbee to the baseball park at Warren. This was as much as he knew about Jacob's actions, he said.

The witness told of having heard Stanley Clark, one of the I.W.W. leaders in Bisbee at the time of the strike, speak in Bisbee during the Warren District trouble. He said he had heard Clark declare in a speech that if the strike then in progress was settled, the I.W.W. would immediately strike again for even more wages and less hours.

The preliminary hearing continued on September 2, 1919. The entire afternoon session was taken up with the testimony of Mrs. Nancy Thomas. The general feeling about the prosecution calling her from her Missouri home to testify for the county attorney was that the prosecution was exploiting a mother's grief in order to push their case.

During the deportation and for several years previous, Mrs. Thomas was a resident of Warren District. It was charged that one of her sons was one of the 1,100 men deported on July 12, 1917, and later this son was killed in France. Grief over her son's death appeared to have affected Mrs. Thomas. From the start of her cross-examination her testimony appeared hopelessly entangled.

The county attorney, using a blanket warrant containing names of all defendants, which had been marked by the witness, questioned her as to her knowledge of actions of the men during the deportation. In a low quivering voice, Mrs. Thomas told of having seen each of the sixty-six men, whose names were read. The majority of them, she said, had walked in front of her home in Bakersville, acting as guards, when the deported men were marched to the baseball park at Warren.

Burges then took on her cross-examination. He first asked her about one of the defendants whom she had not named. Mrs. Thomas described his actions and how he was armed. French vigorously objected, claiming that the questions were unfair, inasmuch as the witness had not testified against the defendant about whom she was being questioned. A legal argument over the admissibility of this testimony ensued, and a recess was declared to afford the county attorney opportunity to look up legal authorities to which he had referred. After he had presented his authorities, the court ruled the questions put by the defense would be permitted if put in simple form that would not allow any possibility of unfairness.

Mrs. Thomas was then asked to identify one of the men she claimed to have seen on the day of the deportation. Although they were sitting in the court room, she was unable to identify them. Time and time again, the defendants stood up and the witness could not identify them. Other defendants whom she pointed out she identified as men whose names she had mentioned. Bob Andreas, a Bisbee miner, was twice identified as another defendant. The first time she identified him as John Hoagan, a Bisbee real estate man, and the second time as George W. Huffman of the Warren District. At last she admitted he was neither of these and she did not know who he was. This procedure was repeated a number of times and at the end of each portion she would always add "but he was one of the men who drove my boy away." She frequently denounced the defendants as "dirty curs" and "dirty rascals." As the grief-stricken woman made mistake after mistake in her attempts to identify the men against whom she testified, her situation became more pitiful and the sympathies of all the defendants went out to her, but as a witness she was through.

The *Douglas Daily International* of September 15, 1919, reporting on the preliminary hearing being held in Justice W.C. Jack's Court stated:

> The preliminary hearing this afternoon was for Harry C. Wheeler. County Attorney French sprang a surprise when he asked the court to dismiss the case against the former Cochise County sheriff on the grounds there has been no evidence to show that he was acting in any capacity other than a peace officer during the deportations. Attorneys for the defense immediately requested the court to refuse the motion, and after conference with Mr. French, it was agreed to waive the preliminary hearing, and he was bound over to the Superior Court for trial with the other 250 men implicated in the kidnapping. Mr. French was quoted as saying to the court, immediately after Court opened:
>
> 'The prosecution is willing to dismiss the case if the defense agrees. There has never been any testimony against Wheeler that would show he had taken an active part in the deportation.'

Burges, as chief counsel for the defense, immediately arose and objected to a dismissal, asserting it was the desire of the defendant to stand trial with the others who have already been bound over to the Superior Court.

This was followed by the conference with French and the agreement to waive the preliminary hearing.

The preliminary hearing of John J. Bowen, county highway commissioner, then began.

Burges did not overlook any possible benefit to his case. Every city had its big celebration on the first anniversary of Armistice Day. He arranged to have his good friend, General John J. Pershing, be the speaker for the event in Douglas on November 11, 1919. General Pershing was a great drawing card, and spoke with authority. During the course of this speech he referred to the great part played by Cochise County in the World War—that its great production of copper was a tremendous contribution, and was one without which the war could not have been won. The point of his statement could hardly have been lost on the people of this county from among whom the jury would be drawn within a few months.

XXV

The Law of Necessity

Who would be free himself must strike the blow.
—Byron

As MATTERS STOOD, by January, 1920, more than two hundred citizens of Bisbee and Cochise County still were formally charged with the 1917 kidnapping and forcible deportation from the county and state of a large number of miners and workmen, members of the Industrial Workers of the World, and others.

The prosecution, headed by County Attorney Robert Napoleon French, chose to try first Harry E. Wootton, who ran a store in Bisbee. French headed a staff of trial lawyers, consisting of himself, A.A. Worsley, and George Roark. Burges' staff consisted of Frank Curley of Tucson and William G. Gilmore of Tombstone. All were active in the trial, with Curley taking a leading part for the defense. Judge Samuel L. Pattee, of the Superior Court of Tucson, was designated as the judge to try the case, and he set it for February 2, 1920. On this date the work of selecting a jury began.

The trial was held in the courthouse at historic Tombstone. Burges took a two-story house as his headquarters, using it as a place of lodging and office for himself and those working with him, including Curley and Gilmore.

The selection of the jury occupied several weeks. The good use to which the "little black books" were put was shown by the *voir dire* examination of a member of the panel who was known to be hostile to the defendant. He had been heard to say, if he could get on the jury, he

Deportation trial was held in this courthouse in Tombstone, Arizona.

Jury members at the deportation trial in Tombstone in March, 1920.

would send Wootton to the penitentiary. Burges asked him, "Have you had any conversation with anyone about this case?"

"No."

"Have you formed an opinion about the guilt or innocence of the defendant?"

"No."

"If chosen as a juror, can you be a fair and impartial juror in this case?"

Burges, using one of the "black books" then asked him, "Isn't it true you were born in Cleveland, Ohio?"

He answered with a surprised look, "Yes."

"And your parents were Josiah O'Rourke and Jenny O'Rourke?"

He appeared even more surprised, and hesitated before answering, "Yes."

"Didn't you in the year . . ."

The would-be juror broke in with the statement, "I have already formed an opinion and cannot serve as an unbiased juror."

He could see what was coming, namely, a question about his having been convicted of crime in his earlier history before coming to Arizona. Witnesses are apt to start answering truthfully when they see you have the goods on them, and the "little black books" helped immeasurably in getting rid of some undesirable jurors.

There were quite a few Mormons in the county, and some were on the jury panel. They were all God-fearing, law-abiding citizens, and had the reputation of convicting in criminal cases. For this reason, lawyers who tried criminal cases in Arizona had a rule, "never take a Mormon on the jury." They convicted. To the surprise of the Arizona lawyers associated with Burges, he took two Mormons on the jury.

"What do you mean taking two Mormons on the jury? Don't you know they are convicters?" they asked.

"Did you ever look at this name on the list of defendants?" he replied, and pointed to the name of a son of the Mormon bishop.

An aftermath was that one day during the trial, the Mormon bishop, a fine looking man, with a long beard that gave him the appearance of a patriarch out of the Bible, came striding into the courtroom, and pulled up a chair behind Burges. He leaned forward, and in a stage whisper that could be heard over the courtroom, said, "How are we getting along?"

On March 10, 1920, the jury selecting process was completed, and twelve men "good and true" were sworn in as jurors, and took their places in the jury box.

Wootton was charged specifically with the kidnapping of Fred W. Brown, and Brown was the county attorney's first witness. He testified that on the morning of July 12, 1917, while on the streets of Bisbee, he was hailed by Ambrose Swoch, who took him before Wootton, who said, "Yes, that is the man," and he was forced to join a group who were being guarded by about fifty men, all with guns in their hands, and each with a white handkerchief tied around his arm. He told of being taken to a ball park at Warren, Arizona, from whence he and about 1,100 others were put into railroad boxcars, and carried to Columbus, New Mexico.

On cross-examination he was asked by Frank Curley, who did a large part of the examination of the witnesses, if he was first accosted by Ambrose Swoch, and taken in charge by him. He answered "Yes," and he was then asked if he did not testify at the examining trial that it was Charles Baer who arrested him, and put him in line? He answered, "Yes, I did so testify, but that is not true." He reiterated it was Ambrose Swoch, but said since Wootton had identified him, he considered Wootton was the one who arrested him. He further testified that most of the working men he knew were in the line of the deportees, while the men on the outside were business men and had handkerchiefs on their arms, and guns. Asked if certain friends of his had not offered to vouch for him, and get him out of the line, he answered this was true, but he elected to stay with his friends.

The value of the examination of witnesses before the justice of the peace at the preliminary hearings was well illustrated on the cross-examination of this witness. He was asked if he had not testified before the justice of the peace, that immediately prior to July 12, 1917 he was engaged in an effort the purpose of which was to run Wootton out of business. He denied having so testified. Curley then read to him from that record, "Didn't you tell him you would close him up or run him out of business?'' To which he replied, ''No, sir.''

''You didn't have any such idea?''

''No.''

''Were you going to injure him in any way?''

''We have a right, when a man is unfair to Union labor, we can tell them not to patronize that man.'' And he then admitted that perhaps he did give the testimony about being engaged in an effort to run Wootton out of business.

Following another series of questions about this same subject matter, he was asked if he had not testified at the examining hearing, ''Is it not a fact you would have done that if you could?'' [run Wootton out of business]

''Oh, yes.''

He then testified he did not now remember it, but if asked, his answer would be ''No.''

''Didn't you testify at the hearing before the justice of the peace that you told Mr. Wootton that you intended to run him out of business? You may not remember telling him that, but the fact is that was your purpose, was it not? And that he had then answered, 'Yes?' ''

He now denied he made such a statement to Wootton.

''Was your testimony before the justice of the peace not true?''

He answered that he may have misunderstood the question or may have answered it incorrectly.

''You were engaged in that as well as you knew how at the time?''

To which, before the justice of the peace, he had answered ''Yes.''

''My answers at that time may have been true to the best of my knowledge at that time.''

''Do you have a better knowledge since then than you had at the time of the justice of the peace hearing?''

''Yes, sir. I have investigated the record since then.''

''What records did you investigate as to your purpose?''

'''I had no purpose in that matter.''

''That is the question.''

He was asked in the same manner about other differences in his testimony given at the examining hearing before the justice of the peace and the testimony which he gave on direct examination in this trial, there being many differences between the testimony he gave on this trial and the testimony which he swore to before the justice of the peace. This included his testimony on the trial to the effect that he was arrested by defendant Wootton on July 12, 1917, and he was asked about having testified before the justice of the peace that Mr. Swoch arrested him on July 12, to which he answered, "He came down to the sidewalk where I was and took me to Mr. Wootton."

He then stated he didn't know whether Swoch had him under arrest or not.

"Didn't you swear at least five times previously that Mr. Baer arrested you?"

To which he said it was a mistaken identity he thought Swoch was Baer.

"Why didn't you testify at the examining trial that Mr. Wootton arrested you?"

"Well, I don't know. Maybe I didn't understand the question the way it was meant, or maybe I understood I was asked who accosted me and took me before Mr. Wootton. I was rather confused and just didn't understand."

He testified he came to Bisbee in 1916 from North Dakota; he went to Minnesota the latter part of July 1918, and returned to Bisbee June 7, 1919, and his business at the time was working for French, the county attorney. The defense made much of the fact that here was a newcomer, from North Dakota, threatening to run an old-time citizen out of business.

"There was a strike, Mr. Brown, in the Warren District, in 1917, was there not?"

The witness wanted to keep from the jury all references to the strike, and French objected to the question. Judge Pattee said he would like to hear counsel on this question. It was then twelve o'clock and the court adjourned until 2:00 P.M.

When the court resumed at 2:00 P.M., Curley made an argument to the court, to the effect the defendant expected to prove the I.W.W.

planned the overthrow of the government of the United States, in connection with which they hoped to see this country defeated in the war then going on, and hoped to foment strikes and other troubles in this country for the purpose of defeating the United States in World War I. The court said he would not rule upon the admissibility of the evidence with respect to its materiality to the case, but ruled this was a matter which had not been inquired about on the examination in chief, and therefore could not be inquired into on cross-examination.

French took the witness Brown back on re-direct examination, and he tried to explain some of the inconsistencies between his direct testimony at this time, and the testimony he had given on the preliminary hearing; and then on further cross-examination, he testified during part of the preliminary hearing he wasn't feeling well; and he didn't know whether he was feeling badly on the day of Wootton's examining trial or not. He admitted he was active during the preliminary trial in riding around and getting witnesses together and was feeling well enough to do that. He admitted he was well enough to testify accurately at those hearings, and any inaccuracies were not due to his physical condition at that time. He admitted he swore to a blanket complaint in the case against the three hundred defendants, and answered he couldn't tell whether these three hundred were working men or not, because he did not know most of them. It thus appeared from his testimony he was willing to testify to one set of facts at this time, but had testified to a different set of facts at the preliminary hearing, and had either perjured himself, or, his testimony, in any event, was not worthy of belief.

The next witness was Freeman Crouch. He said he saw Wootton put Brown in the ring that he (Crouch) was already in. He also told of being taken by freight train to Columbus.

H.L. Grenard then testified to seeing the deportees being rounded up. He was followed on the witness stand by Thomas Green, who was questioned on direct examination by Assistant County Attorney Worsley. The defense attorneys respected French, but they despised Worsley. Green testified that on July 12, he and Oscar Green were near the post office when a man approached him with a gun and with a handkerchief tied around his arm. He said "You will have to go with me."

"And I asked him where?"

"He said, "We are going to send you sons of ______ out of here today."

I said, "I don't know just exactly what you mean."

"Well," he says, "You go with me and you will find out."

"He takes me down in front of the Copper Queen Store, and he turned me over to another crowd that had guns and handkerchiefs tied around their arms, and they kept us there about ten minutes, and they turned us over to another crowd, and they loaded us on a street car, and from the street car they take us down to Warren Park, and at the depot where they stopped. They loaded us in boxcars and took us to Columbus."

On cross-examination by Curley, little by little, and like the proverbial pulling teeth, Green admitted:

That he testified in the preliminary examination, in *State of Arizona v. James Boyd,* but did not then testify he was on his way to enlist in the Navy; and he testified in *State v. Manson, State v. Navarette, State v. Scott, State v. Sims, State v. Slaughter, State v. Sutherland and State v. Tolen,* but in none of them had he testified he was on his way to enlist in the Navy at the time he was picked up. Again, the testimony taken at the preliminary hearing was of inestimable benefit in discrediting a prosecution witness, who was now undertaking to testify differently, and as strongly against the defendant as he knew how.

Curley then asked Green, "Were you a member of the I.W.W.?"

Worsely: "I object to the question. It is outside of the scope of the direct examination."

It was the purpose of the prosecution to keep the I.W.W. out of the case, if it could.

Court: "The objection is sustained. This is not cross-examination."

Curley: "It is five o'clock now. I would like to be heard on this question, I am through with the cross-examination of this witness except on this point."

Court: "The court will be glad to hear you, but in view of the time, court will adjourn for the day."

Burges addressed the court at this point: "I object to counsel (Worsely) stating in the hearing of the jury that the adjournment was asked to try and hatch up something on the witness. I am further away than any of the jury, and I heard it."

Worsley: "I was just whispering, and not facing the jury."

Judge Pattee: "That does not make any difference, it was a highly improper remark to make in the court, and the jury is instructed, if they heard it, to disregard it. Such statements are highly improper and should not be made."

Court thereupon adjourned to 10:00 A.M. the next morning.

It was Worsley who was approached by a friend of the defendant in court one morning during a recess. Everyone had left the courtroom except Worsley, Wootton's friend, and Burges. The friend walked up to Worsley, and Burges, who was standing by the counsel table checking some papers in his file, saw Worsley flush. Tension was intense on both sides of the case, and Burges wanted no trouble started by the defendant's adherents. He called the man over to him, and asked, "What did you say to him?"

"I didn't say anything," was the reply.

"I just saw you. What did you say?"

"I didn't say anything." was again the reply.

"I just saw you," Burges' tone was insistent, "And I want to know what you said to him."

"Well," came the answer, "All I said to him as, I said, 'If you was as big physically as you are mentally, you could kiss a gnat's a____ without bending your knees."

When court convened the next morning, March 11, 1920, at 10:00 A.M, Judge Pattee announced he had looked into the question left open the previous day, and he saw no reason to change his ruling.

Curley said he would like to be heard in it. The court retired the jury from the room, and Curley then presented the argument, that in order for the jury to pass on the credibility of a witness, the defendant is entitled to inquire into his antecedents, history and connections. He said the question was asked for the sole purpose of allowing the jury to determine what credit is to be given to the witness, stating one of the principles of this organization is that right and wrong does not concern them, and it is so stated by Vincent St. John in his book on the history of the I.W.W. Their literature, their papers, show the Christian religion to them is but a joke, and they scorn it. He referred to articles in *The New Solidarity,* an I.W.W. paper published in Chicago, and to an editorial in the I.W.W. paper, *Industrial World* which supported his statements. Will any man seriously contend that we are to sit by and watch the attempt upon the part of a witness to swear away the liberty of another man when he holds up his hand to the Divine Being and it doesn't mean anything to him? He relied principally on the opinion in *U.S. v. Wood,* (Dakota) 33rd N.W. Rep. 59. It was a powerfully stated decision that one accused of crime is entitled to inquire into the antecedents, history and connection of a witness appearing against him. The court rejected the proposition that upon the testimony of witnesses whose own private character (vile and sinful though it may be) is too sacred for inspection by those whose duty it is to give to it such, and only such, weight as it is entitled to receive in the courts of the land.

Curley then said, "In their *Patriotism and The Worker,* I.W.W. Publishing Bureau, Chicago . . ."

French: "I don't understand the ultimate object of this."

The court: "I don't either, unless it is that counsel avows that he will show the character of the organization."

Curley: "That is it exactly."

The court: "Of which he has asked the witness whether he is a member."

The argument continued, to the effect the defendant is entitled to inquire whether the witness belonged to the I.W.W. and, then, the character of that organization. The court indicated he did not follow this argument, since he did not judicially know what that organization was.

Burges then took up the argument, stating the defense could prove only one thing at a time; that it was now entitled to inquire whether the witness was an I.W.W., and if he were, then to show the character of that organization; that he expected to prove the I.W.W.'s purpose was the destruction by force of this government, and the overthrow of every basic principle of our civilization; and if they could show this about the I.W.W., no harm would have been done. It developed in the discussion with the court and the attorneys on both sides that members of the I.W.W. had been denied citizenship for that reason.

The court ruled the objection be sustained at this time, but if later evidence properly showed the character of the I.W.W., the question could then be asked of this witness.

At the conclusion of the cross-examination of this witness, Worsley announced, "The State rests."

It was not far from noon, and Judge Pattee said, "Court will recess until 2:00 P.M."

When Court resumed at 2:00 P.M., Curley made the opening statement for the defendant. The gist of it was:

That about 1908 William D. Haywood, Vincent St. John, and others, running into the thousands, conspired to overthrow the government of the United States, and do away with private ownership of property, all by force. They had continuously disseminated a propaganda of misrepresentation and falsehood to stir up dislike of our government and the private ownership of property; down to July 12, 1917 said conspirators had destroyed private property with the value of millions of dollars, and had destroyed many lives. They had inaugurated a series of strikes in the lumber and copper mining districts of the United States. They intended by these strikes to hinder and obstruct the prosecution by the United States of the war (World War I) against Germany; that as a part of this design, the I.W.W. made demands upon the copper companies of the Warren District in June, 1917, just prior to calling a strike on June 26, 1917, but the demands were made not for the purpose of securing better working conditions or higher wages, but solely for the purpose of embarrassing and defeating the United States in its prosecution of the war. In furtherance of this conspiracy, large numbers of conspirators had gathered in the Warren District for the purpose of destroying lives and property of persons living there, including defendant, and defendant's wife and children. That the conspirators had hidden out and stored large amounts of dynamite and other explosives for this purpose, to be used on, or immediately following, July 12, 1917. That on July 11, 1917, A.S. Embree, one of the leaders of the I.W.W., called the sheriff, Captain Harry C. Wheeler, and notified him that he, Embree, would no longer be responsible for the acts and conduct of the men, meaning the I.W.W. Sheriff Wheeler, being unable to get troops sent into the Warren District to protect the law-abiding citizens, called on said citizens to help him, and deputized them, and the jails being inadequate to hold the large number of conspirators, the sheriff and his posse, to protect the community and the citizens living there, arrested the conspirators, and delivered them to United States troops at Columbus, New Mexico; and Fred W. Brown was not carried there against his will, but went voluntarily and of his own free will.

Following Curley's opening statement, Burges made his celebrated argument on "The Law of Necessity." The theme of his argument was, just as in the law of self-defense, one who is attacked, or threatened with an attack by a person who has both the will and the power to carry out the threat, is entitled to defend himself to whatever extent necessary, just so a community, under the law of necessity, has a right to defend itself against a danger which may threaten it; and, pursuant to this rule of law, the defendant in this case has the right to show he took part in a deportation organized and carried on under the official direction of the sheriff of Cochise County; it was occasioned by the fact that the I.W.W. had a strike going on in Bisbee at the time, and it had made threats of great bodily harm to the community and to the law abiding members thereof; and the I.W.W., as an organization, was dedicated to the overthrow by violence of the government in this country, and it had both the will, and the power, unless restrained, to carry out such a threat. Therefore, he argued, the defendant had the right to introduce in evidence oral testimony and documents which would sustain this position.

The opening two paragraphs of the argument were:

"May it please the court:

"It is not improper for me to say that at least in the judgment of counsel representing the defendant, no more interesting or important case has ever called for the attention of the court. Many months have been consumed in the preparation of this case for trial, no small portion of which time has been given to consideration of the law applicable to the case. We are of the opinion that the principles which should and must govern its determination are as old as our law and enduring as human nature.

"The defense is based upon two propositions, different and yet resembling each other as kinsman—the right of self-defense and the law of necessity."

The argument then ran: It is our contention the right of self-defense is a perfectly valid defense in behalf of a community as well as an individual; that a community, when threatened by the action or threatened action of men armed or unarmed, banded together against the peace and welfare of that community, in such numbers and under such conditions as to imperil the lives of the people in that community or the safety of their property, or of any great part of them, is one form of self-defense and is a right sound in law and in morals. Self-defense is the right of protecting oneself from the unlawful aggression of another. The law of necessity is the law that justifies by virtue of necessity the invasion of another's right. Both find their origin in the primal instinct of man to defend his life and what is his own, whether it be his family or his property—a law stronger than any other in the world—a law before which everything else gives way when the occasion presents itself except the supreme necessity that comes to man of sacrificing his own life for family or community or country. The law of necessity is buttressed by the maxim that the safety of the public is the supreme law, a maxim peculiarly applicable to the facts of this case. We have the right to show all of the facts, circumstances and conditions that existed in the Warren District on the 12th day of July, 1917, and immediately prior thereto, as part of this great transaction. The law of self-defense was discussed, and then: when a community, the law abiding portion of the community, the peaceable portion of the community, the productive portion of the community, has been made the subject of threats of violence; when these threats have been communicated to it or to its representatives, the chosen officers of that community charged with the duties of enforcing its laws and protecting the property and lives of the people, are those who, while wanting in official capacity, are nevertheless their chosen leaders. When these conditions exist and when these threats have been made and are communicated to them, we have the right to show the persons who made these threats were sufficient in number to carry out the threats that had been made, or that they were of the character to justify the belief they meant to carry out these threats; that the making of these threats and the consummation of the purpose indicated by the threats were parts of a well-defined scheme and plan then being carried out in different portions of the country having a common determined end. The defendant is entitled to show that Mr. Embree (I.W.W. representative) and his associates had determined to do violence to the lives and property and business of Mr. Wootton and others similarly situated to him, i.e., the law-abiding citizens of Bisbee; that they had made threats to that effect, and were in position to carry out the threats; Embree and his associates were members of a larger organization existing in various portions of the country and the struggle was then on in other communities; that if the struggle in the Warren District was initiated at the request of members of the same organization at Seattle, Washington, who in turn acted on request of members of the same organization in Butte, Montana, the defendant is entitled to show this unity of purpose between the several branches of the organization as indicative of the character of the threats it is making, the objects to be attained and the purpose that actuated the conspirators in the effort against which Wootton and his associates were defending themselves. We are prepared to show by written documentary proof the character of the organization, its avowed purpose, the objects of which were to be accomplished by what they describe as "The Revolutionary Movement." We have the documentary proof from the minutes of the Bisbee Local of the I.W.W. organization; of their unity of action and purpose with other branches of the I.W.W. at Butte, Sand Point, Idaho, Seattle, Washington and other places. We propose to show a condition existed under which it was the honest conviction of this defendant, reasonably arrived at from credible evidence before him, that unless he took the part he did in the Bisbee deportation, he and those dependent on him, or his neighbors and friends would lose their lives or suffer irreparable injury to their persons and the loss of property. Have we the right to prove it? We say YES. The deportation was under the leadership of the sheriff of Cochise County, Captain Harry C. Wheeler. He led the movement. As sheriff he was charged with the duty of protecting the lives and the property of the people in the community. He believed that a disastrous riot was imminent. He knew a large number of people, strangers to the community, had come in for the purpose of carrying out the avowed program of the organization of which they were members, or with which they were in sympathy, that is, of destroying or so greatly interfering with the industries of the community as to make it impossible for those who owned the mines to operate them, at the same time making it impossible for the government to get the copper it needed for the prosecution of the war. It was a part of the established tactics of the I.W.W. in its efforts to force its will upon the community, or to interfere with the government in the prosecution of the war, to have so many of its members and sympathizers arrested, the jails could not hold them, and they would, therefore, have to be turned loose on that account. The sheriff as the leader of the citizens of the county took the men so seized to a place where they could be held in safety to themselves and to the community until order could be restored and the ordinary processes of government and of life be resumed in the community.

Many legal authorities were then referred to. The first was *Broom's Legal Maxims:* "Regard for the people's welfare, is the highest law." *1 Wharton's Criminal Law,* 107, Sec. 126, 11th Edition: "Necessity a defense when life or other high interest are imperiled." *Hale v. Lawrence, 21 N.J. Law Reports,* page 714, involving the right to destroy property in order to save a city from a disastrous fire. *American Print Works v. Lawrence 21 N.J. Law Reports,* 257, a case growing out of the same fire as the *Hale case.* Hare's *American Constitutional Law,* 2nd Vol., page 917—discussing, among other things, right to do that which is necessary in order to put down a riot of such proportions that it cannot be quelled by ordinary means. *Keller v. City of Corpus Christi,* 50 Tex. 614, the right of a police regulation to meet an impending peril to prevent the spread of fire.

Additional authorities were referred to, both American and

English, a number of them dealing with the necessity for the destruction of property in order to prevent the spread of conflagration by fire. Reference was next made to some criminal cases in which the rule of necessity has been established by the Courts. First in importance is the case of *The Commonwealth v. Blodgett,* 12 Metcalf (53 Mass.) 56. This case is of controlling importance because it is strikingly analogous in facts to the case at bar, being a prosecution for kidnapping, in which the defense relied upon by those charged with the crime, was that they acted under necessity. It is furthermore entitled to highest consideration because it is a decision of the Supreme Judicial Court of Massachusetts, a court whose opinions, in the language of a great chief justice of another state, have been distinguished for their profound ability and wisdom (Chief Justice Hemphill, 10 Tex. 211), and it is the opinion of that court, as expressed by Chief Justice Shaw, and whom no greater has ever occupied the Supreme Bench of any state. The case arose out of the Dorr Rebellion in Rhode Island. Defendants were charged with kidnapping. They acted as members of the military forces of the government of the State of Rhode Island, under command of one of the military officers of the government. Some of the Dorr rebels had escaped into Massachusetts, and were followed there by defendants, who seized them in a tavern and carried them back to Rhode Island for trial. On demand of Massachusetts, those charged with making this unlawful seizure were returned by Rhode Island to Massachusetts for trial. They were tried before Chief Justice Shaw. Among their defenses was the necessity for protecting the safety of the citizens of Rhode Island and their property against these insurrectionists and their threatened activities. Chief Justice Shaw instructed the jury, if there existed a necessity for the defense or protection of the lives and property of the citizens of Rhode Island, or if there was probable cause to suppose at the time the existence of such a necessity, and the defendants did the acts complained of in the indictment for the purpose of such protection, the jury would acquit the defendants. Other legal authorities referred to included, *United States v. Ashton,* 2 Sumner 13, 24 Fed. cases No. 14,470, Opinion by Mr. Justice Storey involving an endeavor to commit a revolt aboard a ship on the high seas, the circumstances relating to action of the crew on finding the ship was unseaworthy. It was found the action of the crew was in line with the necessity of the circumstances, and upon the suggestions of the court, the district attorney, who said his opinions coincided with those of the court, entered a *nolle proseqi*—an Order of Dismissal. Reference was made to *United States v. Vardon,* 1 Sprague, Fed. cases No. 14,625, in which necessity was held to have justified a mutiny at sea. *Republic v. McArty,* 2 Dall. 86 held the compulsory attendance of a man on a treasonable expedition in order to save his own life justified him under the law of necessity. Other cases of similar import were cited.

It was then stated: If on the morning of July 12, 1917, Wootton had reasonable basis to think a large organization had been effected by a group of people whose purpose and intent was to injure or destroy the lives and property of Wootton, his family, friends and associates and his and their properties from such injury or destruction, then he, as the defendant, has the right to show who these people were in said organization, what the organization was, what its purpose and intent was, and what its actions had been in other areas of the country, as stress has not been made in this argument of the fact the United States was then at war and the evidence would also show one of the purposes of the I.W.W. was to embarrass the United States in the prosecution of the war.

A great senator of the United States (Ben Hill of Georgia) once said: "Who saves his country, saves all things, and all things saved will bless him. Who lets his country die, lets all things die and all things dying curse him."

The Supreme Court of California has well said: "Every state and every community, has a right to adopt the means necessary to its own protection, and what those means are, the society must judge. The law of self-protection is as applicable to communities as to individuals. Communities are but corporations, or artificial beings, capable of united action through proper organs. Every member of society forms a part of this artificial being, and the state, therefore, has the greatest interest in preserving the lives of its people. The security, power and greatness of a state, depend upon the number and character of its population. The state, and each member of the body politic, have a reciprocal interest in the welfare of each other, and owe certain mutual duties and obligations to each (*People v. Butler,* 8 Calif. 442)."

The argument continued on Monday, March 15, and through Wednesday the 17th, with lengthy replies by County Attorney French and his assistant, Worsley. Judge Pattee recessed court a part of this time to give him an opportunity to examine the legal authorities cited by counsel on both sides. He also took time to write an opinion on the questions, and on the 22nd he read it in court. In a careful opinion, he upheld Law of Necessity, and in so doing, the right of the defendant to introduce evidence to prove Sheriff Wheeler and those acting under his direction, particularly defendant Wootton, were acting under the Law of Necessity. The legal authorities clearly established this as a correct decision, and, with the court's favorable ruling, Burges scented victory. He knew the facts, and what the testimony would show. And once the testimony was in of the threats of violence and destruction by the I.W.W. against the law abiding citizens of Bisbee, he would have established the basis for putting before the jury the evidence which would unequivocally show the revolutionary character of the I.W.W. and its purpose to overthrow the government and existing order of this country. This would be the clincher.

XXVI

The Scarlet Standard

Then raise the scarlet standard high;
Beneath its fold we'll live and die,
Though cowards flinch and traitors sneer,
We'll keep the red flag flying here.
—I.W.W. Songs To Fan
The Flames of Discontent

THE SCARLET STANDARD would be displayed for the jury, but first it was necessary to put on testimony of witnesses who knew what happened at Bisbee. The lengthy testimony relating the violence and threats of violence by the I.W.W., its members and agents began.

Fred W. Brown was recalled as the first witness. He testified the strike was called by the Metal Mine Worker's Union of the Industrial Workers of the World, commonly known as the I.W.W. He attended their meetings several times, and was in sympathy with the strike, but was never a member of the I.W.W. He belonged to the Retail Clerks Union, affiliated with the American Federation of Labor, which in Bisbee was composed of the barbers, butchers, painters, carpenters, electricians, blacksmiths, stagehands, bootblacks, porters, retail clerks, bakers and printers. The first strike called in Bisbee was on May 24, 1917, called by the painter's union. The next strike was called when the carpenters went out in sympathy with the painters about a week later. And the electricians went out in sympathy with the carpenters shortly after that.

Brown testified he went to the machinists' meeting to see what they were doing. It was his business as organizer for A.F. of L. to keep the A.F. of L. organizations from the I.W.W.'s. The A.F. of L. was not in sympathy with the I.W.W.'s; it was opposed to it.

The next witness was Thomas J. Connor. He was a clerk to Superintendent Ghoring of the C. & A. Mines at Bisbee, and he testified a committee of miners called on him about 1:30 P.M. on June 26 and handed him a paper, which he identified. The committee gave him an ultimatum that they must have an answer by five o'clock that evening.

The paper identified by Connor was placed in evidence. It read:

> Bisbee, Arizona, June 26, 1917. The undersigned committee has been appointed by Metal Mine Workers Industrial Union No. 800 Bisbee Branch to present to the mining companies of the Warren District the following demands:
>
> First, the abolition of the physical examination. Second, two men to work machines. Third, two men to work together in all raises. Fourth, to discontinue all blasting during the shift. Fifth, the abolition of all bonus and contract work. Sixth, to abolish the sliding scale. All men underground a minimum scale of $6.00 per shift. Top men, $5.50. Seventh, no discrimination to be shown against members of any organization. Ben K. Webb, Chairman; M.C. Sullivan; W.H. Davis; J.G. Payne; A.S. Embree; Chas. Tannehill.

Connor said he gave the paper to Ghoring.

Following Connor, the defense read into evidence a number of depositions. They included the depositions of Walter L. Furbershaw, of the Department of Justice, Chicago; Russell H. Lutz, custodian of records, Department of Justice, Chicago; John W. Hughes, deputy clerk, U.S. Court of Appeals, Chicago; Burley H. Wilder, photographer of documents; Thomas J. Sheehan, deputy U.S. marshal, Chicago; Maurice Klein, chief deputy U.S. marshal, Chicago; Philip James Barry, special agent, U.S. Bureau of Investigation; A. Nebaker, U.S. marshal, Salt Lake City; Mrs. Reinhardt, clerk, U.S. Attorney's Office, Salt Lake City. Their testimony was offered for the purpose of identifying and establishing the authenticity of a long list of I.W.W. letters, papers and documents. French objected to nearly every question asked, sometimes at length, so putting the depositions in evidence was a long and tedious task. The depositions went in, but the letters, papers and documents were not offered into evidence until later.

Burges then called Harry C. Wheeler as the next witness. He was the sheriff of Cochise County at the time of the deportation, and was the person who, as the law enforcing officer in charge of keeping the peace of the county, organized and led the posse which rounded up the I.W.W.'s. His testimony, began on March 29, and continued into March 31. He testified:

He was the sheriff of Cochise County for six years from 1912 until 1918, when he entered the Army. The first he knew of trouble in the Warren District was through a telegram from A.S. Embree, secretary of the Metal Workers Union, No. 800, asking him to indicate what stand he would take, as they were about to call a strike in that district. Sheriff Wheeler went at once to Bisbee and mixed among the people to learn just how far that trouble might extend. The first day or two he found a subdued state of excitement, but nothing alarming. After the first couple of days, reports began to come to him of various little disturbances. Men would complain of their lunchboxes being taken away from them and of being harassed while going to work. He began to get telephone messages from women stating they had been visited by people who seemed to be of foreign extraction, threatening them with harm. Many times dynamiting was the threat, in case their husbands didn't cease work. When he reached these places he would ask the men, most of them foreigners, why they were at this time making trouble, why they insisted in attempting to prevent the government from getting a supply of the metal it needed. The invariable reply was that now the government was in trouble, this was the time to raise trouble in order to compel the government to take over these things. They told him that, while they impeded industry in this district, their brethren in the North would do likewise to the lumber and wheat fields, and to the cotton fields in the South.

He attended their meetings and heard their officers state when they got six dollars a day and eight hours they would then demand eight dollars and six hours and after that ten dollars and four hours work and they would never make any agreement. Also that the red button was above the Liberty Bonds; to hell with the draft, and one of the

I.W.W.'s told him if he had a boy old enough to be subject to the draft, he would ship him out of the country. The next thing he noticed was Mexicans daily marching in columns of two to the I.W.W. headquarters for provisions. Most of these people were strangers to him.

Throughout his testimony there were numerous objections. At one point in the testimony, French, being disappointed in an adverse ruling by the court, said to the witness, "Just say anything then. Go ahead and make a speech."

Judge Pattee then said, "No. We might as well understand right here, I am not going to have any remarks from counsel on either side. I am not going to permit any comments. Those can be made on the outside, and the ancient privilege of 'cussing' the court can be indulged in ad infinitum, but not in the courtroom."

A few minutes later, when the witness added to his answer a hearsay statement, Judge Pattee said, "The last will be stricken. I must act as counsel for the state."

Wheeler testified he went to a laundry and was told that Mexican women were greatly frightened through threat of being dynamited if they didn't cease work, as the laundry in Cripple Creek had been previously dynamited. It took most of his time the rest of that day calming the women and designating guards to protect them.

He sent a telegram to the governor and to the president asking for help, stating to them:

> I fear bloodshed and destruction of property; feel unable to cope with situation. Ask federal authorities be placed in charge.

On June 30, 1917, he sent a telegram reading:

> Governor Thomas Campbell
> Phoenix, Arizona
>
> The strike here is most serious and I anticipate great property loss and bloodshed. Majority strikers seem foreign. The whole thing appears pro-German and anti-American. I earnestly request you use your influence to have U.S. troops sent here to take charge of the situation and prevent bloodshed and the closing of the copper industry now so valuable to the United States government.
>
> Wheeler, Sheriff.

Blackie, one of the I.W.W. leaders, told him they had three thousand men in the district, and more were coming. He noticed the men who were at work would band together for protection and pass through the men who were congregated in front of the post office. They came in columns, squads, four abreast. "I afterward learned," said Wheeler, "these men belonged to a Loyalty League which had been formed."

About that time the city marshal invited him to a meeting at the City Hall between the I.W.W. committee, the mayor and himself. The mayor asked the committee to obey the city ordinances and to quit congregating in front of the post office. He stated it was a violation of the city ordinances—and too, in the future, before using the park, a written permit would be needed which he said was a part of the city ordinances. Embree jumped to his feet and told the mayor and the city marshal they would no longer tolerate their rights being trampled upon; they would no longer be responsible for the actions of their men, and he no longer could control them, and said Wheeler, "I replied to them that if he could not control them, I could.

"It was July 11th, the day previous to the deportation. I had heard these men were to go to what was called the 'change rooms' to get their clothing—some of them who had been at work and had ceased; they were to take advantage of that opportunity to close up the tunnels or close the mouths of the men who were working down in the mines. Reports came to me that many of the Mexicans were ex-Villista soldiers who knew of caches of firearms and equipment in the Ajo Mountains; at the proper time they were going to take possession of these weapons and I felt responsible as sheriff for the preservation of life and property. I made up my mind I had to strike first or a large element of that district would be struck. That night I received by telephone from the committee of the I.W.W. the following message: 'If you or any of your deputies come around our headquarters you are going to meet with a hot reception.' I gave the order for a meeting that night of captains of the various companies I had aided to form. And I published in the *Bisbee Review* on the morning of July 12 this proclamation:

Bisbee, Arizona, July 12, 1917. All women and children keep off the streets today. I have formed a sheriff's posse of 1,200 men in Bisbee and 1,000 in Douglas, all loyal Americans, for the purpose of arresting on charges of vagrancy, treason and of being disturbers of the peace of Cochise County, all those strange men who have congregated here from other parts and sections for the purpose of harassing and intimidating all men who desire to pursue their daily toil. I am continually told of threats and insults heaped upon the working men of this District by so-called strikers who are strange to these parts, yet who presume to dictate the manner of life of the people of this District. Appeals to patriotism do not move them, nor do appeals to reason. At a time when our country needs her every resource, these strangers persist in keeping from her the precious metal production of this entire District. Today I have heard threats to the effect that homes would be destroyed because the heads of families insisted upon their rights as Americans to work for themselves, their families and their country. Other threats have, and are being daily made. Men have been assaulted and brutally beaten, and only today I heard the Mayor of Bisbee threatened and his requests ignored. We can no longer stand or tolerate such conditions. This is no labor trouble, we are sure of that, but a direct attempt to embarrass and injure the government of the United States. I therefore call upon all loyal Americans to aid me in peacefully arresting these disturbers of our national and local peace. Let no shot be fired throughout this day unless in necessary self-defense, and I hereby give warning that each and every leader of the so-called strike will be held personally responsible for any injury inflicted upon any of my deputies while in the performance of their duty as deputies of my posse for whose acts I in turn assume full responsibility as sheriff of this county. All arrested persons will be treated humanely, and their cases examined with justice and care. I hope no resistance will be made for I desire no bloodshed. However, I am determined that if resistance is made it shall be quickly and effectively overcome. Harry C. Wheeler, Sheriff of Cochise County, Arizona.

On cross-examination he testified it would have been impossible for him to have jailed all of these disturbers; one hundred and fifty was all his jail would hold. "Other men would have come in from all portions of the country until we had thousands of them here; they told me they were coming in all the time and I knew the loyal men in Bisbee were departing on every train; we were growing weaker and they were growing stronger. Why did I send the men who were deported to Columbus, New Mexico? I wanted the troops to have them. I received no aid from the president or the governor. The ball park was the only place in which I could put them for a time, but it was necessary in my honest opinion to get these men out of there within a short time or see many people on both sides killed or wounded. I was thinking of my country too, as well as of our district. Invariably I asked them why they brought about this trouble in wartime when each man should sacrifice his interest to the interest of his country. I called to their mind the fact that these troubles were going on simultaneously in the mining camps all over the state, and the attempt was undoubtedly pro-German, in view of the effect it would have upon the necessities needed by this government in time of war. Invariably the answer was, now is the time to raise trouble. Now is the time for us to get the things we wish. What does the government care for us? That answer was almost invariably from someone of foreign extraction."

French asked, "When did you learn of the Law of Necessity?"

He answered he had read of buildings being dynamited to save other buildings, prairie fires and forest fires being set in order to save lives and these were Laws of Necessity.

It is the Law of Necessity that permits you to take the life of another man in self-defense. He was asked why he was apprehensive of great crimes being committed? He answered that there were many times the number of men congregated there and the I.W.W. was constantly augmented and was threatening to bring in men from other parts of the country.

In response to other questions propounded in an exhaustive cross-examination, he testified to numerous threats of dynamiting, and other threats of violence to the law-abiding portion of the community, and, when asked, related again,

"I heard that speech that I told you of, where one of them said, 'We demand six dollars and eight hours, and when we get that, we will demand eight dollars and six hours, and when we get that we will demand ten dollars and four hours, and when we get that, we will never make any agreement.' "

E.P. White was the next witness. On direct examination by Curley, he testified he was a foreman in the Cooper mine in 1917 and was well acquainted with the miners in Bisbee. He testified that "eighty percent of the men he saw on the streets about the time the strike was called were strangers to him. In modern slang you would call them hard-boiled guys or roughnecks.

"There was a picket line of 250 to 300 men in front of the Copper Queen Store, and sometimes more would line up and the working men would have to go between them, that is, run the gauntlet. Each one of them would have some slur as he passed along. They were all acting as pickets and trying to hinder other men from going to work. I heard a picket approach a man and say, 'Say, fella, ain't you comin' out with us?'

"The fella replied, 'I have got a wife and two kids to take care of.'

"The picket said, 'We will take care of your kids, and let the old woman get out among the boys and rustle.'

"And this fella got a little hot and it looked as though he was going to take it up and another fella says, 'Oh, let the goddamned scab go. Some of us fellows will be bellying up to his woman in a day or two, anyhow.'

"I asked a man why they were going to strike. He said the I.W.W.'s were going to get $5.50 a day for them. If this government wouldn't make them do it, the German government would."

He further testified, as he came through the picket line coming off work, a picket walked up to him and said, "Say, fella you've only got a day or two more. As an old friend of yours I advise you to stay home on the 13th because there is going to be hell popping in Bisbee. You are married and got a family. Look out for them."

After that, he testified, he didn't stop going to work but he started carrying a lunch bucket.

"What did you carry in your lunch bucket?"

"I carried a forty-five six-shooter."

"With reference to your wife's safety, what did you do?"

"I left a shotgun with her at home, and told her if any strange men came up to the door that she didn't know, to have the shotgun sticking out the door first."

"You believed she was in danger, did you, Mr. White?"

"I did."

On cross-examination, he identified the trouble makers as "Wobblies," a popular name for the I.W.W.

On re-direct examination, he stated:

"Mr. Bendickson and I was going to work together and we got to the corner of the post office and as we passed through the pickets, they were all gathered there and as we went to go through, I had to drop behind Bendickson, and he had a little flag in the lapel of his coat. Somebody said something about coming out with them, and just then another fellow, a picket, came up, a young fellow, he had a big stick or club in his hand, he was a cripple, and he said, 'That is right, you goddamn scab, hide behind Old Glory if you think that will do you any good, but we will damn soon show you how much that damn rag amounts to.' I got mad and started to tie into him, but Bendickson pulled me away."

And so through Wednesday, March 31, and successive days thereafter, except for weekends, the testimony continued.

Burges had rented Mrs. Lowry's home in Tombstone, which was used as his office, and as headquarters of the defense group. He had guards stationed there, among whom were "Shotgun Charlie," remembered for eating his peas with his knife, and "Bulldog Drummond." Their meals were prepared and furnished pursuant to a contract with the El Paso and Southwestern Railroad's dining car service. The cook was Augustus Moody, a Negro who weighed about two hundred and fifty pounds. There were two waiters, both Negroes, "Young Gus," who was a graduate of Tuskegee Institute, and Clarence, a mulatto.

Burges also employed a Pinkerton man from back East, who came into town and voiced his sympathies for the I.W.W., and hung around the places where they congregated. He told them he had promised to write his dear old mother every night, and he sat at a table, in an I.W.W. hangout, and wrote his nightly letter. He then went to the postoffice to mail it, but enroute he passed the Lowry house, and flipped his "letter" over the fence, it being a report to Burges on his observations, information and gossip gathered during the day. One night, shortly after dark, he broke into the house like the dogs were after him, and said, "Get me out of here. They're on to me." So Burges sent him in a car, with guards, down to Bisbee Junction to catch the next train.

The town was divided into two factions, one pro-I.W.W., and one pro-defense, and tension was high. One morning, as the defense group marched down the middle of the street from the Lowry house to the courthouse, Burges saw one of the I.W.W. crowd leaning against a support for a porch, with a leer on his face that was quite provocative. He did not want to see what he anticipated would happen, so he looked the opposite way. In a few moments he heard the sound of blows, and shortly after the group reached the Courthouse, French complained to the court that one of his crowd had been assaulted. Judge Pattee asked Burges if he saw it, but he truthfully answered he didn't see it. Nor did anyone else admit seeing it.

Burges regularly gathered the defense crowd together on a hillside in the afternoon after court adjourned, and talked to them. His constant admonition was, "Don't start any trouble—don't get into any trouble—we are winning, but I have all burdens I can bear, and I don't want any more as a result of your starting any trouble." The crowd would always assure him, "We won't do anything."

J.E. Bendickson, a mine worker in Bisbee in 1917 during the strike, testified he walked through the picket line one morning, with a man on both sides of him, and one fellow came up and said to him, "I see you're hiding under Old Glory, you damn scab. That don't do you any good."

He kept going and never said a word back. Oscar Wynn, a miner in Bisbee, remembered talking to a fellow workman named Lutz, who said he was an I.W.W., that unions were no good, and the Germans would whip us all after the strike began. The number of strangers in the city increased greatly. William J. Jeffries, a miner, worked the night shift; the graveyard shift starting at 11:00 P.M. There were from 300 to 600 pickets present. One of them called him off to one side on the morning of July 10 and advised him to leave, go to the coast or to the mountains,' but get away quick. The pickets looked particularly threatening, and were casting slurs. On July 11 some pickets stopped Charley Blair and asked if he wouldn't come out with them, and when he refused, the picket said, "Go on then, it's the last shift you will make."

Antonio Peralta testified he was a miner who, while going to work, was asked by a crowd of unionists, if he was going to work. "I told them yes," he said, "and that I needed to work because I had a large family. They told me the union had sufficient money and food; that the men would not have to work and the Copper Queen had a large warehouse of provisions and other places there in Bisbee and from there they would have to take either for good or bad at the hour that it was necessary.

"When I came out from my work they commenced hollering at me that I was an instrument of capital, that I was bought by the company. They all wanted to beat me, and then the police came and placed me in jail, and they at the same time wanting to take me from the police. The following day I went to work, and about seven of them caught me, struck a blow to my head and I fell. If I hadn't died in Bisbee it was because of the vigilance of the police. The strikers said I should not go on working; the government was in war and was needing the copper and the company had no one to extract it for them, that the government has to insist on the company that they should pay five and a half on the outside and six on the inside, and if not, the company would not have the workmen, and it would be the triumph of the Germans and the Workers of the World."

Joe Mata, a miner, said, "The strikers would molest us every day with insults and holler at us to tell us we should quit work or they would kill us. While we were helping unload timers from the railroad car, 100 to 150 came towards us, and threw stones at us. Some had pistols, and they called us nicknames on the streets."

William Holmes, a miner, heard the strikers say they were going to win, that it was a government of the rich and they thought it ought to be put on the bum and, by God, they were going to put it on the bum. He heard people say it was a sure thing in their minds the company could not concede to the demands of these people from the fact these men were moving up all the time on their demands and they believed if there was not something done these fellows would destroy the homes and property of the community and walk out and leave them bare. "In restaurants and places around," he said, "I would hear those fellows talking about it, would say the working man hadn't had any say in the matter and the working people were going to show them where to head in; they would show them where to butt in before the thing was through. My recollection from both sides was that something was liable to happen."

Phillip A. Davis, a plumber, saw, after the strike began, several bunches of strikers with pistols and guns stopping men from going to work and he was mobbed by the group of them.

William J. White, a mine foreman, stated that a group of twenty-four or more Mexicans—many of them, including the leader, were strangers—were trying to make some men on a car stop work. He told them to leave. One came up behind him with a rock in his hand, and he knocked the man down. The next day he asked this man why he tried to hit him with a rock, that he had never done anything to him but a favor, and they were friendly. The reply was, "It was orders from the chief, to win the strike, if they had to kill someone."

Charles A. Hines, a miner, saw a Mexican try to hit Mr. White with a rock.

Charles Blair said that as he was going to work, one of the pickets said, "Old-timer, you'd better come with us." When he did not do so, the picket said, "Your time is short, you old son-of-a-bitch." Mark Kentro stated that a striker, Gene Crawford, asked him to quit work. He replied that he couldn't, as he had a family to support. Crawford said, "You better come with us. If you don't, some day you're liable to be blowed up; you and your family."

The defense resumed its testimony on Monday, April 5, 1920. Arthur Notman, who was Assistant Superintendent of the Copper Queen Mine in 1917 prior to calling of the strike said, "We put all the men to work that we possibly could to get as much copper as we could. At the opening of the war in 1914, we had gone on a sliding scale of wages based on the selling price of copper. In May, 1917, we were paying miners $5.50 based on the selling price. In June we were paying $5.60. On the calling of the strike forty percent went to work the day the strike was called, and it fell off for the next two or three days. I was constantly approached by the men, saying they would not be able to work unless they were afforded protection. We were apprehensive because we all knew the reputation of the I.W.W. and their methods of conducting strikes. I did what I could to relieve the apprehension of the men's minds, but there wasn't anything I could really sincerely promise them in the way of protection. All I could urge them to do was to keep a stiff upper lip and stay with it just as we were all doing. There were numbers of men I had never seen before in the district who were stationed on these picket lines and they were rough looking characters. Prior to the presentation of the demands of the strikers, none of the old employees, sixty-five percent men who had worked for us two years or more had even spoken to me or anybody else in regard to conditions or entered any suggestion or complaint that conditions were not good. I had no part in arranging the deportation. I suffered from the same apprehensions everybody else did at that time over the possibility of some serious catastrophe brought about by the actions of these foreigners, not being foreigners in the sense of race necessarily, but men who were not employed in the district, who had come in there to cause trouble and who were members of the I.W.W. organization."

Mr. Burges: "State whether or not you knew of any way or believe there was any way to avert that danger except by what was done?"

Answer: "I knew of no way."

Jack McRea, a watchman, heard men in the picket line say, "Let's beat them up as we did at Globe. You've only got a couple of more days to work, we will take charge of it after that." Frank Barnes, a miner, testified to the same effect. Pedro Garcia, a miner, stated strikers said they were going to tear their houses down. P.L. Walton was in the Copper Queen hospital in April, 1917. A man in the next bunk said he was an I.W.W., and, said Walton, "told me I had better join as there was going to be trouble. They were going to blow up the hospital and blow up the town if they didn't gain their point. They would burn everything in Bisbee. There would be nothing left."

Stiles P. Jones, a miner, employed during the strike to watch the strikers and the Loyalty League, saw numbers of strangers that looked like miners come in to town on every train, some wore I.W.W. buttons. He said he saw them afterwards in the picket line. Charles

Merrill said a lot of rough-looking men came in by train, later saw them on the picket line, wearing I.W.W. buttons and carrying red cards in the coats or vests or shirt pockets. He mentioned that on July 12 one of the deportees said, "You only beat us to it by one day."

George Scott, deputy sheriff, saw rough-looking men come in by train, and later saw them wearing I.W.W. buttons and red cards. James E. Brophy, a merchant, attended a striker's meeting on a lot next to the St. Regis Hotel at which J. Stanley Clark spoke. He said they wanted six dollars and eight hours of work, and that was not what they wanted; they wanted eight dollars and six hours; and that was not what they wanted—they wanted the mines—they are ours—we made them. He advised them to get their red cards, as they were better than Liberty Bonds.

The pickets were mostly strangers and foreigners. When the miners would go on and off shift they (the I.W.W.'s) would grab hold of the men and take their lunch buckets away from them and kick their lunch buckets down the street. At a big parade in Bisbee, one of them said, "It's nothing to the parade you will see here in a few more days."

Robert M. Thursby, a miner who did some work during the strike had a wife and child. "The crowd seemed pretty hostile," he said, "and when I went to work they called me a stiff-legged son of a ______ and we will get you yet!"

W.C. Pope, a miner, was stopped a number of times going to work. "One morning they got me by the coat," he said, "and told me I was not going to work. I pulled away and went to work. They said, 'I hope the dirty son-of-a-bitch gets buried up in the mine.' Not only me but a great many others. A friend of mine said he would advise me not to be a damn fool any longer, to come out with the bunch, that in a few days there would be hell-a-poppin and they were going to start something. Samuel Ryle, a miner, who, two mornings after the strike was called, was going to work. "There were about forty of these men," he said, "who stopped me and asked me to come out with them. "I told them I couldn't see my way to come out, as I felt it my patriotic duty at such a time to work, even if I was called to work for a dollar a day, it was no more of a sacrifice to me than it would be to the boys at the front. The morning following, they stopped me again. I says, 'Now I must be honest with you, I can't afford to come out with you fellas,' I says, 'I have got a wife and a little boy and a crippled brother and a widowed mother to look after and I have to work.' And they told me, they says, 'Well, if you don't come out with us, we will cripple you, too.'

"I told them I would look after that part of it all right. The third morning when they seen me coming, they shouted to each other, 'Well here comes the cripple.' I just gave them a smile and passed on, and I heard one of them in passing call me a scab. That kind of aroused my temper and I says, 'I am no scab and I'm just doing my duty. I feel the flag of this country, and I've got to work if I am the only man traveling this road I must work.' So it went on until the following week. We were ordered out on the night shift, a bunch of us, to keep the thing running. I come down to the post office, and a bunch of them walked up to me and asked would I like to have my wife and child to be a widow and orphan. I told them, 'No, sir, I wouldn't like to see them treated that way.' They says 'They will be if you don't quit working.' I didn't say any more to them but just went on to work. I afterwards took part in the deporting drive, because I thought it necessary for the safety of my wife and child."

W.C. Pope recalled that he knew Fred W. Brown and saw him several times on the picket line taking notes of the men that were going to work.

The same line of testimony continued Tuesday, April 6, through Friday, April 9. It was replete with statements of threats of violence by the strikers, with references of derision to Liberty Bonds for the war effort, and with praise for the red card of the I.W.W. The strikers referred to the flag as "that damned thing," and as "that rag," and they threatened to burn boarding houses run by people unsympathetic to the strike, and to blow up or burn the town of Bisbee. Their threat, about June 11, made it clear the townspeople had only two days left before the I.W.W. crowd would take over Bisbee. Some of the witnesses were examined by Burges, some by Curley and some by

Gilmore, while the State cross-examined them at great length.

The *Bisbee Daily Review* reported with respect to Burges:

> There was never any question during the Wootton trial as to who was chief counsel. Mr. Burges was a barometer for the spectators. If he arose from his chair and walked around the courtroom this action indicated that he considered the point at issue won; if he slid back in his chair and appeared slightly nervous and restless, the spectators knew that some new angle of a point at issue had come to him and he was wondering if his colleagues would catch it without him having to enter the argument; when he looked serious it behooved the defendants to look serious and watch developments carefully and when he smiled or chuckled softly, the spectators knew that 'all's well on the Potomac' as far as the defense was concerned.
>
> But Mr. Burges' inability to put on what is slangily termed a 'poker face' did not hamper him any during the trial for, at every critical moment, his thinking machinery appeared to be just a little better oiled than that of the opposition; if a strong illustration was needed to support some point of law under discussion, Mr. Burges usually had a word picture to hang in the argumentative art gallery that was just a little bit more forceful and clear than any of the other verbal paintings submitted.

Upon conclusion of the testimony as to the action and threats of the I.W.W. in Bisbee the proof of violence and threats of violence by the I.W.W. and its adherents was overwhelming, and the question before the court then was whether to admit in evidence the papers, pamphlets and books published by the I.W.W. stating its position on strikes, agitation, sabotage, violence and revolution.

On April 20, Judge Pattee ruled the testimony concerning the violence and terrorism in Bisbee just prior to July 12, 1917, was sufficient to make admissible evidence concerning a general conspiracy by the I.W.W. and the character of the men charged with doing it. He said that when a condition of terror and violence is charged to exist, the character of those charged with causing that situation is a legitimate and proper thing to be shown in determining whether or not that situation actually existed. That when men are asserted to have been violent, to have caused a situation of violence, you may properly inquire what manner of men it was who were charged with so doing; that the character of the organization may be shown, not as warranting the extreme and summary remedy adopted, but as a circumstance on the same plane, so far as the legal effect is concerned. It is simply the question, what kind of people were there, and it is governed by the same rule that would permit a showing that they were strangers, or that they were short men or tall men, or had this or that appearance. The same principle warrants the introduction of evidence concerning the organization of which they were apprehensive. He therefore ruled the defense could show by oral or documentary evidence the character of the I.W.W.

This was a signal victory for the defense. The testimony of the violence and threats of the I.W.W. in Bisbee was in evidence. Now the defense could put in its written evidence of the conspiratorial and revolutionary character of the I.W.W. Burges first called a number of witnesses, printers and others—most of them by deposition—to show the writings had been printed and published by the I.W.W., or at its order, and then read to the jury many of their pamphlets, circulars, books and other literature. This included the *Preamble to the Constitution of the I.W.W.,* Vincent St. John's booklet, *The I.W.W., Its History, Structure and Methods,* an article by William D. Haywood, the *I.W.W. Little Red Song Book,* several articles on sabotage, a paper entitled "I.W.W. Publishing Bureau of Chicago," and a paper entitled "The Solidarity" issued by the I.W.W.

The defense also read to the jury a book by Gustave Herve, published by the I.W.W. Publishing Bureau of Chicago, entitled *Patriotism and the Worker.* Its tenor is shown by the following quotation from the introduction of this book:

> In issuing this well-known speech of Gustave Herve's as one of the publications of our Bureau we are contributing to an agitation that is now universal in the Capitalist's world, and is of prime importance as well in the United States as in France. Here, as in France, the child's brain is stuffed with stories of alleged 'heroes' of American History from George Washington to Theodore Roosevelt as a preparatory schooling for the future slave to acquire the necessary respect for and obedience to his master—whose mastership, in America as in Europe has resulted from fraud, cunning, financial manipulation, land steals, and by fishing in troubled waters during and after waters of conquest or of expansion, as well as

through the merciless exploitation of the working class in industry.

The Industrial Workers of the World aims to unite all wage workers, without distinction of race, nationality, sex or any other consideration except that they are exploited by a master, into One Big Union of the Working Class, 'To take possession of the earth and the machinery of production and abolish the wage system,' thus putting an end forever to the rule of the robber class.

They then offered in evidence and read to the jury from a book by William D. "Big Bill" Haywood, President of the I.W.W., entitled *The General Strike.* The nature of it is shown by the following quotation from it:

> The working class can't lose anything. While the capitalist class have got all the money and all the credit, still if the working class laid off the capitalists couldn't get food at any price. All the workers have to do is to organize so that they can put their hands in their pockets; when they have got their hands there, the capitalists can't get their hands in. If the workers can organize so that they can stand idle they will then be strong enough so that they can take the factories. I hope to see the day when the man who goes out of the factory will be the one who will be called a scab; when the good union men will stay in the factory, whether the capitalists like it or not; when we lock the bosses out and run the factories to suit ourselves. That is our program. We will do it.
>
> It is war we proclaim, the last war, the international war in which the workers of all lands shall be united against the invaders — the rich who have seized the land and lived on the labor of the poor. This is the war that remains yet to be fought, it is inevitable. It may be delayed but it cannot be prevented.

Reading of exhibits continued on April 15, 1920. There were numerous objections to different exhibits, and Judge Pattee excluded a number of the exhibits which had been offered, on the grounds that they were dated subsequent to the date of the deportation. After lengthy argument over numerous exhibits which the defense offered in evidence, with a substantial number of them being excluded by the court, Curley continued with reading letters written by Grover H. Perry, secretary-treasurer of Local 800. Additional witnesses were then put on the stand, H.D. Palmer, a stenographic reporter, who took down the testimony in the preliminary hearing in the case of *State v. Harry Walkers,* and in *State v. H.E. Wootton,* and identified his transcript of that testimony. He then read from testimony given on the preliminary hearing by Fred W. Brown, who denied he told Wootton he was going to close him up or run him out of business and asked whether he was going to try to injure him. He said, "We have a right, when a man is unfair to organized labor, we can tell people they're not to patronize that man. We intended to do this and would have run him out of business if we could." Whether he told Wootton that or not, that was his purpose, and was engaged in doing so as well he knew how at the time. They intended to force Wootton to meet their demands or else they would break him up in business. In connection with the deportation on the morning of July 12, someone gave orders to fall in, and they formed in twos, not knowing who gave the order. It wasn't Mr. Wootton. They were marched down to the ball park, and never saw Mr. Wootton again.

Vincent Ogwiek, a miner, stated that Bill Kozo, a member of the I.W.W., asked him if he was working. He answered yes. Kozo said, "Well, ain't nobody killed you yet? You kind of lucky still, but I am going to get you now."

"Another one named Mike called me all kind of bad names," said Ogweik. "He called me a __________. He said, 'Are you working?'

"I said, 'I am.' He said 'Well it is just about time to get rid of you. You ain't should live in this world no more, a man like you are.' "

Fred Williams, a miner, stated a mob stopped him while he was going to work. The crowd was rough, so he didn't go to work, because he did not consider it safe. One of them told him on July 10 that he had two more days to work, after that he was going to walk the ties out of Bisbee. "He was one of the pickets," said Williams, "and left the picket line to tell me I had two more days to work."

Stanley Ruse, a miner, heard one of the deportees say to one of the guards, on July 12, 1917, "They just beat us to it by twenty-four hours." Paul T. Lawrenson heard some of the strikers say they were going to bring in gunmen and take over. Mrs. Matilda Borgess' husband was a miner. Three girls who worked in the laundry came to her house crying, and said a lot of men from the picket line told them they were going to blow up the laundry and for them not to work. The pickets, the I.W.W. or the Wobblies told them they were going to blow up the laundry. One man said they should not talk like that to her because she was the shift boss' wife (the witness), but we can make muck of him. She was nervous after that because of the threat.

In the middle of the day, Curley became very ill and had to leave court. At the conclusion of the last witness above named, Burges stated that was practically all of the witnesses except for the defendant, and asked for a short recess in order to see about Curley.

When court resumed, Judge Pattee stated he and French, in company with Burges, called on Curley and Curley's condition was such that he would have to go back to Bisbee, and Burges would need to accompany him. The court therefore recessed until the next morning. Doctors who examined Curley later, determined he had a serious case of appendicitis, and that it was necessary to operate on him at once. The operation was done, and it was during the course of it found his appendix had burst, and gangrene had set in. The doctor later reported there was a gangrenous spot on his intestine about the size of a fifty-cent piece and when he saw it, he thought to himself, "Well, old man, you are still alive so you've still got a chance." He said that he never did a more careful job in his life than he did in getting rid of all the gangrenous part. Curley recovered from the operation entirely, but it prevented his taking any further part in the trial of the case. He was Burges' number one assistant in the case, and his loss was a blow. But fortunately the case was so far along it could be carried on without him, and the defense was not willing to ask for a postponement on this account, as the case was in the best possible condition, and they were anxious to conclude it and submit it to the jury.

On the next morning (April 16) Burges put the last defense witness on the stand, the defendant, H.E. Wootton. His testimony was lengthy but in substance he testified that he was a merchant in the hardware and plumbing business. He told about the strike beginning, the large number of strangers who came into town about that time, and several of them told him they were going to burn up the whole world, they would beat Bisbee to dust and burn the town and put every merchant out of business that had supported, or who they thought supported the copper companies in the strike. And, even if they didn't suspect them, if they didn't like them, they would put them out of the way. They said they were going to win, and when they did win, the fellows that stayed at work would be cleaned up. Wootton stated he believed they meant to try and carry out those threats.

His store was virtually picketed as there was a committee to promote a boycott against his place, one of whom was Fred W. Brown. He said Brown told him they would run him, Wootton, out of town and put him out of business, and he knew it was not idle talk that they were trying to do this, and they were succeeding to a large degree. He denied putting Brown in the line on the morning of the deportation, but said he saw him standing within ten or twelve feet of him. Somebody had asked if anybody knew Brown, and he said he did. Brown said, "What is the matter with me?" and he then said, "Are you not the man up at my place who was going to run me out of business, a few days ago and put me out on the streets?"

Brown replied, "Yes, but that was ten days ago, that was when I was working, but I am not working now." Wootton further stated he had made arrangments to take his family out of Bisbee on Sunday, July 15, because he wanted to get them where they would be safe. Direct examination of Wootton was relatively short, but the cross-examination was rather lengthy. When it was concluded, Burges offered the deposition of Clarence Ingram, who testified that while Brown was in the line on the morning of July 12, he told Brown he could take him out of the line, but Brown replied these were his people and he was going with them, and he did not get out of the line. Burges then stated, except for a Mr. Pennock, who was not present, these were all of the defense witnesses. And subject to getting Pennock later, the defense rested.

Mr. Roark, for the prosecution, then made lengthy motions to strike out various parts of the testimony that had been offered, and the rest of the day was consumed with arguments over these motions, which the court denied.

April 17 through April 26 were taken up with rebuttal witnesses offered by the prosecution, but this testimony was in no way significant. There was already an overwhelming weight of testimony with respect to the strike which had been called on June 26, to the fact that, at the time of and during the strike, a large number of strangers had come in town who were rough looking people; meetings had been held in the city park, at which there were speakers who had made incendiary talks as referred to above. The leaders of the strike were members of the I.W.W., whose actions here and elsewhere in the United States, together with their official statements and documents had said they were against a capitalistic system, were in favor of a dictatorship of the proletariat and the United States' entry into the war with Germany afforded them a great opportunity to overturn the government of this country. They were threatening to take over by force of arms the town of Bisbee and to run out of it those people who had continued to work, and all the merchants and other citizens who had not complied with the demands of the strikers. No amount of rebuttal testimony which, in a way, consisted of picking at little points here, there and yonder, sometimes called nit-picking, was going to upset the overwhelming preponderance of the testimony in favor of the defense, including the numerous letters, books and documents put out by the I.W.W. and which had been read to the jury. The State rested on April 26, which was followed that day and the next with surrebuttal testimony on the part of the defense. After both parties had rested, the court took some time to prepare his charge to the jury, which he read to the jury on the 28th. In his charge to the jury, the court covered the defense based upon the Law of Necessity, carefully guarded any undue extension of such a defense, and strictly limited it to the right of a community to protect itself where there were numerous threats against its safety, and the lives of its citizens, by people who by reputation and appearance were in a position to carry out these threats and who appeared to be both willing and able to do so. Judge Pattee finished reading the charge to the jury at 5:00 P.M. and adjourned to 7:30 P.M. at which time the arguments began. The arguments continued through April 29 and into April 30, until late that afternoon. Gilmore, for the defendant, discussed the evidence in detail. Burges closed for the defendant with a more general type of argument which was not too long, considering the length of the trial. The jury returned its verdict after supper on the evening of April 30.

The crowded court room waited with bated breath while the foreman of the jury handed the verdict to the clerk of the court, who unfolded it and read aloud "Not Guilty."

The *Bisbee Daily Review* reported "District Jubilant.", and in another article headlined, "BISBEE REJOICES AT VINDICATION OF HER CITIZENS," stated: "A pandemonium of joy reigned on the streets last night as the news of the acquittal spread like wildfire throughout the entire district."

XXVII

The Ku Klux Klan and the School Board Election of 1922

I wish to be as free from mobs as kings,
from you, as me.

—Byron

THE *EL PASO HERALD* of January 28 and 29, 1922, carried the announcement that Charles S. Ward and Dr. J.H. Gambrell would run for re-election to the Board of Trustees of the El Paso Independent School District, and Judge S.J. Isaacks would be a candidate for the place then held by Walter S. Clayton.

Burges did not then know he would soon offer himself as a candidate for the school board — his one and only venture into politics as a candidate for public office. But there was talk about the school board approving the use of a questionnaire to teachers and applicants for teacher's positions, inquiring into their religion and church affiliation and rumor had it this was a part of a sinister plot by the Ku Klux Klan to control and shape the El Paso Public Schools to its liking. Against this background, there came to see Burges, late in February or early March, a small group of men who were earnestly opposed to any such influence or control, and they asked Burges to head a ticket, as some dubbed it. Who it was that composed the group that called on Burges can be inferred from those who took part in the campaign: Harris Walthall, U.S. Goen, Richard F. Burges, J.H. McBroom and Judge L.A. Dale—all lawyers.

Thus it was that *The El Paso Times,* on March 10, 1922, announced W.H. Burges, attorney; U.S. Stewart, president of the City National Bank; and Dr. J.B. Brady, dentist, had announced for the school board. The *El Paso Herald,* same date, also carried the announcement, with the added question, whether they were backed by Kelly and the city administration, Charles Davis being mayor at the time. The *Herald,* with H.D. Slater as editor, was for the W-I-G ticket, while *The Times,* James S. Black editor, staunchly supported the Burges ticket. The tide of the Klan was at its height in Texas in 1922. It was commonly understood Earle B. Mayfield won his election that year to the United States Senate with the support of the Klan. It held parades in many Texas cities, and seemed to be riding a tide of public support. The El Paso School Board election that year had a religious angle, which centered around Rev. Van Valkenburg of the First Methodist Church, who supported from his pulpit the opposition ticket, and in which he was aided by several other preachers.

The Burges ticket, which ran on a "non-sectarian and non-partisan" platform, had no intent originally to make a campaign, but expected to rely upon its reputation and standing in the community. But soon ugly rumors were going around – planted and cultivated by the opposition – that Stewart had engaged in shady maneuvering concerning the interest rate and sale of school bonds the previous year, and the City National Bank was trying to get control of the schools; and the ticket, because of Burges' position as defense counsel in the I.W.W. Deportation case, was antilabor. They decided to fight back, and so *The Times,* on March 28, carried the announcement, "Burges, Brady and Stewart will address a gathering at Liberty Hall Tuesday night."

The following day the same paper reported, "2000 citizens cheer when Burges, Brady and Stewart plead for school children." W.W. Turney was chairman, and he spoke for the public schools, eulogized Stewart and Brady, and said of Burges: "For more than twenty-five years William H. Burges has been my law partner, with the exception of a few months he spent in Chicago. I will not enter into that because it is too good and too sacred. But I want to say in passing that in the twenty-five years I sat by him and worked with him I have never known him to do a dishonorable or a questionable act."

Harris Walthall, a lawyer, Presbyterian and a Democrat, was chairman of the campaign committee. U.S. Goen and J.H. McBroom, both lawyers, and men of ability spoke at the rally, as did Stewart and Brady. It came out, of course, that Burges and Stewart were Democrats, while Goen, McBroom and Brady were Republicans; and that Stewart was active in the Episcopal Church, Brady in Trinity Methodist Church, McBroom in the First Presbyterian Church, while Goen's and Burges' lack of church connection was passed over. But this did make it a "non-sectarian and non-partisan" group.

The speakers referred to Rev. Van Valkenburg, and among other things, J.H. McBroom said, "You know, I just missed being a preacher. The more I have observed preachers in recent years, the more I am glad I stayed with the law."

Burges was the main speaker. He straightened out the record about the school bonds sold the year before, and also briefly covered the I.W.W. case. Then, with respect to Rev. Van Valkenburg, he said, "Thirty years before he showed his countenance over the community, this section was struggling against lawlessness, trying to right itself and trying to get itself into a community in which a man wanted to live and rest. There were men, at least two of us, that were in the very midst of that fight, and if he wants to know the truth about what was gone through with, let him look to such men as Mr. (E.A.) Shelton and J.A. Smith, who were here at that time also. And fellows of his kind were hiding out in Kansas. I know what those times were. I lived here, and some hours seemed to me like days, and I lived days in some of those hours. Mr. Stewart did the same thing. Our families are here; all that we have on earth is here, and as far as I am concerned, I expect to close my life in this community, and I want nothing in the way of reward for public service except your approval, and thus leave my own mind clear that the judgment that what we have done has helped make a better El Paso."

Nor did he overlook paying his respects to the Ku Klux Klan. The greatest applause occurred when Burges declared it was true he did not want to belong to the Ku Klux Klan. He continued: "I have nothing but an underlying enmity for an organization that undertakes to set up its methods and its will in place of the constituted process of law. I haven't anything but contempt for an organization that parades in a night shirt and wears a mask. And if there is one in here tonight, I want him to take the news to his kind that I will cordially invite them to vote against me. We do not want them, because we do not stand for the same things. Good men got in to that organization, but got out when they found what they had joined."

He concluded, "With your help next Saturday, we will take the schools of El Paso out of the hands of sectarianism and politics for at least two years."

There were rallies the next few nights at Alta Vista School, at Highland Park, Grandview and at the Stevens Building in Five Points, with a final rally at Cleveland Square, the great place for political rallies in the pre-TV days.

The rally at Alta Vista School was presided over by Mrs. John Wright, formerly Miss Allie Fitzpatrick, for many years principal of Lamar School which stood in the 1600 block of Montana Street. Judge L.A. Dale and Maury Kemp spoke at the Grandview School rally, but Burges was the principal speaker at each of the rallies. Judge Dale lashed out at the Ku Klux Klan, Maury Kemp praised Burges, Brady and Stewart, and Burges, because of an attack on Stewart as president of the City National Bank, said that in 1898, when through some error it was discovered the school taxes could not be collected, and the schools were about to close, Stewart – then cashier of the First National Bank – was one of the signers of an agreement enabling the schools to get the money on which to operate. The newspaper report added, "Burges also signed this agreement." He further said, "What we want is a school system so efficient that every child in this city of scholastic age will have a seat in a comfortable school room during every school day of the year and for a full day; that the schools be kept in good repair and clean; that schools be placed throughout the city where they will serve the needs of the population . . .There should be ample playgrounds, but above all the spirit of the teaching force ought to be kept to the highest level. We will not require them to give an assurance of what church they belong to as a condition precedent to their employment." At the Five Points rally Burges said, "Rev. Henry Van Valkenburg and several other ministers have made a lot of reckless charges against my friend, Mr. Stewart, which I consider in poor taste. This ticket was not cooked up in a Knights of Columbus Hall, or a Masonic Hall or in the Ku Klux Klan camp."

The night before the election, a rally was held in Cleveland Square, with from 1,800 to 2,000 persons present. Judge L.A. Dale presided, and again Burges was the principal speaker. He said he and his two fellow candidates were running on a non-sectarian and non-partisan platform, and they would forever rid the public schools of any taint of religious domination.

"I would rather see this earth melt with fervent heat than turn the public school system over to the Roman Catholic Church (applause), and I would see the same thing occur before I would turn the public schools over to the Baptist Church (applause), or to the Methodist Church (applause), or to the Presbyterian Church or any church or all churches in Christendom combined (applause) . . . It is charged in a scurrilous pamphlet that we were nominated in the Hall of the Knights of Columbus . . .but we were not nominated in that hall, and we were not nominated in the camp of the Ku Klux Klan." And about his personal religious beliefs, "On three occasions I have taken the oath of public office — as city attorney, as a member of the Board of Regents of the University of Texas, and as special judge. The Constitution provides no man can hold public office who does not believe in a Supreme Being. I took that oath of office everytime truthfully . . .I am not going into office the tool of any church or clan. Get that! The state is taking a stand. It has two Ku Kluxers where they belong (jail) . . . I always bet that Texas in the long run does the right thing and it has done it this time."

Both tickets had strong support among the populace. *The Times* supported the Burges ticket vigorously; while the *Herald* plumped for the opposition. *The Times* predicted victory for the Burges ticket, but it was not to be. Burges later said he did not think he could win, but entered the race to expose and combat the Klan. The opposition won by a majority of over a thousand. But although the battle was lost, the war was won. In March of 1923 R.M. Dudley defeated P.E. Gardner, who was supported by the Klan, for mayor; and on April 8, 1923. *The Times* reported "Klan Loses Election" and that Mrs. M.A. Warner, Mrs. John A. Wright, J.H. McBroom and Wyeth Doak were elected to the school board in an election held the previous day. And in 1924 it was anti-Klan votes that elected "Ma" Ferguson governor, and in 1928 elected Tom Connally senator. The Klan was dead.

XXVIII

A Reasonable Fee: $300,000

The fee's the thing.
—Anonymous

ON APRIL 21, 1925, Burges received a telegram, addressed to Turney & Burges, reading:

In suit against the Texon Oil and Land Company we have papers sent you for service and can we use your office address for receipt of proxies? Please wire at our expense. Batts and Brooks.

It was from Judge R. L. Batts of Austin, Texas, a one time judge on the U.S. Court of Appeals, Fifth Circuit, one time general counsel of Gulf Oil Corporation, Pittsburg, Pennsylvania, and one of the great lawyers of Texas. The reply by telegram read:

Yes, our office Eleven Eleven First National Bank Bldg., El Paso, Texas, W.H. Burges.

On April 23, he received a night letter reading:

Judge Batts has given us your name and we wish to employ you in connection with our other counsel in protecting stockholders interests in Texon Oil and Land Company which company has called stockholders meeting to be held at its office at Overland and Santa Fe streets, your city May 5th *STOP* Delaware law requires company have complete list of stockholders entitled to vote at coming election arranged alphabetically and same open to examination of any stockholder *STOP* Wish you in behalf of W.H. Schenck stockholders would ascertain if such list now there and if open to inspection and if so ask you to obtain very speedily complete copy thereof going to such expenses as may be necessary and mail same here *STOP* Please answer by straight message at 120 Broadway this city *STOP* If such list is not there tomorrow please inquire daily and wire me when it is there. Pettigrew & Meyer.

With these two telegrams began an unusual and interesting lawsuit.

The case had an interesting background. In October 1924 Holland S. Reavis, of New York, who had known Judge Batts for twenty-five years, went to his office in Austin, Texas. Reavis, together with friends, including Hugh Lamar Stone, then general counsel of the Gulf Oil Corporation, owned stock in the Texon Oil and Land Company, a Delaware Corporation, which had its head office in El Paso, Texas. Reavis and his friends, in purchasing the stock of Texon, had relied on letters from Texon, and from individuals connected with it. The problem involved the relation of Texon with the Big Lake Oil Company, Group No. 1 Oil Corporation and Group No. 2 Oil Corporation. Reavis advised Judge Batts if Texon owned all the property they understood it owned, the stock was worth $10 per share, but otherwise it had very little value. They thought Texon should own all the property they understood it had, but it seemed other corporations, or individuals may own a large part of these assets, and they employed Judge Batts to examine into the facts and their rights. Judge Batts had long been conversant with the oil business in Texas, and had long been a reader of the *Oil and Gas Journal* and therefore had a background which fitted him for this task. He examined records in the General Land Office of Texas at Austin, corporation records in the office of the Secretary of State at Austin, and the title records in the office of the county clerk of Reagan County, Texas, where the oil properties were principally located. He also investigated the records in the Office of the Railroad Commission of Texas, at Austin, which was the state agency having charge of the oil and gas business in Texas. He prepared a petition to be filed in court, asking for the appointment of a receiver, and upon inquiry it developed Reagan County was in the northern district of Texas, United States District Court, in the San Angelo Division, where Judge Atwell of Dallas held court. He therefore presented the petition to Judge Atwell. Answer to it was filed by C.R. Wharton, who with Judge H.M. Garwood of the Houston law firm of Baker, Botts, Parker & Garwood, represented the defendants.

Land speculators thronged to West Texas as the oil boom moved into high gear in 1925 and 1926.
[*San Angelo Standard Times*]

In Reagan County Judge Batts found no record of the Texon Oil and Land Company or of Group No. 1 Oil Corporation, or of Group No. 2 Oil Corporation. He obtained copies of oil and gas permits issued by the state to Texon Oil and Land Company, or to Group No. 1 Oil Corporation, or to Group No.2 Oil Corporation. It developed Texon had no permit to do business in Texas, and neither had Group No. 1 or Group No. 2 Oil Corporations.

Reavis and the others were principally interested in finding out what the facts were; that is, what properties were owned by the Texon Oil and Land Company, and what properties were held by the other corporations or by the individuals who controlled these corporations, and which were thought by Reavis and his friends to be in the Texon Oil and Land Company. Judge Batts negotiated with Wharton and Garwood about defendants making a full disclosure of the facts, with the prospect this would bring about a dismissal of the case. However, Wharton and Garwood insisted the case be dismissed first, and Judge Batts was unwilling to dismiss the case until he had seen what the defendants were going to produce in the way of a full disclosure of the facts. They could not agree on what was to be done first, and these negotiations came to naught. Judge Batts sought to get information with respect to the status of one million shares of stock issued after the first two million shares had been issued by Texon, but he was unable to get this information either. This situation continued for a period of some months, from the time Reavis came into Judge Batts' office in October 1924, and in April of 1925 a notice was issued of a stockholders meeting of Texon Oil and Land Company to be held in El Paso on May 5, 1925. It was this notice that precipitated the sending of the two telegrams above quoted to Burges.

Upon receipt of the Pettigrew & Meyer telegram, Burges went into action. He immediately went to Haymon Krupp's office, at the corner of Santa Fe and Overland streets, and asked for Mr. Krupp. Haymon Krupp was not present, but he saw Elias Krupp, and asked him if there was a list of stockholders of the Texon Oil and Land Company posted in the office, in accordance with Delaware law. He replied there was, and Burges asked if he could see it. No objection was offered to his looking at it, and he then told the younger Krupp he was representing Mr. Schenck, a stockholder, and he would like to make a copy of the list of stockholders.

Elias Krupp said he did not know whether he was authorized to let him make a copy of it, and he asked Burges to wait until Haymon Krupp returned. Burges said he did not have much time for examination of the list, and asked when Haymon Krupp would be back. Elias said Haymon had left town that morning, and Burges asked him if he could get in communication with Haymon Krupp at once, to authorize him to make a copy of the stockholders. He stated he was entitled to it, and that he wanted it, and Elias said he would communicate with Haymon Krupp. When he left the Krupp office, he went to the office of R.C. Walshe whom he knew to be one of the attorneys either for Texon Oil and Land Company, or for Krupp's business generally. He asked Walshe if he could help him get the list of stockholders. Walshe explained he had no authority in the matter, which would have to come either from Haymon Krupp or Mr. Sachs, his New York lawyer, and neither was in town.

Burges thereupon wired to Haymon Krupp, on the train at Alpine, Texas:

> Am representing W.A. Schenck, stockholder in Texon Oil and Land Company and wish to make copy of list of stockholders posted in your office as authorized by Delaware law. Please wire Eli Krupp to let me make copy *STOP* This very urgent so please wire at once. William H. Burges.

At the same time he sent a telegram to John Perkins, a lawyer at Alpine, asking him to see that the telegram he had just sent to Haymon Krupp on the train at Alpine was delivered to Krupp. He had a reply back from Perkins stating the message had been delivered to a person identified as Haymon Krupp. He did not at that time get an answer from Krupp.

On April 23 he sent a wire to Pettigrew & Meyer, 120 Broadway, New York, stating he had examined the list of stockholders, that it contained about 2,400 names, but no one in the company office would assume authority to let him make a copy of it. He expected to have authority from Haymon Krupp later that day. He wired Pettigrew & Meyer later that day again, explaining the problem about not being able to locate anyone with authority to let him make a copy of the list, but he was pressing the investigation and would keep him advised. On April 24 he again wired John Perkins:

> Understand Krupp still in Alpine *STOP* Please get and wire answer to my telegram quickly as possible. This of utmost importance.

Although he had seen the list of about 2,400 names no addresses were given. On the 24th he was advised by Eli Krupp that Haymon Krupp would be back the next day or possibly the day following and he sent a long telegram to Pettigrew & Meyer stating he would have to wait until Haymon Krupp returned in order to get a copy of the list, and that the list contained approximately 2,400 names holding 4,400,000 shares as of April 15. No addresses given. Four hundred persons held more than one thousand shares each and many of these owned from three to ten thousand shares apiece. Levy Brothers held 423,233 shares; G.A. Loomis & Co., 309,577 shares; R.V. Nuttal & Co., 218,425 shares; Carl G. Cromwell, 1,400,000 shares; that he recognized but few names on the list, and thought a majority of the stock was held by merchants and jobbers in eastern cities.

Pettigrew & Meyer replied requesting Burges to send by night letter as soon as possible, names of all stockholders holding one thousand shares or more, even though he did not have the addresses. He received a second telegram from them telling him to demand the right to copy the entire stockholders list and, if granted, to spare no reasonable expense to make such copy speedily and to mail it to them as quickly as possible, using air mail via Denver and Cheyenne, if this would hasten delivery to them; and also to demand if duplicate stockholders list would be given them in New York or by Corporation Trust company, Texon's agent in Delaware, and to wire them accordingly, together with some instructions as to how the list was to be compiled and sent to them.

He received on the 23rd a wire from H.S. Reavis reading:

> William H. Burges, on behalf H.S. Reavis stockholder send by registered mail immediately to Haymon Krupp as president Texon Frank T. Pickrell treasurer Elias G. Krupp secretary John M. Wyatt, Hon. Charles Davis all at El Paso the following demand quote as a stockholder of Texon Oil and Land Company I hereby demand that you forthwith file or cause to

be filed by the above named corporation in the office of the secretary of state of Delaware a statement showing the names of all the directors of the company and the dates when the terms of each expire and also the date fixed by the by-laws for the holding of the annual meeting for the election of directors. H.S. Reavis

Burges sent a letter by registered mail to each one of the persons named in this last telegram. In the meantime he frequently went to the office of the Krupp Company for the purpose of obtaining the list and was bringing every bit of pressure to bear that he could. Finally he made a suggestion to Walshe that they let him take a stenographer to the Krupp office and copy the list and they could keep the copy, but he would have it ready when Haymon Krupp came in. He did not get an acceptance of this proposition. On April 24 he was at that office late, until about 10:00 P.M., while the people in Texon's office had been trying to communicate with Nathan I. Sachs, general counsel for Texon and its associates, at Big Lake, Texas. Burges finally said to them: "I am not coming down there, I will get it in court, I have wasted all the time I am going to, and I will make you do it now."

They agreed later that night that he could have the list. He stated he had wasted some two or three days in the effort to get it, but he did get it, and had it copied and wired it to New York. He stated every effort was made and every delay was put in the way that could possibly be done, but he got it at last, when a mandatory injunction was going to be applied for by him in court the next morning. He finally had a complete copy on the night of April 27 and sent it as a night letter, by telegraph, to Pettigrew & Meyer in New York.

By Saturday or Sunday, prior to the date the stockholders meeting was called for on May 5, Burges had received proxies for something like $400,000 or $500,000 worth of stock, and just prior to filing the application for the injunction, filed immediately thereafter, he received proxies for approximately a million dollars worth of stock. His testimony later was that they had about $1,500,000 or $1,600,000 in actual proxies. Judge Batts came in on Sunday, and told Burges he wanted him to help in the case. They discussed what probably was going to happen with the officers of the company and the directors. Burges was of the opinion that Hudspeth and Davis, John Wyle and

Haymon Krupp would act properly in the matter and do what they ought to do, and that Frank Pickrell probably would also. He was concerned, however, about what their general counsel might advise them to do and that they would act on his advice.

He and Judge Batts discussed filing a suit for an injunction, including the question of what court it should be filed in, and it was Burges' recommendation that it be filed in the 41st District Court of El Paso County, Texas before Judge P.R. Price. They prepared the petition, and it was sworn to. Judge Batts and he thereupon presented it to Judge Price. In the petition they asked for a temporary restraining order, which was granted by Judge Price. It was then served upon the defendants.

The defendants contended that the District Court of El Paso County, Texas was without jurisdiction, in that it could not do anything to interfere with the internal affairs of a Delaware Corporation, and took the position that plaintiffs could not get the relief they wanted in a Texas court.

Burges was of the opinion that since the defendants had answered in the case, even though merely to raise the question of jurisdiction, under the *York* decision, they were in court for all purposes, and, there could no longer be a question of jurisdiction. This was reinforced by the decision of the 41st District Court in the *Southwestern Portland Cement Company* case, affirmed by the Court of Civil Appeals, and in which the Supreme Court of Texas refused a writ of error. It was decided by Burges, Judge Batts, and their clients, however, there should be someone in Wilmington, Delaware standing by ready to file an action in court there, if there were an adverse decision in El Paso. Accordingly, Warrick M. Downing, a lawyer from Denver, who represented some of the parties on the plaintiff's side of the case, went from El Paso to Wilmington, Delaware for that purpose. It was the distinct understanding he was not to file a suit in Delaware unless he was advised by those remaining in El Paso that things had taken such a turn here that he should go ahead with filing action in Delaware. It is sufficient here to state Burges and the others in El Paso were shortly afterwards advised the suit had been filed and certain restraining orders issued in Delaware, much to their surprise since they had not requested this be done. A little later they learned Downing had changed sides, and had put himself on the other side of the controversy. In the meantime, there had been numerous meetings in El Paso between the plaintiffs, Judge Batts and Burges on the one side, and the defendants, Wharton and Nathan I. Sachs on the other side. At these meetings it developed the facts were all in favor of the plaintiffs, and the defendants, whatever were their motives, held either personally, or through the medium of other corporations which they had organized, large and valuable assets which had been represented to the plaintiffs as belonging to the Texon Oil & Land Company of Delaware. The result was they entered into an agreement for a decree to be entered in the 41st District Court of El Paso County, Texas, pursuant to which said assets were to be transferred to and vested in the Texon Oil and Land Company of Delaware.

The final agreement was negotiated in Chicago, between Arnold L. Davis and C.R. Wharton on the one side and Judge Batts on the other, as a result of which Wharton came to El Paso in November, and a decree was entered by the court in El Paso on November 12, 1925. The effect of the decree was to transfer to Texon Oil and Land Company of Delaware assets of a value of approximately $6 million.

The agreement provided the plaintiffs' costs in connection with the litigation, including their attorneys' fees, were to be paid by the defendants, and if the parties could not agree upon the amount of the attorneys fee, this question would be submitted to Judge P.R. Price, judge of the 41st District Court of El Paso County, Texas, for determination by him. Burges had discussed the matter of the settlement, and decree to be entered, with Judge Batts in Austin prior to its entry in El Paso in November.

Wharton also went to Austin to see Judge Batts about the decree to be entered, and while there he brought up the question of the fee to be paid. Judge Batts had a severe case of laryngitis and could speak only in a whisper. He said, "See Burges. Whatever he says about the fee will be all right with me." While the final papers were being prepared for the entry of the decree in November, some changes in the papers were being made in the Turney & Burges offices and at that time Wharton asked Burges how much they were going to charge the defendants for "licking them" as Wharton put it. There were present at that conference, in addition to Wharton, Maury Kemp, Nathan I. Sachs, Frank T. Pickrell and A.H. Culwell. In answer to Wharton's question, Burges replied, "Five percent of the amount collected, $300,000."

Wharton was very polite in his manner, but indicated in most certain terms the defendants disagreed with the amount of the fee as just stated, and they would have to leave it to the court to decide, and Burges replied, "Let's go." There was no further discussion about the amount of the fee, it being understood both sides would leave it to Judge Price to decide.

The matter was submitted to Judge Price, and Judge Batts testified extensively about the problems that confronted him, the extensive work that he did, and the results obtained, and Burges also testified extensively to the work done by him, and the results obtained. There were others who testified, among them: Holland S. Reavis, Arnold L. Davis, Warrick M. Downing, C.R. Wharton, Nathan I. Sachs and Frank T. Pickrell. During the course of Burges' testimony at the hearing before Judge Price, he stated he had never had but one controversy prior to this over a fee in his life, and this was with some Spaniards. His reference to them was mostly on cross-examination by Wharton, whose approach being that if Burges had been asked to fix a fee in advance for taking this case he would have been satisfied with a fee not to exceed $15,000 and indicating a fee in excess of that sum probably never was heard of in the El Paso area. Burges answered this by saying he had not heard of a court in El Paso fixing a fee of that size, but he had received fees in El Paso larger than he had heard of any other lawyer here getting, or of a court fixing, but he had done work which had earned larger fees, and he was entitled to them. In this connection he referred to the Spanish Cotton cases, in which "we had about $2 million involved, or a little over," and he thought $250,000 was a reasonable fee in that case, and his clients agreed to it. The disagreement over it came up later, occasioned by the loss of the cotton after World War I came on, as a result of which they did not get the full fee, but collected, as he recalled, $113,000 or $114,000. This example, of course, completely refuted Wharton's idea that a $15,000 fee would be a top fee for any kind of work in El Paso. Burges also referred, not by name but by general reference to the I.W.W. Deportation case because he said he also had in mind a case where the fee received, measured by the amount of time he had put in on it (nearly three years) would be in excess of $50,000 per year. He conceded the fee requested in this case of $300,000 was the largest fee ever suggested on the border, but stated in his testimony it is the first fee Judge Price has had before him where over $6 million was involved. His position about it simply was, it had been a case with difficult questions in it, and in which plaintiffs had been opposed by lawyers of the greatest ability, and they had been successful on behalf of the plaintiffs in recovering $6 million and that five percent, to-wit, $300,000 was a fair fee.

At the conclusion of the testimony, Judge Price found $175,000 was a reasonable fee and judgment was entered for that amount in favor of Judge Batts and the Turney & Burges firm. The defendants appealed, but the judgment was affirmed.

One fact thoroughly confirmed Burges in his opinion that a fee of $300,000 was reasonable. In the suit Downman filed in Delaware, the court there, subsequent to Judge Price's judgment and findings in the El Paso case (which included a finding it was due to Batts' and Burges' efforts the assets had been restored to Texon Oil & Land Co.), without a hearing, and with the agreement of the Texon people, awarded the lawyers in the Delaware case a fee of $200,000. It looked like Batts and Burges did the work and others got the fee.

Burges afterwards said that five percent of the amount collected was a reasonable basis for a fee and they were entitled to the fee as fixed by him. He added, the only reason Judge Price did not give them a judgment for $300,000 was, Judge Price did not think there was that much money in the world.

XXIX

The Rio Grande Boundary Litigation and Other Cases

Who may trace the ways that ye have taken,
ye stream and drops?

—Gould

IN THE MEANTIME, in addition to the more or less ordinary, usual run of personal injury damage suits, including those for the A.T. & S.F. Railway Co., breach of contract cases, some of which involved the First National Bank, litigation growing out of bankruptcy cases, such as the case of *H.O. Kane, Trustee in Bankruptcy v. The First National Bank,* and the usual things in a busy office practice preparing papers for real estate transactions, will and probate proceedings, other cases came along that were unique both as to their facts and as to the legal problems, and which are not ordinarily found in a routine general legal practice.

One of these was the case of the *State of New Mexico v. State of Texas.* New Mexico was admitted to the Union as a State in 1912, and in 1913 filed, as an original proceeding in the Supreme Court of United States, a suit against the State of Texas. It involved the location of the boundary between the two states, as the same existed in the Rio Grande River Valley from a point west of Anthony, Texas-New Mexico, southward to the Mexican border, a distance of a little less than twenty miles. The original answer in the case was signed on behalf of the State of Texas by B.F. Looney, attorney general of Texas, G.B. Smedley, assistant attorney general of the State of Texas, and by W.W.

Turney and W.H. Burges, as special counsel for the State of Texas.

While Turney had the laboring oar in the case for Turney & Burges, Burges was familiar with the case, and participated in conferences with the attorney general of the State of Texas and Turney with reference both to the facts and the law relating to the case.

The New Mexico-Texas boundary comes down the west side of the Texas Panhandle along the 103° meridian to the 32° parallel, then west to the center of the Rio Grande where it ran on September 9, 1850, thence down the center of the bed of the river as it ran on that date to the parallel of 31° 47″ on the international boundary between the United States and Mexico. This is an offset in the southern boundary of New Mexico extending nearly to El Paso. New Mexico claimed the river ran near the eastern boundary of the river valley in 1850, while Texas contended it ran near the western side of the river valley, so the difference between the lines claimed by the two parties was approximately four miles. In 1850 this strip was of little value.

In the territory in dispute the Rio Grande flows southwardly through a plain of alluvial and sandy bottom land, composed largely of detritus, and bordered on the east and west by ranges of hills. While the valley is about four miles wide at the northern end, it narrows gradually to a canyon or gorge at the southern end—the pass—that gives El Paso its name. The river in normal times is very shallow, but prior to the building of the dam at Elephant Butte, and the Caballo Dam, at frequently recurring periods freshets caused by melting snow in the mountains and heavy rains or cloudbursts flooded and overflowed the banks of the river, resulting in many changes in the channel both by erosions and accretions and by sudden and violent avulsions.

During the decade of the 1850s, the valley was uninhabited, uncultivated, and covered in many parts near the river with thick bosques (groves or forests of cottonwood or tornillo trees). By the time the suit was filed in 1913, this area had changed considerably, being partly settled and cultivated. The town of Anthony had come into existence, and there were farms, corn fields and alfalfa fields, paved roads and a railroad in many places where they located the old 1850 river. In many earlier years during annual floods, the river occasionally covered the whole valley from its western to its eastern margin.

When the floods subsided, the river sometimes resumed its former channel, and sometimes it did not. The valley was full of old abandoned riverbeds, which were referred to as esteros.

New Mexico relied mainly upon the testimony of a large number of Indians and Mexicans, most of whom had been members of different parties which had accompanied its engineers on various trips down the river between 1912 and 1914, shortly before and after the filing of the lawsuit, for the purpose of pointing out the location of the old river. New Mexico also had the testimony of a former registrar of the land office who had known the river in 1857 and 1858 when he was a conductor on a stage route. He was employed by New Mexico to find witnesses having knowledge of the old river. It also had a survey of the 32° parallel made in 1859 by John H. Clark, United States commissioner, with testimony of its engineers, surveyors and others relating thereto.

The Supreme Court on December 4, 1924 appointed a special master, Charles Warren, Esq., with directions to him to make special findings on all material questions of fact and to report them to the Supreme Court of United States with his recommendations respecting a decree to be entered by that court, and further directing he should accord the parties a full hearing on all questions of fact or law. The facts alluded to here are those taken in the testimony before the special master, which when reduced to writing, covered thirty-five hundred pages of the record, supplemented by about two hundred maps, photographs and other documentary exhibits. This indicates the great extent of the work done in the case by Turney & Burges, since Turney examined or cross-examined all of the witnesses. By this time the direction and control of the case had passed into the able hands of W.A. Keeling, who had become attorney general of Texas, and who carried on the case through the administrations of the attorneys general Dan Moody and Claude Pollard to the end of the case.

The master, in his report, said, "Most of the witnesses were illiterate; they were unable to estimate distances with any degree of accuracy . . . all . . . were old men, some very old, some were only ten years of age or less at the date when they passed along the river between the years of 1850 and 1860. There was much evidence that in those years the country was wild and infested with hostile Indians . . . Many of the witnesses traveled part of the time at night. From White's Ranch to Alamitos, there was but one, if any, house prior to 1857. The things given by the witnesses, therefore, to points along the river with relation to which . . . they located the river . . . , referred to bends, hills, bosques, esteros, cottonwood trees, etc. . . . Many of the witnesses had not traveled along the river since the Civil War, and only a few claimed to have had any continuous knowledge of the river. Moreover, as stated above, most of the river valley had been altered in condition since the 1850 decade down to the time of the hearings in the decade of the 1920s."

Much time and effort was spent in connection with the survey of John H. Clark, United States commissioner, with respect to a survey made by him in 1859 as a member of the United States and Texas Boundary Commission. He located the east bank of the Rio Grande, at its intersection with the 32° parallel at that time and placed a monument there. The monument, however, had long since disappeared. Congress, in February 1911, by a Joint Resolution declared any provision of the proposed New Mexico State Constitution that tended to annul or change the established boundary lines between the territory of New Mexico and the State of Texas, as run by Clark in 1858 and 1860, "shall be of no force or effect," and shall be construed so as not to affect or alter the Clark lines in any way; and the ratification of these lines by the United States and the State of Texas in 1891, "shall be held and deemed a conclusive location and settlement of said boundary lines," and the lines run and marked by monuments along the 103° meridian and the 32° parallel shall, "remain the true boundaries of Texas and New Mexico." The resolution further authorized the president, in conjunction with the State of Texas, to reestablish and re-mark the Clark boundary lines, and, for such purpose, to appoint a commissioner, who, with a commissioner for the State of Texas, should remark the boundary between the territory of New Mexico and Texas on the line run by Clark for the 103° meridian to the southeast corner of New Mexico, and thence west with the 32° parallel as determined by him to the Rio Grande; the position of the boundaries as marked by him to be determined by his old monuments and lines where found on the ground, or otherwise by their original position as shown by parol evidence of his topographical maps and field notes. This commission, commonly called the Scott-Cockrell Commission, undertook to reestablish the location of the Clark Monument No. 1, and this commission placed the riverbank in 1859 substantially in the position claimed by Texas.

The master found, as a matter of law, that New Mexico was bound by the Clark lines as reestablished by the commission and could not challenge the correctness of its acts, and hence, in locating the boundary line extending southwardly from the 32° parallel through the valley, the starting point on the parallel could not be fixed east of the reestablished monument.

Texas further relied upon various old surveys, patents and maps, and the testimony of its engineers in regard thereto, as showing the true course of the river southwardly through the valley from the point where it crossed the parallel. These documents consisted mainly of the so-called Salazar-Diaz Survey of the Rio Grande, made in 1852 by Diaz, a Mexican engineer, by order of Salazar, the Mexican member of the Joint Boundary Commission under the Treaty of Guadalupe-Hidalgo, together with various other surveys, some of which were made under the direction of the American surveyor for the Joint Boundary Commission. Texas also relied upon the long acquiescence by the United States before the territory of New Mexico had been admitted as a state. The master found the Salazar-Diaz survey was authentic. The course of the river as surveyed in 1852 had been reproduced by the engineers for Texas by traverse from the triangulation points with substantial correctness, and even if the engineers for New Mexico were correct in certain contentions, the resultant reproduction would not place the river anywhere near the location claimed by New Mexico. He further found that for many years prior to the admission of New Mexico as a state in 1912, surveys were made by Texas surveyors and patents issued by Texas on substantially all the land in the area in dispute; the occupancy and physical possession of this land by Texas patentees and persons claiming under them had been admitted by counsel at the hearing before him; there was no evidence that from 1850 to 1911 the United States had issued any patents specially covering lands east of the river as located by the Salazar-Diaz survey, or conflicting with any of the patents issued by Texas; and that, for at least thirty years prior to the admission of the territory of New Mexico as a state, the United States made no challenge of the claims to lands asserted by Texas and its citizens and, impliedly at least, recognized the practical line established as the boundary between the territory and Texas. New Mexico also claimed title to some of the lands as having been acquired by accretion to the river where it formerly ran, and the master held with New Mexico that the doctrine of accretion applied.

The net result was, the master made his report of the facts and the law to the Supreme Court of the United States, with his recommendations as to the judgment to be entered. In an opinion handed down on December 5, 1927, the Supreme Court adopted the report of the master, except for his decision on accretion. The Supreme Court thus held in favor of Texas. It held the 1850 river boundary was a fixed boundary, not affected by subsequent changes in the location of the river, and the court ordered the boundary lines as therein described should be accurately surveyed and marked by a commissioner or commissioners to be appointed by the court.

The court appointed Samuel S. Gannett as the commissioner to run, locate and mark the boundary line, and by decree entered March 23, 1931, the court approved the boundary line as so run, located and marked by Gannett. The long litigation had finally come to an end, and Texas had won. The report of the case at 275 U.S. 279 shows the State of Texas was then represented by W.A. Keeling, attorney general of Texas, with whom Messrs. John C. Wall, Walace Hawkins, assistants attorneys general, and W.W. Turney were on the brief for the defendant. We may be sure that Turney, as the man on the ground—that is, the one of the attorneys for the state who lived in El Paso—was busy during a portion of time this case was pending in examining carefully into the facts, locating old maps, plats and surveys talking to possible witnesses among surveyors, engineers and oldtimers, and he was also busy briefing the law on the points which he saw were pertinent to the case. We may also be sure Burges had a hand in this work, as he and Turney conferred on various aspects of the case from time to time, so they were both fully advised as to what was going on, and each had his part in directing the handling of the case, both as to facts and to the law, on behalf of the State of Texas.

The sequel to *New Mexico v. Texas* followed hard on the heels of the handing down of the opinion in the case by the United States Supreme Court on December 5, 1927. Less than sixty days after that date L.M. Crawford, of Wichita, Kansas, filed a suit, on January 25, 1928, in the 41st District Court of El Paso County, against Z.T. White and nine others, in trespass to try title. Crawford claimed title to about two hundred acres of land situated east of the Rio Grande, in El Paso County, in the vicinity of the El Paso Country Club. He had purchased land in the Santa Teresa Grant, an old Spanish Grant in Dona Ana County, New Mexico. His attorney, an El Paso lawyer, had been permitted to intervene, as amicus curiae, in *New Mexico v. Texas.* He was, of course, endeavoring to uphold the claim of New Mexico against Texas, as the means of sustaining Crawford's claim to title to land which, as it turned out, was in Texas, but as to which Crawford had only a New Mexico claim. In the suit against White et al, his claim essentially was, under established rules of law, the boundary of lands abutting on a river follows the river, when the river moves, and additional land is added by accretion. The case was tried in April 1929, with Turney, Burges, Culwell, & Pollard representing the defendant. Testimony was taken for eight or nine days, at the conclusion of which Judge P.R. Price granted defendant's motion for an instructed verdict, and judgment was entered against Crawford, and in favor of Z.T. White and the other defendants. The controlling factor was the decision of the Supreme Court of the United States in *New Mexico v. Texas,* to the effect the Act of Congress of September 8, 1850, which was accepted by the Texas Legislature on November 25, 1850, made the middle of the Rio Grande, as it existed on September 9, 1850, a fixed boundary, not subject to change by accretion. Crawford appealed to the Court of Civil Appeals at El Paso. It is not unusual for the losing side to have some feeling of bitterness at the result of the lawsuit, and so it was in this case. In the brief filed on behalf of Crawford, as appellant, Crawford's attorney digressed from the business of urging his legal points to a personal assault on W.W. Turney, saying:

"It might be explained, that at the time this brief was prepared there was an erroneous map in evidence, being map No. 2 of Texas, prepared by R.J. Owen, a copy of which was introduced in this case as Exhibit "L," which showed the 1905 river between the southwest corner of the Canutillo Grant and Piedras Paradas as running along the foothills at the western edge of the valley, and also showing that the river had changed out of such position by avulsion. Later, when additional testimony was put in to correct this map and show that the 1905 river ran where we claim that it did run, Texas again insisted that the boundary was where the river was in 1850 and that it had not been changed by accretion.

"These changes are peculiarly significant when we learn that Mr. W.W. Turney, the personal attorney of Mr. White, was really in charge of this boundary suit for Texas from its inception. He examined all of the witnesses and controlled the Texas side of the case absolutely.

"His control was so complete that he caused exceptions to be filed by the State of Texas to that portion of the master's report which would have applied the doctrine of accretions to this boundary, and would thus have saved for Texas every acre that Texas had patented. As a result of his direction of the case, Texas lost approximately twelve hundred acres of valley land which it had patented and from which it had collected taxes for more than half a century.

"We firmly believe that the courts of Texas will follow the long continued and correct attitude which the Executive Department of Texas took, prior to 1913, and not the inadvertent and ill-advised action into which it was led by Mr. White's attorney.

"Even after 1916 Texas patented survey 262 just west of the southwest corner of the Canutillo Grant and west of the 1850-1852 river. Texas acted through its Land Office and its governor in patenting this land west of the 1850-1852 river as it had been located by Texas in the boundary suit. The true position of survey 262 above referred to is shown in Exhibit "L." On page 133 of the Statement of Facts, R.J. Owen testified:

'I made the field notes for the patent for Survey 262 for Mr.

White, patented, since 1916. The state issued its patent on that survey. In making that survey the commissioner of the Land Office did not tell me that I should not go beyond the 1852 line. I never heard of that. The State of Texas approved my field notes and survey going over to this old river of 1905, the line considerably west of the 1852 river.'

"Certainly, the conduct of the attorney general under the interested tutelage of Mr. Turney in the boundary case is not conclusive upon the courts of Texas, when every other action of Texas from 1854 to the present time has been to the contrary."

In the brief filed by Turney, Burges, Culwell & Pollard, which brief Mr. Turney determined to forego signing, no doubt on account of the attack on him, and which therefore was signed by William H. Burges, A.H. Culwell, J.M. Pollard, R.W. Yarborough, and William Flournoy, it was said in reply to this attack:

"In this connection we feel constrained to notice those parts of appellant's brief which appear to us to be a criticism of Mr. W.W. Turney for his actions in *Texas v. New Mexico,* or for what is attributed to him by counsel for appellant. We refer especially to pages 63 and 64 of appellant's brief. As there is nothing in the record of this case on which to base this criticism, and nothing in fact upon which to base such criticism, we assume counsel for appellant will not object if we go as far outside the record in reply as they have gone in criticism.

"The firm of which Mr. Turney is a member, was employed by the State of Texas. Mr. Turney never wrote the answer to the original bill in *New Mexico v. Texas,* and never saw it until it was in print. He participated in a conference at the preparation of the brief but did not write it; neither did he argue the case in the Supreme Court, as will be seen by reference to the report of the case in 275 U.S., 279. Mr. Turney represented the State of Texas in taking the testimony in this case and we submit that the result shows that he did it well.

"Probably the best reply that could be made to the strictures of appellant's counsel is in the very language of that distinguished lawyer and citizen of this state, who, as assistant attorney general, attorney general, and, later, as retained counsel by the state after his official connection with the case had ended, the Honorable W.A. Keeling, as contained in a letter to Mr. Turney dated November 30, 1929, after Mr. Keeling had seen a copy of appellant's brief. Not insisting on the adjectives, we quote the letter in full:

November 30, 1929.

Honorable W.W. Turney,
First National Bank Building,
El Paso, Texas.

My dear Mr. Turney:

I feel outraged that Mr. Hardie should have so forgot himself as to indulge in the unethical flings contained in his brief.

I have lying before me now the briefs, motions and the exceptions to the master's report, signed by Clancy and Hardie, attorneys for the State of New Mexico. The only fighting we know that Mr. Hardie did in this case was under the flag of New Mexico. He joined with that state and fought Texas bitterly as he could, and it looks out of taste, to say the least of it, for Hardie, counsel for the State of New Mexico, to complain that the State of Texas did not stand up for its rights and gave away twelve hundred acres of valley land to his client. Of course, the statement that the State of Texas gave away any territory is untrue, but to show the utter ridiculous attitude he places himself in, he complains that his own client was the beneficiary. If Texas is to be criticized, let it come from loyal Texans who stood by the State of Texas in fighting for Texas territory, and not one who for a consideration turned against his sovereign state and fought her at every ditch.

On the matter of accretion which forms the basis of his criticism, you well know that all you had to do with this was upon my urgent demand you came to Austin. We, of course, had decided when the master held against Texas on accretion that we would file exceptions to the report, but I wanted a conference on what should be embraced in the exceptions. You patriotically came at my urgent request to Austin, when you were not in health able to do so. We had a short conference here, and while I do not remember all of the details, I remember that it was decided that I should draft the exceptions. I drafted the exceptions and they were printed and filed in the case just as I prepared them. If there was any doubt as to whether or not these exceptions were proper, we but have to refer to the opinion of the court, which sustained our contention in its entirety.

In the case of the *State of Texas v. The State of New Mexico,* Texas won every single contention that it made. While the Master held against Texas on the question of accretion, when exceptions were filed with the court, the court sustained our contention in regard thereto. Thus Texas won a clear-cut victory and didn't lose a foot of ground it contended for in its pleadings.

I think after I became attorney general, through my administration, through Mr. Moody's administration and Mr. Pollard's administration, every brief, order or paper prepared, at least affecting the policy of the suit, was prepared by me, and while at all times I was delighted and glad to have any suggestion you might make I can truthfully say that as to the policy of this case, which was to contend for every foot of land we could get from the State of New Mexico, there was never a division of opinion among us.

Now, Mr. Turney, I want to do anything I can to help you in your litigation. If it would be of any benefit to you, I can get an affidavit signed by myself, General Cureton, Dan Moody, General Looney and Claude Pollard in effect stating that at no time was there any attempt on your part to inject into the case any pet theory of yours, nor did you at any time ever take into consideration the welfare of any client, and that at all times the services you rendered were patriotic and able. If this would be of any service to you, I will gladly get this and forward it. On the other hand if you had rather risk pointing out to the court the fact that the record discloses that Mr. Hardie was the attorney and counsellor of the state of New Mexico, and who lost every point in his case, who fought Texas in every way possible, this, I think, would dispose of the matter before any Court of Civil Appeals or any other court in Texas, but let me assure you that I am deeply interested in this matter and will do everything possible.

I note in your letter that you ask as to my recollection as to Mr. Hawkins filing exceptions with Mr. Moody. Mr. Hawkins did not file with me any copy of any exceptions and I think I heard something of his doing so, but I did not see the copies he filed with Mr. Moody. All I know is that Mr. Moody asked me to get up the exceptions and they were printed just as I got them up. I recall, however, that in one of our briefs in the case Mr. Moody did rewrite a considerable portion of it. I could refresh my memory by reading the record over again and get these matters all straight, but I shall await your answer as to what you desire that I do.

Sincerely your friend,
W.A. Keeling

"The State of Texas, Mr. Turney's client, is satisfied with his services, possibly including the 'tutelage.' No claimant of land within the disputed area who claims under the State of Texas is protesting against anything he has done. The disapproval of Mr. Crawford is gratifying. The Reverend Sam Jones once said, 'It's the hit pup that yelps the loudest.' We trust Mr. Crawford's grief over the losses of

Texas owners will not prove unbearable. Too much should not be imposed upon one so jealous of the interests of the Texas title-holders as Mr. Crawford has shown himself to be.

"Recognizing, as of course we must do, the entire disinterestedness of that large-minded and unselfish citizen of Kansas, and in order that he may not mourn as one without hope, we refer him to the language of the distinguished associate justice of the Supreme Court of the State of New Mexico, the Honorable Francis W. Parker, who is also the chairman of the Permanent Boundary Commission of the State of New Mexico, used on the 24th of September, 1929, at the hearing before the Joint Committee of the Senate and House of Representatives of the State of Texas, held in the city of El Paso and presided over by the Honorable Joseph McGill, Chairman. For Mr. Crawford's peace of mind we print in full the remarks of Judge Parker, as "Appendix F" to this brief.

"Mr. Turney needs no defense in this or any case and if this had been the first instance of criticism of, and ill will manifested toward him, in connection with this controversy, it would not have been noticed even this much."

The judgment of the trial court was duly sustained by the Court of Civil Appeals, affirming the judgment in favor of Z.T. White.

One day in 1924 the telephone rang in Burges' office. He answered it, to find it was a long distance call from Washington, D.C. The voice at the other end of the line came on, and said, "This is Harlan Fiske Stone, attorney general of the United States."

He went on to say he wanted to secure the services of a Texas laywer in a case in the Federal Court at Fort Worth, and not being acquainted with any Texas lawyers, he had asked some of the justices on the Supreme Court if they could suggest one, and they responded by recommending he call W.H. Burges of El Paso.

Attorney General Stone then referred to the case of *United States v. Frederick A. Cook.* Dr. Cook had earlier become a newsworthy person, whose name was well-known across the country, by reason of his claim of having been the first man to reach the North Pole—a claim disputed by many, who were of the opinion Dr. Cook never reached the North Pole. In the early 1920s he was living in Ft. Worth, which had become something of an oil center, following the discovery a few years earlier of oil in the Breckenridge-Ranger-Eastland area west of Ft. Worth, and in the Burkburnett-Electra areas northwest of Ft. Worth.

Dr. Cook was often in the news. The Ft. Worth papers reported—in 1923—in the Prohibition era: "Dr. Cook Held For Possessing A Bottle Of Gin; Dr. Cook Named On A Liquor Charge; Dr. Cook Quits Paying Dividends; Dr. Cook Sues *Fort Worth Press* For A Million Dollars." References were made to his interest, or claim of interest in the Mexia, Texas, and in the Smackover, Arkansas oil fields, and shortly the news items reported "Story On Dr. Cook Oil Business," "Probe of Oil Frauds Opens in Federal Court," "U.S. Grand Jury At Work In Oil Fraud," "Cook Case—92 Promoters Indicted." Dr. Cook went to trial in October, 1923, on an indictment charging he used the United States mail to defraud. The charges revolved about selling oil interests—real or supposed—by mail, and after a trial lasting five weeks, a verdict of guilty was returned. He was sentenced to fourteen years and nine months in the penitentiary, and the newspapers then reported his friends said Dr. Cook was broke, and they were trying to raise money to appeal his sentence. It was during this time—while the appeal was pending—that Attorney General Stone telephoned Burges. His statement to Burges was, the case seemed not to be moving, and he could not get satisfactory information about it, and wanted to secure Burges' services to see what the status of the case was, and see that it moved ahead.

He said to Burges, "I know you no doubt make more than ten thousand dollars a year." To which Burges answered affirmatively. But the top salary the government can offer is ten thousand dollars a year, and he offered compensation at that rate to Burges, if he would undertake the assignment. Burges did not feel like he could refuse, and did undertake it, going to Ft. Worth, but no record of just what he did, or reported, has been preserved. It can only be reported here that Cook's appeal was heard before the United States Court of Appeals at New Orleans, and on February 3, 1925, that court handed down its opinion affirming the judgment and sentence of the district court. Cook served time until March, 1930, when he was paroled.

A little later, in the mid-1920s, Burges took the Sunset Limited from El Paso to Los Angeles. Lee Orndorff, one of El Paso's prominent citizens was also on the train. The Democratic primary election was just over, and Lee's brother, Seth Orndorff, apparently had been re-elected sheriff. His opponent had announced he was filing an election contest suit, and Lee said to Burges, "Look after Seth." Election contests were not new to Burges, as he had been in many before, not only in El Paso County, but also in nearly all the counties west of the Pecos. In the election contests, the strategy of the contestant was to get an order from the court directing the election boxes be opened, in those precincts where he questioned the accuracy, or correctness, or the honesty of the voting, and of the election returns. Several of Seth's closest advisers and supporters came to Burges, and with tremendous concern said, "Don't let them open the boxes in South El Paso (the area in which most of the Mexican population lived, and long rumored to be the focal point of election irregularities). We stole the other side blind in South El Paso. Don't let them open any of those boxes."

But when the trial came on in the district court, Burges joined in asking all suspect boxes be opened, and when the votes in each box were recounted, with the district judge ruling on each contested vote—whether the voter was a legally qualified voter—or whether the ballot was a valid ballot, properly marked. In each of the South El Paso boxes which were opened, Seth Ordorff gained more votes than he lost, and was declared the winner by a greater margin than shown on the original tally. It all goes to show sometimes amateur politicians who claim credit—with their candidate—for having "stole the election" for him are trying to blow their own horn, and support their pretensions to being astute and knowledgeable in the devious ways of unclean politics, really have not affected the result at all.

In the late 1920s another case arose in a completely different field. Mrs. Mary Cleghorn Hills, a resident of Michigan, died, leaving property in Michigan, and also some downtown business property in El Paso. She left a will in which she named the Michigan Trust Company both executor and trustee, with directions to the trustee what she wanted it to do with her property, after it passed to the trustee. The will was admitted to probate in Michigan, and claims were established against the estate which exceeded the value of the estate's property in Michigan. This left the El Paso property as the only source of payment of the debts represented by the claims allowed by the Michigan probate court.

This was the state of affairs when the Michigan Trust Company employed Burges to represent it in handling the El Paso property. After studying the facts and the law, he advised that an ancillary administration of the estate in the probate court, i.e., the County Court of El Paso County, was necessary and the Michigan Trust Company could be appointed ancillary administrator in El Paso, except for one fact. Business property had to be taken care of and with so many different business actions to be taken, it would be doing business in Texas; and, therefore, the Michigan Trust Company, as a foreign corporation, would have to obtain a permit, from the secretary of state, to do business in Texas as a foreign corporation. The trust company decided not to apply for a permit to do business in Texas, and requested the county court to appoint a local realtor, Otis C. Coles, administrator with will annexed. This was all done on the advice of Burges, and with him doing the necessary legal work. There were many business actions to be taken by the administrator, and each time it required the preparation of motions or applications on behalf of the administrator, and an appearance before the county judge, the drafting of an order, and attending to getting it signed by the judge. The property in El Paso was appraised at $302,350, and the largest claim against it was a claim in favor of Grand Rapids National Bank for $62,000. A large amount of legal and paper work, and time was spent on it, over a period of several years, one consequence of which was the building up of a very thick file. Towards the end of the administration of the estate the question of the fee to the Turney, Burges firm came up. Burges thought $15,000 a reasonable fee, but he sensed some question about it on the part of the Michigan Trust Company, and in an effort to conciliate any adverse feeling on their part, presented a bill for $12,500. It was properly presented as a claim to the ancillary administrator, and he approved it. It was thereafter presented to the county judge, and he allowed it.

The Michigan Trust Company did object to it, and took an appeal to the district court. Its argument was that it could have handled the estate as trustee, and skipped the administration by the ancillary administrator out of which the costs and expenses arose. There was no little amusement among the lawyers of El Paso when they heard that John T. Hill, one of the attorneys for the Trust Company was going to cross-examine Burges on the pertinent questions relating to the probate law. For while Burges was a preeminent legal scholar, Hill, whatever other merits he had, could not make any serious claim to great legal scholarship. There was testimony from judges and others on what was a reasonable fee, and their opinions ranged from $12,000 to $17,000. The jury found it to be $12,500, and from a judgment for that amount the Michigan Trust Company appealed. When the Court of Civil Appeals handed down its opinion in the case, it held (1) the Michigan Trust Company could not have acted as ancillary administrator in this case without having first obtained a permit to do business in Texas; (2) it is the function of an administrator to see that all debts are paid out of the assets, and (3) the Trust Company could not oust the probate court in Texas of its jurisdiction over the estate, to see the debts were paid, and that its claim it could have handled the matter as trustee was therefore erroneous—the ancillary administration was necessary. The Court of Civil Appeals said, in effect, the Michigan Trust Company had been advised correctly by Burges, the services rendered to the estate were proper, and the fee for them should be paid.

XXX

Litigating Over Millions: The Yates Oil Field Cases

Soldiers find wars, and lawyers find out still
Litigious men, who quarrels move.
—Donne

ONE DAY in 1926 a driller brought in an oil well on a dry and scraggly ranch, not far from the Pecos River, in Pecos County, Texas. The well came in with a roar, and oil blew over the top of the derrick, some of it spotting a new dress worn by the young daughter of the rancher whose name was to become synonymous with riches from a fabulous oil field. Ira G. Yates consoled his daughter with the statement, "Don't worry about your dress, you can have a new dress now whenever you want it." Thus came into existence the fabulous Yates oil field of West Texas.

It was not long before it was the source of much litigation.

The California Company, a subsidiary of Standard Oil Company of California, had taken oil and gas leases from Yates on parts of his ranch in 1924, and also had taken oil and gas leases from Mrs. M.A. Smith, who owned an adjoining ranch. Other persons and companies obtained leases on other parts of these two ranches.

Litigation over these leases broke out early in 1927. It was multipronged, consisting of the Relinquishment Act cases, which were said to be the most important litigation ever to take place in Texas, the celebrated Turner vacancy case and related cases, the Mrs. M.A. Smith litigation, involving not only suits filed by her children, but also a multitude of suits filed by the receiver appointed by the judge of District Court of Pecos County to take charge of her estate, and finally, the suit by the state to recover parts of the Yates oil field lands.

The handling of this litigation on behalf of the California Company was undertaken by Burges and A.H. Culwell. It could not have been in better hands, for no greater lawyer ever lived than A.H. Culwell, and as already stated, Burges was preeminent in the legal field. In addition to being in contact with the representatives of the California Company in Texas, whose office was in Colorado City, Texas, the principal contact with the client was Oscar Sutro and Felix T. Smith of Pillsbury, Madison and Sutro, Attorneys, San Francisco, who were counsel for the company. The representation of the Calfornia Company in the Yates oil field litigation meant not only days and weeks but years of work and effort on the part both of Burges and Culwell in the Relinquishment Act cases, in the vacancy cases, in the Smith cases, and in the State cases. An additional lawsuit surfaced a short time later—an offshoot of the Smith cases—when in 1934, two of the Monroe children, Mrs. Ramsey and Mrs. Seeley filed suit against a number of parties, but principally directed at judges James Cornell, C.R. Sutton and Brian Montague, as well as L.W. Elliott, all of whom had had some connection or another with the receiverships of the M.A. Smith estate, and had been connected with various aspects of the litigation resulting therefrom.

The Turney, Burges, Culwell firm was engaged in the Relinquishment Act cases first. These cases had an interesting historical and legal background. Much of the lands of West Texas were set aside to the Public School Fund, and when sold by the state of Texas, each section was classified by the General Land Office as Dry Grazing or Mineral and Dry Grazing. If classified as Dry Grazing, the purchasers had title not only to the surface but also to any minerals thereafter discovered. But if a section of land was sold as Mineral and Dry Grazing, the purchaser received title to the surface only, and title to any minerals remained vested in the state. The state law set up a permit system under which anyone could apply for a permit to search, prospect for, and produce any minerals on land covered by the permit. Permitees were thereby authorized to go on the land of ranchers who owned only the surface and dig, drill, blast and whatever it took to do a job of mineral exploration, including driving across the ranch, creating tracks and ruts, destroying grass needed for cattle, and at times leaving open gates they had opened for passage way. They were, in general, a nuisance to the rancher, and were destructive of his property.

Moreover, once it got around there might be oil in West Texas, the ranchers felt they were entitled to its benefits, just like those who had purchased land classified as Dry Grazing. The legislature was in sympathy with the ranchers, and in 1919 passed the Relinquishment Act. It recognized the ownership of the oil and other minerals in the state, but authorized the landowner to act as the agent of the State of Texas in executing oil and gas leases on the land, the surface of which the rancher owned. For this service he would recieve one-half the bonus, delay rental and royalties, the other one-half going to the state.

Some of the Yates and some of the Smith lands leased by the California Company was "Mineral and Dry Grazing." The company had taken leases from the surface owners on the strength of the Relinquishment Act. But now the state had instituted suits in the District Court of Travis County, asserting the Relinquishment Act was unconstitutional, and other people were applying for "permits," and were likewise contesting the Relinquishment Act on the ground it was unconstitutional and void. Some of them filed suits for writs of mandamus directly in the Supreme Court of Texas. If they prevailed, the California Company stood to lose some valuable properties. The litigation over the constitutionality of the Relinquishment Act began early in 1927, and it was the subject of correspondence in the Turney, Burges, Culwell & Pollard office begun in June, 1927.

Culwell wrote to Felix T. Smith on June 14, 1927, advising that he and Burges had concluded Culwell should go to Austin the next week and investigate the pending litigation affecting the Yates' leases, and he should also go to Houston and Dallas and confer with lawyers for other parties there who were involved in the litigation. He stated in his letter, "It will be our purpose, unless you direct otherwise, to as actively participate in this litigation as the circumstances will permit." At this time, while there were other cases pending, the California

First gusher, Yates Field
[San Angelo Standard Times]

Company was not party to them, but he stated to Felix T. Smith the facts indicated that they should become familiar with the litigation so as to be ready for any developments.

His actions are indicated, at least partly, by the correspondence he carried on about the pending cases. On June 16 he sent a telegram to Claude Pollard, attorney general of Texas, requesting the style and court where pending cases were filed by the state involving the Relinquishment Act. On that same date he wired E.F. Smith, an Austin lawyer, inquiring if any of the cases involving the Relinquishment Act were likely to be tried soon. On the 17th, he wrote Oscar Sutro saying he would send him a list of the pending suits as soon as they came, and copies of the pleadings. On the 18th he wrote Sutro, and stated the pending cases were: *State of Texas v. Yates, et al; State of Texas v. Skelly Oil Company,* each pending in the District Court of Travis County; and also *Greene v. Robison, Commissioner of the General Land Office,* pending on a petition for writ of mandamus in the Supreme Court of Texas. He referred to Section 34, a Public School Land section, which Yates had leased to the California Company, as having been purchased by Yates from the state with the classification of Mineral and Dry Grazing; and indicated there were vast interests involved in the Relinquishment Act cases. He referred to provisions of the Constitution of Texas, and to a number of decided cases, and stated, "We are rather fixed in the view that the Relinquishment Act will be held constitutional." He proposed to intervene in the cases pending in the district court in Austin, and to assist in the defense of them.

On the 20th Culwell wrote about going to San Francisco for a conference and also sent telegrams to E.F. Smith, Austin, Judge John J. Hiner, Fort Worth, and H.M. Garwood, Houston, about going to see them for conferences about these cases. On the 23rd, he advised Felix T. Smith, he would leave El Paso Sunday night, be in Ft. Worth Monday afternoon, and be in Austin Tuesday morning. Shortly thereafter he was in touch with Judge Nelson Phillips of Dallas and Judge F.A. Williams of Galveston about meeting them in Dallas for a conference. About the same time he sent Felix T. Smith a copy of the Hickox application on Section 34, which he had obtained from the commissioner of the Land Office, and this was followed by a copy of the petition in the Greene case. There was still another mandamus case in the Supreme Court of Texas, *Thiesen v. Robison,* involving University lands, and he forwarded copies of an opinion by the Commission of Appeals in this case, which the Supreme Court refused to adopt.

About this time Burges wrote Felix T. Smith that Culwell had been hit by a car the previous week, and would be out of the office another week. He was soon back at work, and the next item we find is a letter to Charles L. Black of Austin, requesting a copy of his brief in the Greene case.

On August 12, 1927, Culwell sent a telegram to W.F. Vane, California Company, in San Francisco to the effect that "party" will hold open the matter of eighty acres in Section 34 until Tuesday, with a request that Vane be present for a meeting in El Paso on that day. On the 19th he reported to Felix T. Smith that on Tuesday Vane had been in El Paso, and had secured an assignment from "Bowen" covering the remaining eighty acres in Section 34, and this meant assignments have been secured covering all permits on Section 34. Bowen agreed to go forward with a mandamus suit, the work to be done by Culwell, at no expense to Bowen. He advised the mandamus suit should be filed against the land commissioner before December 7 to protect rights obtained under these permits. He also expressed his fear the validity of the Relinquishment Act would not be determined by the Supreme Court in the Greene case as counsel for Yates had injected a fact question, as to whether the land involved had been classified Mineral and Dry Grazing, which would cause the Supreme Court to dismiss the case for want of jurisdiction. He further stated that before he filed the mandamus suit, he would undertake to get an agreement from Yates' counsel they would not raise a fact question in it. Otherwise, suit would have to be filed in District Court of Travis County.

A month and a half later, in the first week of October, he urged that nothing must be left undone to perfect the title to Section 34, and to other sections similarly situated. He stated the mandamus suit would have to be filed, and as soon as he finished the trial of some cases in federal court, he would go to San Angelo to try to get Judge Hill, attorney for Yates, to waive any issues of fact, and proceed on the mandamus suit. By November he had prepared a petition for mandamus against the land commissioner and the California Company, and committed it to Paul D. Thomas, a prominent El Paso lawyer, to file and handle on behalf of the plaintiff. It was filed that month, and the case was headed for a decision by the Supreme Court of Texas.

Culwell was then in contact with Judge Nelson Phillips, of Dallas, and Judge F.A. Williams, of Galveston, both outstanding lawyers. Judge Phillips was a former chief justice, and Judge Williams was a former justice of the Supreme Court of Texas. Culwell suggested they should meet soon "to congregate our forces," and outline a brief for the respondents in the several pending Relinquishment Act cases. They agreed first to meet in Galveston, but decided later to meet in Dallas, where it developed Judge Williams did not intend to write a brief, and Judge Phillips was pressed for time in other matters, with the result they asked Culwell to prepare the brief, and he wrote it. These cases were argued before the Supreme Court of Texas on March 16, 17, and 19, 1928.

On August 29, 1927, the Turney, Burges, Culwell & Pollard firm became involved with another facet of the Yates Field litigation. They were employed by the California Company to look after its interest, as one of the defendants, in *Fred Turner v. A.N. Lea et al,* District Court of Pecos County. Culwell wired Hill, Neill & Hill, Attorneys, San Angelo, for information about Sections 34 and 35, Block 194, being Yates land, as affected by this case. This was followed soon by telegrams to Joe Montague, attorney at Ft. Stockton, to find out if the case would be tried at the next term of court, and a letter to H.L. Winfield, District Clerk, enclosing an answer to be filed in the case. It developed the case would not be tried at the next term, but the district judge directed the County Surveyor to make "a preliminary survey," and Culwell urged Felix T. Smith to see that the company had a surveyor of its own choosing present when this was done. On September 23, he was able to send the company office at Colorado City, Texas, and Felix T. Smith, copies of the court's order, and again urged the company to have a surveyor present when the county surveyor made his survey. He reported on it again on October 4, adding, it was his understanding the county surveyor does not really believe there is any vacant land. This was important, because the Turner suit was a "vacancy" case. Turner claimed there was excess land between, or partly on, the Yates and Smith ranches, not covered by existing surveys, and he had filed an application to purchase the alleged excess, at what was a nominal price. It was facetiously said, a vacancy is a long, narrow strip of land studded with oil wells, between existing surveys. It is an apt definition, and the battle was on, whether Turner could, in effect, muscle in on part of a great oil field.

And then the third ring broke out. On October 6, 1927, Culwell sent a telegram to H.L. Winfield, district clerk of Ft. Stockton, to send a copy of the petition and order appointing a receiver in *Smith v. Monroe.* They were then in the litigation wherein the Monroe children, and the receiver, were attempting to set aside leases on the Monroe Smith ranch on the ground Mrs. M.A. Smith did not have the mental capacity to execute valid leases.

Pollard, who had examined the abstract of title covering leases taken by the California Company wrote a memo to Culwell giving him the background of the Smith family controversies.

It appeared the M.A. Smith ranch, composed of some 22,000 acres, originally belonged to Mr. and Mrs. Monroe. He died many years before the discovery of oil, leaving his widow and six children. She then married M.A. Smith, and a part of the settling of this litigation is the fact he and Mrs. Monroe's children were at odds with each other, and the public apparently sided with the children. There had been an application for guardianship filed against her in 1916, and the court records show the question of her mental condition was tried before a jury, resulting in a hung jury. Another suit involving these parties was filed in 1920, but it was inconclusive. She had signed the various leases to different parts of her ranch, and they were outstanding when the Yates oil field was struck in 1926.

In early 1927 the case of *Smith v. Monroe* was filed in the District Court of Pecos County at Ft. Stockton. It was styled *W.A. & M.A. Smith v. Henry Monroe,* No. 1775 on the clerk's docket. On April 15, 1927, Jerry Monroe filed an intervention in the case, alleging

W.A. Smith was trying to acquire title and possession of Mrs. M.A. Smith's estate, and he had caused her to execute leases and mineral deeds. He also alleged she was incapable of handling her affairs, and prayed for a receiver. Judge Claude Sutton, the district judge, on that same day appointed W.H. Colquitt of Marfa, Texas as a receiver for the estate of Mrs. M.A. Smith. About this same time Ida May Ramsey, one of the Monroe children, employed James Cornell, a very able San Angelo lawyer, to look after and preserve the estate of her mother, and Mrs. Smith's children's rights in it, and she gave him a power of attorney in that connection. It was also about this same time the receiver employed Belcher & Montague of Del Rio as attorneys to represent him. They soon filed numerous suits against various oil companies and individuals to set aside deeds and leases on the ground Mrs. Smith had been mentally incompetent at the time of their execution. Among those sued were the California Company.

In the meantime, the Turner case required attention. Culwell was in touch with both Oscar Sutro and Felix T. Smith, in San Francisco, and with the California Company representatives in Texas about it. This case carried the threat of encroaching on the boundaries of several sections which the California Company had under lease, and taking away valuable oil lands. Felix Smith, under date of August 26, 1927, had advised of the filing of the Turner suit, but stated it only involved the Clint Jacobs lease, which was of slight value, and not worth an elaborate defense. But Culwell was always of the opinion it carried a definite threat to valuable leases of the California Company, and at all times urged on the company the necessity for making full preparation for the trial. Hill, Neill & Hill, of San Angelo reported if Turner was successful, the acreage in Sections 34 and 35 probably would be reduced, and Culwell again urged Felix Smith not to conclude, without additional, serious investigation that the company had no interest in it, stating, "Indeed, I have a distinct feeling at this time that sooner or later boundaries of Section 34 will be affected." He urged a study of the field notes in the Turner application and that the situation be analyzed. This all occurred in 1927, and it is of interest that Felix Smith wrote under date of March 3, 1928, just before the case went to trial, "I am glad you gentlemen finally concluded this litigation involves serious situations,'' to which Culwell replied, ''We knew so all the time, and have devoted lots of time to it.''

In January 1928, Culwell and Burges met A.J. Cunningham, who was the company's chief representative in Texas, for a trip to the Yates Oil Field. They stopped in San Angelo, and discussed it with Hill, Neill & Hill, and then went on to Iraan, in Pecos County. A surveyor went with them to point out the fixed objects on the ground, such as a mound of rocks, or an iron pipe set in the ground, which marked the corners and lines of the various sections of land involved. This enabled them to have a better understanding of the facts, including the visualization of corners and lines as delineated on maps they were using. The country was rocky, hilly, with ravines and arroyos across it, and as the objects they went to see were to be reached only by walking, they had a rough time of it, but they covered the entire area. They saw the original points used by Dodd, who made the surveys in 1918, and on which the company's holdings were based. They also saw the bearing points called for in the descriptions prepared by Dodd. Culwell reported all this to Felix T. Smith, stating, ''The time is at hand to actively prepare the defense of these cases.''

Culwell and Burges were both on hand in Ft. Stockton for the trial of the Turner case, which began March 6, 1928. Culwell could only stay for the first part of the trial, as the Relinquishment Act cases were set for argument before the Supreme Court of Texas on March 16, 1928, and he needed to be in Austin. He stayed for three days, during which time he helped present questions of law to the court, but he reported the judge knocked them all down as fast as they were presented. Burges remained for the rest of the trial, which lasted until March 19, 1928. Among the lawyers representing the several defendants were Hiner & Pannill of Ft. Worth, for the Transcontinental Co., W.F. Dean, for Mid-Kansas O. & G. Co., Rex Baker, for Humble Oil Company, Hill, Neill & Hill, for Ira G. Yates, and Wright & Gibbs, for the Smith-Monroe interests, which were also represented by Belcher & Montague under appointment of the court as attorneys for the receiver for Mrs. Smith's interests. Plaintiffs were represented by Gillis Johnson and Mark McMahon, of Ft. Worth, and Gossett &

Collard of Odessa. The case necessarily involved lengthy testimony about old surveys, corner monuments and boundary lines. At the close of the testimony all counsel for defendants were of the opinion they were entitled to an instructed verdict, but, instead, the judge instructed the jury to return a verdict for the plaintiff. The defendants ordered a transcript of the evidence from the court reporter, and began the work necessary to taking an appeal to the higher courts.

In the meantime, the Smith cases were burgeoning. In a short time after the appointment of a receiver and the appointment of Belcher & Montague as attorneys for the receiver, more than eighty suits were filed against various persons and oil companies holding leases from Mrs. Smith, undertaking to set aside these leases on the ground that she was not mentally competent to make them. They got around to suing the California Company in early October, and on October 6, Culwell asked the district clerk at Pecos for a copy of the petition and for a copy of the order appointing the receiver. The next day he advised Felix Smith, it was apparent the Monroe children would attempt to set aside the Smith leases on the ground that Mrs. Smith was non compos mentis.

Culwell at this time was engaged in a trial, in the federal court at El Paso, of *General Finance Corp. v. Penn National Hardware Mutual Ins. Co.,* a case of considerable importance to General Finance Corp., his client, and to him, and which it took all week to try. He was, nevertheless, at the same time keeping the wheels in motion with respect to the Relinquishment Act cases and the Turner case, and by the middle of October was engaged in work on the Smith case. He left on a Sunday for Colorado City, Texas, where the California Company had its office, and from there went on to San Angelo to investigate the Smith case and to confer with Hill, Neill & Hill, attorneys who were familiar with it. At the same time he discussed with the company the desirability of getting a written document from the Monroe children ratifying the leases which had been made by Mrs. Smith. He later reported a satisfactory meeting with the San Angelo lawyers, and shortly thereafter was on his way to Dallas to confer with lawyers there, who also were concerned on behalf of different defendants with these cases. This conference was held in Dallas on

October 24, at which attorneys for Humble, Gulf, Simms, Roxana, Mid-Kansas, Transcontinental Oil Companies, as well as attorneys for royalty holders, were all present. Some of them suggested the formation of a steering committee to handle the cases but Culwell and the attorney for Mid-Kansas opposed it, and they prevailed, although they all agreed to work together. The group agreed it was desirable to retain the services of a local attorney at San Angelo, and possibly one at Ft. Stockton, who had influence in the community and whose standing was good, for the purpose of collecting evidence on the questions of the sanity of Mrs. Smith, and not for the purpose of controlling or dictating policy of the litigation. Culwell was confident the fight between Mrs. Smith and her children was genuine, but he was also concerned whether they might later get together and join forces against the oil companies. He advised the California Company the interest involved to the defendants was so important they could not afford to sit idly by and make no preparation for a fight until it was actually upon them. Wright & Gibbs, San Angelo attorneys representing Mrs. Smith, stated she would defeat the intervention filed by one of her sons on behalf of all of them, and they declined any aid from the oil companies in that connection. They said Mrs. Smith contended she received value for these leases, she knew what she was doing and had no desire to rescind them. Culwell suggested the employment as local counsel in San Angelo of Hill, Neill & Hill. He advised Felix Smith, he assumed the company's Colorado office would shortly get in touch with the Monroe boys and undertake to feel out in a diplomatic way their attitude towards the California Company leases, but added he did not believe it safe to take anything for granted, saying, "Human nature is about the same all over the world, and as these properties become more valuable, the greater is the incentive to undertake to set aside the present holdings, and as soon as the Colorado office gets any advice we shall appreciate it if same will be communicated to us."

The latter part of November, the committee tentatively employed Williams & Jackson at Ft. Stockton, and were negotiating with Hill, Neill & Hill with reference to their employment. The question at issue in the negotiations seems to have been the amount of the fee, which was to be divided among the various defendants who were working together, in the proportion of their holdings, as determined by some of the geologists. There were other meetings thereafter, some in Dallas, some in San Angelo, and some in Ft. Stockton. The Smith litigation was many-faceted, involved many different people and companies as well as many lawyers representing various clients. It was a complex task merely keeping in touch with all those concerned, and being conversant with, or helping to direct, the different angles involved, and it took a great deal of time, legal acumen, and diplomacy. Culwell, in reporting on the status of the cases in December 1927, was opposed to entering into settlement negotiations with the Monroe children, as Mrs. Smith was insisting she knew what she was doing when she signed the leases, and he said any show of a feeling of insecurity weakened the company's position. He was, in short, in favor of complete preparation for a fight and not giving in an inch.

In January, Culwell was in San Francisco conferring about all the pending litigation. A short time later he arranged to get a copy of the proceedings of the 1920 case of *Smith v. Monroe,* and shortly thereafter he ordered from the district clerk at Ft. Stockton copies of the petition in *Colquitt, Receiver v. Whitesides, Monroe, Smith et al,* and which petition necessarily involved the sanity of Mrs. Smith. He had in the meantime filed in United States District Court at Pecos, Texas the case of *California Company v. Colquitt, Receiver,* for the purpose of trying the question of quieting titles to the California Company leases. It was his opinion the filing of this suit and the service of summons out of that case on the defendants would aid in effecting a desirable compromise, as it would show the defendants the California Company really meant business. In the middle of February, 1928, he advised, along this line that he would shortly be in San Angelo where he would try to ascertain what approach, if any, should be made to the receiver and to the Monroes. He was also busy keeping up with other similar litigation. The Roxana Petroleum Company had filed a suit in the federal court at Pecos, Texas, on January 25, 1928. He learned Roxana was not anxious to settle, and that it had advanced a substantial sum to Wright & Gibbs as attorneys for Mrs. Smith, assisting Mrs. Smith in that way in the payment of their fee. It appeared the cases at Pecos, Texas would not be tried before the end of April, whereas the state district court at Ft. Stockton would convene on March 5, 1928, where the California Company had three important cases, the *Turner* case, *Reid v. Lea,* and *Newman v. Lea,* all involving boundaries in the oil fields, and Culwell expressed the opinion these cases doubtless would be tried at that time. At the same time, in considering his March schedule, he noted the Relinquishment Act cases were due to be argued March 16 before the Supreme Court of Texas in Austin.

Early in January, 1928, Culwell indirectly sent word to Judge Cornell that he might be willing to take up with him the question of an adjustment with respect to the California leases obtained from Mrs. Smith. It was the opening feeler to see if a compromise settlement could be made. It was about this time he heard the Simms Oil Company had made a settlement with them, paying $50,000 as the consideration for the settlement.

Culwell and Sutro discussed the matter of trying to effect a compromise settlement, and they both were of the opinion, since extremely valuable properties were involved, that, even though the anticipated testimony in support of Mrs. Smith's competency to make the leases appeared to be very strong, and therefore they had reasonable expectations of winning such a suit, still they knew there would be testimony to the contrary, which would result in submitting questions of fact to a jury for determination, and this necessarily made the outcome somewhat uncertain. The result was, they both agreed it would be wise to explore settlement possibilities. Many suits involving other companies and people were filed, but neither Culwell nor Burges had any connection with most of them. A few other suits were also settled, as well as the Simms Oil Company case. While these matters were pending Culwell went to Ft. Worth for a meeting with lawyers in some of the other cases and came back by San Angelo. He advised Sutro he would be in Ft. Stockton on the first Monday in March, and Judge Cornell would be there, and, of course, he expected to see him. Things took a different turn the first week of March. Mrs. Smith had discharged Judge Wright from representing her in the cases, and the word was out she had made peace with her children, and was joining them to fight to cancel the leases. This is just what Culwell sometime earlier had anticipated was likely to happen. The defendants in the several cases pending were immediately of the opinion Judge Wright, who was aligned on their side of the cases while he was representing Mrs. Smith, should be continued in the defense of the cases, and they understood they would have to pay his fee.

Culwell wrote to Sutro outlining this, and stating what it was anticipated the fee would be, and added to his letter, "Mr. Burges has read this letter and fully concurs," and advised that he and Burges were leaving the next day for Ft. Stockton, for the trial of *Turner v. Lea.* He added "the fight at the present time is intense. Necessarily feeling is somewhat high . . . we are not the least bit panicky."

He reported under date of March 9 that certain non-resident defendants in the cases at Ft. Stockton had presented to the court a Petition for Removal, in which they alleged the joinder of their clients as defendants was a fraudulent joinder, in order to try to get the court to sign the Order for Removal on that ground. He advised the allegations of a fraudulent joinder had created intense feelings between parties and counsel on opposite sides of the case, and that some of the actions in the courtroom were disgraceful. The court signed no Order of Removal.

The intensity of the feeling in these cases was illustrated by Burges' account of an incident at one of the trials at Ft. Stockton. This was a small, western county seat, set amidst the great rolling ranches of Pecos County. It was typically western, and was still on the edge of pioneer life. Two of the lawyers from San Angelo, whom I will call Smith and Jones, on opposite sides of the case bore considerable ill will toward each other. Smith, wanting to look at a paper the other one had, asked Burges to get it from Jones for him. Burges did so, promising to return it shortly. During a recess, Jones asked Burges for his paper. Smith was standing outside the Courthouse, and when Burges asked him for the paper, Smith said, "Tell Jones if he wants it, to come and get it." This spelled trouble, but Burges said, "John, I promised to return that paper. Now give it to me." He did get the paper and returned it, avoiding what might have been an ugly incident.

It was at about this time Judge Cornell got in touch with Burges and Culwell and asked them not to take part in the controversy, stating he did not want to litigate with them. It was apparent he greatly preferred them to be out of the lawsuit, instead of opposing him. Culwell reported he would be in Austin the following Friday, for the Relinquishment Act cases, and while in Austin he would see Judge Cornell, and see what he had to say about a settlement. He did have conferences, a little later, with Judge Cornell and Brian Montague representing the Monroe children and the receiver, respectively, and during exploratory talks about a compromise settlement, Judge Cornell and Brian Montague intimated they might be willing to settle for a figure which they named, which was substantially higher than the Simms settlement, plus a certain percentage of oil that might be found in wells thereafter to be drilled until the value of the oil they obtained reached $100,000. They professed the greatest anxiety to settle with the California Company, and said they wanted Culwell and Burges out of the way, and they were willing to make considerable concessions to accomplish that result. To this Culwell replied their offer did not so indicate. These conferences lasted over a period of two or three days. One of the problems that developed was, recently there had been eight additional so-called "strip" cases, being vacancy cases similar to the Turner case, wherein the boundaries of most of the surveys in the Yates field were involved. Culwell said if it looked like they could reach a favorable conclusion with Judge Cornell and Brian Montague, some provision would have to be made to take care of the contingency that the boundaries of the California Company leases might be moved. He stated he did not express fear of the ultimate outcome of the strip cases, but said, "I discovered quite a while ago that any lawsuit is dangerous, and it is not impossible that a vacancy will ultimately be established somewhere in that territory, and this contingency should be considered in an adjustment with the receiver and the children, provided any of our lands are so located that they could be seriously affected."

Culwell's settlement negotiations obviously bore fruit, for on April 5, 1928, he sent a telegram to Oscar Sutro advising the Smith litigation had been settled, the consideration being the payment of a sum of money substantially larger than paid by Simms Oil Co., but without giving the other side any interest in oil to be produced in the future.

All that remained to do was close the settlement. This required a determination of just what papers needed to be written and executed, and what orders entered by the court. Culwell discussed this with Sutro, following which he made a trip to San Angelo for the purpose of having the proper papers executed. On May 12, 1928, he was able to report the settlement had been closed, and all papers and orders signed. There was an interesting follow-up on May 14, 1928, when he wrote Sutro, just as a matter of interest, that the testimony of the nurse upon whom he was relying as one of the best and strongest witnesses with respect to Mrs. Smith's good mental condition, showing she was of sound mind, had had her testimony taken in a case wherein Gulf Oil Corp. was the defendant. It turned out in this case that her testimony was very, very weak. She did not throw in the sponge entirely, but she was certainly not too strong about Mrs. Smith's mental condition, and this information was passed on to Sutro simply to indicate how wise they had been to effect the settlement which had just been concluded.

Culwell, in the meantime, early in the year had written his brief in the Relinquishment Act cases. The cases, of course, had been argued before the Texas Supreme Court on March 16, 17 and 19, 1928. The *Dallas Morning News* of Saturday, March 17, 1928 reported "Arguments involving millions of dollars in oil leases were begun Friday and will continue Saturday and Monday before the Supreme Court. The largest assemblage of lawyers ever attending the court was present for the arguments. So many interests were affected and so many lawyers here that at noon they held a meeting to apportion the presentation of the University of Texas Mineral cases." Friday and Saturday were devoted to cases with similar issues to be decided, but the Relinquishment Act cases were argued on Monday.

The entire group of cases brought some fifty lawyers to the Supreme Court of Texas on this occasion. They represented, variously, the State, oil companies, patentees of State land and their lessees, the University of Texas Board of Regents and others. They had expected adequate time for the lawyers interested in each of the two groups of cases to present their respective arguments to the court. Culwell, in January, had advised the clerk of the court he would make an oral argument, and he went to Austin intending to make an argument in the Relinquishment Act cases, but the Texas Supreme Court limited the arguments to six hours, each side to have three hours. This meant revising the schedule for arguments. They confided the task of making the oral arguments to Judge R.L. Batts, a former judge on the United States Court of Appeals, Fifth Circuit, and then a distinguished member of the Bar of Travis County; Judge F.A. Williams, a former judge on the Supreme Court of Texas, and one of the state's eminent lawyers, then residing in Galveston; Judge Nelson Phillips, of Dallas, who was a former Chief Justice of the Supreme Court of Texas, of preeminent standing and ability; ex-Senator J.W. Hill of San Angelo, who represented Ira G. Yates and had 91,000 acres of valuable oil lands involved; and H.C. Young of St. Louis, who represented Roxana Petroleum Company. They were giants in the legal profession, and Culwell was the equal of any of them, but in scheduling the arguments he agreed to forego making one, so the above schedule could be adopted. Judge Batts told the court the Relinquishment Act was constitutional and valid under a broad interpretation recognizing the desire of the Constitution's authors to develop the state school fund in a "common sense and democratic manner." Judge Hill was reported to have waxed eloquent, stating "sage brush, rattlesnakes and coyotes" are the main characteristics of some of the West Texas lands besides their value to the purchasers as oil producing acreage.

On June 25, 1928, the Supreme Court handed down an opinion in *Thiesen v. Robison,* upholding the Act, in a university lands case, and in *Frank v. Robison,* also a university lands case. At the same time it handed down opinions in six public school lands cases, *Greene v. Robison,* and others, including *Bowen v. Robison.* The main opinion was in the Greene case, and it sustained the validity of the Relinquishment Act. This meant the leases taken by the California Company on Section 34 and other public school lands in the Yates oil field, under the provisions of the Relinquishment Act, were valid, and the company was safe in its ownership of the minerals under these leases, at least insofar as they had been jeopardized by the attacks on the Relinquishment Act.

The situation at that time can be summarized by saying one assault upon the company's titles to its leases in the Yates oil field had been turned back by the favorable decision in the Greene case and the Bowen case. The attack made on the Smith leases by her children, and in which she later joined, and also by the receiver appointed by the court for her affairs, had been settled on a very reasonable basis, considering what was involved. This left the vacancy cases, the leading one being *Turner v. Lea.* The company, of course, had taken assignments of those who had filed for permits on Section 34, on the theory that a portion of it might be within a vacancy, and it was safely situated in that respect. Under date of March 23, 1928, however, and again on March 27, 1928, Culwell had advised the California Company that seven additional cases, similar to the Turner case, had been filed in Pecos County and in three of them the California Company was named as defendant and was interested in all of them. On May 4 he wrote the company and said they needed to prepare for the trial of these cases, and "lots of work remained to be done."

While all of the foregoing matters relating to the Yates field litigation had been going on, other matters were transpiring at the office as well. Turney was participating with the attorney general of Texas in the case of *New Mexico v. The State of Texas.* At the same time Burges was advising the interested parties in the method of handling the Hills estate, which had some novel questions in it. He was also getting ready for trial in another case involving Yates oil field property, this being done by him on behalf of a Major Quinby of New York. Culwell, while corresponding about the Yates oil field cases, had occasion to mention the trial of *General Finance Corporation v. Penn National Hardware Mutual Ins. Co.* and *Galveston Wharf Co. v. American Grocery Co.* During the same period of time one or another of Burges, Culwell or Pollard were busy with obtaining title to a site which had been selected just outside the city of El Paso for the location of an oil refinery by Standard Oil Company of California. In addition to the title work, there were questions to be resolved about the nature of the corporate organization to be set up, the naming of the company, which eventually was named Pasotex Petroleum Company, the organization of the corporation to hold it, obtaining a permit for it as a foreign corporation to do business in Texas; and similar questions for another corporation which would own a pipeline to run from Wink, Texas, to El Paso, i.e., from the closest oil fields to the refinery site in El Paso. This involved not only the other questions mentioned above in connection with the refinery, but also becoming familiar with the rules relating thereto issued by the Railroad Commission and complying with them. On February 28, 1928, Culwell sent Sutro the permit for the Pasotex Petroleum Company to do business in Texas, and on the 16th he advised Sutro it was satisfactory for the company to name W.H. Burges and A.H. Culwell to the Board of Directors of the Pasotex Pipe Line Company. Burges, in the meantime, was engaged in acquiring title to an additional twenty-six-acre tract of land adjacent to the refinery site. He went to Los Angeles to negotiate with one of the owners, and dealt with the others in El Paso, principally through C.M. Bassett, who had an interest in this tract, and who was anxious to see the company acquire it. He also reported the public reception in El Paso of the announcement that Standard Oil Company of California would build a refinery here was excellent. In fact, it may be said, the city was jubilant over the news the El Paso Natural Gas Company was building a line to bring natural gas to El Paso, and Standard, the Texas Company and Phelps Dodge Corporation all planned to build refineries in the vicinity of the city.

Phelps Dodge Corporation, which had mines and smelters in Arizona, had decided to build an electrolytic copper refinery in El Paso, doing it through a closely associated company, the Nichols Copper Company. Mr. Nichols insisted, as a condition of going forward with the project, that the City Council pass a resolution, agreeing never to take the refineries into the city. The resolution was passed on May 31, 1928, and it read:

WHEREAS, it had been made known to the Mayor and Council of the City of El Paso, and to the people of this municipality, that the Phelps-

Dodge Corporation and its associates, through a Company to be known as the Nichols Copper Company, or otherwise, contemplate the construction of a Copper Refinery in this section of country; and

WHEREAS, in the judgment of the Mayor and Council of the City of El Paso, as well as of the people of the City of El Paso, it is to the great interest of the City and its inhabitants that said Copper Refinery should be located at El Paso, Texas; and

WHEREAS, MR. WALTER DOUGLAS, for himself and his associates, had taken an option on approximately Five Hundred and Eighty (580) acres of land lying immediately North of the North Loop Road and East of the Spur Track on the Southern Pacific Lines from the main line of said Road, being Fort Bliss Spur several miles Easterly of the Eastern Boundary line of the City of El Paso; and

WHEREAS, it had been made known to the Mayor and Council of the City of El Paso that a reasonable assurance to those contemplating the construction of the said Plant that it would be left without the City limits of the City of El Paso and thereby relieve from municipal taxation until such time as it may, if ever, become necessary in the municipal life of the City to include it within the City Limits, would be effective in securing the location of said Plant on said property;

NOW, THEREFORE, for the purpose of inducting the location of said Plant at the point hereinabove designated, and for the purpose of expressing to such Mayors and City Councils as shall come after us, and to such people as may hereafter move into the City of El Paso, this consideration for the location of such plant at El Paso;

IT IS HEREBY RESOLVED by the Mayor and City Council of the City of El Paso, Texas, in meeting duly assembled, that during the period of time for which the present Mayor and City Council have been elected, the corporate limits of the City of El Paso will not be extended as to include any part of the said Plant as hereinabove referred to, and it is their opinion that said corporate limits of the City of El Paso should never be extended so as to include said Plant until and unless it becomes absolutely necessary to the future welfare and growth of the City of El Paso so to do, and to this intent and action on the part of the City of El Paso and its citizens, we pledge the good faith of the City and people of El Paso.

PASSED AND APPROVED this 31st day of May, 1928.

R.E. Thomason, Mayor

Attest: Herman Rosch,
City Clerk

It lasted for only about twenty years, before the city, in spite of said resolution, reached out and annexed the area in which the three refineries were located. Thus ended the solemn promise not to annex these properties. At the time of annexation, the city administration acknowledged the city was not in a position to furnish services to the refineries, and that the refineries did not need them, and promised to compensate for this by giving them a reduced tax valuation. But like other city promises, this did not last long.

Burges was concerned with the coming of all three refineries, and in addition to the work referred to above, wrote title opinions to each company with respect to the land each of them purchased.

On May 17, 1928, Burges reported the federal court in El Paso had set the cases of the Roxana Company and the Douglas Oil Company for trial on June 11. This, of course, referred to cases involving the Smith leases. He also stated there would be a special term of the District Court of Pecos County at Ft. Stockton on the next Monday following May 17, and he anticipated the plaintiffs would make every effort to try some of the cases pending at Ft. Stockton before the cases pending at El Paso could be heard. Apparently, they intended to make their first fight against the Gulf Oil Corporation.

Burges went to Ft. Stockton for the first day of the special term for the purpose of seeing that all the cases they were interested in were continued for the term, as he did not expect them to be tried at that time.

On May 21, Culwell reported the *Turner v. Lea* appeal by other companies was under way, but "our interest in this case is practically nil, indeed, our only interest is as it may affect other boundaries in that area." He then suggested the desirability of his client's representatives and he having a conference soon concerning all the litigation affecting boundaries in that field. On the 26th, he reported he had an appeal bond, and other necessary papers for an appeal by the California Company. He also referred to *Fred Turner v. Adams Royalty Company, et al* at Ft. Stockton, stating he was not required to answer in it until the first Monday in September, and it was improbable it would be tried before a decision by the court of civil appeals in *Turner v. Lea.*

Culwell was in Ft. Stockton in June, 1928, and on the 18th he reported what he learned there about the trial in the Gulf case.

On June 27 Culwell reported it seemed, that as an inducement to

Mrs. Smith to join forces with her children, the promise was made to her that no attack would be made upon her sanity. During the trial of the Gulf case at Ft. Stockton however, Mrs. Smith got word they were attacking her sanity and called for an explanation. The children gave her a letter saying no attack was made upon her sanity but they were simply endeavoring to show she was in feeble health. This partially satisfied her. But during the hearing before the master in the *Roxana Petroleum Company* case, testimony was published in the San Angelo paper wherein it definitely appeared they were directly attacking her sanity. Without notice to anyone she came to El Paso, went before the master and demanded to be put on the witness stand. Her examination consumed some two days. She dissolved partnership with the children, denounced everybody connected with the case and proceeded to tell the master she was thoroughly sane.

He further reported that opinion was divided as to the effect of her testimony, both sides contending they were helped by it.

On that same day, Culwell wrote Collins, Jackson & Snodgrass, attorneys, San Angelo, about the payment of rental on the Smith leases. His opening paragraph was typically Culwellian:

> It will be admitted that it is my purpose to make a sort of clearing house out of your firm. One particular reason for doing so in this instance is that I am not certain as to the particular attorney with whom to take up my subject, but am satisfied that if I happen to be in the wrong church, to say nothing of the pew, you will not disappoint me but will do the needful.

The question was whether annual rentals on certain Smith leases should be paid to Mrs. Smith or to the receiver for her properties. There seemed to be some difficulty in getting this ironed out, and the company did not want to pay twice, but at the same time it wanted to be sure it paid the right party.

Culwell wrote that if he could talk to Cornell, he felt he could make a satisfactory arrangement, but Cornell had had a serious breakdown and was not available. He also advised he was unable to secure a joint order from the receiver and Mrs. Smith covering payment of the rental, and eventually they decided to pay both parties, and see later about getting it back from the party shown by the court's decision not to be entitled to it.

On June 30 Burges wrote Sutro to the effect he had inflammatory rheumatism and was going to Long Beach, California, to the Virginia Hotel for ten days. This was a favorite place with both Mr. Burges and Mrs. Burges. Mrs. Burges had trouble with her health, and often found the climate of the southern California coast to be beneficial, and for several years Burges occasionally had rheumatism or neuritis, and when he felt like he needed a complete rest he would go to the Virginia Hotel. Between the time Mrs. Burges spent there, and the time he spent there, he said he felt like he had bought the Virginia Hotel, but never got a deed to it. Long Beach was a comparatively small place in those days, and the Virginia Hotel seemed to have been a delightful place to stay, and they enjoyed it to the utmost.

In the meantime, on June 26, Culwell advised Sutro the Supreme Court of Texas had handed down an opinion on June 25 sustaining the validity of the Relinquishment Act, and on July 3 he forwarded Sutro a copy of the opinion in *Greene v. Robison.* On July 27 he sent Sutro a copy of the opinion in *Ehlinger v. Clark,* the third important land case decided by the Supreme Court within a few weeks time. He stated the opinion in the Thiesen case was more satisfactory than the others, and that it was prepared by a judge who seemed to have greater ability than either of the other two judges on the court. On July 11 he advised Hill, Smith & Neill of San Angelo that *Smith v. Turner* was set for submission in the Court of Civil Appeals for September 4, and on the 12th, he wrote them about *Reid v. Lea, Surveyor,* stating the case was pending at Ft. Stockton, where court would convene the first Monday in September. His question to them was whether they were getting ready for the trial of that case, and whether there was anything they wanted him to do. On the next day he wrote Sutro acknowledging receipt of a check for the fee in the Smith litigation, and expressed to Sutro his sincere appreciation for the kind letter which accompanied it.

On December 20, 1928, the Court of Civil Appeals at El Paso had handed down an opinion in *Turner v. Smith,* reversing the judgment of the trial court, and holding there was no vacancy. The Supreme Court of Texas however granted a writ of error in the case, and it had quite a checkered career before that court. At that time the Supreme Court consisted of three judges, but to assist them in the work load, there had been created a Commission of Appeals. There were two branches of it, Commission A and Commission B, each having three judges. The Supreme Court referred the case first to Commission A, which wrote an opinion affirming the Court of Civil Appeals. The Supreme Court then withdrew the case from Commission A, and gave it to Commission B. It wrote an opinion also affirming the Court of Civil Appeals, and the Supreme Court then withdrew the case from Commission B. The court thereafter, in 1933, handed down an opinion written by Judge Pierson, joined by Judge Greenwood, with Chief Justice Cureton dissenting, in which they reversed the Court of Civil Appeals and upheld the district court. This of course had the result of holding there was a vacancy, and giving the title of it to plaintiff Turner. The California Company was not adversely affected directly by this particular holding, since Culwell had already effected a settlement insofar as the California Company's interest in the case was concerned.

The state, however, got into the vacancy suit business, and had filed among other cases *The State of Texas v. The Douglas Oil Co., et al,* this particular one being known as the California Company case. It likewise asserted there was a vacancy, and in its pleadings claimed all of Section 34, on which the California Company had a lease.

Burges handled this case for the California Company and spent a great deal of time in 1929 preparing for trial, and then spent most of January, February and part of March, 1930, in Austin in connection with the trial. In April of 1929 he was in San Angelo for depositions being taken by the state. When they were concluded, they went on to Iraan, in the Yates oil field, where the state took further depositions. When these were over, he and the others present for the California Company walked over the ground looking at and fixing in their mind the location of corners, markers, and boundary lines, so they would be familiar with them. This done, he went to San Angelo for a conference with Yates and his attorney. Burges was not satisfied with the survey that had been made of the land in question, and arranged to have another survey of it made.

He spent several days in September in Dallas working on various aspects of the case, and advised Sutro the court would take up all questions of law and preliminary matters and dispose of them on October 7. He also reported those interested on the other side of the case had offered to settle for $500,000, but they were told the figure was so high it would not even be submitted to the company. Nevertheless Burges passed the information on to Sutro, with the comment he thought the company had a better-than-average chance of winning, but that Section 34 was immensely valuable, and while plaintiff's case might not have been worth $500,000, the company was gambling a great deal more than that. He added it was a hard, bad case, and Sutro might wish to consider exploring the possibility of a settlement.

He was in Austin for the hearing on October 10.

In December he received notice that *Turner v. Smith* would be argued before the Texas Supreme Court on January 30, 1930, and advised the Clerk he would be present. He was busy in December seeing that his witnesses would be available, and was also preparing to argue before the Court of Civil Appeals at El Paso on January 9 the case of *Crawford v. White.* Part of the latter half of December, and including a portion of the Christmas holidays he spent in Pecos in connection with some injunction suits there relating to other parties.

After the argument before the Court of Civil Appeals in *Crawford v. White,* Burges went on to Austin and remained there in connection with the trial of the *State v. Douglas Oil Co.,* the California Company case, until the first week of March. The case was tried to a jury, but before the end was reached, he negotiated a settlement in it. There were several different questions in the case, as to vacancies, boundary lines and the like. He settled the whole controversy for $250,000, and reported some two or three days later to the company that from information learned after the settlement it had turned out to be very wise and fortunate. He learned the judge had said after the case was settled, he would have ruled for them on part of the case and against them on part of the case. The part on which he would have ruled against them would have required the company to make a refund payment to the state for oil taken from wells in the Bob Reid vacancy, and would also have lost the company this alleged vacancy, which was a sizable tract of land producing large quantities of oil. The net result was the company preserved its ownership and rights in oil lands worth a great deal more than the amount of the settlement, and therefore considered it had come off very well indeed.

XXXI

The Ateca Case: Suitcases Filled with $750,000

How quickly nature falls to revolt,
when gold becomes her object.
—Shakespeare

EVENTS IN MEXICO in late winter and early spring of 1929, gave rise to a situation which a little later brought Burges into another unusual and interesting case. In the revolutionary decade of 1910 to 1920, the state of Chihuahua, the north boundary line of which is, in part, the Rio Grande, was the spawning ground of numerous revolutionary movements. All had been quiet there, however, after General Obregon, ably assisted by General Elias Plutarco Calles, took over as president of Mexico in 1920, and effectively suppressed all other revolutionary movements.

In the first few days of March, 1929, there were reports of another revolution in Mexico. The first news of it however, was not from the state of Chihuahua. It was reported on March 4, 1929, that the state of Sonora, lying just west of Chihuahua, and Vera Cruz, on the Gulf Coast, were in open revolt. General Aguirre was said to be leading the revolt in Vera Cruz, which at the moment, seemed to be making headway. This news was followed on successive days by reports of heavy fighting at Torreon, where the Rebels were commanded by General J. Gonzalo Escobar. General Escobar continued to be a leading figure in the Revolution, and this episode was known, at least in the El Paso and Juarez area, as the Escobar Revolution. Ten days later it appeared a battle was expected south of Juarez that day; General Caraveo had joined the Rebels, and the Juarez groups had left Juarez for Samalayuca. The next day the Federals were still holding Juarez, and General Matias Romas crossed from El Paso into Juarez, and was in charge of the Federal forces there. El Pasoans also heard the Federals had arrested a number of officials in Juarez, including Mayor Augustine Gallo, Jorge M. Cardenas, the state tax collector at Juarez, Edmundo Herrera, night chief of police, as well as several others, and they were being held under heavy guard at the Military Garrison for possible court martial. This latter phrase had a fateful sound, as captured revolutionaries were apt to be dealt with in a summary fashion by a court martial.

On the 8th it was reported Rebel troops had moved up to within eight miles of Juarez, and were encamped at Mesa, and it was expected they would soon launch an assault on Juarez. Because of the imminent hostilities in Juarez, General George Van Horne Mosely, in charge of Fort Bliss, announced no firing across into El Paso would be permitted, and placed troops, with artillery, tanks and armored cars in position to enforce it. Soon the Rebels assaulted Juarez, and descriptions of the fighting appeared in El Paso newspapers. From various vantage points in El Paso, including those on the hillsides of Sunset Heights, the fighting in Juarez could be seen. The Federal troops were soon forced back from the center of Juarez to a position behind the levees along the banks of the Rio Grande, and El Pasoans could see them firing at houses held by the Rebels and the Rebels shooting back at the Federals. The battle did not last long, however, for the Federals were soon routed, and they crossed over into the United States. The United States interned 325 Federals, who were held at Fort Bliss after having crossed to the U.S. side for the purpose of surrendering. Juarez, it was announced, was again under revolutionary control, and Augustine Gallo was again mayor of that city. The news soon carried items ominous to the cause of the Rebels. Ambassador Morrow, American ambassador to Mexico, assured President Portes Gil of support by the United States of the Mexican government. The United States agreed to sell war supplies to the Mexican government, and Washington laid an embargo on the shipment of commercial planes to Mexico. This was to prevent planes being secured by the Rebels.

Two days later Rebel troops left for Torreon, and it was believed there was a big push on by the Rebels to capture Mexico City. But on the 11th it was learned the Mexican government had bought planes from the United States, and General Calles, commander of the Federal forces, had moved on Torreon. It was also learned General Jesus Aguirre had been defeated at Vera Cruz, and he offered to surrender if the government would guarantee him safe passage out of Mexico, but the government replied his surrender must be unconditional. This too had a fateful sound.

On the 12th it was heard a skirmish had been fought on the Torreon front, and the Federals claimed the Rebel forces had fled. El Pasoans read of an air attack by the Federals on troop trains moving south from Juarez, and the Rebels, on the 14th, claimed two victories below Torreon. But only two days later it was announced General Calles had captured Durango. Families of the Rebel leaders soon fled to El Paso, and Mrs. Escobar was a refugee there. Jorge M. Cardenas, a tax collector, as well as others connected with the Rebel movement in Juarez, had also crossed over into the United States at El Paso.

The Federals soon took Torreon, and General Escobar moved his Rebel troops to Juarez. The Rebels sent envoys to President Hoover to ask the revolutionists be considered as belligerents, and not as Rebels. On the 21st it was announced General Aguirre was to be courtmartialed. The following day General Escobar arrived in Juarez, where he was given an ovation and a huge parade. Juarez seemed to be in strong support of the Rebels, but at the same time it was reported the Rebels were seeking to smuggle gold and silver money into the United States, and the customs and immigration officials along the border had been directed to look out for this most particularly.

In short, it soon developed the Escobar Revolution had failed. All of its leaders who could, escaped across the Rio Grande into El Paso, and sought refuge there. They included not only General Escobar's family, but General Escobar himself, and among others, Salvador Ateca.

William Burges in his office on the 11th Floor of the First National Bank Building in the late 1920s.

Ateca was a native of Spain, a Spaniard who had become a naturalized citizen of Mexico, and who lived in Juarez where he was described as a capitalist and gambling concessionaire. He had attached himself to the Escobar Revolution, and was paymaster for the revolutionary forces. He was said to have brought into El Paso with him a large sum of money and negotiable securities of a value of over three-quarters of a million dollars, and the Mexican Government was moving high and low in the United States to have him and the money thrown back into Mexico, with the prospect his money and securities would be taken over by the Mexican Government, and he himself undoubtedly would face a firing squad.

Ateca probably would not be able to remain long in the United States. It was contemplated he would either be deported to Spain, his native country, or extradited to Mexico, where an unpleasant reception awaited him. The Mexican government was putting down the revolution, and the revolutionaries were persona non grata. Ateca obtained the services of W.H. Fryer, a well known El Paso lawyer, who had one time been county attorney, and later assistant United States district attorney. Through his efforts it was arranged with the U.S. Immigration Service for Ateca and his family, consisting of his wife and three children, to go by train to New York City, and there take a ship for Spain. Even so, it looked like it might be touch and go, for the Mexican government was exerting every effort to have him sent back to Mexico.

On April 30, 1929, Ateca and his family, accompanied by his secretary, A.G. Maquero, and R.B. Matthews, assistant director of immigration at El Paso, and W.H. Fryer left on the Golden State Limited for New York. On the night of May 1 they were in the Union Station at Kansas City when officers came up and arrested Ateca and Maquero. A complaint had been filed before the U.S. commissioner at El Paso, charging them with violation of American neutrality laws, to-wit, a conspiracy to purchase an airplane in the United States, and to transport it to Mexico, and warrants were issued for their arrest. Red Mohun, charged as a co-conspirator, was in jail in El Paso in lieu of making bond fixed at $2,000.

Fryer, however, had no trouble in securing their release on

posting bonds of $500 each. But it was evident the pack was baying closely on their heels, and he telephoned to Burges. He wanted Burges to be apprised of the situation, and to be ready to come to their aid, if needed, for with this arrest, the spectre of death for Ateca at the hands of a Mexican firing squad loomed nearer.

They proceeded to New York City, arriving May 4, 1929, and registered at the McAlpine Hotel. They had not been in the hotel long when there was a knock at the door of Ateca's suite. His ten-year-old daughter opened the door, and was thrust to one side as twenty officers—six members of the New York bomb squad, twelve secret service agents, and two detectives—headed by Assistant U.S. District Attorney George Mintzer, burst into the room. Ateca, Fryer and Matthews were arrested. The officers pushed on into the adjoining room, which was used by the children, and where several suitcases were located. They opened the suitcases, saw that two of them were filled with money and securities. They picked up Mrs. Ateca's purse, went through it, took out the money she had in it for her and her family's needs, and took Ateca, Matthews and Fryer, and the two suitcases to the U.S. commissioner's office at the old Post Office Building at City Hall.

El Paso buzzed with news of the arrests. R.E. Cunningham, law-partner of W.H. Fryer, and a fine lawyer who later became a district judge, was quoted in the newspapers as saying the arrest was wholly unwarranted, and was caused by someone ignorant of the facts, acting from the vilest of motives. G.C. Wilmoth, district director of immigration at El Paso, said Matthew's arrest was at the instance of a representative of the Mexican government, and was entirely without justification. He wired his department in Washington to call for a public apology by the representative who caused the arrest.

Wilmoth stated he had sent a telegram to the Bureau of Immigration at Washington saying Ateca could not return to Mexico without jeopardy and telling of his desire to go to Spain with his wife and children. He recommended authority be given to permit Ateca to proceed to New York under guard and to depart thence to Spain unless the Mexican Government indicated it would institute extradition proceedings. Wilmoth further said that prior to his sending the telegram a representative of the Mexican Government called at his office and criticized the Immigration Service for letting Ateca stay in El Paso. Wilmoth told him it was not the policy of the United States to deport even undesirable aliens when it might result in their execution as political offenders. On April 29 Washington advised him it would permit Ateca and family to proceed in transit to New York on posting a $100,000 bond. The bond was made. Matthews went along as a guard. Fryer went for the special purpose of giving legal advice for just such perplexities as had now arisen.

Burges' telephone rang May 4, 1929. It was Fryer, calling from New York City. He related the facts about the arrest, that he and Matthews were each allowed to make bond in the sum of $2,500, but Ateca was being held without bond. Come at once. Urgent.

It was urgent. The hue and cry raised by the Mexican government to have Ateca arrested and returned to Mexico was on. The complaint filed April 30 before the United States commissioner at El Paso, and Ateca's arrest in Kansas City on the night of May 1, 1929, were done, no doubt, by officers of the United States at the instance of the government of Mexico. It was made clear at the proceedings on May 4, 1929, before U.S. Commissioner Francis A. O'Neill, in New York City, the government of the United States was moving against Ateca in every way possible at the instance of the Mexican government. The United States was represented in these proceedings by Charles H. Tuttle, the U.S. district attorney. It quickly developed no written complaint against Ateca had been filed, nor had a warrant for his arrest been issued, nor had a search warrant been issued to search his hotel rooms and effects, and to take away any property he had in his possession.

Tuttle opened the hearing about 4:00 P.M. before Commissioner O'Neill with the statement, "As this matter, Mr. Commissioner, is one of some urgency, I have not as yet had an opportunity to prepare a formal written complaint, but I will do so immediately. However, at this time I make a formal charge to you verbally . . . on information and belief that these persons named (Salvador Ateca, Antonio Gomez Maquero, W.H. Fryer and "John" Matthews) have been in a conspiracy to aid the departure from this country as a fugitive from justice of Salvador Ateca, he having been arrested in Kansas City and there held on $5,000 bail on the charge of having violated the Neutrality Proclamation of the president of the United States and having sought to import into Mexico for the use of the so-called Mexican rebels certain munitions of war without permission of the secretary of state of the United States."

He went on to say that he, on information and belief, and the Mexican consul, charged Ateca and Maquero had looted certain Mexican banks and the public treasury of Chihuahua, and this was the source of the moneys and securities found that day in Ateca's possession in New York; and the Mexican government had formally laid claim to the money.

The commissioner said he did not know on what theory Tuttle was proceeding, and asked if it was on the basis of the Mexican government claiming a crime was committed in its territory. Tuttle replied he claimed the crime was committed in the Southern District of New York by the defendants, who were about to have Mr. Ateca take a ship to Spain.

In a hearing May 7, before U.S. Commissioner Garrett W. Cotter, Tuttle said the force behind these proceedings was not the Mexican government, but was the United States government, and read a telegram he had received from the attorney general of the United States, "Apprehend and if possible hold without bail Salvador Ateca, sailing for Spain with $200,000 loot. Mexican government claims stolen by him from Mexican banks in rebel area. Also take appropriate action to return loot to Mexican government. Appropriate instructions have been forwarded." It appears from the face of the telegram, contrary to Tuttle's statement, the motivating force was the Mexican government, but the proceedings showed the United States government was doing everything it could to satisfy the requests of the Mexican government. Tuttle also referred to a telegram he held from the Mexican government, and further said the United States government had an interest in backing up law and order in Mexico and in not taking a course which encourages fugitive revolutionaries. Further, the Mexican government was preparing extradition papers for the purposes of extraditing Ateca to Mexico, and this prevented allowing bail to Ateca. With this statement the commissioner agreed, and it appeared Ateca would be held without bail—in jail.

It thus appeared the forces of the United States government were being exerted fully, at the instance of the Mexican government, to return Ateca and the moneys he had, to Mexico.

When Ateca, Maquero, Fryer and Matthews were arrested and taken to the U.S. commissioner's office, the urgent need for the services of a New York lawyer was evident, and therein lay a problem. Fryer met one, apparently at the U.S. commissioner's office, or in the building where this office was located, on the 4th, and being in dire need of a lawyer, retained him on the spot. This was David P. Siegel, and he turned out to be an able advocate. The problem, as it developed over the next few days, lay in the fact that so many other lawyers wanted to represent Ateca. No doubt word got around quickly that, when arrested, he had over three quarters of a million dollars in cash and securities. Fryer wired Burges, who was still in El Paso on May 11, " . . . situation here involved because shysters and jail combers reached Ateca promising immediate relief STOP suggest wiring Ramiro Diaz McAlpin Hotel Atecas confidante it is inadvisable having multiplicity of counsel and to close with nobody until you arrive because Dudley Field Malone against our wishes interviewing Ateca STOP have been unable to see Ateca personally because rule Federal Detention Headquarters."

Burges, following Fryer's suggestion, wired Diaz on May 13, "I will be in New York Thursday and will see you on arrival suggest that you say to Mister Ateca that it is inadvisable to have too many lawyers in his case and I suggest he make no arrangements with anyone until my arrival."

On that same date Mr. Diaz sent a telegram to Burges in care of The Golden State Limited, stating that upon Diaz's strong representations to Ateca, "We compelled latest head counsel appointed by him to await your arrival. Meantime all matters are at a standstill. I had to fight too much politics and from now on you are to be the head advisor to handle all matters at your complete will in every respect. Suggest you telephone Fryer tomorrow on board Twentieth Century Train at Chicago station to get latest views, if any."

Fryer sent another wire to Burges on May 11 saying, "You will be here a week probably wire time arrival". On arrival in New York he had a busy time. He saw Fryer, talked with Ateca, conferred with Siegel and examined the papers filed in the proceedings in New York. He then had to determine what should be done next, for the control and direction of the case was in his hands. There were numerous telegrams to his partner, A.H. Culwell, in El Paso. On the 19th he wired Culwell to get all the cases in the federal court in El Paso, in which Fryer was counsel, continued, as Fryer could not possibly get home for cases set for trial. Four days later he wired Culwell the Mexican government claimed property given by husband to wife while solvent may be taken under Mexican community property law for subsequently incurred debts of husband, and to check Mexican law and advise whether this was correct. The answer was, it was correct.

On the 30th he wired Culwell he expected to leave New York on the following Wednesday, June 5, and reach home about the 10th, going to Dallas immediately, then to Denver, probably back to New York, and then to Austin. It showed a busy schedule, as all related to pending lawsuits or legal matters. But he did not get away from New York on the 5th. It developed Fryer was required to give bond on May 4 on the charge he was wanted in the El Paso District on account of being charged there with having conspired to violate neutrality laws by exporting arms to Mexico, and requesting he obtain a telegram from the federal district attorney's office saying no complaint of any kind pending against Fryer had been under consideration. And quick action was desired.

On June 4 he wired Culwell again. Matters had taken such a turn he could not leave, but hoped to be through by end of the week, and requesting he see the district attorney, and if warrant for Ateca and application for his removal have not already been sent, to have it done at once, and wire him when it is done, as "this is a necessary part of our program." On the 5th he sent another telegram, asking Culwell to have the commissioner (in El Paso) fix Ateca's bond at $5,000. On that same date Culwell wired Burges stating only one complaint was filed, and one warrant issued, the one served in Kansas City, where Ateca made bond for appearance in El Paso to await action of the grand jury. The matter had not been presented to the grand jury because the district attorney did not consider the evidence justified such action. Therefore, there was no warrant to send, and no application for removal was necessary or contemplated.

He mailed Burges a certificate from U.S. Commissioner Schmidt and an affidavit by Assistant U.S. Attorney Dodson. He added he had tried and won the International Sheep Co. case, and the Raynolds-Hatfield case. Burges wired Culwell again on the 5th that things were progressing satisfactorily, but fearfully slow and he might not be able to leave until the 15th, when the forty days allowed to present extradition papers had expired. On the 6th, he sent another telegram to Culwell—that he had copies of two complaints filed before Commissioner Schmidt giving the file numbers and requesting a certificate that no others had been filed, and asking for an affidavit from the district attorney that there are no pending indictments against Ateca and Maquero, and there is nothing pending on which an application for removal from New York will be made. A few days later there was another telegram to Culwell: "I think I am coming as well as could be hoped here, but I am making no rash promises as am up against the hardest game I have ever gone up against and no one can tell what or when the end will be."

In the meantime, the Banco de Laguna of Torreon, Mexico was pressing a claim against Ateca for $168,000. This was money which the bank asserted General Escobar had taken from it while the revolution was in progress, giving his receipt therefor, and the bank claimed the taking of the money was part of a conspiracy to which Ateca was a party, and he was liable. It further claimed the money which Ateca had with him was a part of the $168,000, but this it was impossible for the bank to establish, and indeed, there was little likelihood of it being at all true. A part of the pressure from Mexico came from the bank asserting this claim, which, for handling in the United States, it had placed in the hands of a Los Angeles lawyer by the name of Zach Lamar Cobb. He was well known to Burges, having earlier resided in and practiced law in El Paso. Burges sent Cobb a telegram on May 31 stating "Believe I can arrange settlement your claim against Ateca for twenty-five cents on the dollar, possibly a little more, I think this settlement is a win for your client, and I would make it if I were in your place.'' Burges, on that same date, sent a telegram to Culwell saying Fryer had been required to give bond, and asking Culwell to get the United States district attorney at El Paso to send a telegram to the effect that no complaint had ever been filed in El Paso against Fryer. He had his reply from Culwell that same date stating McCune had sent a telegram as requested, and adding the somber note that Lyons and Oppenheimer were both killed by a Spaniard today. They were El Paso lawyers, partners, who were shot in their offices by a deranged client. There was still another telegram on this date, a reply from Zach Lamar Cobb stating he appreciated the suggestion the case be settled by compromise, and, ''I hope you may be able to arrange acceptable basis. Have talked over long distance phone with one director and he insists on fifty cents on the dollar. If you can get fifty cents on the dollar I will insist on settlement.''

There were additional telegraphic communications and some letters back and forth, principally between Burges and Culwell. In one of them Burges stated he would be unable to leave until the 15th, when forty days had expired. This was the forty days prescribed in the treaty between the United States and Mexico, under which it was agreed a person held for extradition would not be released for a period of forty days, to give that much time for extradition papers to be forwarded.

On June 6, Burges again wired Culwell the affidavit from the U.S. district attorney with reference to Fryer was not satisfactory and to get the district attorney to send a telegram that no complaint was ever filed in El Paso against Fryer, and that there were no indictments pending in El Paso against Ateca and Maquero. This resulted in affidavits being forwarded by L.V. Dodson, assistant U.S. district attorney at El Paso, certifying no indictments were pending there against Salvador Ateca, A.G. Maquero or W.H. Fryer and no application for removal had been instituted on the complaints filed before the U.S. Commissioner A.J.W. Schmidt. There was also the affidavit of A.J.W. Schmidt, United States commissioner at El Paso, certifying to the complaints filed of May 1, 1929, against Ateca, Maquero and Phillip Mohun, relating to a conspiracy to export munitions of war to

Mexico and of exporting munitions of war, to-wit, one Eagle airplane to Mexico; and there are no other charges pending.

Work was going on day and night by Burges and those working with him to show there were no indictments pending against Ateca and the others at El Paso, the two complaints referred to were the only two pending in El Paso; bond had been made by Ateca on them at Kansas City, guaranteeing to appear in El Paso on these legal proceedings when required; and undertaking to defeat the complaint made in New York, to the same general effect about Ateca and the others entering into a conspiracy to violate the neutrality laws of the United States; and to undertake to prevent an extradition of Ateca to Mexico, if and when extradition papers might be received in New York from the Mexican government. It remained highly desirable to settle the claim of the Banco de Laguna, and efforts to make this settlement were under way. In connection with all of these proceedings, Burges went down to Washington to have a conference with the people in the State Department who were handling the Ateca case there. U.S. District Attorney Tuttle had stated at the initial hearing on May 4 that Ateca had been arrested upon directions of the United States attorney general, and these directions had come from the State Department. The State Department, of course, was acting upon the request of the Mexican government. Burges was outraged by the attitude of the people in the State Department with whom he talked, as he thought they were not well advised as to what the facts were, or what the consequences might be of the return of Ateca to Mexico, and that their attitude was arbitrary and completely pro-Mexican government.

Some progress was being made, however, as indicated by a letter written by Ateca on June 11, 1929, to Senor Tellez, Mexican ambassador to the United States at Washington, stating he was willing to return to El Paso when required in connection with the complaints filed there.

Other matters came to his attention while he was in New York on this case, as indicated by a letter of June 11, 1929, from W.W. Turney to him advising White & Case, a correspondent New York law firm, had approved a fee of $7,500 in the Candelaria case, and an order would be obtained to have the receiver proceed with the payment of same.

Burges had urgent business in Chicago and on June 15 went from New York to Chicago, where he stayed, as usual, at the Congress Hotel. A telegram to him there on the 16th from Fryer stated, "Our party may insist on settlement, even to the extent of one-half, and he would like for Burges to return to New York." On the 17th he received a telegram from Zach Cobb asking when and where he could see him. On the 18th there was another telegram from Fryer to him at the Congress Hotel stating he would like for Burges to return to New York and conclude the settlement. There was a second telegram that same date from Fryer urging him to use every effort to get the bank to reduce its claim to $40,000. He stated, "My knowledge of your important engagement is only thing preventing me from insisting on your return, practically the only thing interfering with closing matter is the attorney's fees which I believe you could resolve even in one day."

There was still another telegram from Fryer on the 18th stating, "Geer insisting on $50,000. Newly employed counsel conferred with us today. Ateca being arraigned on extradition this afternoon, and date will be fixed for hearing."

Another telegram from Fryer to Burges at the Congress Hotel stated Ateca's wife had employed a lawyer to recover her half interest in the funds; that Ateca offered to relinquish $200,000, but insisted that their fee and Siegel's must come of out of that amount, the balance of which would be paid to claimants. "In my opinion things are headed for a bad blowup due to outside interference and intrigues again developing. Your return advisable."

Cobb wired to say in order to get a settlement, Ateca must tender cash or the equivalent.

On the 20th Siegel sent a wire stating, "Ateca agrees to accept $214,000 provided he receives a Mexican passport to Spain. Important U.S. attorney at El Paso wire me either conspiracy action is dismissed or that no bail is required on it and that no removal proceedings will be initiated on conspiracy complaint."

There was also a telegram from Fryer on that date stating "parties plan is to leave for Spain immediately on release. Ateca's gruffness and insolence intolerable. Intervention of outsiders is creating nasty complications."

On June 21, McCune, U.S. district attorney at El Paso, advised Tuttle: "Two complaints are pending here against Ateca one for violation Presidential Proclamation and one for conspiracy to violate Presidential Proclamation Bond given in Kansas City on complaint charging violation Presidential Proclamation was held by the commissioner as sufficient for both cases STOP No removal proceedings have been instigated by this office and do not contemplate so doing STOP Bond requires Ateca to await grand jury here in October."

On the same day, Burges sent a telegram to Fryer stating the settlement was going through, adding, "I caused Cobb to come down $8,000 on the Torreon claim by staying in Chicago an extra day."

But three days later Siegel wired Burges again the El Paso district attorney's telegram "is insufficent, have him wire Tuttle immediately the present bond given by Ateca is sufficient for all purposes concerning any case in Texas against Ateca."

On the 25th Fryer sent a wire to Burges at the Driskill Hotel in Austin, Texas, stating, "No word from Mexico yet. Looks hopeless, will you be able to be here for the hearing? Ateca's attitude entirely changed and sound sense prevailing." There were efforts by Culwell in El Paso to get McCune, who was attending federal court at Del Rio, Texas, to send the telegram requested by Siegel and still another telegram on June 26 from Fryer to Burges at the Driskill Hotel in Austin stating the settlement had been rejected; that "Siegel as an attorney was entirely satisfactory but prefer you here. If we win extradition matter we still have the civil suits and questions of policy therein to determine. Your good judgment invaluable to Ateca."

On the 28th Fryer sent him a telegram stating, "Hearing set for Tuesday. Come without fail. Siegel expending large additional amounts for expenses and request you wire $700." He also sent a wire asking Burges to bring a copy in English of the penal code of Chihuahua. The next day Burges advised Fryer, "Leaving on Golden State, arrive New York, 8:25 A.M. Tuesday."

The extradition hearing began on June 29. It was not concluded until July 3. It developed there was not sufficient showing of an extraditable offense, and on July 3, the U.S. commissioner discharged Ateca. He was, for the first time since his arrest on May 4, free from jail. Burges sent a telegram to Culwell that Ateca had been discharged after the hearing, and he would be in El Paso the next week on civil cases. However, progress in the civil cases was slow, and he soon found he would be in New York until the middle of the next week or possibly longer. Burges did stay there for a week or so working on the civil cases, and finally felt compelled to leave, returning to El Paso. On July 15, Siegel sent a long telegram to Burges at El Paso with respect to the affidavits supporting an attachment which was made for the purpose of attaching the funds Ateca had with him, and advising that the Motion to Vacate the Attachment had been adjourned until July 23 for hearing. He requested evidence, if available, to controvert these affidavits.

One affidavit for the attachment was by E.C. Monteverde, residing in Los Angeles, who was employed by the Mexican government as an agent in the Department of Labor and Commerce. His affidavit stated he was stationed at Torreon in March of 1929; he became a revolutionist with Escobar in Escobar's personal headquarters; was directed by Escobar to telegraph from Chihuahua City to Ateca in Juarez concerning purchase of an airplane, and that Ateca replied he had paid for an airplane. Another affidavit was by Elena de Goldbaum Padilla, then living at the La Salle Apartments in El Paso. She stated her husband, Enrique Goldbaum Padilla, was a lieutenant colonel on the Escobar staff; he was wounded and brought to El Paso on April 7, 1929, and was removed to Providence Hospital in El Paso; she asked Escobar for funds, and he wrote an order to Ateca to deliver her $1,500 for medical attention, and the photostat of that order was attached to the papers; and she tried to get the money from Ateca, but he never paid it. There was a similar affidavit from Enrique Goldbaum Padilla. A fourth affidavit was made by Francisco Lascas of Los Angeles who stated he saw Juan de la Vega in March 1929, go to Ateca's headquarters in Juarez and obtain money and casually pay it to troops. Still another affidavit was to the effect that it was the general understanding Ateca was acting as financial agent for

General Caraveo. Licenciado Jose Zurita of Torreon made an affidavit that Escobar, under command of Castellanos, entered the banking house of the Banco de Laguna and took moneys and gave receipts for them; and Ateca was considered as the person in charge of handling the moneys. And there were other affidavits to similar effect.

Burges replied to Siegel by telegram of July 16 stating he would give these affidavits immediate attention and tried to obtain contradictory affidavits.

On August 29, Siegel was able to wire Burges, the state supreme court had that day vacated the Banco de Laguna attachment against Ateca, and also had decided the court would not entertain jurisdiction, and therefore dismissed the entire cause of action against Ateca. His telegram added, "Believe you are in position to close out matter. My opinion imperative this must be done immediately."

There remained the matter of clearing up the civil suits, and getting Ateca, with his funds, on his way to Spain. Ateca was still in New York through August and into September, but before the month was over he had been able to leave New York for Spain. The suit of the Banco de Laguna was settled by Burges with Zach Lamar Cobb for $10,000 and Ateca's waiver of any action against Banco Laguna for damages or libel. It was also ascertained the U.S. district attorney at El Paso did not expect to secure the indictments against Ateca out of matters pending here, and the complaints against Ateca in El Paso were not apt to be brought up for hearing. It thus developed Atecas's troubles were mostly over. There remained only the matter of payment of fees to Siegel, Fryer and Burges. Burges' fee was $25,000 including all expenses, including outlays on behalf of Ateca (an itemized statement of which showed they amounted to approximately $10,000) leaving a net balance for his fee of $15,000. It had been a long hard summer. There was much he was trying to keep up with on other matters pending which took him to Chicago, Denver, Dallas and Austin, and as soon as he could get away in the middle of August, he went to Long Beach, California to join Mrs. Burges at the old Virginia Hotel for a well-earned vacation.

XXXII

Thomas B. Love: "Tellest Thou Me of Ifs?"

Off with his head! So much for Buckingham.
—Shakespeare

IN 1930 THERE AROSE a case of unusual political interest, and which raised interesting legal questions.

In 1928 the National Democratic Party nominated Al Smith of New York for president. The Republicans nominated Herbert Hoover. Smith had a long and distinguished political career in New York and in 1928 was governor of that state. But he was an antiprohibitionist—a wet—and he was also a Catholic. Hoover, born a Quaker, likewise had a long and distinguished career in government service, and in 1928 he was secretary of commerce.

The prohibition sentiment was strong in Texas in 1928, and, the people, overwhelmingly protestant, had a strong current of anti-Catholic feelings. A majority still lived in rural areas, or in small towns, and the urban influence was small.

No sooner was Al Smith nominated and his supporters singing "The Sidewalks of New York" than some of the rock-ribbed Democrats of Texas began to show signs of disaffection, so much so, that a majority of the Texas voters, in 1928, voted for Hoover. Those Democrats who remained regular, and voted for Smith, felt outraged that other Texas Democrats would bolt the party and turn against its nominee.

Tom Love, long active in political circles in Texas, and who had held various political offices, was one who bolted. I am not prepared to say whether he was influenced mostly by Al Smith's pro-wet pronouncements, or by his religion, but Love voted for Hoover.

In 1930 Thomas B. Love filed with the State Democratic Executive Committee his petition to have his name placed on the ballot in the Democratic primary as a candidate to be the Democratic nominee for governor of Texas. In his application he stated he was a resident of Dallas County, giving an R.F.D. number, Lancaster, Texas; his occupation was "lawyer and farmer." He was a member of the Democratic party, and he voted for everyone on the Democratic ticket in 1928, except he voted for the electors for Hoover. His statement read:

> I am a Democrat, affiliating with the Democrat Party as I have all my life. At the last general election I voted for every candidate on the Democratic ticket for United States senator to constable, inclusive, and I voted for the Hoover electoral ticket. I participated in the Presidential Primary Convention of 1928, and in the county and state Conventions and took the required pledge, expressly declaring that neither in law nor in morals could any such pledge bind a voter to violate his conscience in casting his ballot at the general election.

He continued with a statement or argument in favor of his conscience not being bound by the pledge. It was, in effect, a statement he would vote the ticket straight "if his conscience would permit him to do so."

At a meeting thereafter of the State Democratic Executive Committee, a resolution was adopted to the effect that no one's name would be placed upon the ballot in the Democratic Primary unless it appeared:

> That in the last preceding general election he must not have voted against any nominee or presidential elector of the Democratic Party, if he participated either in the primary election or conventions of the Democratic Party in 1928, and took a pledge to support the nominees of the Democratic Party.
>
> That he must in good faith, without any reservations, pledge himself in writing filed with the chairman of the Executive Committee not later than the date set for filing applications.
>
> And that he does not now advocate a voter's entering a party primary or convention and taking the prescribed pledge, with reservations, mental or otherwise.

The committee refused to put Tom Love's name on the ballot in the Democratic primary, and on Februrary 24, 1930, he filed in the Supreme Court of Texas a petition for a Writ of Mandamus against the committee to require it to put his name on the ballot. The petition was signed by Thomas B. Love as relator and by twenty lawyers, all well-known, prominent attorneys in the State of Texas. Seven of them were from Dallas, but geographically they covered a wide area extending from Beaumont to Alpine and from Del Rio to Dangerfield.

The Democratic Executive Committee was represented by six of Texas' most eminent lawyers, all of whom volunteered their services. They were: F.A. Williams of Galveston, H.M. Garwood of Houston, William H. Burges of El Paso, Rice Maxey of Sherman, V.W. Taylor of Brownsville, and C.C. Renfro of Dallas. They divided among them the work of preparing a brief on behalf of the committee. They countered Love's petition with four propositions: (1) The Committee was legally authorized to prescribe the qualifications of those who participate in the party primaries. (2) The Committee was vested with the duty of determining whether a prospective candidate is a Democrat or not, and entitled to be on a Democratic ballot. (3) Relator is not entitled to be put on said ballot, since the committee has filed a verified answer denying he is a Democrat and affiliates with the Democratic party, and (4) Relator has not come into court with clean hands, but has violated and repudiated his pledge to support the nominees of the party and now asserts he has a moral and legal right to repudiate the pledge which he will be required to take in 1930, and this honorable court should refuse any relief to relator. The fourth point Burges undertook to cover in the brief. He did not spare Tom Love. He stated Love shamelessly alleged in his petition that in 1924 he supported the Repubican candidate (Butte) for governor of Texas, and in 1928 he entered the Democratic primaries, both presidential and state, and took the pledge prescribed by the State Executive Committee and authorized by the statute of this state . . . expressly declaring his purpose to violate his pledged word, if to be true to said pledge violated what he is pleased to call his conscience. He then quoted at length from Edmund Burke's "Thoughts on the Causes of the Present Discontents" where Burke described a political party and discussed the necessity of party members remaining true to the party and its nominees, and scoring those who would not do so, i.e., the bolters. He thereafter stated:

> We submit it as inconsistent with good morals or even common honesty to declare one's affiliation with men whose principles and desires he avows agreement with only to thwart.
>
> When a man enters a primary with the formed design, and purpose of voting aginst the nominees of that party, if such nominees happen not to be those of his choice; takes a pledge he intends to break in order to act with thousands of his countrymen with whom he, with falsehood on his lips and party treason in his heart, pledges his loyalty in order to get the double chance of defeating enemies within the party if he can at the primary or afterwards in the general election, if the first act of perfidy prove ineffectual, he stains his hands so that by no rule of authority or reason is he entitled to invoke at the hands of a court of justice the issuance of a discretionary writ to put him in a position to either lead or betray as time and circumstance may in the future determine.

He quoted the language of Chief Justice Phillips in *Westerman v. Mims,* 111 Tex. 29, at 38; 227 S.W. 178:

> If in the face of this statute one who makes that pledge is only morally, but not legally, bound to observe it, the statute is a farce. It means that the statute has no virtue as a law, but is only a moral sanction. It was not needed as a moral sanction. It would be bad morals to violate such a pledge though there were no statutes on the subject. The moral obligation would exist without the statute.

The exact language covered by this point was quoted by him from *Love v. Taylor.* The opinion was written by Chief Justice Fly of the San Antonio Court of Civil Appeals in July 1928. In this case the same Thomas B. Love in 1928 had sought to compel the Democratic Committee to place his name on the ballot as a candidate for lieutenant governor, but was unsuccessful because he had announced he would not support the nominee of the party for president, and now Burges quoted in the brief from Judge Fly's language in the opinion in the 1928 case:

> However that may be, and regardless of whether the County Committee or its sub-committee did not have the authority to refuse to place appellant's

name on the primary ticket, he is in no position to seek aid and assistance from a court of equity, under his own admissions. The maxim is as old as equity itself that 'he who comes into a court of equity must come with clean hands,' or as sometimes forcefully expressed, 'he that hath committed inequity shall not have equity.' Pom. Eq. Jur. 397. Under the facts of this case, which perhaps has not a parallel in the history of political parties, a man is seeking not only to participate in the counsels of the party, but to have himself presented as a candidate for the second highest office of the executive department of the state, at the same time that he is entering into a conspiracy with the enemies of the party whose honors he is seeking, and endeavoring to defeat men who have already been nominated by the highest authority of the party to the two chief offices of the republic. Can he be said to come into a court asking for equitable relief 'with clean hands?' He makes professions of loyalty to and faith in the Democratic party, but his acts belie his words and besmirch his political record with insincerity and disloyalty. His works destroy his profession of party faith, and break down all protestations of love and fealty. As said in holy writ: 'for as the body without the spirit is dead, so faith without works is dead also.' In this instance, however, it is worse than a profession of faith without works to evidence it, for it is a faith professed with works directly against it.

But the stinger was yet to come, because at the end of the brief on this proposition, Burges ended it with the following statement:

The rule of conduct for a great party fighting for its life, and for the welfare of the state, and the very language of its answer to one who asks for its honor, but offers only a conditional loyalty can be found in the second scene of the fourth act of Colley Cibber's version of Shakespeare's *Richard III.* Richard says to Buckingham:

Tellest thou me of ifs? Thou art a traitor!
Off with his head! So much for Buckingham!

At the subsequent hearing before the supreme court the only thing that seemed to get under Love's skin was the Shakespeare quotation.

The supreme court, however, took the attitude it was not a man's past record, but his present promises that governed whether he was entitled to be considered a member of a political party or not, and ruled in favor of Love. *Love v. Wilcox,* 119 Tex. 256, 28 S.W. 2d 515. Based upon the prior decisions of appellate courts in this state, this was bad law, but it was good politically. Tom Love was making loud and resounding noises, and claimed to be the leader of a dominant faction in the Democratic Party in the State of Texas. The supreme court settled that point. They ordered his name put on the ballot, and when the election came off, he got only a minority of the votes. His political career was ended.

XXXIII

The Banco Cases

Our lands from foreign judgments free.
—Anonymous

IN JANUARY 1931, Mrs. Allie D. Clardy and her daughter, Mrs. Josephine Clardy Fox, who in prior years, had been occasional clients of Turney & Burges, came to see Burges. She brought citations served on them on January 21, 1931, in the case of *San Lorenzo Title & Improvement Co. v. Allie D. Clardy, Josephine Clardy Fox and Eugene Fox.* It was a Trespass to Try Title case. The San Lorenzo Title & Improvement Company, which described itself as a common law trust composed of Sydney Smith, an El Paso lawyer; Edward D. Tittmann, a lawyer then living in Hillsboro, New Mexico; Alfredo Urias, a lawyer of Juarez, Mexico; John W. Penn, an El Paso lawyer associated with Sydney Smith; and Felipe Seijas, of Juarez, Mexico. The trust sued for title and possession of a farm belonging to Mrs. Clardy and Mrs. Fox, containing approximately six hundred acres. It was a part of the San Lorenzo banco, situated approximately where the Clardy-Fox Addition to the city of El Paso now lies. The International Boundary Commission in 1930 declared this tract had been segregated from Mexico in 1898, and the commission took action to transfer jurisdiction to the United States. There was, in fact, a whole series of cases filed about that time by the San Lorenzo Title & Improvement Company, covering the entire banco.

Burges was also counsel, with his brother Richard F. Burges, in the City Mortgage Co. and the Caples cases, as well as in the Willis case in the U.S. District Court at El Paso.

These cases grew out of the vagaries of the Rio Grande. The First Congress of the Republic of Texas, meeting in 1836, by an act passed by it, fixed the boundaries of the Republic of Texas, "beginning at the mouth of the Sabine River, and running west along the Gulf of Mexico three leagues from land, to the mouth of the Rio Grande, thence up the principal stream of said river to its source . . . " This boundary was confirmed by the Treaty of Guadalupe Hidalgo which settled the affairs between the United States and Mexico at the end of the Mexican War, and the middle of the river or of its deepest channel remained the boundary between Texas, which before then had become one of the United States, and Mexico.

The Rio Grande could be turbulent at times, before several dams were built on it to impound flood waters for irrigation, and at the same time protect the lands below the point of origin of flood waters from its ravages. The floods meant that from time to time, sometimes annually, the channel of the river was changed by the floods, sometimes by eating away, piece by piece, a sandbank forming the bank of the channel of the river, so within a few days – or perhaps hours, by the process of erosion, the location of the river channel shifted toward one side or the other of the river valley. At other times, flood waters would cut sharply across a piece of land, cutting a new channel, and leaving the old one dry, this being termed avulsion. Under international law, the boundary between the two countries followed the center of the main stream of the river when it was changed by erosion, but the boundary did not change with the river when the change was by avulsion.

This had resulted in hundreds of areas, most of them comparatively small, up and down the river, from Brownsville to El Paso where, due to an avulsive change, a tract of land belonging to one country was on the other side of the river. The Mexican term "bancos" was applied to them.

Later treaties between the United States and Mexico undertook to solve the problems arising out of the existence of the bancos. The Treaty of November 12, 1884 declared the middle of the river, or its deepest channel to be the boundary, except in cases of avulsive changes.

The Treaty of March 1, 1889, set up The International Boundary Commission to determine whether changes in the river were by erosion or avulsion. The Treaty of March 20, 1905, provided for the elimination of bancos avulsively created. In essence, it provided for the relevant facts to be determined by the commission, and for the transfer of the bancos to the nation on whose side of the river they lay. The treaty was negotiated on the basis that sovereignty of the bancos was in dispute, and their elimination would not amount to ceding of Mexican territory, as the representatives of the Mexican government steadfastly maintained they had no authority to cede Mexican territory.

Burges went to work briefing these cases with his usual indefatigable energy. The lands comprising the San Lorenzo banco had long been on the north bank of the Rio Grande, with sovereignty exercised over it by the State of Texas, and in possession of various owners who held under patents issued by the State of Texas. He did not propose to allow claimants under a recent Mexican title to take this land away from its long-time owners.

The San Lorenzo Title & Improvement Company, on May 26, 1931 filed its First Amended Original Petition, and in it set out fully the facts and circumstances on which it relied. They alleged that prior to October 2, 1930, plaintiff was lawfully possessed of the land in question, about six hundred acres, and on October 2, 1930, defendants unlawfully ejected the plaintiff from said premises and withheld possession of same. This property was alleged to be part of the San Lorenzo banco No. 302, which plaintiff described by metes and bounds.

Plaintiff further alleged, prior to March 21, 1930 the San Lorenzo banco was located within the limits of the state of Chihuahua, Republic of Mexico, but was on the left side of the Rio Grande, and on March 21, 1930 the International Boundary Commission classified said land as a "banco" and eliminated the same as the San Lorenzo banco No. 302; that the Treaty of 1848 between the United States of America and the United States of Mexico provided the center of the then "deepest channel of the Rio Grande River" should be the boundary line between the two countries, and it was surveyed and fixed by a line known as the Emory-Salazar Boundary Line of 1853, but thereafter there were frequent changes in the course of the river and many tracts of land were cut off from the country to which they belonged. Plaintiff further alleged the Treaty of 1889 created an International Boundary Commission, and later the two countries executed the Treaty of 1905, one purpose of which was to eliminate the bancos in the Rio Grande River from the effects of Article II of the Treaty of November 12, 1884. It also alleged, on March 21, 1930, the International Boundary Commission found the said San Lorenzo banco No. 302 was a true banco; in 1898 it had been cut off from Mexico by avulsion; and on the date of said finding and prior thereto it had been a part of the United States of Mexico, and on said date the International Boundary Commission eliminated San Lorenzo banco No. 302, whereby the said land was ceded to and became a part of the territory of the United States of America. Plaintiff asserted this land had been carried on the tax books in the city of Juarez, Mexico since 1898, and that Alfredo Urias of Juarez, on August 6, 1926, filed a petition in the Court of First Instance of the Municipality of Juarez, Republic of Mexico, alleging this was vacant land and, after publication of notice in Mexico, the court entered an order declaring it to be vacant, and ordered it sold. Urias bid on it, and purchased the land under the order of the court, for $300 pesos. Urias thereby purported to have acquired, for the equivalent of $150 U.S., title under Mexican law to the San Lorenzo banco, the value of which was in the hundreds of thousands of dollars at that time.

The litigation therefore appeared to focus on the claim that the San Lorenzo banco, which had long been held as a part of El Paso County, Texas, was in fact a part of Mexico up until March 21, 1930, and Alfredo Urias, by legal proceedings in Juarez, Mexico purchased it for $300 pesos by a sale made under order of a Mexican court, and approved by that court on August 31, 1927.

While Sydney Smith was the moving person among the El Paso lawyers involved in this lawsuit on behalf of the plaintiff, he did not sign the petition. It bore the names of McKenzie, Walthall and Gamble, Knollenberg and Cameron, Joseph U. Sweeney and J.E. Quaid as attorneys for plaintiff and was signed on their behalf by E.F. Cameron.

Plaintiff having pled its case in detail, including detailed references to and quotations from the Treaty of Guadalupe Hidalgo in 1848, the Treaties of 1884, 1889, and 1905, and from the court records in Juarez upon which it relied, together with the quotations from the laws of Mexico alleged to be applicable, Burges filed an answer consisting of a general demurrer. This, in effect, said plaintiff had not stated a cause of action. The legal position which he took was that the treaty, under which the plaintiff claims, was effective, if ever, as between the United States of Mexico on March 20, 1905, and as between all others not later than June 5, 1907; and since plaintiff affirmatively pleads the first step it took in acquiring title of this property was on August 6, 1926, long after title to it was vested in the United States under said treaties, plaintiffs acquired no title to the premises in controversy by reason of judicial proceedings in Mexico begun in 1926. Burges urged that since plaintiff pled the land had been in the actual territorial jurisdiction of the United States since 1898, and since the treaty was entered into in 1905, the proceedings in the Mexican court begun in 1926 and terminated, as plaintiff claims, in October 1930, were void because the land affected was without the jurisdiction, *de jure* or *de facto,* of the Mexican court, and such proceedings therefore vested no title in the plaintiff.

He also attacked the regularity and sufficiency of the pleadings in the Mexican court as shown by the allegations contained in Plaintiff's First Amended Petition. He stated, additionally, it must be held the treaty did not undertake to make a cession of the territory, but merely made a readjustment of boundary, and therefore it must be assumed the land had always been in Texas, and the proceedings in the Mexican court concerning it were therefore void. He added the government of the United States is without authority to cede any portion of the territory of a state, and by the terms of the treaty did not attempt to do so. The main issue in the case thus outlined was whether the San Lorenzo banco was transferred to the United States by the terms of the Treaty of 1905, or was the transfer not effected until the International Boundary Commission acted on March 21, 1930.

He cited a number of cases from the Supreme Court of Texas, and from the Supreme Court of the United States, as well as from other jurisdictions. The leading case cited was *Kennedy Pasture Co. v. Texas,* from which he quoted at length. The opinion in that case, written by Chief Justice Phillips for the Supreme Court of Texas, and relating to the title to certain land lying between the Nueces River and the Rio Grande River in South Texas, was a controlling authority. In substance, it said and held that following the Battle of San Jacinto in 1836, the Republic of Texas fixed the southern boundary line of Texas at the Rio Grande, and this was confirmed at the end of the Mexican War, in the Treaty of Guadalupe Hidalgo, 1848, where it was agreed the title between the two nations begins at the mouth of the Rio Grande, and follows the principal stream of that river upward to the point above El Paso where the boundary line leaves the river, and strikes out westward toward the Pacific. The holding was, a grant by the governor of Tamaulipas, a state in the northeastern corner of Mexico, issued on April 12, 1848, purporting to grant land lying between the Rio Grande and the Nueces, was invalid, for the reason, Mexico had no jurisdiction or right of title, into and over land lying north of the Rio Grande at that time, the same belonging to the State of Texas, and being within the jurisdiction of Texas and the United States. Burges applied the holding of that case to the facts in the Clardy case, i.e., since the plaintiff pled the land in controversy had been in the actual territorial jurisdiction of the United States since 1898, and the treaty having been entered into in 1905, the proceedings under which plaintiff claims, begun in the Mexican court in 1926, were void for the reason that land affected was without the jurisdiction, *de jure* or *de facto* of the Mexican court. It followed, such proceedings vested no title in the plaintiff or any of its grantors, immediate or remote. In other words, the land was not in Mexico at the time the Mexican legal proceedings were begun in 1926, and any orders or decrees of the Mexican court with respect to the title of said land were therefore void.

Burges marshalled his historical evidence that neither Mexico nor the United States could cede any land, but could straighten disputed boundaries. His brief gave the history of the negotiations leading up to the signing of the Banco Elimination Treaty in 1905, the reference made being taken from "Chamizal Arbitration 'Appendix to the Case of United States,' " printed by authority of the government in 1911. This included a reference to a letter dated January 6, 1898 from Ambassador Romero to Secretary of State John Sherman, following directions received by the ambassador from Senor Mariscal, secretary of foreign relations of Mexico, instructing Ambassador Romero to disapprove certain decisions of the Boundary Commission, because the commission, "attributes to itself the authority to change the jurisdiction from one country to another, which is contrary to the agreement that created it," and then announces, under such instructions from the Mexican secretary of foreign relations:

> The government of Mexico is not impowered to cede any portion of Mexican territory, not even when, as is stated in the protocol of the commission of December 3rd last, the land may be of a particular kind and it may be wished to cede it; and for this reason the Mexican government has refused to approve the part of the protocol to which I refer.

Again, on December 2, 1899, Senor Mariscal, in a communication to Ambassador Clayton, confirming formal verbal statements, raises the objection to the proposed treaty that his government is powerless to cede territory, stating, "in regard to the project of a treaty in the matter of the bancos of the river Bravo, there arises a grave constitutional question which requires profound and long study; that of the lack of power on the part of this government to cede portions, limited although they may be, of the Mexican territories."

This problem was solved by eliminating the bancos, not on the basis of its amounting to a cession of territory, but on the basis of its fixing and determining a boundary line. The treaty itself, however, was changed to eliminate from a preliminary draft the provision the bancos on the left side should be transferred to the United States, etc., and recited in lieu thereof, that the treaty as agreed upon eliminated the bancos in question from the effect of Article 2 of the treaty. The treaty gave the commission power to mark upon the ground, with suitable monuments, the bed abandoned by the river, so that the bancos should be clearly defined. Burges noted in his appellate court brief that since the trial of the Clardy case in the trial court, and as late as November 12, 1931, Senor Estrada, Mexican secretary of foreign affairs, announced to the press, "Mexico will not sell or relinquish its claim," to certain lands in El Paso County, and Estrada went on to explain a cession of national territory is prohibited under the Mexican Constitution. Burges then stated Secretary Hay, supported by the highest legal authority, might have said the United States of America also was without constitutional power to cede territory of any state, and this want of power had been recognized from the very beginnings of the government. He quoted from Thomas Jefferson, when Jefferson was secretary of state, in connection with negotiations in 1792 between the Spanish government and our government as to the southern boundary of the United States. Mr. Jefferson stated:

> The power to alienate the unpeopled territories of any state, is not among the enumerated powers, given by the Constitution to the general government, & if we may go out of that instrument & accommodate to exigencies which may arise by alienating the unpeopled territory of a state, we may accommodate ourselves a little more by alienating that which is peopled, & still a little more by selling the people themselves. A shade or two more in the degree of exigency in all that will be requisite, & of that degree we shall ourselves be the judges. However, may it not be hoped that these questions are forever laid to rest by the Tenth Amendment once made a part of the Constitution, declaring expressly that, 'the powers not delegated to the U.S. by Constitution are reserved to the states respectively?' And if the general government had the power to alienate the territory of a state, it is too irresistible an argument, to deny ourselves the use of it on the present occasion.

Again, on March 18, 1822, Mr. Jefferson stated:

> For as to territory, we have neither the right, nor the disposition to alienate an inch of what belongs to any member of our Union. Such a proposition therefore is totally inadmissible, & not to be treated of for a moment.

Mr. Jefferson further stated to the commissioners to Spain, when delivering to them their commissions, that said observations had been reported to the president and approved by him.

It appeared abundantly clear, since the United States had no power to cede territory, and since plaintiff alleged the San Lorenzo banco had been in the territorial jurisdiction of the United States since 1898, together with the fact that the Treaty of 1905 provided for a settlement of the boundary, as distinguished from a cession of territory, the actions of a Mexican court in rendering judgment concerning the ownership of land in the San Lorenzo banco beginning in 1926, when the land was not within the judicial jurisdiction of Mexico, was void. The court so held, and the title of the American owners was upheld.

In an opinion written by Chief Justice Pelphrey, the Court of Civil Appeals at El Paso stated the San Lorenzo Title & Improvement Company relied upon the proposition the resolution of the International Boundary Commission dated March 21, 1930 transferred title to the San Lorenzo banco to the United States, whereas defendants assert it was transferred in 1905 by the treaty of that date. The court held the defendants were correct, and that the Mexican legal proceedings of 1926-1930 were void.

The court's opinion quotes from the Romero letter, quoted above. It also quotes from a letter from Mr. Hay, secretary of state, to Mr. Clayton, wherein Hay stated that Clayton might suggest, as the sovereignty of the bancos in question proposed to be eliminated as in dispute, it could hardly be construed as a ceding of Mexican territory, but rather the fixing of the boundary separating territory, the sovereignty of which is questionable; that this is a power understood to be assumed by nations in similar questions, and one which is generally referred for adjudication to commissions like the one now having the question under some consideration, and only requiring the approval of the treaty-making powers of the countries involved to make its results effective and binding upon the contracting parties. It was on this basis the respective governments found a means of settling title to bancos without unlawfully ceding national territory.

The Supreme Court of Texas granted writs of error in these cases, and handed down opinion on June 30, 1934, in the City Mortgage Company case, and Clardy case, and the Caples case, writing the main opinion in the City Mortgage Company case. The Supreme Court of Texas there held:

> Treaties between nations are binding from their effective dates, and

where a treaty was entered into between the United States and Mexico in 1905 providing for the elimination of bancos along the Rio Grande River, and in 1930 the International Boundary Commission declared the land in controversy to be a "banco" according to the terms of the treaty, said land was a territory of the United States from the date of the treaty and the Mexican government had neither de facto nor de jure jurisdication over it and consequently no authority to grant title or rights to it subsequent to that date. The judgment of a Mexican court, having no jurisdiction to adjudicate title to said land was void.

This opinion and decision was followed, in a brief opinion, in the Clardy case and in the Caples case.

Sydney Smith filed a motion for rehearing in the Supreme Court of Texas which opened with some fourteen numbered statements setting out why the opinion of the court was wrong, including the allegation that the opinion is, "untrue in its application of the facts, unsound in its process of reasoning; is subversive of all public law and destructive of private rights; is careless, loose, indifferent and superficial in its treatment of the questions involved; and in purporting to approve all previous opinions rendered in said litigation it exhibits a carelessness and disregard for consistency and well-established law not compatible with the dignity and ancient renown of this court."

Many thought this language overstepped the line, and was carelessly close to exhibiting contempt, and the court should have dealt with it as such. The court, however, seemed to prefer to overlook it, and merely overruled the Motion for Rehearing without further comment, with the result title to the San Lorenzo banco remained in its Texas owners.

XXXIV

The Jimmie Allred Antitrust Case and the Blue Buzzard

The eagle suffers little birds to sing.
—Shakespeare

THE DEPRESSION of the 1930's was on. Franklin D. Roosevelt was president, and many panaceas were recommended to him. One was the National Industrial Recovery Act, passed by Congress, and signed by the president on June 16, 1933. It provided for groups of business men to get together, and adopt codes of fair conduct in their respective businesses, envisioning a help to businesses then struggling to stay alive, by cutting out some of the competitive practices which made it difficult to show a profit. Under the leadership of its vigorous director, General "Iron-Pants" Hugh Johnson, it put out its emblem, soon to be seen in thousands of stores and businesses — the Blue Eagle. It was a square-drawn bird, with a bright blue color. Burges saw the N.I.R.A. or N.R.A., as it was usually called, as a threat to individual freedom and to a democratic government, and he promptly dubbed its emblem "The Blue Buzzard." It almost saved the day in a historic anti-trust case — but did not quite make it. This is the story of the Jimmie Allred antitrust suit against the oil companies.

On November 12, 1931, James V. Allred, attorney general of Texas, filed a suit, in the name of The State of Texas against fifteen oil companies. He named as defendants Standard Oil Company of New Jersey, Socony Vacuum Corporation, formerly Standard Oil Company of New York, Standard Oil Company of California, Shell

Union Oil Corporation (none of these corporations did business in Texas, but each owned the majority stock in a subsidiary company which did), Humble Oil and Refining Company, The Texas Company, Gulf Refining Company, Pasotex Petroleum Company (which was Standard of California's subsidiary), Continental Oil Company, Sinclair Refining Company, Magnolia Petroleum Company, Simms Oil Company, Shell Petroleum Corporation, Cities Service Oil Company, Texas Pacific Coal and Oil Company, Texas Petroleum Marketers Association, and American Petroleum Institute. The suit was based on alleged violations of the Texas antitrust laws constituting a conspiracy in restraint of trade, and was based on defendants having become parties, some of them reluctantly, to a Code of Fair Practices in the oil business. It was alleged the code had been prepared by the American Petroleum Institute, of which defendant companies, together with many other companies and individuals, were members. It was also alleged the A.P.I. had obtained approval of the code by the Federal Trade Commission. The code contained twenty-one rules, and among the practices it forbid was one of loaning or leasing tanks, gasoline pumps and other equipment free of charge, as being unsound and uneconomic; the leasing or licensing of service stations at less than cost; the running of lotteries, prizes or other games of chance in connection with sales of gasoline or oil; selling gasoline or oil below cost in order to injure a competitor and lessen competition, and so on. The State asserted the various items set out in the Code of Fair Practices were in restraint of trade, had the effect of fixing prices, and lessening competition. The petition was signed by James V. Allred, attorney general of Texas, Everett L. Looney, assistant attorney general, three other assistant attorneys general, Cofer & Cofer, who were engaged in private law practice in Austin, Bernard Martin, a lawyer in private practice in Wichita Falls, Texas, and George Mendell, who was in private practice in Austin. Cofer & Cofer, Bernard Martin and George Mendell were all employed as special counsel to assist in the prosecution of the case against the oil companies.

Burges was in Houston when the suit was filed, attending a meeting of the committee on pipe line rates on behalf of the Pasotex Pipeline Company. He immediately heard of the suit, and soon had a copy of the petition, since he was the agent for service of the Pasotex Petroleum Company. Six days later the state secured the issuance of writs of attachment against the property of the Pasotex Petroleum Company, directing the seizure of said property, apparently on the theory they could make the Pasotex property liable for any judgment obtained against Standard Oil of California. Burges had already caused Pasotex to send its records in El Paso to San Francisco, stating these records would be needed in preparation of the defense, and he did not want them left in El Paso, where they might be seized by the state under some kind of attachment proceedings. He expressed amazement at the issuance of the writ of attachment, as he thought it would be wholly ineffective.

Herewith began a long series of trips. He had other business away from El Paso, but this case called for frequent trips to Houston and Austin, with some to San Francisco and other cities. By letter of November 19, 1931, he advised Felix T. Smith, of Pillsbury, Madison & Sutro, San Francisco, he would leave El Paso on the 20th for Washington, and expected to come to San Francisco as soon after as possible, but in the meantime, he was expecting a call for a meeting of the defendants' lawyers in Houston. The fifteen defendants had an imposing array of counsel. They included among others, Andrews, Kelley, Kurth & Campbell, E.E. Townes, Hines Baker, C.R. Wharton, all of Houston; Williams, Neethe & Williams, of Galveston; Thompson, Knight, Baker & Harris and Walace Hawkins, of Dallas; David Trammell, Burney Braley and Cantey, Hanger & McMahon, all of Ft. Worth; Chas. I Francis, of Wichita Falls; and Charles L. Black, R. L. Batts, Ben H. Powell, T.H. McGregor, W.A. Keeling and Henry Brooks, all of Austin.

His first decision in the case was to obtain an Austin lawyer as local "on the ground" counsel. The company's general counsel in San Francisco told him to use his own judgment, and, after making some inquiries, he secured Charles L. Black, whom he had not previously known, as local counsel. It turned out to be a happy choice, and was the beginning of a long and pleasant personal and professional friendship.

The state moved at once with another writ—obtaining a writ of garnishment to impound the stock of the out-of-state companies in their subsidiaries in Texas. Every effort was made by the state to reach the out-of-state companies. The purpose was obvious. Antitrust suits of this kind and magnitude have a distinct political flavor, and the attorney general wanted to catch the "big fish," Standard Oil of New Jersey, Socony-Vacuum Corporation, Standard Oil Company of California, and Shell Union.

Black wrote him on January 6, 1932, that Judge Wheeler, the trial judge, had reversed his tentative ruling, and held the Shell stock was not subject to garnishment in Texas, and refused to enter a default judgment against Shell Union. The question of permitting the attorney general to take a default judgment, providing the court would enter it, was a prime question at the time, and Black wrote Felix Smith, advising Standard of California to let a default judgment be entered against it. At about the same time, however, Smith wrote Burges, saying Oscar Sutro, chief legal advisor to Standard of California, wanted Burges' opinion on the question. It was his opinion the company should permit the default judgment, on the ground the court had no jurisdiction over the company, and the judgment would be void. The company eventually decided not to pursue this course.

On January 12, 1932, Judge Wheeler, apparently at the instigation of the attorney general entered an order transferring the case to the 98th District Court, over which Judge Moore presided. Ordinarily, this would indicate the state was not happy with Judge Wheeler, and was looking for a judge more to the attorney general's liking. This, it turned out, was not to be the way with Judge Moore.

The state immediately filed an amended petition, applied for new process, in the nature of non-resident notices, and filed new affidavits for writs of attachment and garnishment. It then obtained from the clerk of the court writs of attachment and garnishment, and apparently directed the sheriff to return the writs of garnishment "no property found." This was crowding on an upcoming hearing, one having previously been set for January 18 on all dilatory pleas and exceptions.

In the meantime, the attorney general had dispatched two of his assistants, H.D. Bishop and H.D. Noonan, to San Francisco. They appeared at the offices of Standard Oil Company of California on January 15, 1932, and were ushered in to see Oscar Sutro and Felix T. Smith, the two chief attorneys for the company. Bishop and Noonan said they wanted to look over the records of Pasotex Petroleum Company, and Sutro asked him to specify what records he wanted to see, as he was not inclined to meet a mere omnibus request. Bishop said a statute authorized them, and Sutro asked, "What statute?" They referred to Articles 1366 and 1372 of the Texas statutes. Bishop said it was made a part of the written authority he brought from the attorney general, but he had left it at his hotel. After some discussion, Biship said he would request in writing the records he wished to inspect. He left to get his written authority from the attorney general, and to prepare his written request for the records he wanted to see. On January 16, Bishop and Noonan had not returned, and Sutro and Smith were concerned lest they take some drastic action directed toward Pasotex's permit to do business in Texas. But Bishop was back to see Sutro and Smith on the morning of the 18th with a request to see the records of the Marketing Department in connection with the operation of the code. They went to Collier's office, but he had no file, and his secretary, Marr, had none. After some searching, some files were produced, but Bishop had seen them previously, and had made copies of some parts of them. He then wanted to know how the accounting was handled on consignments to agents, and was taken to the office of B.W. Letcher, the auditor. Letcher said the books that would show this were in El Paso, not San Francisco.

Correspondence between Burges and Smith continued, reanswering the writs of garnishment, amounts of business done in Texas, amounts of taxes paid, etc., and to a letter of February 10, 1932 to Burges, Smith added a postscript in longhand:

"I am just finishing *The Raven.* It has been most delightful, and will afford the foundation for my conversations for a good while." Burges had sent him a copy of this biography of Sam Houston, and he obviously enjoyed it.

In February the parties were in court, presenting arguments on the suggestion of "friends of the court," arguing jurisdiction had not been established against the non-resident defendants. The state followed with four arguments, one by Looney, one by Powers, one by John Cofer, and one by the senior (R.E.) Cofer, which lasted for six and one-half hours. Burges thought R.E. Cofer's argument was especially extreme, and showed the state's position in the case would be extreme. The court took the question under advisement, but ruled a few days later against the defendants. The ruling appeared to the defendants to be a harbinger of an adverse attitude on the part of the court, and was, therefore, very disturbing. There was a further letter from Burges to Smith on March 5, 1932. He had just arrived in El Paso from Austin, and said he was returning to Austin that night. He advised the court had ruled against the defendants on the order to require the presence of the witnesses in Texas, and also, the non-resident corporations are required to file an answer. He wrote that the state's counsel, including the attorney general himself, had all the appearances of men pretty badly used up by the arguments on the misjoinder of parties, and they are going to be worse used up "before we are through with the arguments on demurrer which will commence immediately on the action of the court being announced on the pleas."

He had the impression the court was inclined to go along with the attorney general's theories about the case, and he, and the other defendants' attorneys decided the only course for them to pursue was to fight hard on every point, and they told the court they were not asking any favors, but they were demanding their rights, and intended to have them. They kept the record so as to save points of appeal to the United States Supreme Court, particularly on the jurisdiction question, relying on the due process clause of the 14th Amendment. He accumulated a list of cases, some of them recent ones, from the U.S. Supreme Court which he thought indicated an appeal to the Supreme Court of the United States would not be in vain.

Burges advised Smith he had complete confidence in the judge's integrity, but the judge was completely unfamiliar with the subject of this case, and his actions on the bench so indicated. The attorney general, he said, was getting more and more obstreperous as the difficulties of the case in its final phases became more apparent to him. He had some hope—but not a very strong hope—the court would hold the antitrust law unconstitutional. He noted with interest that John Cofer, in one of his arguments to the court, stated more than once, the defendants had not done anything wrong, if done by an individual, but the only wrong was in agreeing with others to do it, i.e., to do what was right for each one as an individual to do.

Burges, nevertheless, was exploring gently the possibility of a compromise settlement. He heard the attorney general might settle for an injunction to the effect that defendants were not to agree to the code, or perhaps just to rule out certain parts of the code, as designated by the attorney general. He later heard the attorney general might also want two or three of the smaller companies to pay a small fine. Burges thought if they could settle by ruling out part of the code, and with a judgment which did not find the defendants guilty of violating the law, but with small fines paid by two or three small companies, to which, of course, all defendants would contribute, it might be the best way out of the case.

On April 1, 1932, he advised Felix Smith by telegram from Austin, after arguments to the court on special exceptions, the court had struck out paragraphs 2, 4 and 6, appearing as 5 on page 8 of the printed copy, and sustained all special exceptions except those attacking the constitutionality of the antitrust law and those raising the question of misjoinder. The state was given fifteen days in which to replead, and the defendants would then have fifteen days in which to answer. May 2 was set as date for hearing exceptions to the new pleading, and testimony before the commissioner was to begin on May 2, at which time the Texas Company witnesses would be examined.

In due time the state's amended petition was received and Burges went to work at once analyzing its legal sufficiency, the facts alleged, and the proof he would need. On May 3, 1932, he wrote Smith, and gave him a list of facts he needed to know; how many filling stations were in Pasotex's area when it began business, what happened to them, how many there were now, etc., and requested the work be done by R.G. McIntyre, who headed the company's business office at El Paso.

On May 9 the state began taking the testimony of R.C. Holmes, president of the Texas Company, before Commissioner Shelly, in Austin, in day long sessions, May 9 through May 13. One hundred twenty exhibits were introduced, all taken from the files of the Texas Company, either at New York or Houston, when the assistant attorneys general investigated that company's records the previous summer. Very little testimony was obtained from Holmes, other than his identification of the papers, and it appeared to the defendants the attorney general's case had narrowed down to the contention that the acceptance of the code is of and in itself a violation of the Texas antitrust laws. Burges sent Felix Smith a clipping from the *Dallas Morning News* of May 14, stating it covered the high points of the hearing on Friday (May 14), and advised that exceptions to the pleadings were to be heard on May 23. In the meantime, Smith sent him the information he had requested re number of filling stations, etc.

The code was the subject of considerable correspondence between them. It appeared from a letter by Burges of June 4, 1932, that he was of the opinion the fact the Federal Trade Commission approved the code was not a defense to the charge of violating the Texas antitrust laws. He referred to the fact that Pasotex Petroleum Company had not participated in anything about the code after the company's organization and before Mr. Kingsbury, president of Standard Oil Company of California, signed the notification to the Federal Trade Commission, as requested by the latter. But he did think he could get considerable advantage from the fact that Kingsbury's letter was addressed to the F.T.C., and that he signed no agreement with any oil company or any other person in the oil industry on behalf of Pasotex. He hoped to get this before the jury, and on this basis, to obtain a finding from the jury that Pasotex had not entered into an agreement with any other company or person. Even in view of the rule that one who enters into a conspiracy makes himself liable for what had already been done by co-conspirators, the evidence Pasotex entered into the agreement only at the request of an agency of the federal government, and had participated only to a minimal extent, should minimize any penalties against it, if not relieve it entirely of them. He was of the opinion the state was not going to be able to prove anything against Pasotex that looked like interfering with competition, except the mere language of the code itself.

There had been considerable thought that the filing of the antitrust was instigated by the Quaker State Oil Company, which wanted all service stations to handle its motor oil. Many stations handled only the oil distributed by the oil company with which it was affiliated, hence the unhappiness of Quaker State. One of the special counsels for the state was Bernard Martin, of Wichita Falls, Texas, which was Jimmie Allred's home town when he was elected attorney general. Many of those connected with the defendants' side of the case understood Martin was an attorney for Quaker State, and this was the reason he was in the case. The defendants went to work to prove the connection, when in June 1932, the attorney general admitted it. The question was, how best to take advantage of it, and Burges was strongly of the opinion it should not be sprung until the time of the trial, as this would give it the biggest impact on the case. A majority of the defense counsel agreed. He was a little put out, then, when two of the defense lawyers filed a motion to restrain Bernard Martin from participating in the case, and to restrain the attorney general from permitting him to see any papers he acquired under the visitorial powers given him by the statutes. He said the motion was most inadequate, and the court promptly overruled it.

The attorney general was in Houston on a political speaking trip on the day the motion was overruled, and his assistants did everything in their power to get the court to refuse to hold the paper was a filed paper in the case, and to prevent the newspapers from getting it or using it. They hurt, instead of helped, the attorney general. Allred was in court himself the next day, furiously angry with everybody and everything and showed it repeatedly, just as his assistants had done the day before. Just before the court adjourned at noon, he tried to get the court to let him make a speech, but the court declined to permit him to do so. Allred responded that he was going to San Antonio to make a speech that night, and he wanted to get through with this before he left. The court refused again, and told him he would hear anything he had to say at 2:00 P.M.

After the court adjourned, Cofer and Looney went to the court and urged him not to let the matter come up, and not to give the attorney general an opportunity to speak, as it might result in very serious trouble in court, and it would be injurious to the attorney general whom, of course, they wanted to protect.

When the court met, Judge Moore announced he was not going to have any argument of any kind on the amended motion; he had read it, thought it was still inadequate, and refused to let the movers discuss it, or the attorney general to make any speech at all. A good deal of temper was shown by movers and the attorney general, but the court had his way, and announced a recess in the case until the first Monday in October.

The attorney general asked to have the case set down for hearing at that time. The court declined, stating it would have to be brought to his attention at a later time, and fixed the last Saturday in July as the time to present such a motion, but he was in doubt whether it would then be in order, as he questioned whether the taking of evidence would have progressed enough to justify a final setting of the case. The court was right about this for it was fairly well understood there was to be no taking of testimony before the first of September, and the matter stood continued to the October term of the court.

The defendants thought they lost some advantage by having the Quaker State matter brought up at this time, but were of the opinion they would be able to use it to their great advantage, and planned to insist upon an inquiry as to who else, if anyone, had been employed and what other companies or individuals had contributed to the prosecution of the case.

The court overruled practically all defendant's exceptions. He overruled exceptions to the amended petition that were identical with the exceptions sustained with regard to the same allegations in the first amended petition, even to the very language used. There was no satisfactory explanation for such ruling.

Burges was busy, getting the company to furnish him with statistics on the percentage of the oil business done in Texas by

Pasotex, knowing it would be very small. He also asked for the percentage of business done by the Panhandle Refining Company of Wichita Falls. He had learned that Roy Jones, president of Panhandle, who had presided over one of the meetings of the A.P.I. at which the A.P.I. finally committed itself to the code, was willing to testify to the conditions which led to the adoption of the code, the necessities for it, and the good accomplished by it. Panhandle was not a party to the suit, and it was generally assumed Jimmie Allred was protecting his home town business and friends, although it appeared Roy Jones wanted to testify in favor of the code.

On July 11, 1932, he reported the Third Amended Petition had been filed, and a few days later sent a copy of it to Felix Smith. He advised a committee of defendant's lawyers was going to Washington to call on Judge McCullough of the Federal Trade Commission with respect to his being a witness, and also, the defendants were making progress in assembling evidence of the effect of the code on competition in Texas, and it looked like this evidence would be helpful.

On July 30, 1932, he was advised the testimony of W.R. Boyd, Jr., executive vice president of the American Petroleum Institute was to be taken before the commission in Austin beginning September 5, and also that the attorney general would insist on going to trial on October 5. Burges was concerned about the trial date. He did not want to move for a continuance or postponement, but he thought it would take two or three months to try the case, and he did not want the defendants to find themselves with the case ending just before the Christmas holidays.

When September came, Clarence Wharton, one of the attorneys for Sinclair Oil Company, was ill and unable to appear for Boyd's testimony, and the commissioner reset it for October 3, which meant the case would not be set for trial before January, 1933. By September 28, it appeared the taking of Boyd's testimony had been postponed to October 12, and defendant's attorneys heard the attorney general was not as enthusiastic as he had been for an immediate trial, and would probably agree to a postponement in January.

Boyd made a splendid witness. The state questioned him

first—over a period of several weeks—and he stayed with it although he had occasional attacks of appendicitis, and was expecting to have an operation.

In the meantime, more "feeling out" about a possible settlement went on. The word was out the attorney general would agree to a judgment finding the code legal, but on the condition the one hundred percent contracts, i.e., those tying a service station to the products of one company, were to be perpetually enjoined, and he wanted a cash judgment of $650,000. Burges concluded all the attorney general wanted was to protect the Quaker State Oil Company against the effects of the one hundred percent contracts, which kept Quaker State Oil Company out of many stations, and to recover enough money to make a political showing, and have money to pay the private counsel assisting the state. The defendants sent back word all they would agree on was a judgment recognizing the validity of the code, and they might be willing to pay court costs, including reasonable attorney's fee, but not an excessive one; and if anyone wanted to institute a suit to test the legality of the one hundred percent contracts, defendants would enter an appearance and expedite the hearing as much as possible.

Burges was back in El Paso on December 12, 1932, and immediately was engaged in a controversy with the county tax assessor over taxes leviable against the Nichols Copper Company on copper stored in El Paso subsequent to being refined, and then held in storage pending sale and shipment. This took his time for most of the week following December 12. After that, he had time to advise Felix Smith that Boyd was a very sick man, his condition being aggravated by some of the internal affairs of the A.P.I. He was so manifestly unwell the commissioner suggested he did not want to require him to go on with the hearing, and as a result, the further taking of his testimony was postponed to January. This seemed to make it clear the case would not be set for trial until after the legislature adjourned (it met in January for one hundred twenty days) as the defense counsel were strong in their opinion the case should not be tried while the legislature was in session. The attorney general offered all the opposition he knew how, and, as Burges wrote Felix Smith "made a perfect ass of himself in the way he protested against the postponement, but the commissioner disregarded his objections and adjourned the hearing until 10:00 A.M. on Tuesday, the 3rd of January."

They finished taking Boyd's testimony on the last Saturday in January, 1933. The defendants were pleased with the way it had gone, and Burges advised Felix Smith the state had not begun to make out a case, unless the court holds the mere agreement to abide by the provisions of the code is per se a conspiracy in restraint of trade under the Texas Statutes. He also reported defense counsel were all working harmoniously, and probably would agree on a small committee to actually try the case.

Early in March, Judge Moore entered an order postponing trial of the case until after the legislature adjourned, which meant sometime after May 9, 1933. Burges meanwhile combed through Boyd's testimony, and the exhibits attached to it, making notes of objections to various parts of it—a slow, time-consuming job. Shortly, the attorney general served a notice on him to produce certain papers at the trial, but they were not to be found in his client's files, and he thought they were of no importance, anyway. Other documents were called for from time to time, and in April he was served with notice from the commissioner the state had applied for an order to take the testimony in Austin of H.L. Flynn, executive secretary of the Texas Petroleum Marketers Association, on May 8, and had called for exhibits, listed on forty-nine typewritten pages. It was later postponed to May 22.

Thereafter, the case was set for trial on October, 22, 1933. The defense attorneys met in Houston in August, and while there chose their committee to try the case. This was done, partly, to obviate the necessity for seventeen or so lawyers each making objections to introduction of evidence, and arguing the objections, as it was thought this would be an intolerable and disadvantageous situation.

They chose Frank Andrews of Houston who represented Standard of New Jersey; Charles L. Black of Austin who primarily represented the Texas Company; and Burges. He told Felix Smith he made every effort to avoid being on the committee, as he did not see how anyone could want to undertake to represent and act for thirteen groups of lawyers whose opinions on almost everything conflicted somewhere. Several different groupings of personnel for the committee were suggested, but Burges was on everyone of them, some of the lawyers stating they would not be satisfied with any committee which did not include him. He felt he could not refuse under the circumstances, and so accepted. The only problem was that Sutro and Smith felt that Pasotex Petroleum Co. did such a small portion of the oil business in Texas, they did not want Burges to do a disproportionate share of the defense work in the case, with Pasotex and Standard of California bearing the expense. Burges said, however, he would not permit it to result in an unfair burden to his client. Smith wrote him:

"As we know, it is hardly fair for these other lawyers to ask you to take such a prominent part in the case in which our interest is, of course, quite small. Nevertheless, that is the penalty of your ability. Nothing could be more flattering, or more deserved."

Burges summarized his position in the case: "So there is nothing to do but give the attorney general the very best fight that is in us and, in the language of the old common law, 'trust to God and your country to give us a good deliverance.' This may be carrying confidence in divine protection a long way in a case like this, but we'll have to let it go at that."

In the meantime, the National Industrial Recovery Act had been passed by Congress and became the law on June 16, 1933. Soon the Blue Eagle—the Blue Buzzard—would be widely displayed, and Codes of Fair Competition rapidly came into existence. A notice was soon issued there would be a meeting open to all marketers of petroleum products in Texas to consider a proposed code under the National Industrial Recovery Act, at the Adolphus Hotel, in Dallas, on Tuesday morning, July 18, 1933. Burges did not attend.

The trial committee went to work at once, and shortly had an eighteen-point memorandum setting out the assignments of various defense lawyers. It began: "Mr. H.H. Brooks will daily examine the court records and report to the counsel of all companies the names and residencces of all witnesses for whom subpoenas may be issued together with such other information as Mr. Brooks may be able to obtain."

Subsequent paragraphs allocated work and responsibility among various lawyers. For example, Polk Shelton, Senator McGregor and Black, all Austin lawyers, were designated to examine jurors as to qualifications, and as to suggestions for challenges to jurors. W.R. Harris, Ben H. Powell and W.H. Burges were to look after the right to preemptory challenges, the method of handling, the time of making exceptions, and the bills of exceptions in the event the court should deny each defendant the right to six challenges. Judge Batts, Alfred McKnight and Hines H. Baker were to present a motion to suppress the depositions of Holmes, Boyd and Flynn, and such objections and motions as may from time to time be necessary with reference to the form and manner of taking and the admissibility of the testimony already taken when it is offered in evidence in court. Judge Batts, E.E. Townes, Clarence Wharton and W.H. Burges were to be prepared to re-argue the general demurrer in event the occasion arose that justified their doing so. Governor Moody, Black, Charles I. Francis and General Keeling were to look after consultation with the attorney general's forces as to preliminary agreements that would expedite the trial. Other assignments related to various phases of testimony, and the final paragraph assigned to Judge F.A. Williams, Judge Batts, Black and Tomlinson the task of being prepared to argue both on the facts and the law, how far the N.R.A. code supersedes local law and regulations. It recited this was one of the most important subjects for consideration, and suggested each defendant would probably desire to file an amended answer setting up the effect of the N.R.A. code, the interstate character of commerce, and that the N.R.A. code superseded all other regulations on the subject.

A short time later another matter arose which raised the question whether the attorney general's side of the case was being run on the "up and up." One day in September 1933, Chris P. Fox, who was then sheriff of El Paso County, telephoned Burges and told him he had in his office five subpoenas issued in the antitrust case for persons living in El Paso County, and which were forwarded to him by the attorney general's office. Burges went to the sheriff's office and examined the subpoenas, saw they appeared to be in due form, duly signed and sealed by a deputy district clerk of Travis County, Texas, and he noted the names of the five persons to whom the several subpoenas were addressed. He made some inquiry as to who these persons were, and learned what he could about them, and what they might be in position to testify.

Two days later, which fell on a Saturday, he left El Paso for Austin, for a conference of defense attorneys on the following Monday. At this conference, he complained to the others that Henry Brooks was not getting the job done which had been assigned to him, namely to examine the docket in the office of the district clerk every morning, and ascertain whether any subpoenas had been issued the previous day, and if any had been issued, to promptly advise defense counsel. Brooks was present, and he maintained no subpoenas had been issued, and insisted he was keeping watch on things as per his instructions. Brooks and Charles I. Francis, who represented the American Petroleum Institute, then went to the office of the district clerk, and asked the clerk if any subpoenas had been issued at the request of the state, and the clerk told them none had been issued. They told the clerk one had been served in El Paso County, and the clerk ducked by saying he had been away on vacation and perhaps his deputy had issued a subpoena. They then contacted the deputy, who at first denied any subpoenas had been issued, but upon being confronted with the fact that five subpoenas had been seen in the hands of the sheriff of El Paso County for service upon persons living in El Paso County, he admitted he had issued six subpoenas at the request of Assistant Attorney General H.D. Bishop, who asked him to give to him six blank subpoenas containing the names of no witnesses. The name of the county and the name of the witness was to be filled in on each subpoena at the pleasure of the attorney general when he was ready to use them. The deputy clerk said he had objected to this as being irregular, because the statute expressly requires it shall be addressed to the sheriff of the proper county where the witness resides, and shall contain the name or names of the witnesses desired, and shall designate the date on which they are to appear, and the cause, and a record of this must be kept in the clerk's office. Bishop apparently told the deputy clerk he wanted to keep the matter from the knowledge of the defendant's lawyers, did not want any record made of the issuance of the subpoenas, and advised the deputy clerk this was customary procedure in antitrust cases in the State of Texas, although contrary to law. In order to accommodate him the deputy clerk took six subpoenas from the back of the book furnished for that purpose, signed them and sealed them, and turned them over to Bishop to use as he saw fit.

Francis and Brooks then went to the attorney general's office and asked Bishop if he had any subpoenas issued. He said, "No," he had not. He was asked if anyone else had done so. He replied, no one that he knew of had done so, but said he would ask the attorney general about it. Francis and Brooks waited for about twenty minutes, when Bishop returned and said the attorney general said he had not had any subpoenas issued, and did not know of the issuance of any. Later that day Brooks and Francis telephoned Burges at Ft. Worth, where he had gone for the purpose of reviewing records of the Sinclair Oil Company which it was anticipated might be used in the trial of the case, this being done in connection with the attorneys for Sinclair.

On receiving the information telephoned to him, Burges returned to Austin that night. The next day they obtained an affidavit from the deputy district clerk as to what had transpired, and Burges wrote and filed a motion, attaching the affidavit to it, to require the attorney general to return the subpoenas, and directing the clerk not to issue subpoenas in blank again. He also had a subpoena duces tecum issued to the attorney general and to his assistant, Bishop, to appear in court at 2:00 P.M. the next day, being the time set by the court for the hearing of the motion, and to bring with them all correspondence and records of every kind connected with the use of these subpoenas.

At 2:00 P.M. the following day, Allred and Bishop appeared in the court together with Everett Looney, who had charge of the antitrust case. All exuded the attitude of being in a bad humor, and exhibited the feeling they had been greatly outraged. Burges had two objects in view in filing the motion and having it heard before the court. One was to find out the names of all who had been subpoenaed so defense counsel would know who they were, and undertake to ascertain what they might be going to testify. The other was for the purpose of airing the deliberate statement made by Bishop at a 180 degree angle to the truth, and the apparent connection the attorney general had with it.

Looney, on behalf of the attorney general, presented a demurrer to the motion. They took no other position, because this raised only a legal argument as to the legality of what had been done, and did not put the facts in controversy about the issuance of subpoenas under such circumstances. Indeed, the attorney general could not argue against facts in the matter, for he had been "caught with his pants down."

After a full day's argument, the court overruled the attorney general's demurrer and preemptorily ordered the attorney general to return the subpoenas which had been issued, together with any other blank subpoenas he might have, and entered a rule that the clerk should issue no more subpoenas under such circumstances. The general impression of all the lawyers connected with the defendants' side of the case was that real good had been accomplished, as they had made it perfectly plain to the court, and to the newspapers throughout the state, there was positive proof of the skulduggery going on in the attorney general's office.

On the following Friday the defense had the benefit of another action on the part of the attorney general, namely, on that day the attorney general filed in the district clerk's office a notice that Bernard Martin, who had been employed as private counsel by the attorney general in the case, and who was understood to represent the Quaker State Oil Company, would not appear as counsel. The attorneys for the American Petroleum Institute and for the Texas Petroleum Marketers Association, both of which were defendants in the case, immediately set to work to have subpoenas issued to take the testimony of Martin, and one or two others, in Austin before the commissioner on the following Tuesday to show what Quaker State's connection with the case had been. The witnesses who were subpoenaed had been interviewed by the Quaker State Oil Company's Austin representative, and it was through his activities they were taken to Austin as witnesses. Burges stated they did not intend to let Martin's withdrawal take the Quaker State out of the case, and they were proceeding with evidence to show that Quaker State was up to its ears on the attorney general's side of the case.

The court's ruling against the attorney general on his demurrer to Burges' motion about the subpoenas was the first favorable ruling the defendants had had from the court, and it was a boost to their morale, as up to that point they felt they had been getting the worst of the deal.

In the meantime, Burges had prepared a short brief containing nine points in support of a general demurrer based upon the proposition the N.R.A. had superseded the state antitrust law with respect to the basis of this case. He first referred to a part of Article VI of the Constitution of the United States, containing the provision that the Constitution and the laws of the United States shall be the supreme law of the land and the judges in every state shall be bound thereby, anything in the Constitution or laws of any state to the contrary notwithstanding. He next referred to Section VIII of Article I of the Constitution of the United States to the effect that Congress shall have power to regulate commerce with foreign nations and among the several states and with the Indian tribes. He then quoted from the National Industrial Recovery Act, where it was declared to be the policy of the Congress to remove obstructions to the free flow of interstate and foreign commerce which tend to diminish the amount thereof, and to provide for the general welfare by doing the several things in the act specified, and in the manner and form therein set forth, one of which is the promulgation of codes of fair competition, and under which the president, on August 19, approved and promulgated a code of fair competition for the petroleum industry.

His next point was, the power of Congress to regulate commerce between the states has been held to extend to those things which, while apparently intrastate, nevertheless aided or impaired or retarded, or affected, commerce between the states, and when it has acted, it occupies the entire field and its authority is paramount.

Under this item he cited a long list of cases, first from the United States Supreme Court, and then several from the Texas courts. His next point cited a number of authorities for the proposition it was the duty of the court to accept and act upon the president's finding of fact, whether justified or not, it being within his discretion. He then stated the federal courts alone have the authority to pass on the validity of the president's code, citing authorities. His seventh point was that to inflict punishment or impose penalties, or to permit a recovery in a civil action authorized by statute, it is necessary the act complained of should be unlawful when done and unlawful at the time the court awards judgment. If either element is absent, the court is without authority to enforce, citing authorities from both the Supreme Court of the United States and the Supreme Court of Texas. He next stated the N.R.A. had created such uncertainty and confusion as to make the Texas Act unenforceable, citing one authority from a Texas court, and finally stated the effect of approval of the code by the Federal Trade Commission, citing several authorities.

The case was set for trial on October 2, 1933, and a meeting of all of the defense attorneys was held on Friday, September 29, in Austin. Burges suggested to the group that when the case was called for trial on October 2, they should present to the court the question whether or not the federal government, through the National Recovery Act, had taken over the entire field of interstate commerce, and things affecting it insofar as the refining and marketing of petroleum products were concerned. Black fully concurred with Burges, and a majority of the lawyers present agreed. Townes and Andrews, however, indicated they doubted the court would go with them on this proposition insofar as acts had already been done and penalties already incurred were concerned. It was discussed for some time, during which Burges submitted the authorities which he had collected, and Townes thereupon joined with Burges in his opinion, and later Andrews became fully convinced by the decision in the case of *Erie Railroad v. New York,* 234 U.S. 671. Everyone agreed that not even a whisper should be made with respect to the decision to present this demurrer on Monday morning, so it would come as a complete surprise to the attorney general.

When court opened October 2, Burges stated to the court defendants desired to argue their general demurrer. The court heard the arguments, with Judge Batts closing for the defendants. He was a large man, with a leonine head, great ability, onetime judge on the U.S. Court of Appeals, Fifth Circuit, and onetime general counsel for

Gulf Oil Corporation at Pittsburgh. He made a very effective argument, citing several cases where the N.R.A. had been held to be paramount, and urged the court not to be the only court to impede the efforts of the president to make the N.R.A. effective. Judge Moore took it under advisement, and on the following Thursday afternoon announced he had resolved every doubt as to constitutionality of the Texas Antitrust Law in favor of the state, but he had fully concurred with the defendants, the N.R.A. had suspended the Texas Antitrust Law insofar as these defendants and the issues in this case were concerned. The despised "Blue Buzzard" had been called into action, and, for the nonce, at least, was entitled to fly proudly under its usual designation of the "Blue Eagle."

Felix Smith sent his congratulations, and Burges took pains at this point to pass on to the officials of the Standard Oil Company of California, in San Francisco, the information that all of the information he requested at any time during the course of this lawsuit from either R.G. McIntyre or E.W. Endter was furnished by them promptly and efficiently. These two men went on to hold high positions with that company, Endter later becoming president of one of the other subsidiaries of Standard of California, and McIntyre became president of Standard Oil Company of Texas.

The state appealed from the judgment of the district court to the court of civil appeals at Austin. The defendants, among other things, urged the Texas Antitrust Laws were unconstitutional because they denied them the equal protection of the laws in that there was an exemption in the penal code of Texas of persons dealing in agricultural products and in livestock, as well as an exemption for unions, from the provisions of the antitrust statutes. The defendants also urged the defense of the N.R.A. having preempted the field, i.e., the federal law had taken over in this area, and the state laws could not, therefore, be enforced. In June 1935 the court of civil appeals, with an opinion written by Judge Baugh, handed down its opinion, holding the Texas Antitrust statutes were indeed unconstitutional for the reason asserted by the defendants. The court having so held, affirmed the judgment of the trial court, although saying it was not necessary for them to pass on the effect of the N.R.A., since they had ruled in favor of the defendants on another ground.

The state then appealed to the Supreme Court of Texas. In the meantime the N.R.A. had received a death blow from the Supreme Court of the United States. In May 1935 the Schecter case had been decided by that court. This was the so-called "Sick Chicken" case and although the N.R.A. was at that time the heart of the New Deal, and although Mr. Justice Louis D. Brandeis was accounted to be a very liberal member of the court, he wrote an opinion which put the quietus on the Blue Buzzard. The applicable N.R.A. codes required a purchaser of chickens on the New York poultry market to take a whole coop full, even though some of them might be sick. The Supreme Court of the United States said the way the N.R.A. was set up, the promulgation of such codes was an unconstitutional delegation of legislative power, and the N.R.A. was, in effect, void. It turned out the "sick chicken" case in New York had a direct effect on the Jimmie Allred antitrust case in Texas.

The Supreme Court of Texas handed down its opinion approximately two years later, in June 1937. It disagreed with the court of civil appeals, and said the Texas Antitrust Laws were not unconstitutional, and of course the N.R.A. and the "Blue Buzzard" were already out of the case, since they had been relegated into limbo by Mr. Justice Brandeis' opinion. The Supreme Court of Texas said, however, with respect to the F.T.C. and its codes, the Federal Trade Commission cannot regulate intrastate business in Texas, and therefore the F.T.C.'s sponsorship of these codes afforded no protection to the defendants with respect to what they did in intrastate business in the State of Texas. The court therefore remanded the case to the district court for trial. The upshot of it all was the defendants again pursued the question of making a compromise settlement, and did so by means of a judgment in favor of the defendant oil companies, but with the marketing associations paying a substantial sum of money to the state as a compromise settlement of the state's claim for a penalty. Thus ended the Jimmie Allred antitrust case, and it turned out the "Blue Buzzard" fell flat on its face, having eventually afforded no protection to the defendants.

XXXV

Wanted: a Day in Court

Those sculptured halls my feet shall never tread.
—Smollett

ONE DAY IN 1937, the telephone rang. It was long distance from San Francisco. Oscar Sutro, of Pillsbury, Madison & Sutro, and chief legal advisor of Standard Oil Company of California was calling. He asked Mr. Burges to become one of counsel for Standard of California in what was known as the "Section 36" case, officially styled *United States of America v. Standard Oil Company of California.* It was a case with a long history, and more than one lawyer had spent years on it, only to retire or die, and leave the case in other hands. New blood was being injected into the defendant's legal counsel, and Mr. Sutro wanted Mr. Burges to help the defense. Thus began his connection with a case that was to take a large part of his time until it ended in 1940.

The proud boast of the law is that everyone is entitled to his day in court. The real fight in this case, however, was over the question, will Standard of California be given its day in court, or will the decision of a bureaucratic officeholder, who never saw a witness or read a word of the record be held the final decision as to the rights of a party who is engaged in a controversy with the government.

The battle was over the ownership of Section 36, Township 30 South, Range 23 East, Kern County, which had become a fabulously rich oil producing section of land. Congress, in 1853 had granted to the state of California Sections 16 and 36 in each township for public schools, but this did not apply to lands known to be mineral on the date the survey of it was accepted and approved by the General Land Office, which, in this instance was January 26, 1903.

In 1908 a man named George Hay applied to purchase this land from the state of California, and thereafter, in 1909, assigned his certificate of purchase to Oscar Sutro, who transferred it to Standard Oil Company of California. As early as 1914, initial steps were taken by the General Land Office to claim Section 36 as a mineral section, but it was not followed up until 1921, when amended charges were filed. These charges were heard before Secretary of Interior A.B. Fall in 1921, and after hearing arguments, he dismissed the charges. In 1924, Congress directed the secretary of the interior to institute, forthwith, proceedings to assert and establish the title of the United States to Section 36. The then secretary of the interior reversed the action of Secretary Fall, and ordered proceedings to begin, which order was sustained by the Supreme Court on January 2, 1929, in *West, Secretary of the Interior v. Standard Oil Company,* 278 U.S. 200.

Walter Spencer, as substitute register for the government, held extensive hearings, and under date of February 24, 1932, filed his "Decision by the Register."

The question was, was Section 36 known in 1903 to have commercial quantities of oil in it?

It is difficult for men knowledgeable in the oil business to look at a producing oil field, and admit that prior to the discovery of oil on that land, they would not have been able to see the geology of an oil bearing structure. Hindsight here, as in other walks of life, is so much smarter than earlier opinions. The testimony before Mr. Spencer, nevertheless, was to the effect that the general opinion of people in that area, in 1903 and some subsequent years, was, there was no oil in Section 36. There was oil in some other areas of Kern County, but it was in different geological formations, and Section 36 was "written off" as having no oil. Indeed, the geologists of the time who looked at Section 36 gave it a cursory examination, and condemned it as being non-oil bearing. This opinion was concurred in generally, both before and after 1903, by local citizens, prospectors, speculators, oil men and geologists, who considered it worthless.

Oil was discovered eight years later in Elk Hills, not far away, in

1911. And in 1912 the Naval Reserve including Township 30, was established. In 1916, in order to settle title questions in Naval Reserve No. 2, Buena Vista Hills, it was suggested the government would be better off to have a compact block of land, and if it would give up opposition to a leasing bill, with respect to Naval Reserve No. 2, certain private lands, including Section 36, would be surrendered to the government.

At this point not only did the local people in Kern County, California, and geologists and other oil men concur in the opinion and belief that Section 36 contained no oil, but high ranking officials of the federal government joined in the chorus that Section 36, for oil producing purposes, was worthless. When the offer above mentioned was made to give Section 36 to the Federal government, Secretary of the Navy Josephus Daniels said to Governor Gillette and Mr. Titus, who went by appointment to see the secretary of the Navy, "You California boys are pretty smart, but you aren't smart enough to put this over on me. We don't want that Section 36 and that associated land. What we need is some oil land. We have investigated this Naval Reserve No. 1 thoroughly, and we are satisfied there isn't any oil there, and we don't want it."

Secretary Daniels had the benefit of the opinion and advice of geologists, one of whom was E.B. Latham. E.J. Justice, of the Department of Justice, the attorney in charge of the California land suits for the government, stated to Secretary Daniels that E.B. Latham, who was educated as a geologist at Harvard and Columbia, was, in his opinion, the best practical oilman and best expert in the country. He had more experience and observation in drilling and operating wells, and knew oil conditions in California better than any other Justice knew.

Latham gave his opinion not only to Secretary Daniels, but he also testified before the Senate Committee on Public Lands, "In my opinion Naval Reserve No. 1 is not suitable for a reserve. I do not think the Navy should depend upon that. I do not think it is commercial oil land at all, and I think it is very limited in its content of oil."

Other geologists, oilmen and government officials expressed the same opinion. The negotiations with the Navy went on from February

1916, to February 1917, with the negotiations being based on the premise that Section 36 was owned by Standard Oil Company of California, and the Navy never questioned this. In one of the hearings, Senator Phelan asked, "Will the Navy surrender its claims to two thousand acres in No. 2, in consideration of getting a clear title to No. 1? That is a tangible proposition. I would like to ask the secretary, will the Navy agree to that?"

It was answered by Assistant Secretary of the Navy Franklin D. Roosevelt, "Certainly not, Senator."

To a further question, Roosevelt replied, "Practically speaking, in No. 1 there is only one section with undisputed ownership to private persons, and the rest of the Reserve No. 1 — nearly all the rest of it — is absolutely unproven land. Therefore, the Navy on the basis of surrendering one in order to get the other, would be surrendering proven land for something we know very little about."

Accordingly, when Spencer filed his "Decision By the Register" on February 24, 1932, he reported there had been no oil development attempted in Section 36 until 1918, when Standard began drilling there. He held that in 1903 it was not known to be oil bearing, and his decision if it became final, would quiet title in Standard.

His decision was affirmed on February 23, 1933, by C.C. Moore, commissioner of the General Land Office. It then came on for action by a new secretary of the interior, Harold L. Ickes, who, in his autobiography, described himself as an "old curmudgeon." Ickes never saw the record of the testimony and exhibits in the case, but did hear arguments on it, and on January 24, 1935, held Section 36 was known in 1903 to be oil bearing land, and this holding, if upheld, had the effect of divesting Standard of title to Section 36.

On January 30, 1937, the United States filed suit in the Federal Court for the Southern District of California, to establish its title to Section 36. Shortly after this Burges was employed in the case.

The government attorneys filed the case on the equity side of the docket. In those days the federal courts maintained two dockets, one a Law Docket, and the other the Equity Docket. In trials in equity cases, the parties were not entitled to a jury, as the guarantee of a jury trial related only to cases at law. One of the first things done by

Standard was to file a motion to transfer the case to the Law Docket. The company was represented by Oscar Lawler, an eminent attorney of Los Angeles, who had been counsel for the company through all of the prior proceedings before the representatives of the General Land Office, and the Department of the Interior, and also by Eugene M. Prince, of the firm of Pillsbury, Madison & Sutro, San Francisco. It was after this motion had been prepared and filed that Burges came into the case, and a little later a fourth lawyer also became one of counsel for Standard of California. This was Donald R. Richberg, an excellent lawyer from Cleveland, Ohio, and whose name had come into national prominence by having become at one time the administrator of the National Industrial Recovery Act.

Burges, for his part, found it necessary to go through the record of the previous history and evidence in the case, and to join with his fellow counsel in preparing briefs for the court. Some were prepared before he came into the case, and others were prepared after he became one of counsel. The gist of the argument to the court was the government's action was in fact one to recover title and possession to real property which was in the possession of Standard Oil Company of California, and the recovery of title and possesssion of land was an action at law, and therefore properly belonged on the Law Docket. It was strongly urged, since the company then would be entitled to a trial by a jury on the facts of the case, which it could not get on the equity side of the docket. They invoked the Seventh Amendment to the Constitution of the United States, preserving inviolate the right of a trial by jury in cases at law, and cited numerous cases to support their position. The government attorneys contended, however, that the defendant's claim of an offset for expenses which had been incurred in connection with drilling and producing oil was an equitable remedy, and therefore the case belonged on the equity side of the docket. For all of the apparent correctness of the position of counsel for the company, the court nevertheless overruled them, and retained the case on the equity side of the docket.

The government moved for a judgment based upon the proposition the decision by Secretary Ickes was an administrative determination of the controversy, which was final and conclusive, and the company was not entitled to a trial of the facts in the court. This is what is known as the substantial evidence rule, which holds where there is a controversy before a governmental agency, and that agency is authorized to hear the controversy, and to make a decision upon it, if there is any evidence before the agency to support the decision it reaches, then that decision is final and there can be no further hearing on the facts. The result is, where this rule is applied, one side, usually a citizen, an individual or a corporate one, may have an abundance of evidence that is overwhelming in its proof, but if the person on the other side—or the antagonist—or the government, has any evidence at all to support its position, and if the government agency decides in favor of such person, or the government, then the citizen is stuck with that decision, and he cannot get a hearing in court.

What the substantial evidence rule does is to deny a person his day in court, where he has a controversy that has been decided by a government agency, if there is any evidence at all to support the agency's decision. No matter how overwhelming or how convincing the evidence is in favor of the citizen, no matter how fair his position is, no matter how prejudiced is either the elected or appointed agency offical who decides the matter, no matter how unfair the decision of the agency obviously may be, under the substantial evidence rule you have no recourse, but must take the unfair, the prejudiced, the purely political, the anti-factual decision of the agency, as determinative of the facts. Of course, the government agency can always get somebody, even if it is only a clerk working in the agency's office, to give some testimony so the substantial evidence rule will be applicable.

This is not only a rule in federal government area, but is also the rule in many state and local governments.

The government, therefore, took the position that Secretary Ickes had determined that Section 36 was known to be oil bearing land at the time the government conveyed it to the state of California in 1903, and no further inquiry into the facts could be made in court. The Standard Oil Company, on the other hand, asserted it was entitled to a trial *of the facts* in court, and that, indeed, Ickes had never examined the testimony and facts in evidence—being those in the record of the hearing before the Register—and that Ickes could not hold contrary to the decision of the Register, who had heard all the evidence. In other words, Standard insisted on its right to its "day in court." Judge Yankwich held, however, Ickes did not have to examine or be familiar with the testimony and evidence in the case, but it was sufficient he had heard arguments in the case and moreover, he was entitled to adopt the findings and conclusions of his subordinates. He specifically held Ickes, as secretary of the Interior, could make this decision dated January 24, 1935, although by an executive order in 1912 Section 36 was placed in Naval Reserve No. 1, and Congress, in 1920, passed a law giving the secretary of the Navy possession of the properties in the Naval Reserve. The judge brushed aside the argument that the matter was within the province of the secretary of the Navy, and also the arguments: that title to the land was a legal question, and could be decided in a court only after hearing all the facts; to let a cabinet member make such a decision would amount to an unconstitutional delegation of judicial power to the executive branch of the government; the secretary of the Interior had no right to reverse the decision made by the Register, which had been affirmed by the commissioner of the General Land Office; that the secretary could make such a decision only if he himself was personally familiar with the record of testimony and evidence before the Register; and, the government, by various acts, was estopped to claim title to Section 36. While the opinion, as printed in 20 F. Supp. 427, is twenty-five pages long, it all boiled down to the fact that (1) whereas, the Register who heard all the testimony and evidence found that Section 36 was not known in 1903 to be oil bearing, and this decision was affirmed by the commissioner of the General Land Office, still, Secretary Ickes legally was authorized to make a contrary decision, without even having examined the record, and (2) more fundamentally, the landowner was not entitled to try his case in court, where he could put on all relevant evidence. In other words, the judge held the landowner is bound by a decision by the secretary of the Interior, without even having "his day in court."

This is the "substantial evidence" rule, and many a citizen since 1935 has been made the victim of ignorant, or prejudiced, or biased, or arbitrary decisions of executive and administrative personnel decision, without even getting his day in court, on the ground of the "substantial evidence" rule.

Even Judge Yankwich must have had some misgivings, because he said in a later case, "if we consider the meager evidence on which the administration decision in *United States v. Standard Oil Company,* D.C. Cal. 1937, 21 F. Supp. 645, was based . . ."

But the Ickes decision was upheld, regardless of the facts in the case, and this prompted some one to produce a parody, which read:

In "36" the poppies grow
    Between the derricks row on row.
In "36" wildflowers bloom
    Above that most official tomb
Where oil the life of "36"
    Was buried under Harold Ickes.
Pink Margolds and red daffydills
    Cover the gold in them there hills,
Black gold that once was Standard Oil
    Until the New Deal came to foil
The Sixty Families and their tricks
    With law made up by Harold Ickes.

In "36" where poppies grow
    Men lived in hope not long ago.
They dug deep in the stubborn soil
    To find if there was hidden oil —
Unknown to human kind, these riches —
    But not "unknown" to Harold Ickes.
Theories were wet and wells were dry
    Oilless, alas! the years went by.
Yet now we're told, since oil did flow,
    "You must have known what now we know,
Contrary proof shall never stick us,
    We are the judge," says Harold Ickes.

In "36" where poppies grow
    The torch of oil and gas burns low.
Only a "Beehive" lights the sky
    To tell us where the experts lie:
Experts that someone, maybe, likes
    Someone who thinks like Harold Ickes.
In "36" the crosses show

> Where men went West who did not know
> That there was wealth – forgotten men –
> Who in their graves turn over when
> They hear that back in nineteen three
> This land was known as oil and free!
> "Tell the marines! Tell all the mikes"
> "They must have known," says Harold Ickes.

Although Standard had, by the Yankwich decree, lost Section 36, and would be liable for the net profits it had made from the sale of oil produced from this land, there was still a battle to come over how much the net profits were, that is, what allowance, as a cost of producing the oil, were to be made. The gross proceeds from the sale of the oil produced was approximately $25 million. The question was, how much was the net?

The attorneys for the company went to work on this question, assembling the facts and records as to the gross amount, and as to the breakdown of various times entering into the cost to be charged against it. It was a question to which they devoted a great deal of time, both as to the facts and the law. Burges was active in preparing a brief on the law, and in reviewing the facts relative thereto.

The government conceded Standard was entitled to deduct drilling and development expenses. It also conceded the law of the state of California was the controlling law, but the government and Standard disagreed as to which California statute was applicable. In allowing expenses of production against the gross income, the question of good faith was also involved, and this too required a briefing of the law. The law was likewise briefed with respect to various expense items, including the payment to prior owners of a part of the land of sums necessary in order to drill on it, which amounted to nearly $2 million. There was also the item of state and local taxes paid on the land, in the sum of $574,351. There was likewise an item of income taxes paid to the United States government, amounting to $500,010.89, together with various other items of smaller sums. Judge Yankwich had no difficulty in reaching the conclusion Standard should be allowed the taxes paid. He noted a California statute specifically provided in such a case the cost of production should include taxes paid, and this took care of the state and local tax question. With respect to the income tax paid to the federal government, he noted Standard had no choice about paying it, but was compelled to do so under the law, regardless of the fact that a dispute over the title to the land existed. He stated the law with respect to the government coming into court as a litigant, which should always be kept in mind in case of litigation with the government, where the government so often claims special rights and prerogatives, where, in his opinion at 21 F. Supp. 645 at 655 he said:

> With all due regard for the powers and attributes of sovereignty, it is well to remember that, when a sovereign comes into a court of equity seeking its aid to enforce its rights, even as the owner of the public domain, its claim should be tested by the same equitable principles which govern suits between private litigants, unless there is a special statute commanding a contrary rule (citing authorities, and quoting from *U.S. v. Thekla,* 266 U.S. 328), ' when the United States comes into court to assert a claim it so far takes the position of a private suitor as to agree by implication that justice may be done with regard to the subject matter . . . the reasons are strong for not obstructing the application of natural justice against the government by technical formulas when justice can be done without endangering any public interest.' If the principle thus stated is not strictly applicable, it at least suggests that the court should not affirm what is clearly an unjust and inequitable result unless under plain compulsion of law.

Judge Yankwich then said:

> It would be a shocking injustice, under these circumstances, to allow the government to retain the one-half million dollars paid to it as income tax under circumstances which would preclude all possibility of a refund. That the tax can only be approximated is not ground for denying reimbursement, the more so as the method of computation is one sanctioned by the government in income tax matters.

The court also allowed to Standard the cost of building a compressor plant which was necessary, the expenses after shutdown, and disallowed the government's claim for interest on the amount of damages being paid to the government. The final result of Judge Yankwich's judgment is given at 21 F. Supp. 645 at 663, where he decreed the quieting of title to Section 36 in the United States, thus giving it title to the land, and entering a judgment in favor of the government against Standard for $6,214,102.42.

Thus, for lack of a day in court where undoubtedly the overwhelming proof would have shown Section 36 was not known to be oil bearing land in 1903, the government, by Ickes' decree and Yankwich's judgment, took Section 36 away from Standard, and obtained a judgment ordering it to pay the government the six million-odd dollars above stated.

Judge Yankwich's opinion was dated December 4, 1937. Messrs. Prince, Lawler, Burges and Richberg set themselves to the task of appealing the case, with the hope of securing a reversal of the judgment upholding the Ickes' ukase. This entailed the preparation of the appeal, and writing the appellant's brief and a great deal of time was devoted to this. The appeal was to the United States Court of Appeals for the Ninth Circuit, at San Francisco, and in due time, that court handed down an opinion which, by a divided court, two judges to one, affirmed Judge Yankwich's decision. Judge Healy of the court of appeals, dissented.

There was one further step left; the petition for writ of certiorari to the United States Supreme Court was prepared and filed, but on January 29, 1940, the clerk of the United States Supreme Court advised the petition for the writ had been denied. The case therefore came to an end, and Prince went to Los Angeles in order to pay the judgment, receive the necessary receipts and releases in connection therewith.

XXXVI

Politics, Demagogues, and Public Utility Rates

Men who can stand before a demagogue.
—Holland

IN THE DECADE 1932-1942 Burges was active in several public utility rate cases. Public utilities are often considered fair game by politicians holding public office, who want to seek favor with the voting public by beating down utility rates, regardless of the facts.

Turney & Burges had long represented the telephone company in El Paso, and Burges was soon involved when a rate fight began in 1931. The afternoon newspaper urged the city to investigate all utility rates, and before long, Mayor Sherman initiated demands on the Mountain States Telephone & Telegraph Company. He was quoted saying, "I feel we are entitled to lower rates," although at that time he had no facts on which to base the statement.

The telephone company requested the opportunity for a full hearing, but instead of holding a hearing, the city council, on September 22, 1932, passed an ordinance on first reading, lowering the rates, and one week later the ordinance was passed on final reading.

Burges was prepared for this, and immediately filed a Bill of Complaint in federal court attacking the ordinance on the grounds the rates set were confiscatory, and that the failure to give the company a hearing violated the due process of law and equal protection of the law provisions of the 14th Amendment to the Constitution. Judge Boynton issued a restraining order against the city enforcing the ordinance, and set it for hearing a week later.

Preparations for hearings on the case went on apace, and on October 11, 1932, E.R. Campbell, of the company's legal staff in Denver, wrote Burges, "You seem to have this case in splendid shape." Meanwhile, the hearing on the case was postponed to March, 1933, which fell during a city election campaign. The court refused to dismiss the injunction Burges had obtained, and the city was put in the position of starting over. The *Herald-Post,* the most avid backer of the city in this rate fight, ran a headline reading, "Phone Rate Case Muddled." It became official on August 4. The *Herald-Post* headlined, "City Loses Phone Rate Fight; Forced to Repeal Ordinance; Starts New Rate Reduction Battle." The subhead read, "Company Outmaneuvers Municipal Government in Federal Court; Kills Bill Lowering Cost of Service in El Paso." The final line was "Court Costs Will Be Charged to the City."

The city started over with another rate hearing, which began on August 16, 1933. The witnesses offered by the telephone company finished their testimony on August 17, and the city attorneys asked the council to recess the hearing while they studied the matter. The city had struck another snag the day before, when its demand for administrative reports showing earnings of other exchanges of the Mountain States Telephone & Telegraph Company was refused by Burges on the ground it was not material to the issue before the council. Burges added, "It would cost an enormous amount of money to get such data, and would involve an infinite amount of time. We have already spent $40,000 in amassing information asked for by the city in this hearing." Burges also told the city attorneys the city rate engineer could not collect this data in the company's Denver office. He pointed out the city had the earning reports of the El Paso exchange and they were sufficient for this hearing.

The city demanded the telephone company compile evidence for use by the city in the rate hearing, but Burges compiled instead a list of authorities holding it was too general to require compliance, and therefore this burdensome demand need not be performed.

The hearing was recessed by the mayor on August 17 to

September 18, 1933. It actually resumed October 4 and ran to October 12, when the mayor recessed it to December 4 in order to give the telephone company time in which to prepare counter exhibits to the ones introduced by the city.

An additional hearing was held December 4 to December 8, 1933, but no action was taken by the city. On July 18, 1934, *The El Paso Times* stated, if the city decides to reduce the telephone rates, the cut will be much less than the one the council tried to put into effect back in 1932. On July 23, 1934, the *Herald-Post* reported the city had spent $32,058 on rate investigations and fights, and had saved the people of El Paso $324,000, but the breakdown given in the newspaper article showed these savings were all on electric bills and gas bills, and it only predicted the phone saving eventually would be $8,690. No further ordinance was adopted by the city at this time reducing telephone rates, and it can only be concluded the telephone company had so firmly established its position that the idea of compelling a reduction of telephone rates by ordinance was dropped. What started out as a political wingding to compel, willy-nilly, a reduction in telephone rates, regardless of the facts—indeed, completely indifferent to the facts—had been forestalled, and hearings compelled at which the telephone company had ample opportunity to present the facts. The true valuation of the company's El Paso properties used and useful in rendering telephone service to the citizens of El Paso, its expenses, and its income, showed a rate reduction would be confiscatory, and an ordinance purporting to make such a reduction would be void. Burges, and those with whom he was associated in the case, had made the right moves, and presented the evidence to sustain their position, and success crowned their efforts.

A little more than three years later Burges was again engaged in a rate controversy with the city. This time his client was the Texas Cities Gas Company, the local natural gas distributor. Once again the city, with a new mayor and council in office, rushed forth, regardless of facts, to curry favor with the public by assaulting the rates of a public utility.

On Monday, February 16, 1938, the El Paso City Council met in the office of Mayor M.A. Harlan in secret session, and, in what they described as "emergency action," adopted a resolution and ordinance for the investigation of the gas rates. The ordinance delegated the authority to do this work to two employees of the Railroad Commission, naming them as "city agents" for this purpose. The resolution and ordinance, although passed on Monday, were kept secret until 10:00 A.M. on Tuesday, when they were submitted to R.S. Reading, manager of the El Paso business of Texas Cities Gas Company.

The ordinance adopted at the city council's secret meeting made refusal to comply with it a misdemeanor, subjecting the company, and its officials, to a fine ranging from $150 to $200 for each violation. The refusal of any utility to submit its records to the scrutiny of the city employees "shall constitute a ground for forfeiture of the franchise granted such person, firm or corporation."

Reading, using a statement prepared by Burges, told the Railroad Commission agents who were designated by the city to act for it, the company would cooperate, under protest, and would recognize them "as agents for the city, but not as representatives of the State Railroad Commission." He pointed out the appointment of Railroad Commission employees as "city agents" was "against ethics, human nature and all fundamental conceptions of right and justice."

The company obtained a restraining order in a Dallas court to prevent employees of the Railroad Commission from acting as agents of the city of El Paso in the rate investigation, and the city council threatened to pass an ordinance "ordering wide arbitrary reductions in El Paso gas rates" if the city and the Railroad Commission lost the injunction suit filed in Dallas. Olin Culberson, chief of the gas utilities division of the Railroad Commission was in El Paso, ready to give the city "any advice on rates."

The Texas Cities Gas Company, in the meanwhile, had offered a reduction in rates which would save the El Paso users upward of $50,000 but this was not accepted by the mayor and council, who declined to say what reduction would be satisfactory to them. Civic leaders, including B.M.G. Williams, as president of the Chamber of Commerce, and S.J. Isaacks, as chairman of the Tax and Economy Committee of the Chamber of Commerce, Maurice Schwartz and other leading citizens proposed the controversy be settled by arbitration. The company agreed, but this proposal fell on deaf ears at the City Hall.

The city council thereafter passed an ordinance lowering the gas rates. There was no notice to the company, and no hearing was afforded it. The rate fixed was confiscatory, and was ordered without the council having any facts on which to base it. The city council's theory was put on the gas company the burden of making the next move. It was not long in coming.

Burges and the company's Legal Department immediately prepared a Bill of Complaint, asking for an injunction against the city enforcing said ordinance on the ground the failure to give notice and a hearing violated the 14th Amendment to the Constitution of the United States, as well as sections 33 and 41 of the City Charter, and that the rate fixed was confiscatory. The facts showing the rate fixed was confiscatory were alleged and a copy of the ordinance was attached. The Bill of Complaint was filed in the United States District Court at El Paso on March 31, 1932, and on the same day, Judge Charles A. Boynton signed an order for the issuance of a temporary restraining order, restraining the city from enforcing the new ordinance.

The case came on for hearing before Judge Boynton on April 8, 1938, and at the conclusion of the testimony he held the city's failure to give the company notice of its proposed ordinance, and a hearing on it, made the ordinance void and unenforceable, and granted a preliminary injunction against the city, enjoining the enforcement of the rate ordinance.

The city appealed to the United States Court of Appeals, which held the company should have appealed to the State Railroad Commission, and therefore the injunction should be dissolved, after allowing a reasonable time for the company to appeal to the Railroad Commission and to supersede the order of the city of El Paso. But the court of appeals also said in its opinion "The ordinance as passed, we agree with the district court, was not lawfully passed, and cannot lawfully be enforced."

The Supreme Court refused to review the case, and Burges staked his position on the quoted statement from the court of appeals that the ordinance was not lawfully passed and could not lawfully be enforced.

Thus supported, the company was prepared to stand its ground and an article in the El Paso Times stated:

W.H. Burges, utility attorney, said the company had no intention of filing 'any kind of a motion.'

'The courts have held the ordinance is invalid,' Mr. Burges said.

'Let's see them enforce it.'

The gas rate matter was next mentioned in the *El Paso Herald-Post* on May 1, 1939. Mayor M.A. Harlan had been defeated for reelection. J.E. Anderson and a new council were elected, and they explored the question of a fair gas rate for El Paso. On May 6 the *Herald-Post* ran an editorial stating the gas company had offered to reduce the rates $100,000 a year and again said, referring to Burges,

The company's attorney has hitherto said the city's ordinance means nothing—'it's invalid, let'em try to enforce it.'

The editorial further said:

But he requests that the injunction against this 'invalid' ordinance be extended, and the company offers to tilt the ante if that is done.

The parties reached an agreement on a rate reduction some time in the summer of 1939, and the controversy was brought to an end. The *Herald-Post* headlined an assertion the mayor had made a utility "deal," but what happened was, the valuation of the company's property was reduced for rate purposes, and so had to be reduced accordingly for tax purposes.

The Harlan administration mishandled its gas rate ordinance, and the new city administration which succeeded it took a more reasonable approach, with the result it was able to work out something with the gas company that was both fair and reasonable to all parties concerned. But while the controversy was on, the watchword was, as Burges stated, "The ordinance was not lawfully passed—let 'em try to enforce it."

A year later Burges was again in a utility rate controversy. The summer of 1941 saw the beginning of a multipronged attack on the Mountain States Telephone & Telegraph Company by both the county and city of El Paso. Mayor J.E. Anderson wrote to F.E. Farwell, manager of Mountain States at El Paso, stating the city council felt the citizens of El Paso were entitled to a rate reduction, and he and the Council would be glad to confer with Farwell and negotiate new telephone rates. The council did not have an opinion that lower rates were in order, for it had not investigated the facts, and did not know the fair value of the telephone company property used and useful in rendering telephone service to the people of El Paso, nor had it determined what was a fair rate of return on the company's investment, nor what the latter's net profit in El Paso was. It knew only the *Herald-Post,* which mounted first one assault and then another, was fanning the flames for lower telephone rates, and that rate reduction campaigns are popular with the voting public.

Milton Smith of Denver, general counsel for the company, telephoned Burges about the mayor's letter. Burges expressed surprise that Farwell and Speechly, the latter being the company's El Paso district manager, had called on the city council and promised to furnish information about the rate question. Ordinarily this would not have been done without legal counsel. He wrote he had not seen the mayor's letter of the 28th until "today," and added, "we are in for all the trouble the *Herald-Post* can stir up."

In August, 1941, the county of El Paso mounted its attack. County Commissioner Moliere Scarborough was acting county judge in the absence of the County Judge McGill. He lived a short distance west of the town of Ysleta, and in those times Ysleta was a separate town, twelve miles from El Paso, with the intervening area being primarily rural in nature. El Paso and Ysleta each had its telephone exchange, and in order to protect each exchange, boundary lines between them were drawn, with the result, one telephoning beyond the exchange boundary of the area in which he lived paid a long distance toll charge. Scarborough was in the Ysleta exchange area, and consequently paid a toll charge on calls between his house and El Paso.

Early in August, Scarborough sent a letter to the telephone company demanding telephone rates in the unincorporated areas of the county be equalized. The telephone company agreed to meet with Scarborough and County Attorney Guinn to discuss the matter. The *Herald-Post* continued to rail against the telephone company, but *The*

El Paso Times stated while the people of El Paso had good reason to complain of the telephone service, the telephone company had a good excuse, namely, El Paso had grown rapidly in the last few months, thus increasing the demand on all utilities, and further stating, "The telephone company had great difficulty in training operators fast enough to meet the situation." Implicit in these statements were the facts, well-known in El Paso, that the war in Europe had resulted in beefing up the armed forces in the United States, Fort Bliss was enlarged, and required a greatly enlarged telephone service. The conference between Scarborough and County Attorney Guinn, and Farwell and Speechly—described by the *Herald-Post* as "stormy"—had lasted three hours, but nothing was resolved. It was followed immediately by the *Herald-Post* editorial, the tone of which was indicated by the heading which read, "So They're Going To Get Tough?"

In the meantime the city and the *Herald-Post,* in parallel acts, pushed for a rate fight. City Attorney Andress, who had been in office less than two weeks, announced the city was pushing its demand for a phone rate cut, and the *Herald-Post* publicized the statement. Between the two of them, announcement was made that a formal rate hearing would be set before the council, following which the rates would be lowered. The council's decision was announced before the hearing was held.

Before long the city attorney and the county attorney announced they were joining their efforts to force a reduction in telephone rates, and Scarborough did his part by calling a mass meeting at the Lower Valley Community Center, where he could hope to whip up a demonstration against the telephone company. The *Herald-Post,* meanwhile, editorialized the telephone company did not have a franchise, had not had one since 1932, and could be expelled from the city unless it obtained a franchise, and agreed to lower its rates. The city attorney joined in with an announcement he had drafted an ordinance to make the company pay the city's expenses in a rate contest. The *Herald-Post* urged the passage of an ordinance requiring the company to have a franchise, and imposing penalties for not doing so.

Meanwhile Burges and Milton Smith studied the factual basis and legal authorities for an injunction against the city in the event it quickly passed a rate ordinance that denied due process of law to the company, or amounted to confiscation. Burges was ready on that question, as well as the question of not having a franchise. He relied on an opinion to Southwestern Bell Telephone Company by Nelson Phillips, its general attorney in Texas. Phillips previously had presided with great distinction and ability as chief justice of the Supreme Court of Texas. His opinion stated a city in Texas could not require a telephone company to obtain a franchise, basing this on a Texas statute authorizing telephone companies to place their construction on the streets of cities, subject to the reasonable exercise of the police power of the cities to ensure the public is not incommoded. Burges was also ready on the law questions arising from the ordinance requiring the company to pay the city's expenses in a rate contest.

City Attorney Andress announced a meeting scheduled for 10:00 A.M., August 19, 1941, of the city council with Frank Farwell and George Speechly, at which time the city would demand lower rates. Guinn and Scarborough were also scheduled to be at the meeting. The meeting was followed by a headline across the top of page one of the *Herald-Post,* "Utility Refused Phone Rate Cut: City Fights On." Farwell told the council the company's return in 1940 of 2.9 percent on its capital investment was not a fair one, and cited figures to support it. The city, nevertheless, started negotiations for employment of a rate engineer, but declined to identify with whom it was negotiating.

The council met and passed the city attorney's ordinance obligating El Paso utilities to pay the city's costs of investigating their rates. The county attorney announced the commissioner's court would hold a public hearing on August 27 on its demand for equalization of telephone rates outside the city. City Tax Collector Graves obliged by stating he raised the telephone company's tax valuation by an additional sum of $463,000, and the county tax assessor followed suit.

The *Herald-Post* and Scarborough continued their efforts to fan the flames of discontent against the telephone company. Scarborough, as acting county judge, called a public hearing on the question of the telephone rates between El Paso and Ysleta. Burges represented the company at the so-called "hearing." Few people were present, indicating the lack of public interest on the part of the public. Two or three of those present—stooges of the acting county judge—made vehement talks, all smoke, with little fire and no light. One of them, in particular, not only denounced the telephone company in as vitriolic a manner as he could muster, but also made a vicious, verbal assault on Burges, while Scarborough sat behind the judge's desk making no effort to keep the meeting within bounds. He obviously was content to let hatchetmen do their worst. Burges appeared to take no notice of the assault on him, no doubt considering its source, for he had been in bigger and better fights than this.

The action moved forward on three fronts, the attack by the city, another by the county, and a continuous barrage fired almost daily by the *Herald-Post.* The city announced it was moving toward hiring a telephone rate expert, and Scarborough invited everyone in the county who had a complaint against the telephone company to bring it to him, and the county attorney asked the company for an accounting of its profits in the three telephone zones west of Ysleta. It was clear the county attorney was only groping around, since the county had no authority to regulate rates. Two days later the city announced it had selected a phone rate expert, but refused to give out his name. On the same day, the *Herald-Post* editorialized that the city and its legal department were not waging a real battle, but were only "fighting with marshmallows at forty paces."

The El Paso Times took no part in the controversy except to report the news factually where there was news, and occasionally, to print a letter from someone who took the side of the telephone company. In one such letter the writer took care to point out he was not, and never had been an employee of the telephone company. The tone of his letter was set in the opening sentences, "I was mildly taken back some several days ago. 'Captain' Anderson and his private crew have set sail on another political policy raid against what it claims are 'unfair rates' on the gallant city of El Paso." He continued to upbraid the city fathers, stating, "our streets are a shame and disgrace; vacant lots are overgrown with weeds; alleys...are littered with garbage and rubbish...very few police are ever around...tax valuations have been increased..." He asked why they picked on the telephone company when everyone knows the good wages they pay and how well they treat their employees.

Shortly thereafter, the city demanded an inventory of telephone plant property, listing separately what was in the city and what was outside the city. At the same time county officials announced they were considering filing a suit against the telephone company. They set a public hearing, and invited those with complaints to come forward. County Attorney Guinn outlined the possible legal action to be taken:

(1) A series of suits filed in justice of peace courts to recover allegedly excessive charges assessed by the utility in the past.

(2) A petition for a permanent injunction, filed in district court by several county subscribers, seeking to prevent the utility from charging excessive rates in the future.

(3) A petition for a similar injunction filed by a subscriber in an area where rates were discriminatory. The court's ruling, it was said, would apply to other subscribers in similar areas.

The county commissioners held their hearing on September 12. Burges was the principal spokesman for the company, and he told the commissioners any ultimate rate changes in the county hinged upon the city council's decision as to whether its demand for a reduction of telephone charges should be confined to the city or should extend into the entire El Paso exchange area, which included the unincorporated districts. "We can't do anything to change county conditions until the city answers the questions of whether any rate changes would apply only within the city, or outside, too," he said. "There is nothing we will do or try to do until the city controversy is out of the way." He added the telephone company executives will do anything possible to improve rural service, but obtaining equipment for improvement of service had become difficult since the defense program started, and for that reason preference is being given to the development of the Fort Bliss and Logan Heights cantonment telephone service. He explained to the commssioners, if the city confined its rate reduction demands to the city limits, the county's rate picture would not change. However, if the city's fight extended to the county, present county rates would be affected. The hearing ended abruptly when

Burges said flatly the company did not intend to make any revisions of its Lower Valley service while the city's litigation against the utility was pending. The *Herald-Post's* editorial was headlined, "Well, The Telephone Company Got 'Em A Lawyer."

The Times again printed a "Letter to the Editor," this one from John T. Hill, an oldtime El Paso lawyer. Hill had long played the role of one who helped the poor, and fought the rich, a substantial part of his practice being the representation of plaintiffs in damage suits against business concerns. He espoused a liberal philosophy, on the basis of which he often had been adverse to Burges. Nevertheless, he now found this to be "an inopportune time to make an attack on our telephone company for reduction of charges." He believed it to be a political move by certain public officials...who were interested in the coming election to feather their nests. The war was causing everything to go up in price, and the city was fortunate the telephone company was not asking for an increase in its rates, and many rural telephones had been installed since World War I, at a loss to the company. He added, "I have fought corporations all my professional career, not to rob them, but to make them be just, as their aggregated wealth and stockholders, employees, financial and political influence gives them an advantage over individuals, and they should be justly and carefully regulated, but these quasi-public corporations are a great necessity and must be permitted a reasonable profit so they can pay good wages, give good service, improve their plants and pay their stockholders a good dividend, and mind you, many of their stockholders are poor people as well as the public that patronizes them."

The county soon announced its major move in the case being pushed by Scarborough. The afternoon paper headlined, "County Prepares Phone Rate Suit," and Guinn confirmed preparation of the suit had begun. It was based on Article 4013 and 4015, of the Texas statutues, and alleged subscribers in the three "zones" paid higher rates than are charged other county subcribers. The next day the *Herald-Post's* editorial surmised the attitudes of the courts had changed in recent years, and "nowadays the people are having their innings," and further, the successful prosecution of this case would cost the

American Telephone & Telegraph Company millions. Guinn filed his suit a few days later, naming five subscribers as having been discriminated against, and asking for penalties of $25,000.

The suit, styled *"The State of Texas v. Mountain States Telegraph & Telephone Co."* set off a train of action by Burges and two of his younger partners, as well as by Elmer Brock of Denver, general attorney for the company. There were pleadings to prepare and file, questions of law to brief, and witnesses to interview.

Meanwhile, the city was grinding away on its rate case. The city council passed an ordinance to require a utility company to present to it all the evidence the company had on the question of rates, reciting evidence not presented to the council would not thereafter be presented to a court in a suit over rates. Burges sent Brock a copy of the ordinance, with the comment he saw no objection to it, except for "the fact that the investigation is manifestly being conducted in extreme malice and with the desire of doing any harm that can be done, directly or indirectly, to the company and the A.T. & T. Company. He also forwarded a letter from the city attorney asking for a history of the formation of the local exchange, its ownership by previous companies, and its acquisition by its present owner.

In November, 1941, Elmer Brock and Ray Morris, both of Denver, presented arguments to the city council on not separating the city from the exchange area. The council thereafter authorized Mayor Anderson to sign a letter to the telephone company, stating the council would include unincorporated areas in the survey which would be the basis of its demands for reductions in the telephone rates. Farwell was asked to furnish at the hearing a report on the "property revenues and expenses" of the utility in the entire exchange area, and a similar report confined to properties within the city limits. At the same time, the city attorney told the council he was not ready to recommend whether the entire exchange should be used as a basis for telephone rate revision, but the letter stated any adjudication by the council as to the telephone rates would be confined to the city limits. The city soon notified the company the rate hearing was set for January 12, 1942.

About this time Burges received a note from William H. Duls, an attorney in Dallas for Southwestern Bell Telephone Company, attached to a copy of Judge Phillips' opinion concerning a franchise. The note, typical of statements, written or oral, made to or about Burges read:

Dear Mr. Burges:

Thought you might be interested in this opinion by Judge Phillips.

Best wishes and regards. I live over often, as I shall do for a long time to come, the day I had the privilege of spending with you in Austin recently.

Cordially,
William H. Duls

Preparation continued for the county's penalty suit. The county attorney gave notice of intent to take the oral deposition of George Speechly. He had been in the company's employ many years, and knew the telephone business inside out. Burges wrote Smith, Brock, Akolt & Campbell that Mr. Speechly, in his deposition testimony, was a perfect witness, and that the county attorney got nothing out of it. With respect to the taking of this deposition it was reported, "Guinn and Phone Firm Attorney Clash in Court—W.H. Burges Tells County Attorney To Expect 'No Help' In Penalty Suit." The county attorney asked Speechly about bringing certain records to the trial, but Burges broke in to say, "I can tell you right now you will not get those records. This isn't a friendly suit and we're not going to help you in any way."

The penalty suit was set for trial, first on Monday, December 1, 1941, and then changed to December 8, 1941. Brock, general attorney, Morris, vice-president, financial, and several others arrived in El Paso for the trial. They were all at dinner on the evening of December 7, 1941, with members of the Burges, Burges, Scott & Hulse firm, but the telephone case was not then uppermost in their minds, for this was the "Day of Infamy," when Japan made its sneak attack on Pearl Harbor, and war with Japan occupied everyone's attention.

The trial of the penalty suit styled *The State of Texas v. Mountain States Tel. & Tel. Co.*, began the following Monday morning in the 41st District Court, Judge D.E. Mulcahy presiding. Guinn had demanded a jury, and one was empaneled. Although each side had several witnesses, it turned out there was no dispute about the facts.

Ysleta, twelve miles distant from El Paso had its own telephone exchange, and the question was whether company could draw an exchange line between the El Paso and Ysleta exchanges to protect the service in each exchange area. At the conclusion of all the testimony both sides moved for an instructed verdict, that is, for the court to decide in its favor as a matter of law. Because of the obvious differences which had been pointed out between the several areas referred to in the evidence, Burges and his co-counsel were confident they were entitled to a favorable judgment at the hands of the court, and felt they would get it. The court first set about writing a charge to the jury, but a little later announced he was granting the state's motion for an instructed verdict. This meant a judgment against the company for $25,000, being a penalty of $5,000 for each of the five persons named as complainants in the petition.

An appeal followed. Judge P.R. Price, chief justice of the court of civil appeals at El Paso recused himself, because he owned some A.T. & T. stock. This resulted in the case being transferred to the court of civil appeals at San Antonio. The main effort was in preparing a brief. Brock wrote the part pertaining to the two different exchanges, the necessity to protect each, and the justification from the standpoint of service and rates, for what had been done. Burges and two of his younger partners wrote the rest of the brief.

The brief pointed out the services to the five complaining parties were not rendered under substantially the same circumstances and conditions as the services to the parties in Sunrise Acres and the Country Club areas, respectively, with which they were compared. It was also shown that in other states with public utility commissions, and with anti-discrimination statutes, the establishment of exchange boundary lines was recognized as being both necessary and right.

The point was raised that the penalties imposed by the judgment were so excessive as to be in violation of Article I, Sec. 13 of the Constitution of the State of Texas, which provides excessive fines shall not be imposed. It seemed obvious a penalty of $5,000 for levying what was claimed to be an excess charge of $1 per month was indeed excessive, and this argument was supported by the citation of a case from the Supreme Court of Texas. Burges supplied a quotation from Gilbert and Sullivan,

> My object most sublime,
> I shall achieve in time,
> To make the punishment fit the crime.

Another point urged the statutes relied on by plaintiff were too indefinite to authorize the assessment of a penalty, since a penalty statute must be as definite and certain as a criminal statute. The authorities cited plainly stated this to be the law. In addition to a long list of legal authorities, there was a quotation, also supplied by Burges:

> Let the mark be set on the door where the
> plague is, and then let him who will enter die.

Articles 4004 and 4013 were analyzed in detail, with a clear and positive showing they were too indefinite and uncertain to be enforced as penalty statutes. This section of the brief ended with another quotation, taken from the Chinese Penal Code.

> Whoever is guilty of improper conduct, and of such as is contrary to the spirit of the laws, though not a breach of any specific part of it, shall be punished by at least forty blows; and when the impropriety is of a serious nature, by eighty blows.

While the brief was being written, and the case argued before the court of civil appeals at San Antonio, the rate case before the city council continued. A hearing before the council was set for January 12, 1942, but the company's schedule of preparation for the case showed it could not be ready by that date, and the opinion was expressed the city should take into consideration that two weeks had been taken in the penalty suit. Burges advised Brock he had heard nothing from the city about a postponement, but *The El Paso Times* reported the company would ask for a postponement, and the city would refuse it. He added, "The city will have handed us a temporary injunction."

The hearing opened on January 12, 1942, but it did not last long. As the *Herald-Post* reported, after commenting the city had spent four months and $14,000 on preparing:

The city found itself embarrassed by the quick and utter demolition of a set of earnings figures prepared by one of the experts.

Thousands of dollars had been added in one place and other thousands omitted in another and the resultant inaccurate figures gave a picture that was not even a near likeness.

The telephone men pounced on this and knocking it down was as easy as shooting ducks in a barrel.

The city, for all its adamant position of not granting any postponement to the telephone company suddenly found itself in the position of giving a postponement to its own attorney and experts, and it recessed the hearing to April 6.

The county attorney, in the meantime, filed a suit, asking for an injunction to prevent the company from charging the rates to subscribers in the Ysleta exchange that was the subject of the penalty suit. Burges filed a petition to remove it to the federal court, and the county attorney moved to remand it to the state court. It was remanded, and a hearing on it set in September.

In April, *The Times* printed another "Letter to the Editor," written by Nap F. Lucero. It began:

The daily attack on our telephone company and their officials is becoming boresome. The paying off of political pledges 'to obtain reductions' of this and that expense...may be all right during normal times as a favorite smokescreen to cover up other and more glaring deficiences; but these are abnormal times. These intelligent and highly trained men, now engaged in legal battle, could be used to better advantage in other and more urgent work.

...if half of the business and industrial establishments of the country would hire help and officials of the high moral, education, ethical and intellectual standards that the American Telephone and Telegraph Company and their subsidiaries use, we would have little need for drastic legislation to control labor, capital and antitrust conspiracies.

After a lengthly, spirited defense of the telephone company, he concluded:

No, the telephone company did not hire me to write this; they may not even read it. But let's be fair, and friendly, and cooperative with our public utilities. Let's not make political footballs out of them but treat them as we would like to be treated in our own business.

A formal rate hearing was held before the city council, but it appeared to be only a legal formality, insofar as the city was concerned, before passing an ordinance to lower the telephone rate substantially.

The company's attorneys prepared to file suit for a temporary restraining order in the event of adverse action by the council. They had until May 25, 1942, to file a brief with the city council, and therefore anticipated a rate ordinance would not be passed before May 28. On the 28th, the *Herald-Post* reported that on the previous day, the city council and City Attorney Andress met behind closed doors for three hours. The long-expected ordinance was passed on June 4, 1942, and it adopted certain findings on which it was based. But somewhere along about this time negotiations were begun to settle all litigation and outstanding issues at El Paso. In addition to the rate case, where an injunction suit was imminent, there were also the penalty suit, pending before the court of civil appeals at San Antonio, the suit for the city's expenses in the rate case, and the injunction suit filed by the state as an aftermath of the penalty suit. There was also the question of getting a city franchise. So in July it developed a compromise settlement was announced. It included a compromise on the telephone rates lowering them to a certain extent; the dismissal, with prejudice, of the suit for the city's rate case expenses, amounting to \$33,000; the granting by the city to the company of a twenty-five-year franchise for \$33,000; and a satisfactory agreement on the telephone charges to Scarborough, and the others living in his neighborhood, together with a dismissal of the penalty suit. The settlement included the agreement the city would no longer get free telephone service, and a dial telephone system would be installed when World War II was over. The *Herald-Post* congratulated all those involved, and said:

> And, finally, we congratulate the telephone company officials—particularly Mr. Morris, Mr. Farwell and Mr. Brock—for the spirit of cooperation they showed in negotiating the settlements.
>
> It was a nice little scrap while it lasted, but peace is always preferable to war.

There was one aftermath: The company's ad valorem tax values in the office of the county tax collector and the city tax collector. The city had reduced the company's valuations for rate making purposes and the company insisted upon, and received, a lower valuation for tax purposes. It was roundly denounced by the *Herald-Post,* but on balance that's the way it had to be.

XXXVII

Last Years

Sunset and evening star,
And one clear call for me.
—Tennyson

THE LAST FEW YEARS of Burges' life were uneventful. He was in his seventies, and hard of hearing. His hearing difficulties kept him from active participation in trial work. This is illustrated by the occasion when he sat in with Louis A. Scott on the trial of a case before Judge P.R. Price. The judge, universally regarded as a good one, was an old bachelor, and frequently indicating nervousness by grimaces, fidgeting in his chair, and moving arms and legs in an uncertain fashion. At one point during the trial, Judge Price exhibited all these indications of uncertainty and momentary indecision, and Burges—in a way characteristic of hard-to-hear persons—leaned toward Scott and said in a stage whisper audible all over the courtroom, "He's a-woolgathering now. God Almighty doesn't know what he's going to do."

He well knew that soon after one is gone from this earth how little is remembered of him, much as Thomas Gray wrote:

Some village Hampden, that with dauntless breast,
The little tyrant of his field withstood,
Some mute, inglorious Milton, here may rest,
Some Cromwell guiltless of his country's blood.

On occasion, obviously recalling his preeminence in so many facets of life, and the oblivion that comes thereafter, he said, "Yes, in the years to come, someone may say, 'Oh yes, there was a man named Burges who lived here.' "

His name has not gone unhonored in the city where he lived and which was the scene of so many of his endeavors. The College of Mines at El Paso, later Texas Western College and now the University of Texas at El Paso, recognizing his contributions to that institution in its earlier days, has a building named for him, "Burges Hall." The city of El Paso named W.H. Burges Street for him. Then the board of trustees of the El Paso Independent School District, in recognition of his significant contributions to the cultural and educational life of El Paso in its early days, named the William H. Burges High School for him.

But at last it was,

> Sunset and evening star,
> And one clear call for me.

He suffered a severe angina attack, and was placed in Southwestern General Hospital where death came to him on March 11, 1946. He left behind a life full of kindnesses and good deeds to his fellowman—a life full of accomplishment and successes in his chosen field of the law, and a life where he was ever fighting for the liberty and freedom of the individual. Wordsworth asked,

> Who is the Happy Warrior,
> Whom neither shape of danger can dismay,
> Nor thought of tender happiness betray.

He might well have answered, "William H. Burges."

> For all in all, he was a man.

His life fitted well the last lines of Thanatopsis:

> So live that when thy summons come to join
> The innumerable caravan that moves
> To that mysterious realm, where each shall take
> His chamber in the silent halls of death,
> Thou go not, like the quarry slave at night,
> Scourged to his dungeon, but, sustained and soothed
> By an unfaltering trust, approach thy grave
> Like one who wraps the drapery of his couch
> About him, and lies down to pleasant dreams.

Index

Alderete, Frank, 122
Alderete, Ike, 120, 122
Allred, James V., 336-337, 346, 352, 357
Anderson, J.E., 374
Arbitration Commission, 167, 170
Ateca Case, The, 303-319
Austin, W.H., 32

Banco Cases, The, 326-335
Bassett, O.T., 36
Batts, R.L., 250-251, 253 256-260, 294, 350, 355
Beecher, Henry Ward, 110-114
Beltran, Fernando y Puga, 170
Black, James S., 245
Brady, J.B., 245-247
Bryan, William Jennings, 69
Burges, Anna Pollard, 67-70
Burges, Bettie Rust, 15
Burges, Richard Fenner, 16, 31, 49, 118, 120, 137, 244
Burges, William Henry (Sr.), 15
Burns, Jim, 43

Campbell, "Poker Bob", 45-50, 53, 62
Chamizal, 167, 169-170
Chew, Ben Mar, 83, 87
Chew, Wu Li, 87-88
Chicago, Illinois, 17, 19, 175-183
Chinese Exclusion Act, 82-90
Clark, John H., 264-265
Cobb, Z.L., 124
Coldwell, Ballard, 102
Coldwell, W.M., 52, 101-102, 104, 119
Coles, A.P., 43
Coles, Otis C., 275
Crawford, L.M., 267-268, 271-272
Culberson, C.A., 54-55, 62-64
Culwell, A.H., 259, 269, 278, 282-283, 285-287, 289-293, 295-296, 298-299, 312-314, 317-318
Cunningham, R.E., 308
Curley, Frank, 206, 208, 210, 212, 214, 227, 235, 240

Dale, L.A., 244, 247-248
Davis, Arnold L., 258-259
Davis, Beall & Kemp, 33, 36
Davis, B.H., 33
Davis, Charles, 136-137, 245, 255
Davis, W.H.H., 22
Davis, W.J., 151-152
Diaz, Porfirio, 96, 155-157, 159
Dudley, R.M., 249
Dwyer, Jim, 121-122
Dwyer, Pat, 120-122
Dwyer, Sam, 122

Edwards & Edwards, 101
Edwards & Neill, 33
Edwards, Peyton, 36, 45, 119-120
Escajeda, Joseph, 118-119, 124
Escobar, J. Gonzalo, 303, 305 313, 318
Extradition—Richardson, Mason, Harle, 127-135
Eylar, A.S., 123, 136

Falvey, T.A., 27, 30, 34, 65
First National Bank of El Paso, 29, 261
Fitzsimmons, Bob, 62, 64
Foster, A.G., 31-32
Fox, Chris P., 350
French, Robert N., 197, 201, 203, 212, 220, 224, 227, 240
Fryer, W.H., 307-309, 311-312, 314, 316-317, 319

Gaines, Ruben R., 17-18
Goen, U.S., 244, 246
Goggin, J.M., 102
Grant, Walter B., 170
Gregg, Josiah, 21
Gregory, Burges & McNabb, 175
Gregory, S.S., 175, 177-178
Griest, N.L., 121, 123-124

Hammett, B.F., 116, 118
Hardin, John Wesley, 58-61
Harlan, M.A., 371, 374
Hart, Juan S., 119-120, 136, 151
Hart, Simeon, 22
Hasam, T.R., 32
Haywood, William D., 188, 195-196, 213, 238
Hill, J.W., 294
Hill, Neill & Hill, 283, 285-288
Howard, Tillie, 78-79, 81
Howe, W.D., 42, 118-119, 131-133
Hunter, F.E., 176
Hurt, James M., 17-18

Industrial Workers of the World, 184-243
International Boundary Commission, 169
International Water Co., 151-154
Isaacks, S.J., 244

Juarez, Benito, 21

Keeling, W.A., 270-271
Kelly, C.E., 138, 245
Kemp, Maury, 247, 259
Kemp, Wyndham, 119
Kohlberg, Ernest, 75
Krupp, Elias, 253-254
Krupp, Haymon, 253-257
Ku Klux Klan, 244-249

LaFluer, Eugene, 170, 172
Langtry, Texas, 65
Lea, Tom (Sr.,), 138
Littlefield, George W., 179-181
Love, Thomas B., 320-325

Madero, Francisco, 162
Magoffin, James Wiley, 22
Magoffin, Joseph W., 27, 136
Maher, Peter, 62, 64-65
Martinez, Felix, 117-120, 122
Masterson, Bat, 63, 66
Mills, Anson, 157, 170, 172
Mills, W.W., 53, 45
Milton, Jeff, 59-61
Monroe, Henry, 284
Moore, Henry T., 110-111

Morehead, C.R. 25, 117, 119-120, 123-124, 126
Mountain States Tel. & Tel. Co., 369-370, 374-375, 381-382
Mayar Opera House, 25-26, 30, 107, 120, 123, 125, 138

McBroom, J.H., 246, 249
McGill, Joseph, 272, 375
McGown, W.C., 50-51, 55
McIntyre, R.G., 356

National Industrial Recovery Act, 336-357
Newman, S.H., 119

Pasotex Petroleum Co., 337-339, 343, 346, 349
Patee, Samuel L., 302, 211, 213, 220, 224, 230, 236, 238, 240, 242
Patterson & Wallace, 128
Patterson, Charles, 83
Pershing, John J., 108, 174, 202
Peticolas, W.M., 117, 120-122
Pettigrew & Meyer, 253—256
Phelps Dodge Corp., 296-297
Phillips, Nelson, 283, 294
Pickrell, Frank T., 255, 257 259
Pillsbury, Madison & Sutro, 358, 362
Pollard, J.H., 138
Pollard, J.M., 269
Price, P.R., 257-260

Quaker State Oil Co., 344-345, 347, 353-354

Raynolds, Joshua, 25
Reavis, H.S., 251, 253, 255-256, 259
Roberts, Oran M., 17, 19
Rosenthal, Abraham, 147
Rosenthal, Max, 147
Roxana Petroleum Co., 289, 299

Sachs, Nathan I., 256, 259
Salazar-Diaz Survey, 265-266
Seguin, Texas, 15-17, 19-20
Sing, Dock, 24, 56, 82, 107
Slater, H.D.; 245
Smith, Felix T., 278-279, 281-283, 285-286, 288, 340, 342, 346-349, 356
Smith, Mrs. M.A., 277, 284-285, 287-290, 299
Standard Oil Co. of California, 277-302, 336, 338-340, 343, 356, 358, 365-366, 368
Stanton, M.W., 83, 119
Stewart, U.S., 245-247
Sutro, Oscar, 281, 285, 290-292, 296, 299, 301, 339, 349, 358
Sweeney, Joseph U. 138, 153, 157, 160

Taft, William Howard, 157, 159, 172
Texon Oil and Land Co., 250-260
Texas Cities Gas Co., 371-372
Thomas, Paul D., 283
Thomason, R.E., 297
Toltec Club, 108-109, 162, 176
Turney, W.W., 56, 71-74, 118, 137, 266, 268-269, 295
Tuttle, Charles H., 309-310, 315, 317

University of Texas (Austin), 17, 19, 106-107, 248

Van Valkenburg, Henry, 246, 248

Villa, Francisco, 172-174

Walthall, Harris, 244, 246
Warren, Charles, 263
Wells Fargo Building, 29, 31, 56-57
Wharton, C.R., 258-259
Wheeler, Harry, 190-191, 194, 201, 214, 217, 220, 223-226
White, James H., 117-118, 120
White, Owen P., 125
White, Zach T., 74-75, 267-269, 272
William, F.A., 283, 294
Williams & Jackson, 288
Wootton, Harry E., 191, 205-209, 211, 216, 219-220, 238-239, 240-241
Wrenn Library, 178-181
Wright & Gibbs, 288-289
Wyatt, John M., 255

Yandell, Dr., W.M., 16, 20, 45
Yates, Ira G., 277, 286, 294, 301
Yates Oil Field, 277-302
Young, H.C., 294

This Book

is lithographed by Guynes Printing Company, El Paso, Texas.
Text is set in 12-point Baskerville, leaded two points.
Paper is 70-pound Warm White Mountie Book.
Binding is by Gerhard Schermer.